Quick Reference Card

Macworld Guide To Micr

By David Maguiness

Note: Extended keyboard is needed to use Function keys.

File shortcuts

To do this . . .	*Press . . .*
Create a new chart	F11
Create a new document	Command-N
Create a new macro sheet	Command-F11
Create a new worksheet	Shift-F11
Open an existing document	Command-O or Command-F12
Print the active document	Command-P or Command-Shift-F12
Quit Excel	Command-Q
Save a document with File Save As	Command-Shift-S or F12
Save a document with File Save	Command-S or Shift-F12

Formatting shortcuts

To do this . . .	*Press . . .*
Bold	Command-Shift-B
Comma format - two decimals	Control-Shift-!
Currency format - two decimals	Control-Shift-$
Date format - dd/mm/yy	Control-Shift-#
Exponential format - two decimals	Control-Shift-^
General number format	Control-Shift-~
Italicize	Command-Shift-I
Percentage format - no decimals	Control-Shift-%
Plain format	Command-Shift-P
Select Style box	Command-Shift-L
Shadow	Command-Shift-W
Strikeout	Command-Shift-_
Time format - hh/mm am/pm	Control-Shift-@
Underline	Command-Shift-U

ISBN 1-878058-40-1. Quick Reference Card — $5.95 value.
For more information on IDG Books call 1-800-762-2974.

Editing

To do this . . .	*Press . . .*
Activate formula bar	Command-U
Copy selection	Command-C or F3
Copy selection down	Command-D
Copy selection right	Command-R
Cut selection	Command-X or F2
Enter formula bar contents into the selected cell	Return
Halt editing	Command-. (period) or Esc
Paste selection	Command-V or F4
Repeat preceding task	Command-Y
Undo preceding task	Command-Z or F1

Other shortcuts

To do this . . .	*Press . . .*
Activate AutoSum	Command-Shift-T
Activate/deactivate Add mode	Shift-F8
Activate/deactivate Extend mode	F8
Calculate active document	Command-= or F9
Calculate all open documents	Command-Shift-= or Shift-F9
Display context sensitive help	Command-Shift-? or Shift-Help
Display formulas	Command-' (apostrophe)
Display Help window	Command-/ or Help
Go to a desired cell	Command-G or F5
Go to cell A1	Command-Home
Go to Column A of current row	Home
Go to last cell in current row with contents	Return
Go to last cell with contents	Command-End
Show/hide Standard toolbar	Command-7
To select this . . .	***Press . . .***
Entire column	Command-spacebar
Entire row	Shift-spacebar
Entire worksheet or chart	Command-A
Menu bar	/ or . (Num Lock off) or F10
Shortcut menu	Shift-F10

Quick Reference Card

Macworld Guide To Microsoft Excel 4

By David Maguiness

IDG BOOKS

Personal Finance

Managing Your Checkbook

Check Register

Number	Date	Description of Transaction	Payment/ Debit (-)	Fee (If Any) (-)	Deposit/ Credit (+)	Balance
						1,000.00
1001	9/23	Power & Light	55.25			944.75
1002	9/30	Rent	600.00			344.75
	10/1	Payroll deposit			800.00	1,144.75
card	10/1	Cash	20.00			1,124.75
1003	10/2	Acme Food Store	72.35			1,052.40

Copy the formatting from these rows to other rows to accommodate new transactions.

Copy this formula =G4–(D5+E5)+F5 to other cells in Column G as needed.

Reconciliation

Outstanding Deposits and Credits	
Date	Amount
10/01	800.00
Total	800.00

=SUM(C5:C9)

Outstanding Checks and Debits	
Check # or Description	Amount
1003	72.35
Cash	20
Total	92.35

=SUM(C16:C18)

Statement Balance	344.75
Plus: Outstanding Deposits	800.00
Subtotal	1,144.75
Less: Outstanding Checks	92.35
Adjusted Balance	1,052.40

Enter the balance from your checking account statement here.

=C10

=F2+F4

=C19

=F6-F8

Use Edit Insert with the Shift Cells Down option to enlarge these ranges. Be sure to select one cell each from columns B and C.

Calculating Your Monthly Payments

Payment Calculator

Interest rate	9%
Number of years	5
Amount of loan	$12,500.00
Payment occurs at: Beg=1 or End=0 of month	1

Monthly payment	$257.55
Payments:	
Total number	60
Total principal	$12,500.00
Total interest	$2,952.87
Total amount paid	$15,452.87

=-PMT(D2/12,D3*12,D4,0,D6)

=D3*12

=D4

=CUMIPMT(D2/12,D3*12,D4,1,G5,D6)

=G7+G8

You must have the Analysis ToolPak add-in macro open to calculate this number.

Corporate Finance

Expense Planning

To create another scenario, substitute current year plan for current year actual expense on an annualized basis.

Copy these formulas down their respective columns:

=D5-C5 =E5/D5 =D5/$D$9

Planning

Department	1992 Plan	1993 Plan	Increase/(Decrease) Amount	Percent	Percent of 1993 Plan
Accounting	500	490	-10	-2.04%	21.6%
Administration	750	800	50	6.25%	35.3%
Marketing	350	350	0	0.00%	15.5%
Production	600	625	25	4.00%	27.6%
Total	2,200	2,265	65	2.87%	100.0%

=SUM(C5:C8)

Expense Reporting

Copy these formulas down their respective columns:

=C4-D4 =E4/D4

Reporting

Department	Actual	Plan	Over/(Under) Plan Amount	Percent
Accounting	460	500	-40	-8.0%
Administration	770	750	20	2.7%
Marketing	400	350	50	14.3%
Production	525	600	-75	-12.5%
Total	2,155	2,200	-45	-2.0%

=SUM(C4:C7)

About *Macworld Guide To . . .* Books

Macworld Guide To Microsoft Excel 4 is part of the *Macworld Guide To . . .* series of books, brought to you by IDG, the leading publisher of computer information worldwide. This is a new kind of book designed to meet your growing need to quickly find what you want to do and learn how to do it.

These books work the way you do: They focus on accomplishing specific tasks — not learning random functions. *Macworld Guide To . . .* books are not long-winded tomes, manuals, or even quick reference guides, but are the result of drawing from the best elements of these three types of publications. These books have the easy-to-follow step-by-step sections of a manual; the comprehensive coverage you'd expect to find in a long tome; and the brevity you need from a quick reference guide — it's all here.

The designers of the *Macworld Guide To . . .* series use the following visual elements to make it easy to find the information you need:

Overview sections provide a summary of the Topic's subject and are meant to be read when you want help accomplishing your goals without having to work through the tutorials. This is a good learning tool for the intermediate user who does not need/want any hand-holding.

Step-by-Step sections demonstrate the concepts given in the Overview sections with easy-to-follow instructions. If you're a beginner, these Step-by-Step sections will go a long way toward getting you up to speed on unfamiliar topics.

Quick Tip sections include tips and insights contained on the material in each Topic which enable you to get the most out of your application or operating system no matter what level user you are.

The authors of the *Macworld Guide To . . .* books are leading *Macworld* columnists, technology champions, and Mac gurus, who are uniquely qualified to provide you with expert advice and insightful tips and techniques not found anywhere else. We're sure you'll agree that the *Macworld Guide To . . .* approach is the best.

— David Solomon
Publisher

MACWORLD

GUIDE TO MICROSOFT

EXCEL 4

MACWORLD
GUIDE TO MICROSOFT
EXCEL 4

By David Maguiness

Foreword by John Walkenbach
Contributing Editor, *PC World* and *InfoWorld*

IDG BOOKS

IDG Books Worldwide, Inc.
An International Data Group Company
San Mateo, California 94402

Macworld Guide To Microsoft Excel 4

Published by
IDG Books Worldwide, Inc.
An International Data Group Company
155 Bovet Road, Suite 310
San Mateo, CA 94402
(415) 312-0650

Library of Congress Catalog Card No.: 92-72340

ISBN 1-878058-40-1

Printed in the United States of America

10 9 8 7 6 5 4 3 2

Distributed in the United States by IDG Books Worldwide, Inc.

Distributed in Canada by Macmillan of Canada, a Division of Canada Publishing Corporation; by Computer and Technical Books in Miami, Florida, for South America and the Caribbean; by Longman Singapore in Singapore, Malaysia, Thailand, and Korea; by Toppan Co. Ltd. in Japan; by Asia Computerworld in Hong Kong; by Woodslane Pty. Ltd. in Australia and New Zealand; and by Transword Publishers Ltd. in the U.K. and Europe.

For information on where to purchase IDG Books outside the U.S., contact Christina Turner at 415-312-0633.

For information on translations, contact Marc Jeffrey Mikulich, Foreign Rights Manager, at IDG Books Worldwide; FAX NUMBER 415-358-1260.

For sales inquiries and special prices for bulk quantities, write to the address above or call IDG Books Worldwide at 415-312-0650.

Dedication

To the millions of Excel users that have made the program the number one spreadsheet for the Apple Macintosh.

Acknowledgments

First and foremost, hats off to the folks at Microsoft for a class A-1 product. Excel is one of the best reasons to go out and get a Macintosh, or to get down on your knees and beg your boss for one.

Many thanks to the entire IDG team, especially Jeremy Judson, for his management of this project, and Bud Smith, technical editor extraordinaire, for keeping me on the straight and narrow. And my eternal gratitude goes to Terrie Solomon for giving me another once-in-a-lifetime opportunity.

Last but not least, thanks to Karen and Kyle for being patient and understanding while I was working on this project. With your help I was able to carry the day.

(The publisher would like to give special thanks to Patrick J. McGovern, without whom this book would not have been possible.)

About the Author

David Maguiness has been working with and writing about spreadsheets since 1981, when (thankfully) electronic spreadsheets put scissors, glue, and adding machines out to pasture as financial planning and analysis tools. He has written or co-written more than a dozen books on spreadsheets for the Apple Macintosh and IBM PC, including *PC World Excel 4 For Windows Handbook*, IDG Books, 1992. Maguiness also contributes to *Lotus Magazine* and was editor-in-chief of *Absolute Reference: The Journal for 123 and Symphony Users*. An alumnus of several Fortune 500 companies, Maguiness is currently a freelance writer and lives north of Indianapolis with his family.

Credits

Publisher and Vice President
David Solomon

Project Editor
Jeremy Judson

Production Manager
Beth Jenkins

Acquisitions Editor
Terrie Lynn Solomon

Copy Editor
Michael D. Welch

Technical Reviewer
Bud Smith

Proofreader
Shirley Coe

Indexer
Anne Leach

Editorial Assistant
Megg Bonar

Book Design and Production
Peppy White
Francette M. Ytsma
(University Graphics, Palo Alto, California)

About IDG Books Worldwide

Welcome to the world of IDG Books Worldwide.

IDG Books Worldwide, Inc., is a division of International Data Group, the world's largest publisher of computer-related information and the leading global provider of information services on information technology. IDG publishes over 194 computer publications in 62 countries. Forty million people read one or more IDG publications each month.

If you use personal computers, IDG Books is committed to publishing quality books that meet your needs. We rely on our extensive network of publications, including such leading periodicals as *Macworld*, *InfoWorld*, *PC World*, *Computerworld*, *Publish*, *Network World*, and *SunWorld*, to help us make informed and timely decisions in creating useful computer books that meet your needs.

Every IDG book strives to bring extra value and skill-building instruction to the reader. Our books are written by experts, with the backing of IDG periodicals, and with careful thought devoted to issues such as audience, interior design, use of icons, and illustrations. Our editorial staff is a careful mix of high-tech journalists and experienced book people. Our close contact with the makers of computer products helps ensure accuracy and thorough coverage. Our heavy use of personal computers at every step in production means we can deliver books in the most timely manner.

We are delivering books of high quality at competitive prices on topics customers want. At IDG, we believe in quality, and we have been delivering quality for over 25 years. You'll find no better book on a subject than an IDG book.

John Kilcullen
President and C.E.O.
IDG Books Worldwide, Inc.

IDG Books Worldwide, Inc. is a division of International Data Group. The officers are Patrick J. McGovern, Founder and Board Chairman; Walter Boyd, President. International Data Group's publications include: ARGENTINA's Computerworld Argentina, InfoWorld Argentina; ASIA's Computerworld Hong Kong, PC World Hong Kong, Computerworld Southeast Asia, PC World Singapore, Computerworld Malaysia, PC World Malaysia; AUSTRALIA's Computerworld Australia, Australian PC World, Australian Macworld, Network World, Reseller, IDG Sources; AUSTRIA's Computerwelt Oesterreich, PC Test; BRAZIL's Computerworld, Mundo IBM, Mundo Unix, PC World, Publish; BULGARIA's Computerworld Bulgaria, Ediworld, PC & Mac World Bulgaria; CANADA's Direct Access, Graduate Computerworld, InfoCanada, Network World Canada; CHILE's Computerworld, Informatica; COLOMBIA's Computerworld Colombia; CZECH REPUBLIC's Computerworld, Elektronika, PC World; DENMARK's CAD/CAM WORLD, Communications World, Computerworld Danmark, LOTUS World, Macintosh Produktkatalog, Macworld Danmark, PC World Danmark, PC World Produktguide, Windows World; EQUADOR's PC World; EGYPT's Computerworld (CW) Middle East, PC World Middle East; FINLAND's MikroPC, Tietoviikko, Tietoverkko; FRANCE's Distributique, GOLDEN MAC, InfoPC, Languages & Systems, Le Guide du Monde Informatique, Le Monde Informatique, Telecoms & Reseaux; GERMANY's Computerwoche, Computerwoche Focus, Computerwoche Extra, Computerwoche Karriere, Information Management, Macwelt, Netzwelt, PC Welt, PC Woche, Publish, Unit; HUNGARY's Alaplap, Computerworld SZT, PC World, ; INDIA's Computers & Communications; ISRAEL's Computerworld Israel, PC World Israel; ITALY's Computerworld Italia, Lotus Magazine, Macworld Italia, Networking Italia, PC World Italia; JAPAN's Computerworld Japan, Macworld Japan, SunWorld Japan, Windows World; KENYA's East African Computer News; KOREA's Computerworld Korea, Macworld Korea, PC World Korea; MEXICO's Compu Edicion, Compu Manufactura, Computacion/Punto de Venta, Computerworld Mexico, MacWorld, Mundo Unix, PC World, Windows; THE NETHERLAND'S Computer! Totaal, LAN Magazine, MacWorld; NEW ZEALAND's Computer Listings, Computerworld New Zealand, New Zealand PC World; NIGERIA's PC World Africa; NORWAY's Computerworld Norge, C/World, Lotusworld Norge, Macworld Norge, Networld, PC World Ekspress, PC World Norge, PC World's Product Guide, Publish World, Student Data, Unix World, Windowsworld, IDG Direct Response; PANAMA's PC World; PERU's Computerworld Peru, PC World; PEOPLES REPUBLIC OF CHINA's China Computerworld, PC World China, Electronics International, China Network World; IDG HIGH TECH BEIJING's New Product World; IDG SHENZHEN's Computer News Digest; PHILLIPPINES' Computerworld, PC World; POLAND's Computerworld Poland, PC World/Komputer; PORTUGAL's Cerebro/PC World, Correio Informatico/Computerworld, MacIn; ROMANIA's PC World; RUSSIA's Computerworld-Moscow, Mir-PC, Sety; SLOVENIA's Monitor Magazine; SOUTH AFRICA's Computing S.A.; SPAIN's Amiga World, Computerworld Espana, Communicaciones World, Macworld Espana, NeXTWORLD, PC World Espana, Publish, Sunworld; SWEDEN's Attack, ComputerSweden, Corporate Computing, Lokala Natverk/LAN, Lotus World, MAC&PC, Macworld, Mikrodatorn, PC World, Publishing & Design (CAP), DataIngenjoren, Maxi Data, Windows World; SWITZERLAND's Computerworld Schweiz, Macworld Schweiz, PC & Workstation; TAIWAN's Computerworld Taiwan, Global Computer Express, PC World Taiwan; THAILAND's Thai Computerworld; TURKEY's Computerworld Monitor, Macworld Turkiye, PC World Turkiye; UNITED KINGDOM's Lotus Magazine, Macworld, Sunworld; UNITED STATES' AmigaWorld, Cable in the Classroom, CD Review, CIO, Computerworld, Desktop Video World, DOS Resource Guide, Electronic News, Federal Computer Week, Federal Integrator, GamePro, IDG Books, InfoWorld, InfoWorld Direct, Laser Event, Macworld, Multimedia World, Network World, NeXTWORLD, PC Games, PC Letter, PC World Publish, Sumeria, SunWorld, SWATPro, Video Event; VENEZUELA's Computerworld Venezuela, MicroComputerworld Venezuela; VIETNAM's PC World Vietnam

The text in this book is printed on recycled paper.

Contents at a Glance

Table of Contents

Foreword

Electronic spreadsheet programs have been around for more than a decade. During this time, I've watched this class of software evolve at a rapid clip. The first spreadsheets were simple accountant's tools, used primarily to add up rows and columns of numbers. But over the years, spreadsheet manufacturers have added a nearly endless list of features, and today's spreadsheets are used in virtually all disciplines — business, education, science, manufacturing, and who knows what else.

But as these products become more sophisticated, they also become more complex and it's easy to be overwhelmed by the power at your disposal. I've seen too many spreadsheet users who were ready to throw in the towel after spending several frustrating hours attempting to perform an operation that should have taken minutes.

David Maguiness wrote the *Macworld Guide To Microsoft Excel 4* to help reduce your frustration level so you can get up to speed quickly. It's a handy guide to the most frequently used spreadsheet operations, and makes no claims to cover every aspect of Excel. While there's certainly a place for thick, comprehensive computer books, not everyone needs to know every nuance of their software. Rather, their main concern is solving the problem at hand. If you're a bottom-line kind of person, you'll be glad you picked up a copy of this book.

What I like most about the *Macworld Guide To Microsoft Excel 4* is that it helps you locate information you need quickly. It's well-organized and has a great index — which means you don't need to wade through a lot of extraneous material to get an answer. Even better, Maguiness makes the material easy to understand and tosses in plenty of time-saving tips along the way. Maguiness has certainly paid his dues. He's a widely-published author who has years of experience under his belt working with all the major spreadsheet programs on a wide variety of computer systems.

Regardless of your experience level, you'll find that this book will help maximize your investment in Microsoft Excel and help you work smarter and more efficiently. Enjoy.

John Walkenbach
Contributing Editor
PC World and *InfoWorld*

Introduction

About This Book

Welcome to *Macworld Guide To Microsoft Excel 4* — a different type of book about the most popular spreadsheet for the Apple Macintosh. *Macworld Guide To Microsoft Excel 4* isn't a quick reference booklet, a manual, or an encyclopedia-sized handbook.

The *Macworld Guide To . . .* series is the result of IDG Books' analysis of the current computer book market and the subsequent effort to provide an unmet need in personal computer software information. Quick reference booklets, for example, typically provide fast answers to specific questions at a low price. But because of their brevity, quick references always fall short in providing in-depth information about the nuances of a program.

The documentation that comes with a program has been getting better over time, with the use of step-by-step instructions being their strong suit. But user documentation's organization and structure doesn't always reflect what a real-world user encounters when using a program.

And what about those door stop-sized computer books? Few of us have the time or inclination to curl up in the evening with a good computer book and leisurely find what we need to know to get a job done. And you shouldn't need to plow through 500 pages of text to learn something as essential as printing. Typically, these books contain helpful insights and tips, but because they try to cover every aspect of a program, many useful features end up getting short changed.

What is needed is a book that contains the best of all three types of books — the brevity and structure of a quick reference booklet, the step-by-step tutorial of a manual, and the insights and tips of an epic computer book.

That's where *Macworld Guide To Microsoft Excel 4* fits in. Think of the book as your travel guide to Microsoft Excel. A travel guide lets you look up a place, and then learn about it and find out what to do and where to do it. In a similar vein, this book enables you to look up a task and learn how to do it. And if you wander into unfamiliar territory, this book enables you to quickly find the information you need to get back on track.

And as you explore other new worlds in the Macintosh galaxy, IDG's other books in this series can act as guideposts: *Macworld Guide To Microsoft Word 5*, *Macworld Guide To Microsoft Works 3*, and *Macworld Guide To System 7*.

Whom This Book Is For

Macworld Guide To Microsoft Excel 4 is for anyone who uses version 4 of Microsoft Excel for the Macintosh:

- If you're a beginner, the Step-by-Step tutorials help you get up to speed quickly with common, but unfamiliar, Excel Topics.
- If you're an intermediate Excel user — someone who needs only the Excel essentials but doesn't want any hand-holding — the Overviews in the beginning of each Topic explain how to accomplish a task without working through the tutorial.
- If you're an Excel guru, the tips and insights in each topic will help you get the most from Excel. You'll find the Quick Tips sections, icons indicating new Excel 4 features, and the Quick Reference Pull-Out Card handy tools for your Excel toolbox.

How This Book Is Organized

Rather than chapters, this book has Topics — tasks you're likely to perform in Excel. Each Topic covers a specific task, such as working with worksheet files, charting data, creating macros, and so on. When you need to perform an Excel task, scan the table of contents to locate the Topic that addresses your needs. You can also fan the pages of the book to quickly find the topic you need — each topic's name appears at the edges of each page. Every topic contains the following three sections:

Overview provides a summary of the Topic's subject. This section provides you with a flavor of the topic and describes how to accomplish the task.

Step-by-Step provides you with a hands-on opportunity to try out the task covered in the Topic, whether or not you read the Overview section. The numbered "To do" lines in each Step-by-Step spell out specific instructions for a task.

Quick Tips gives useful tips about the task covered in a Topic. This is the spot to look for the inside scoop (and how to avoid those occasional pitfalls) on how to accomplish an Excel task quickly and efficiently.

Other icons used to help streamline your learning experience include the following:

Excel version 4 alerts you to features that are new to Excel.

Caution alerts you to areas that you should read before proceeding with the task at hand. Use these to avoid the hidden traps that sometimes occur when using a program.

This book's Topics are organized into five parts:

- **Part One, "Excel Worksheet Fundamentals,"** explains basic worksheet tasks, including working with worksheet files, entering data, and printing worksheets.
- **Part Two, "Worksheet Data Manipulation,"** teaches you how to change the contents of cells by deleting, cutting, copying, and pasting.
- **Part Three, "Intermediate Excel,"** shows you how to create formulas, use worksheet functions, add pizzazz to a worksheet, create and enhance charts, and draw objects on a worksheet.
- **Part Four, "Advanced Excel,"** describes how to link and consolidate worksheets, and how to use Excel's database features.
- **Part Five, "Customizing Excel,"** describes how to use Excel toolbars, create macros, use the add-in programs that come with Excel, and exchange data with other programs.

The back of the book contains the following four appendixes:

- **Appendix A** provides information on how to install Excel. See this section to learn how you can customize Excel for the way you work.
- **Appendix B** lists Excel's vast arsenal of keyboard shortcuts. If using a mouse is new to you, or you don't want to take your hands off the keyboard, you'll want to check into this appendix. The Topics contain the keyboard shortcuts you're most likely to use, but this appendix is your keyboard shortcut one-stop shop.
- **Appendix C** is a glossary of common Excel and spreadsheet terminology. If you run across an unfamiliar term, turn to this appendix for the inside track.
- **Appendix D** is a Task Index that lists all the instructions that appear in each Topic's Step-by-Step section for easy reference.

How To Use This Book

If you're new to Excel or spreadsheeting, you should read and work through the first few Topics to get a feel for the program. If you've been around the block with Excel previously, jump in wherever you like — one advantage to this book is that you don't have to read the Topics in order.

This book has a number of features that enable you to locate the information you need quickly. Here are some pointers for putting these features to work.

When you need to . . .	***Use . . .***
Learn how to accomplish a certain spreadsheet task such as entering a formula into a cell	The table of contents to locate the Topic that describes the task
Look up a specific set of instructions within a Topic — for example, those that describe how to enter a formula with a mixed cell address	The task index

What You Should Already Know

This book assumes that you know the basics behind operating an Apple Macintosh.

Specifically, you should know how to start programs and manipulate windows (making a window active, moving and sizing a window, and zooming a window). In addition, you need to know how to choose commands from pull-down menus and understand pointing, clicking, and double-clicking. If all this sounds strange to you, take another look at the documentation that came with your Macintosh, or better yet, read David Pogue's *Macs For Dummies*, IDG Books, 1992 — a fun way to learn about your Macintosh.

Part I:

Excel Worksheet Fundamentals

Topic 1

Creating and Saving Worksheets

Overview

This chapter, or "Topic" as they are called in this book, introduces you to the world of Excel and worksheets and serves as your launching pad to learning and using the program with confidence. Specifically, you'll become acquainted with opening, creating, closing, and saving Excel worksheets.

To get the most from this and future Topics, you should have Excel running and onscreen so that you can follow along with the discussion. In addition, you'll have an opportunity to practice what you've learned in the Step-by-Step section, so if you haven't already, now is a good time to start up Excel on your Macintosh.

Creating a new worksheet

In Microsoft Excel, a worksheet is a document that resembles a large grid, similar to accounting paper. Excel's worksheet is much bigger, however — 16,384 rows and 254 columns. The intersection of the rows and columns of the worksheet are known as *cells.* You enter text, numbers, formulas, and functions (Excel's built-in formulas) in cells to calculate results quickly. Excel enables you to find the answers to a variety of business problems, including the following:

- ✦ Totals and averages
- ✦ Depreciation and investments
- ✦ Planning and budgeting
- ✦ Actual and variance reporting

In fact, Excel can help you solve any problem that can be expressed in numerical terms. But first you need to know how to view different areas of the worksheet, and how to enter data into it.

Viewing the worksheet

Because the Excel worksheet is so large, you can view only a small portion of the worksheet at a time. You view different areas of the Excel worksheet by using the scroll bars, just like any other Macintosh program. The horizontal scroll bar lets you display different columns on your screen, while the vertical scroll bar lets you choose which rows to display, as shown in Figure 1-1.

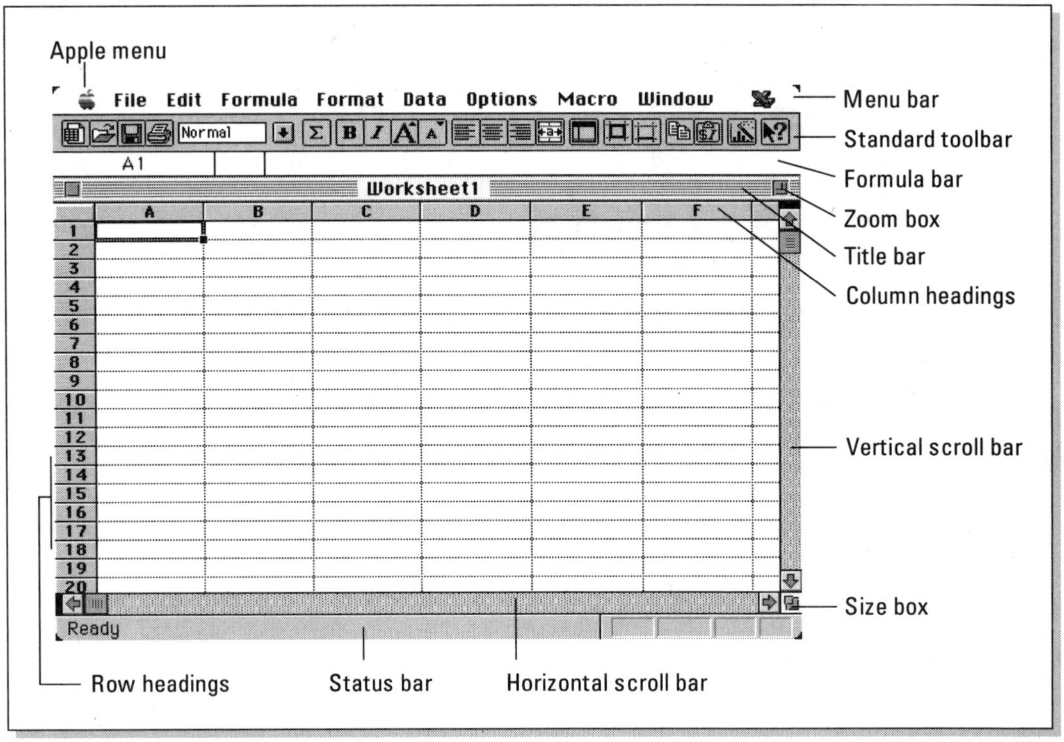

Figure 1-1: The standard elements of an Excel worksheet.

Hey Microsoft! Why so large?

If you're new to Excel, you may be scratching your head — why such a large worksheet? Does anyone *really* create an application that requires that many rows and columns?

That's a fair question. Since the dawn of personal computing, there's been what industry pundits call a "spreadsheet war" going on. And the battlefield is features. The earliest feature that drew attention was size. Each new program that came on the market boasted a larger worksheet, a type of row-and-column one-upmanship.

Even if you could create an application that used every row and column (you'd run out of memory long before you did), it's not in your best interest to do so. It's much more efficient to create smaller, more compact worksheets that perform a single, dedicated task. In this manner, Excel can perform calculations, execute commands, and redraw screens that display several small worksheets much more quickly than a single huge worksheet.

Fortunately, the battle has shifted to ease-of-use features, such as the toolbars, and analytical capability, with worksheet functions to meet every need. The winner in all this is you — the user — by providing you with a spreadsheet program that not only has great capacity but is also easy to use, powerful, and continually improving.

As you view different areas of the worksheet, you move the *cell pointer*. The cell pointer is the rectangular border around a cell that appears when you click in a new cell making it the *active cell*. You enter text or values into the active cell in the worksheet through the formula bar. You can make a cell the active cell using the mouse or the keyboard. To move around the worksheet using the mouse, simply click in the cell in which you want to enter data. If the cell you want to move to doesn't appear on-screen, use the scroll bars to scroll the worksheet, and then click the cell when it appears.

To move around the worksheet using the keyboard, use the keys as shown in Table 1-1:

Table 1-1: Manipulating worksheets using the keyboard

Keystroke	*Action*
All Macintosh keyboards:	
Right arrow or Tab	One cell to the right
Left arrow or Shift-Tab	One cell to the left
Down arrow	One cell down
Up arrow or Shift-Return	One cell up
Extended keyboard:	
Home	First cell in the current row that contains data
Command-Home	Cell A1
End	Last cell in the current row that contains data
Command-End	Intersection of the last row and column that contains data
Command-up arrow	To next cell up containing data, next range of data, or row 1
Command-down arrow	To next cell down containing data, next range of data, or row 16,384
Command-left arrow	To next cell left containing data, next range of data to the left, or to column A of worksheet
Command-right arrow	To next cell right containing data, next range of data to the right, or to column IV of worksheet
Scrolling the screen (extended keyboard):	
Page Up	Up one screen
Page Down	Down one screen
Command-Page Up	Left one screen
Command-Page Down	Right one screen

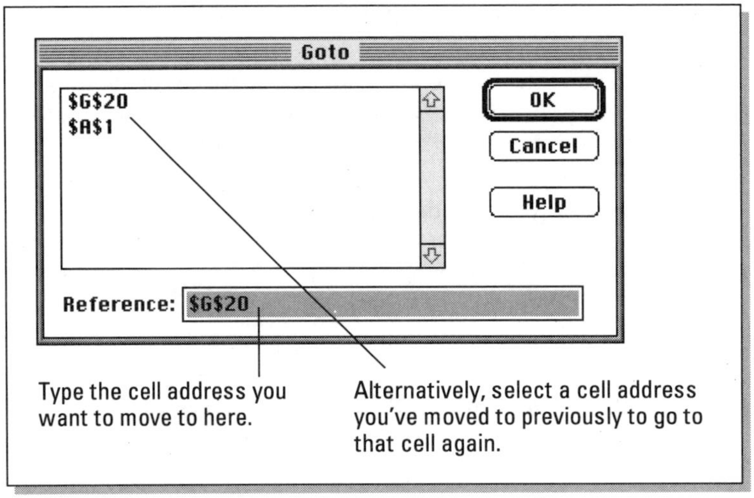

Figure 1-2: Moving within a worksheet using the Goto dialog box.

You can also move to a cell by pressing F5 (extended keyboard) or Command-G (all keyboards). When you do, the dialog box shown in Figure 1-2 appears. Type the cell address (the column letter and row number) in the Reference text box and click OK. Excel will make the cell you chose the active cell and display it in the upper-left corner of the worksheet window.

Entering data

When you start Excel, the program displays a new worksheet (named Worksheet1) in its own window. (*Worksheet1* appears in the title bar of the worksheet). This worksheet is like a blank piece of paper because it does not contain any text, numbers, functions, or formulas. As you enter text and data, you add structure to the empty worksheet and create a worksheet *application*. Text, and especially values, are essential for Excel's worksheet functions and formulas to perform calculations.

Each cell in the worksheet can hold one text entry, value, worksheet function, or formula. To enter text or values, do the following:

1. Make the cell you want to enter data in the active cell.
2. Type the data. The data will appear in the formula bar.

To enter data in a cell, press Return, press an arrow key, or click the Enter box in the formula bar. Pressing Return moves the cell pointer down to the next cell. To cancel entering the data, press Esc or click the cancel box in the formula bar.

As you type the data, Excel evaluates your typing to determine whether it's text or a value. Any entry containing alphabetical characters or other keyboard symbols are considered text by Excel. In addition, data entered in one of the following formats are considered dates, and can be used in calculations:

Format	Example
mm/dd/yy	12/31/92
dd/mmm/yy	31-Dec-92
mm-dd-yy	12-31-92

Creating a worksheet is basically a three-step process. First, make sure your problem is clearly defined, and think about how you can use Excel to help you solve it. Second, use text as labels to give values or the results of calculations meaning, as shown in Figure 1-3. Third, enter data, functions, and formulas into the worksheet. Finally, you save your completed worksheet to disk for use in future Excel sessions.

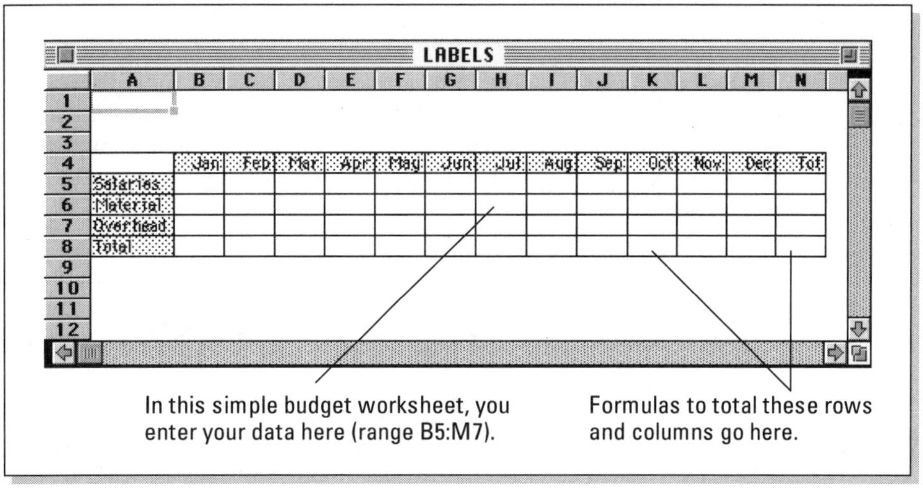

Figure 1-3: Using text as labels in the creation of a worksheet.

Help! I've made a mistake and can't get up!

It happens to all of us — entering a number in the wrong place, entering a wrong number over a right number, moving or copying the wrong data, and on and on. What's an Excel user to do?

The first rule to remember is: Don't panic. Like all other Macintosh programs, the Undo option on the Edit menu is only a mouse click away. The Undo command can undo, or reverse, just about all of the most potentially destructive mistakes: overwriting cell entries, wrong commands that can affect your data, and so on. Remember, the good folks at Microsoft want you to do your best, and like a silent spreadsheet friend, the Undo command stands by you through thick and thin, bailing you out of many potentially unpleasant situations.

The Undo command can't reverse everything, of course. Undo won't be able to stop a copy of a worksheet going to your printer (you'll have to do that yourself). And if you close a changed file without saving it first, you've lost your changes. But you can do an end-run around that problem by saving frequently to disk, a good habit whatever your Excel skill level is.

Saving a worksheet

Saving a worksheet to disk periodically is one of the most important Excel activities. As you create or revise an existing worksheet, labels or values are only temporarily stored in your Macintosh's memory. If you should experience a power interruption, or system problem, or you turn off your computer, your work will be lost permanently. To use a worksheet again in future Excel sessions, you must save it to disk.

You use the Save command from the File menu or Command-S to save a worksheet to disk. If this is the first time you've saved the worksheet, Excel displays a dialog box that you use to name the worksheet file and to specify where to save it (appropriate disk and folder). After you type a name (with a 31-character maximum), click the Save button, and Excel will save the worksheet to disk. Try to use descriptive names for your worksheets so you can quickly identify their purpose in future Excel sessions.

As a shortcut, you can forego the File menu and click the File Save tool on the Standard toolbar, as shown in Figure 1-4. The Standard toolbar is the gray rectangle directly below the menu bar and contains icons, or tools, you click to perform common worksheet tasks quickly. The File Save tool, the third tool from the left on the toolbar, resembles a computer disk.

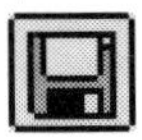

The File Save tool

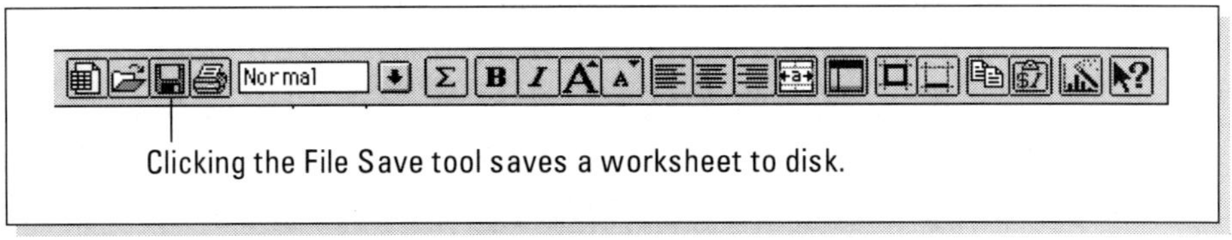

Figure 1-4: Saving a worksheet using the File Save tool from the Standard toolbar.

The next time you use File Save, Command-S, or click the File Save tool with a worksheet you previously saved to disk, Excel will save the worksheet to the same disk or folder using the same name. Excel will not display the File Save dialog box this time, though you can see the progress of the file save operation in Excel's Reference area, expressed as a percentage (see Figure 1-5).

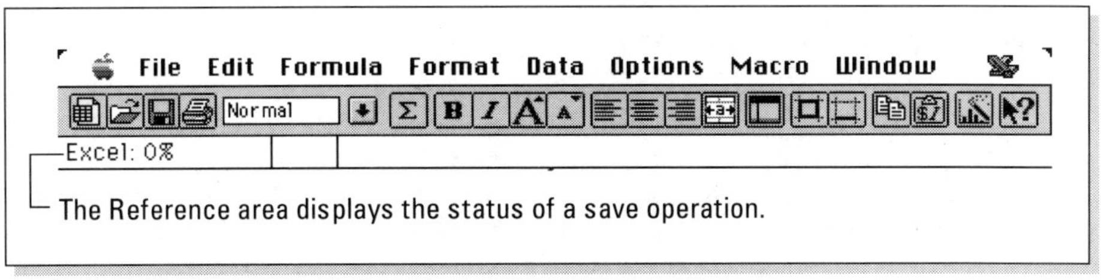

Figure 1-5: Monitoring a save operation from Excel's Reference area.

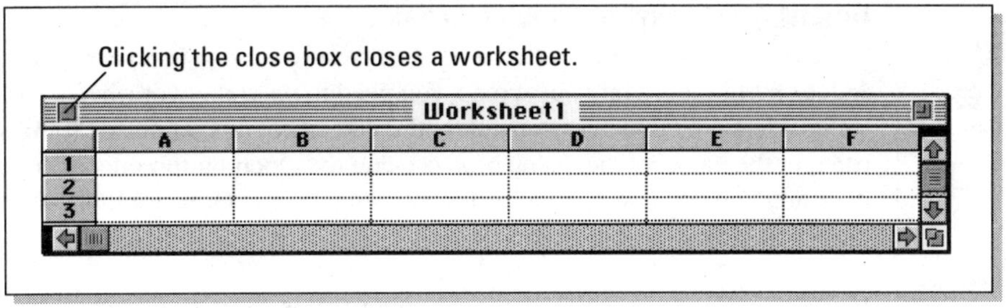

Figure 1-6: Saving changes to a worksheet.

If you want to save the worksheet in another folder or under a different filename, you'll need to use the Save As command from the File menu. The File Save dialog box will appear which will let you specify a different folder, disk, or name for the worksheet.

Closing a worksheet

As you become more proficient with Excel and create more advanced worksheet applications, you may need to have more than one worksheet displayed on-screen. To reduce screen clutter and free up memory, you can close unneeded worksheets. Closing a worksheet is similar to putting a piece of paper back into a file folder until you need it another time. To close a worksheet file, you use the Close command on the File menu, Command-W, or click the close box, as shown in Figure 1-6.

If you've never saved the file and have entered data or modified the file since the last time you've saved it, Excel displays the dialog box shown in Figure 1-7. Press Return or click Yes to save any changes you've made since your last save operation; click No to close the file, or click Cancel to stop closing the file. If you choose No, however, any changes to your document are permanently lost, so be careful.

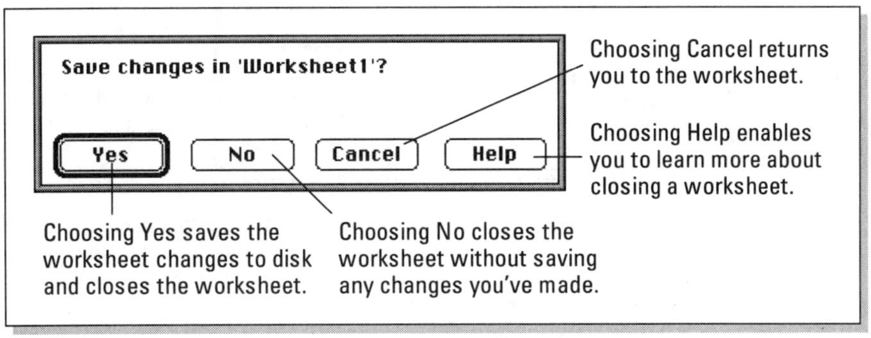

Figure 1-7: Saving a worksheet that has been modified since it was saved last.

Opening a worksheet you've created

The File Open tool

If you would like to work with a worksheet you've created in an earlier Excel session and it isn't displayed on your screen, you need to *open* the worksheet. To open a worksheet, you use the Open command on the File menu, or Command-O, and select the name of the file from the dialog box, clicking the Open button once you've selected the filename. You can also open a document using the File Open tool. The File Open tool, the second from the left on the toolbar, resembles an open file folder.

If you're fortunate enough to have a monitor that is 13 or more inches in size (measured diagonally), Excel displays the names of the last four previously opened worksheets at the bottom of the File menu. Select File from the menu bar, and then select the name of the file to quickly open it.

Opening a new worksheet

You may encounter a situation during an Excel session where you'd find it useful to have another blank worksheet to work with. For example, you may want to create another scenario by copying the information from the first worksheet to the second worksheet, add a product or cost center to a budget consolidation application, and so forth. Opening a new worksheet is easy. Simply choose New from the File menu or press Command-N. Excel displays the dialog box shown in Figure 1-8, asking you the type of document you need. If you want a new worksheet, click the Open button or press Return. Excel displays a new worksheet as the active document, named in sequential order (*Worksheet1*, *Worksheet2*, and so on).

Every time you open a new worksheet, each worksheet is displayed smaller than the last. To enlarge the display of a worksheet to its full size, click the zoom box on the title bar. The zoom box is the small square on the far right side of the title bar, as shown in Figure 1-9.

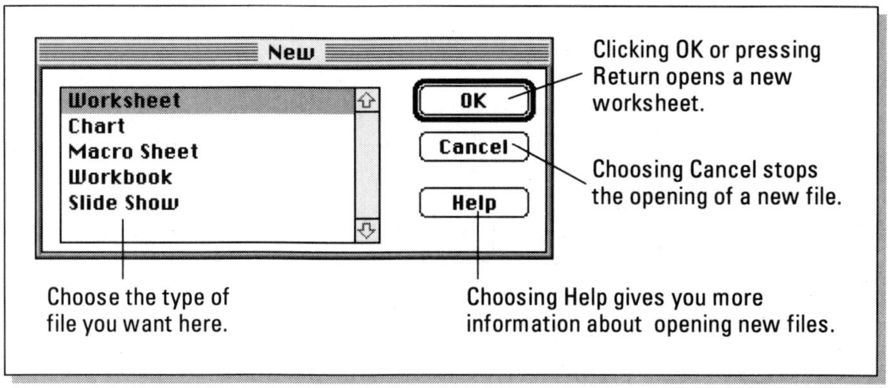

Figure 1-8: Opening a new worksheet.

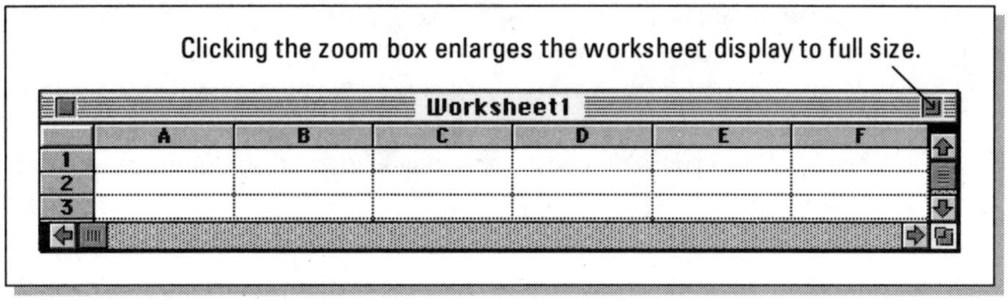

Figure 1-9: Resizing a worksheet using the zoom box on the title bar.

Enlarging a worksheet to full size will prevent you from clicking on other open worksheets, making them active. To make another worksheet active, select its name from the Window menu. The currently active worksheet has a check mark to the left of its name, as shown in Figure 1-10.

VERSION 4 Microsoft

The File New tool

You can also bypass the File menu when creating a new worksheet by clicking the File New tool on the toolbar. The File New tool, the first tool on the toolbar, resembles a grid on top of a document.

Calling it quits

When you're through using Excel, or need to call it a day and turn off your Macintosh, or want to exit from Excel to free up memory, you end your Excel session by choosing Quit from the File menu or by pressing Command-Q. Depending on any other activities during your current computer session, you'll be returned to another open application or the desktop — unless you have an unsaved file open.

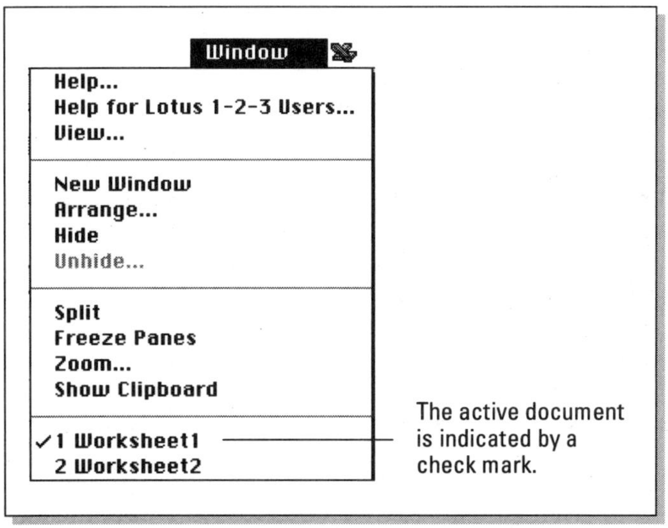

Figure 1-10: Making worksheets active using the Window menu.

If you've made changes to any open Excel documents since your last file save, Excel will display the dialog box you saw in Figure 1-7. Remember, choose Yes or press Return to save the file to disk (then you'll exit), choose No to exit from Excel without saving, or choose Cancel to stop quitting Excel and get back to work. If you choose No, however, any changes to your document are permanently lost, so don't be too hasty about leaving Excel.

Step-by-Step

This section lets you practice creating, saving, closing, and then opening a simple Excel worksheet. First, you'll enter text and values into a worksheet, and then save it to disk. Second, you'll close the worksheet, and open it again.

Creating a worksheet:

Step 1. Start Excel if you haven't already, or make Excel the active application with a new blank worksheet on screen.

The Worksheet1 window appears:

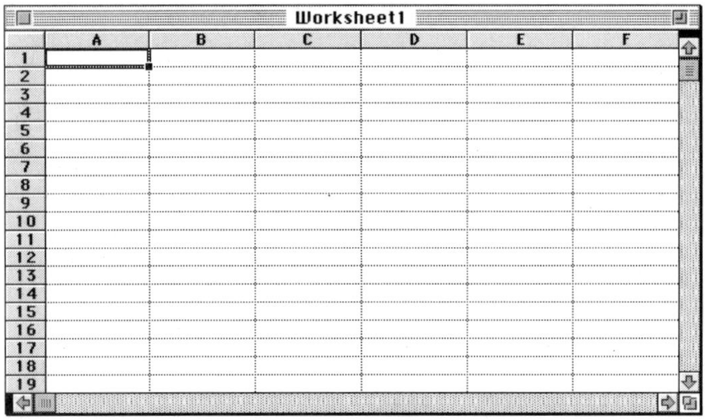

Figure 1-11: The window that is displayed when starting up Excel.

Step 2. Enter the text and values in the cells, as shown in Figure 1-12. Point and click on the cell or use the direction keys to make the cell active, and then type the text or a value. When you finish typing, press Return. Repeat this process until each cell in your worksheet contains the appropriate data, as shown in Figure 1-12.

If you make a mistake entering text or values, select Undo from the Edit menu, and then try again. (Don't worry if you do make a mistake; you'll learn how to make changes to the worksheet in Part II of this book).

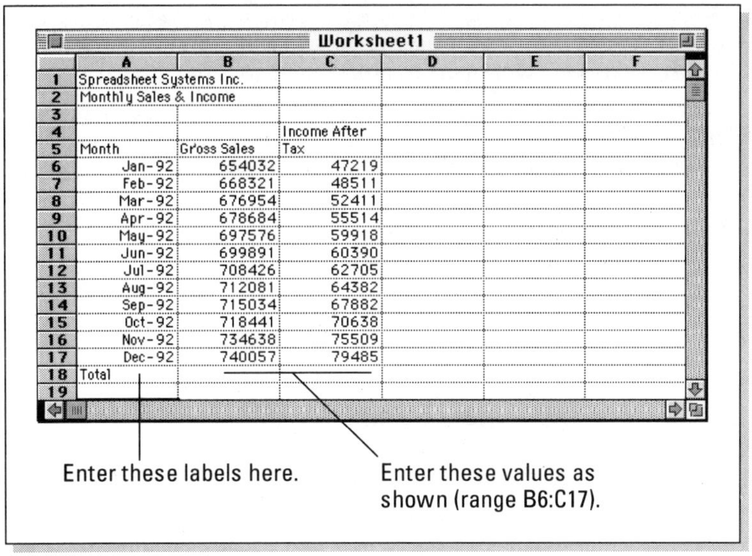

Figure 1-12: The sample worksheet with text and values typed in.

You may think this spreadsheet could look better, but don't worry about that now. We'll spruce it up in the next Topic.

Saving a worksheet:

Step 1. Select Save from the File menu.

The Save dialog box appears:

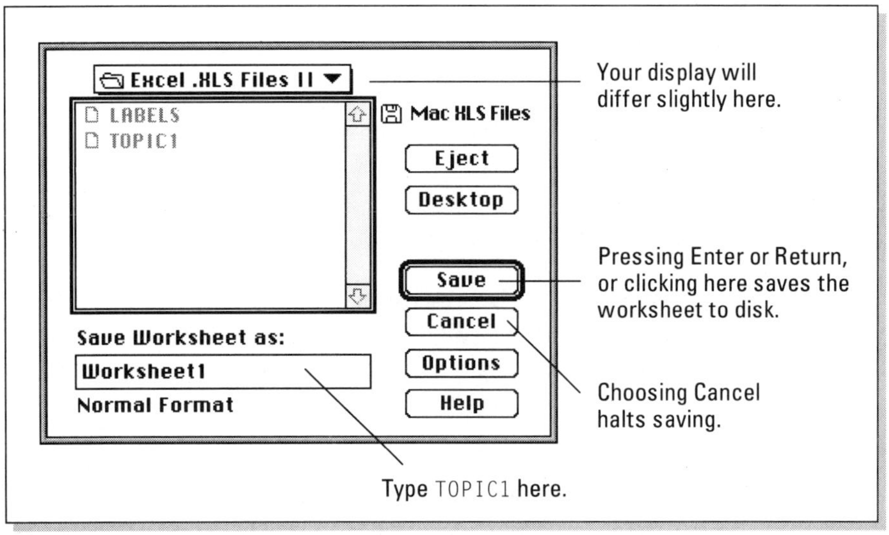

Figure 1-13: Choosing Save from the File menu displays the Save dialog box.

Step 2. Type TOPIC1 in the Save Worksheet as box and press Return or click Save.

Excel saves the worksheet to disk.

Closing a worksheet:

Step 1. Select Close from the File menu or click the worksheet window's close box.

Opening a worksheet:

Step 1. Select Open from the File menu.

The Open dialog box appears:

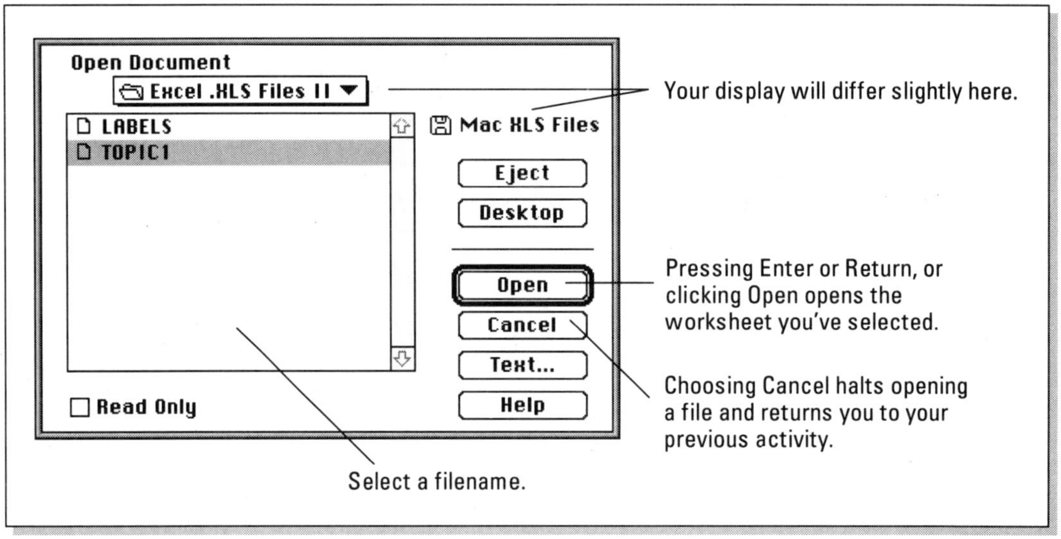

Figure 1-14: Choosing Open from the File menu displays the Open dialog box.

Step 2. Select TOPIC1; then click Open or press Return.

Excel opens TOPIC1 and displays it on-screen in its own window.

Quick Tips

This section provides you with tips on how to create and save your Excel worksheets.

Taking advantage of Excel's rows

In most cases, you should design budget worksheets so that time periods are your column text and item names are your row text. This enables you to take advantage of the greater number of rows than columns that Excel displays; you can also display more data on-screen at a time.

Cycling through worksheets

If you have more than one worksheet open at a time, pressing Command-M will cycle through all open worksheets.

Opening Excel worksheets automatically

If you find you use the same worksheet(s) each time you use Excel, see Topic 15, for information about how you can specify which Excel documents open automatically each time you start Excel.

Saving worksheets frequently

Remember to save worksheets frequently to guard against accidental errors or losing data in a power failure. If you are just starting out with a new worksheet, you probably have not saved it if the worksheet's title bar displays *Worksheetx* (where *x* is the number of the worksheet).

Using the Save As command

If you have made changes to an existing worksheet but want to preserve the original version on disk, use the Save As command from the File menu. This command enables you to save worksheets sequentially (BUDGET_01, BUDGET_02, and so on) so that you can keep track of prior versions of the worksheet.

Undoing changes made on a worksheet

If you've made changes to a worksheet that you now regret, don't save it to disk. Use the Close command from the File menu; choose No when the dialog box appears, and then choose Open from the File menu to start over with the worksheet's original contents unscathed.

Saving worksheets automatically

Excel includes a macro named Auto Save that saves worksheets automatically at a time interval you specify. See Topic 15 for more information about the add-in macros furnished with Excel.

Using the Return key in dialog boxes

Remember, any time a dialog box contains a button with a bold border, you can choose that button by pressing Return. This enables you to avoid having to take your fingers away from the keyboard.

Saving worksheets in different file formats

Excel can save a worksheet file in many popular program file formats, including Lotus 1-2-3 and dBASE. If you want to save a worksheet in a file format different from Excel, use Save As from the File menu, and then choose the format you want in the File Format box. For more information about exchanging data with other programs, see Topic 16. You can use worksheets created in Excel for Windows directly with Excel for the Macintosh.

Closing worksheets simultaneously

All open worksheets can be closed simultaneously by holding down Shift and choosing Close All from the File menu. Excel will prompt you with the dialog box shown in Figure 1-7 for each unsaved open worksheet.

Deleting files on disk while still in Excel

You can delete files saved to disk without leaving Excel by using the Delete command from the File menu. The dialog box in Figure 1-15 appears enabling you to choose the file that you want to permanently erase.

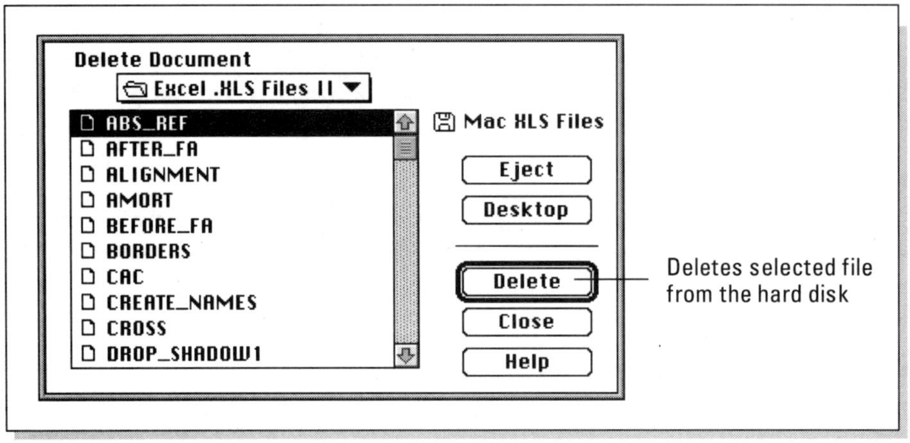

Figure 1-15: Deleting a file saved to disk without leaving Excel using the Delete command from the File menu.

Summary

- Every Excel worksheet contains 16,384 numbered rows and 256 lettered columns.
- You display different areas of the worksheet by using the mouse and scroll bars or keys on the keyboard.
- Data can be text, values, worksheet functions, or formulas that you enter into the active cell, the cell surrounded by a rectangular border.
- Mistakes can be reversed by immediately selecting Undo from the Edit menu.
- Save your work frequently to disk by using the Save command from the File menu, pressing Command-S, or clicking the File Save tool.
- Previously saved worksheets can be saved with another name or in a different folder or disk by choosing Save As from the File menu.
- Close a worksheet by choosing Close from the File menu, pressing Command-W, or clicking the worksheet's close box, the small square on the left side of the worksheet's title bar.
- Open a previously created worksheet by selecting Open from the File menu, pressing Command-N, or clicking the File Open tool.
- Exit Excel by choosing Quit from the File menu or by pressing Command-Q.

Topic 2

Changing the Display of Your Data

Overview

Now that you've successfully created your first Excel worksheet, you may want to spruce it up a bit. For example, wouldn't it look better if the text lined up over the values?

Now look at the text. If you're used to working with dollar amounts, you may prefer to display a dollar sign in front of each number. Or you may want a comma to separate the thousands in each number. Perhaps you'd like both.

With Excel, you can change the display of text and numbers, known as *formatting* your data. You can choose Alignment from the Format menu to align values or text left, center, or right in a cell, or to apply other options. Choosing Number from the Format menu enables you to add dollar signs, commas, and decimals to the display of values.

Aligning: The first step

To change the alignment of the text or values in a worksheet, first *select* a cell or range of cells containing data you want to align. Selecting a range is a snap. Simply move the cell pointer to the desired cell with the mouse or arrow keys. To select more than one cell, press and drag the mouse until all the cells you want to align are highlighted, and then release the mouse. Or press and hold down Shift and use the arrow keys to select the cells. Once you've selected the cells, you can perform as many worksheet operations on the cells as you want.

Aligning text and numbers

Excel's normal cell alignment displays text left-aligned and values right-aligned. Most of the time, you'll only align text. Figure 2-1 shows you the various alignment options.

Once you've selected the cells you want to align, choose Alignment from the Format menu, and then select the alignment option you want from the dialog box, as shown in Figure 2-2. Clicking OK changes the alignment of the selected cell entries.

You can also align cell entries quickly by clicking on one of the alignment tools from the toolbar, as shown in Figure 2-3.

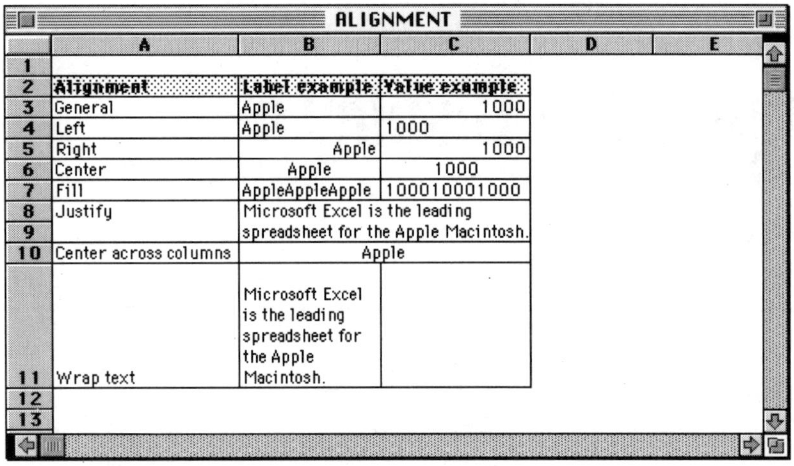

Figure 2-1: The alignment options available in Excel.

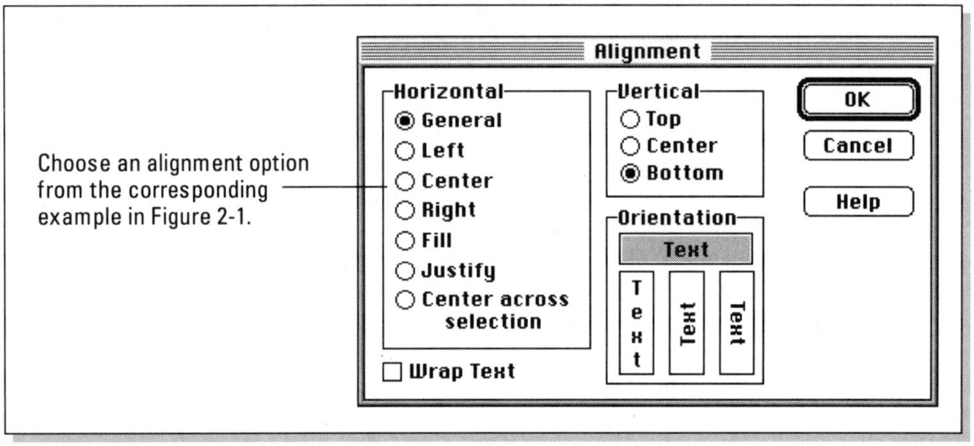

Figure 2-2: Choosing Alignment from the Format menu displays the Alignment dialog box.

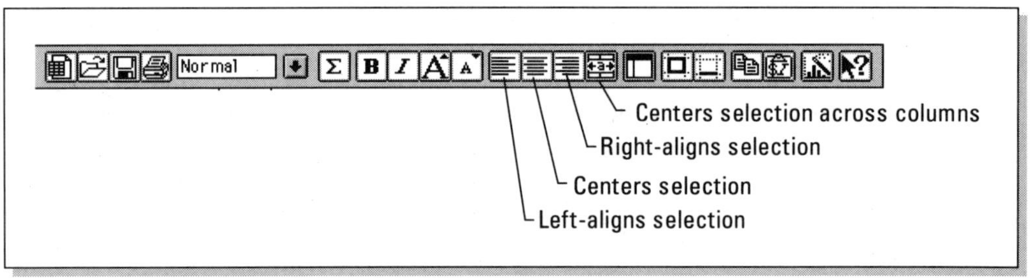

Figure 2-3: Using the alignment tools from the toolbar to align cell entries.

Formatting numbers

You use the same technique to format numbers that you use to format text, but you have a few more ways you can go about it. First, select the range of cells containing the numbers you want to format. You can then format the numbers using one of the following:

- ✦ The Number command from the Format menu
- ✦ A style from the Style pull-down menu
- ✦ A shortcut key combination

When you choose the Number command from the Format menu, the Number Format dialog box appears, as shown in Figure 2-4. Select a format category from the Category box that's appropriate for the type of values you're working with (when in doubt, use the All category). Then select a format from the Format Codes box. Note how the format looks in the Sample area of the dialog box. When you're happy with the format you've chosen, click OK to format the selected values.

You have a variety of formats that you can apply to values. Table 2-1 lists the formats available to you and how they affect the display of numbers.

To help you decipher the format types in the previous table: The pound symbol (#) represents numbers, and the semicolon (;) separates how the format displays positive and negative values. If a format type contains [Red], negative values will be

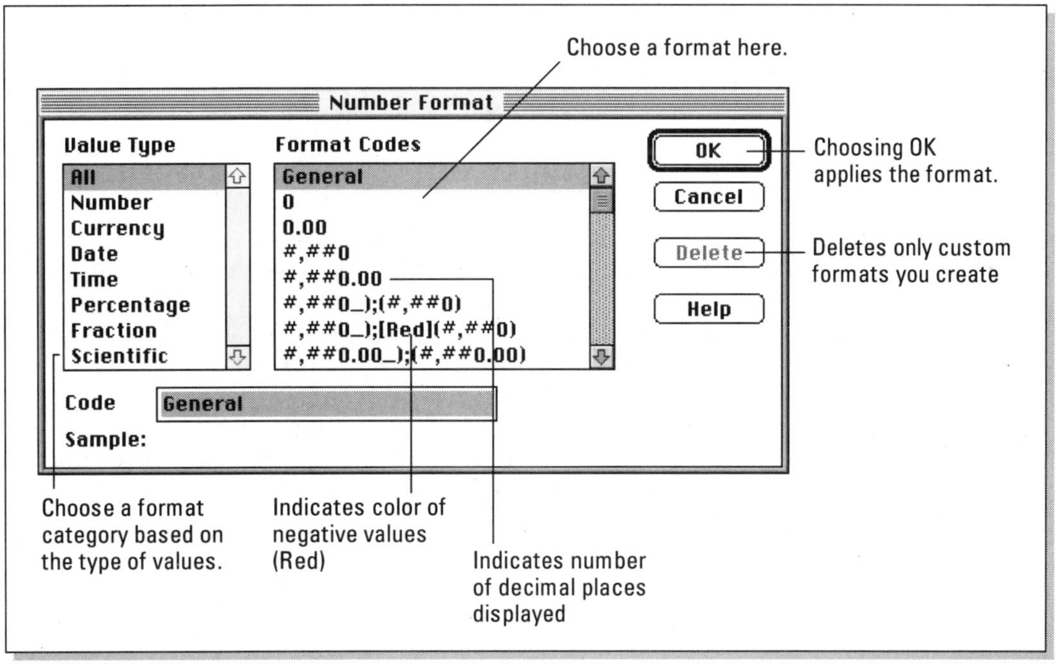

Figure 2-4: Choosing Number from the Format menu displays the Number Format dialog box.

Table 2-1: Available number formats

Display format	*Positive*	*Negative*
General	1234.5	-1234.5
0	1235	-1235
0.00	1234.50	-1234.50
#,##0	1,235	-1,235
#,##0.00	1,234.50	-1,234.50
#,##0_);(#,##0)	1,235	(1,235)
#,##0_);[RED](#,##0)	1,235	(1,235)[1]
#,##0.00_);(#,##0.00)	1,234.50	(1,234.50)
#,##0.00_);[RED](#,##0.00)	1,234.50	(1,234.50)[1]
$#,##0_);($#,##0)	$1,235	($1,235)
$#,##0_);[RED]($#,##0)	$1,235	($1,235)[1]
$#,##0.00_);($#,##0.00)	$1,234.50	($1,234.50)
$#,##0.00_);[RED]($#,##0.00)	$1,234.50	($1,234.50)[1]
0%	123450%	-123450%
0.00%	123450.00%	-123450.00%
0.00E+100	1.20E+103	-1.20E+103
#?/?	1 2/3	-1 2/3
#??/?? [2]	1 2/3	-1 2/3

[1] Displays negative values in red.
[2] Left aligned in cell.

displayed in that color. Note the way Excel treats decimal places: Formats with a single zero round off the display of a value, and those with 0.00 display two decimal places.

Some of the formats are available to you from the Style pull-down menu, or by using shortcut keys, as shown in Table 2-2.

To use the Style pull-down menu, press and hold down the mouse button on the arrow next to the Style box, as shown in Figure 2-5. When the pull-down menu appears, drag and release the mouse button on the style you want.

To use the shortcut keys, simply press all three keys simultaneously. Whichever method you choose to format with, make sure you have the cell or range you want to format selected first.

Table 2-2: Other number format options

Style	*Keystrokes*	*Format*	*Example*
Normal	Command-Option-~	General	1000
Comma (0)		#,###0	1,000
Comma		#,##0.00	1,000.00
Currency		$#,##0.00_);($#,##0.00)	$1,000.00
Currency (0)	Command-Option-$	$#,###0;($#,##0)	$1,000
Percent	Command-Option-%	0%	10%
	Command-Option-^	0.00E+00	1.00E+03
	Command-Option-!	0.00	1000.00

Figure 2-5: Using the Style pull-down menu to format cell entries.

Menus vs. tools vs. shortcut keys

You've undoubtedly discovered by now that there's more than one way to accomplish a task with Excel. You can format numbers, for example, using the Number command from the Format menu on the menu bar or the shortcut menu (discussed in the Quick Tips section at the end of this topic). Or you can apply a format from the Style pull-down menu, or by using shortcut keys. Which is the best method?

Actually, it comes down to personal preference. If you're a Macintosh veteran, you're probably accustomed to using the mouse, so that is probably the most efficient way for you. If you're new to graphical computing (or would rather keep your hands on the keyboard), you may want to continue using shortcut keys on the keyboard until you get comfortable with the idea of using a pointing device. Of course, there's nothing that says you can't use a combination of keyboard and mouse. You'll need both to enter text and values anyway.

Don't let the multiple ways of performing an Excel operation confuse you. Look at it as an opportunity to select what works for you, and I'll give you some helpful advice along the way to decide what's best.

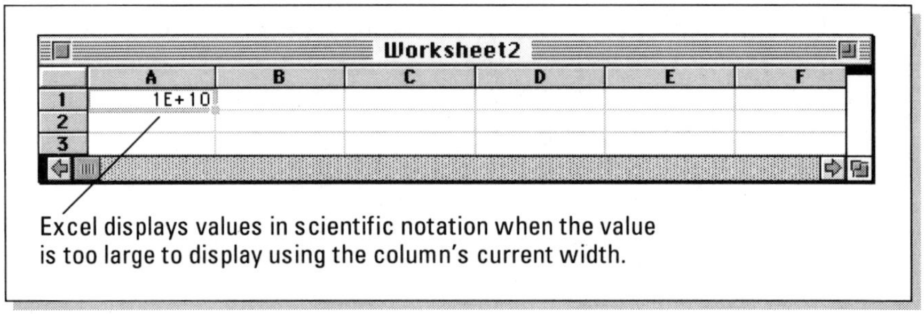

Figure 2-6: A value represented in scientific notation before changing Excel's display settings.

Changing the width of columns

If you haven't made any changes to Excel's display settings, entering the number 10,000,000,000 displays *1E+10* in the cell, as shown in Figure 2-6.

The number (10,000,000,000) is displayed this way because the column is not wide enough to display the contents of the cell. To get the entire number to display in the cell, you must widen the column.

Two-headed arrow

Changing the width of a column to display long text or a large number is easy. You click and drag on the right line that separates the column letters in the worksheet's column headings. The pointer, which appears as a black two-headed arrow, should be positioned on the right column heading line of the column whose width you want to change, as shown in Figure 2-7.

Click on the line and drag it to the right to expand the column width; drag to the left to reduce the column width. As you drag, watch the Reference area to see the actual width of the cell, which will be the number of characters you can display in a cell in that column for the current font and size. When the column is at the width you want, release the mouse button.

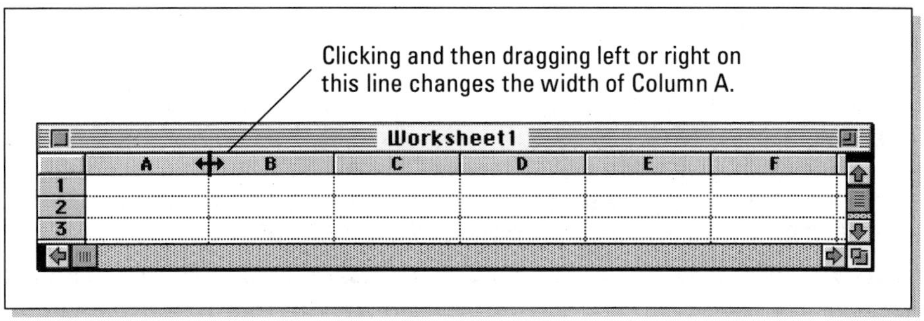

Figure 2-7: Changing the width of a column in a worksheet.

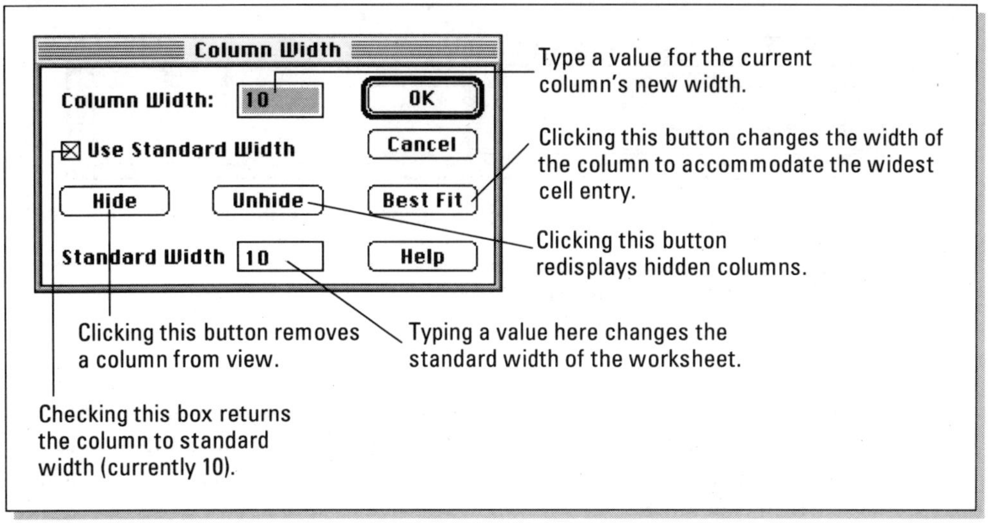

Figure 2-8: Choosing Column Width from the Format menu displays the Column Width dialog box.

You can also choose Column Width from the Format menu to change the column's width. When the Column Width dialog box appears after you choose the Column Width command, enter an integer or decimal fraction that represents the number of characters for the current font, and click OK, as shown in Figure 2-8.

Simultaneously changing the width of multiple adjacent columns is just as easy as changing the width of a single column. Click on a column's letter, and then drag the mouse left or right to select other columns. Now, drag on the line separating any two selected columns in the column headings area. Excel increases or decreases the width of all selected columns based on the one column width you change.

Changing the height of rows

You may want to manipulate rows just as you did columns. For example, if you work with solid lines to create boxes and tables, you may want to reduce the height of rows containing horizontal lines to enhance their appearance.

Changing the height of a row is very similar to changing the width of a column. You click and drag on the bottom line that separates the row numbers in the worksheet's row headings. The mouse pointer appears as a double-headed arrow, and should be positioned on the bottom line (the line immediately below the row's number) of the row whose height you want to change, as shown in Figure 2-9. Click on and drag the row down to increase the height of the row; drag up to decrease the height of the row. Release the mouse button when the row is at the height you want.

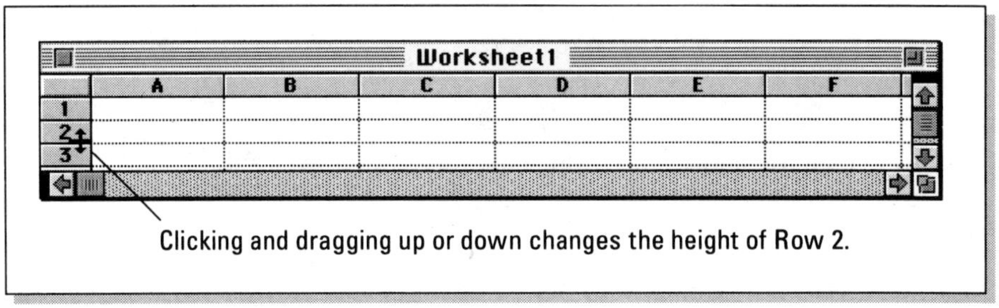

Figure 2-9: Changing the height of a row in a worksheet.

If you prefer to use commands to change row heights, choose Row Height from the Format menu. Choosing Row Height from the Format menu displays the Row Height dialog box shown in Figure 2-10. Enter the number of points you want the row's height to be, and then choose OK.

Be sure to specify a number larger than the point size of the font you're using in the row. If you don't, the cell entries will be cut off, as shown in Figure 2-11.

Either way you choose to change the height of a row, be careful not to make the height so small that you can't see the data. If you specify a row height that's too small, select Undo from the Edit menu (or press F1) to return the row to its previous height, and then try again.

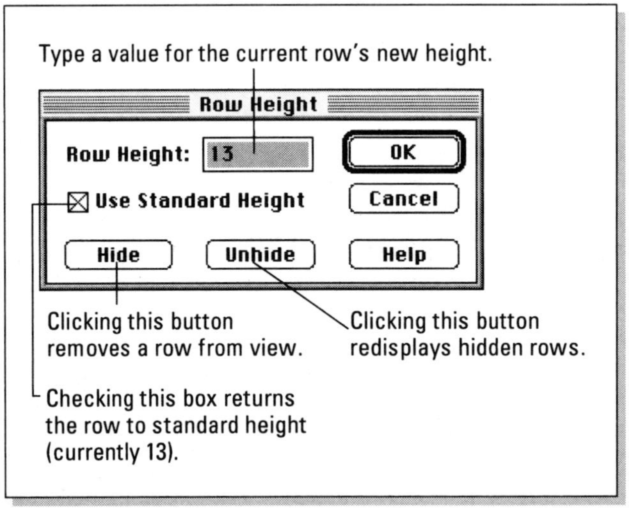

Figure 2-10: Choosing Row Height from the Format menu displays the Row Height dialog box.

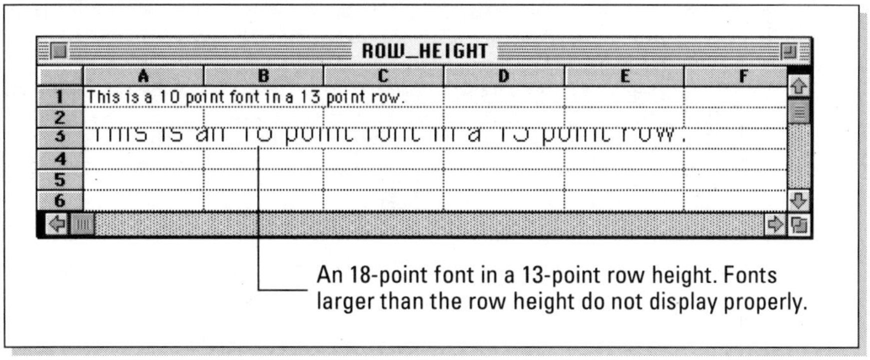

Figure 2-11: An example of how data looks when the font size is larger than the row height in a cell.

You can also change the height of multiple rows simultaneously much like you can with multiple columns. Click on the number of the first row whose height you want to change, and then drag up or down. After you've selected two or more rows, click and press down on any line separating the selected row numbers and drag down (or up) until the row is at the height you want. When you release the mouse button, each selected row has the height you just specified. Alternatively, choose Row Height from the Format menu to specify a row height.

Step-by-Step

This section gives you practice aligning text, formatting values, and changing row heights and column widths. First, you'll align text and format the numbers in the worksheet you created in Topic 1. Second, you'll practice changing column widths and row heights. For the second part of the exercise, you can use the worksheet from Topic 1 or a blank worksheet.

Set up your worksheet by doing the following:

Step 1. Start Excel if you haven't already, or make Excel the active application.

The Worksheet1 window appears.

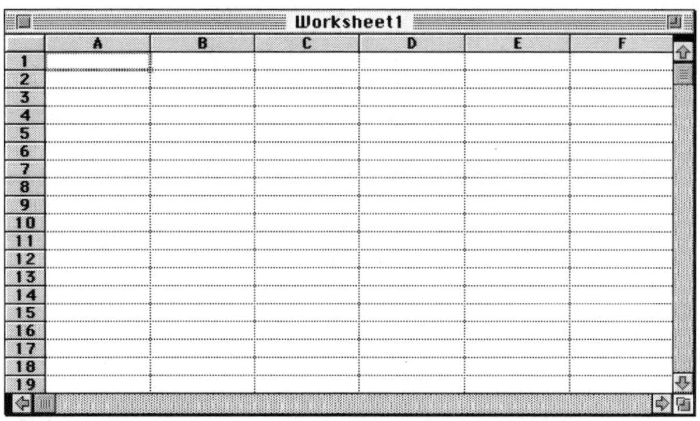

Figure 2-12: Starting Excel displays the Worksheet1 window.

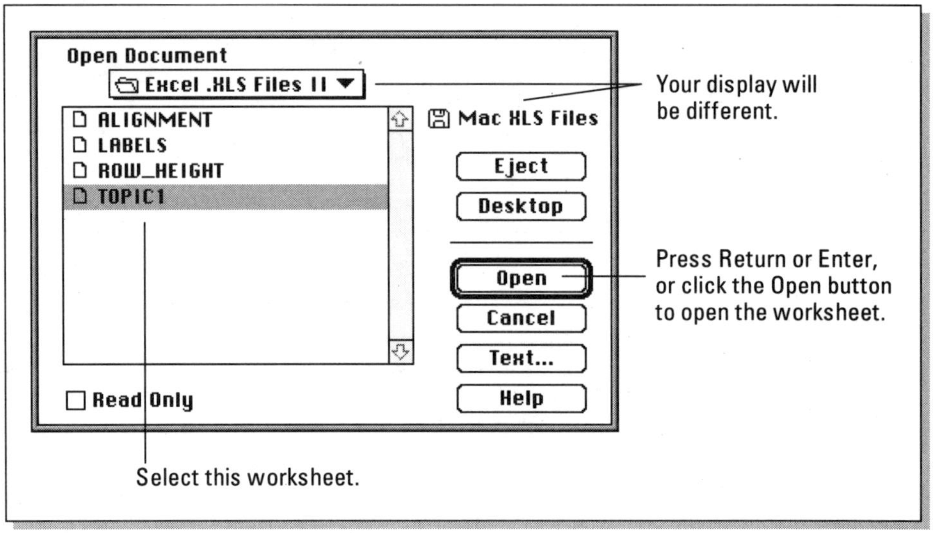

Figure 2-13: Using the Open dialog box to open a worksheet.

Step 2. Choose Open from the File menu.

The Open dialog box appears (see Figure 2-13).

Step 3. Select TOPIC1 and choose Open or press Return.

The TOPIC1 worksheet appears.

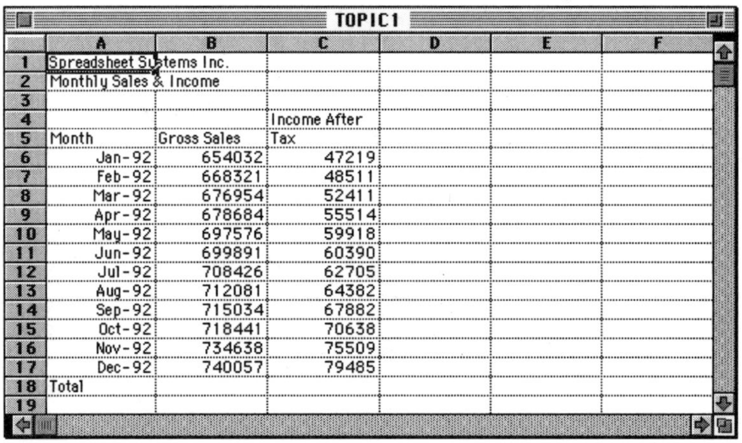

TOPIC1

	A	B	C	D	E	F
1	Spreadsheet Systems Inc.					
2	Monthly Sales & Income					
3						
4			Income After			
5	Month	Gross Sales	Tax			
6	Jan-92	654032	47219			
7	Feb-92	668321	48511			
8	Mar-92	676954	52411			
9	Apr-92	678684	55514			
10	May-92	697576	59918			
11	Jun-92	699891	60390			
12	Jul-92	708426	62705			
13	Aug-92	712081	64382			
14	Sep-92	715034	67882			
15	Oct-92	718441	70638			
16	Nov-92	734638	75509			
17	Dec-92	740057	79485			
18	Total					
19						

Figure 2-14: A worksheet that was opened using the Open dialog box.

Aligning labels:

Step 1. Select the range A4:C5, and choose Alignment from the Format menu.

The Alignment dialog box appears.

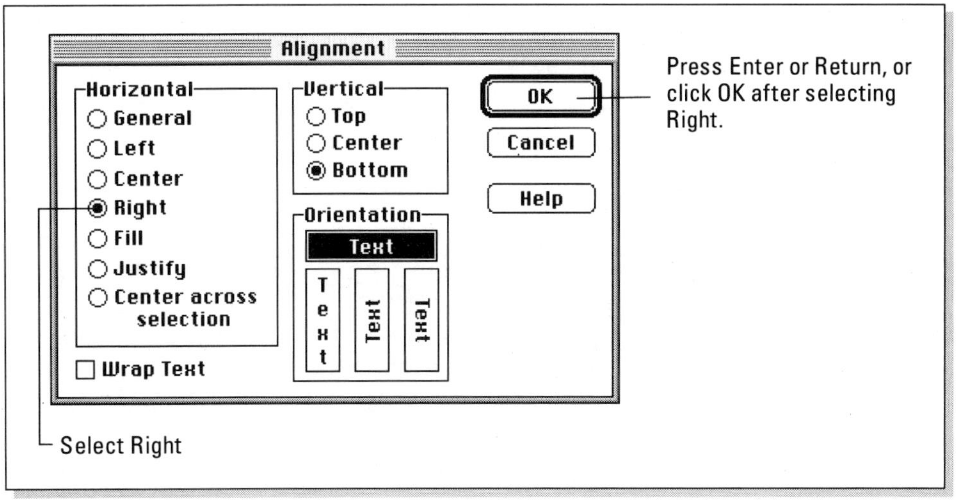

Figure 2-15: Aligning labels using the Alignment dialog box.

Step 2. Select Right and click OK.

Excel aligns the selected labels flush right in the cell.

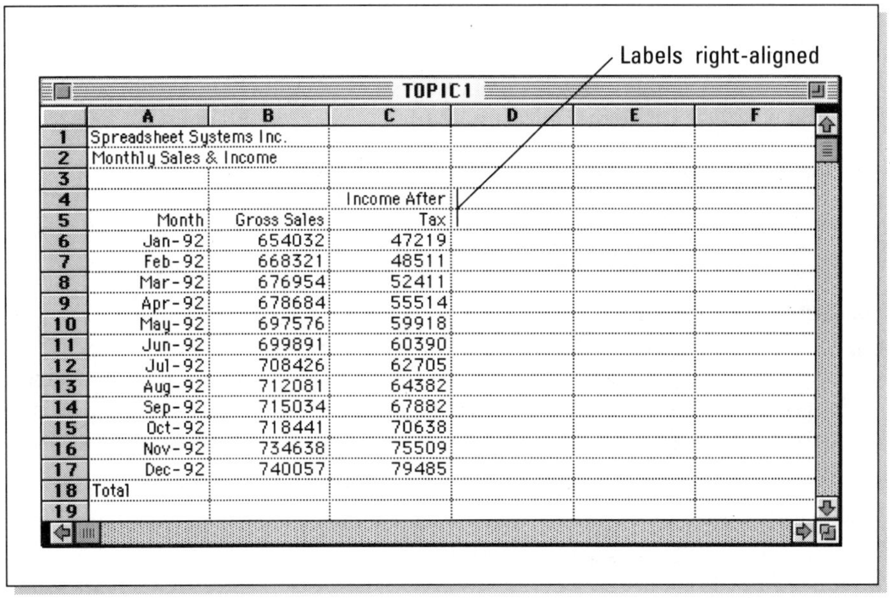

Figure 2-16: Selecting Right from the Alignment dialog box results in values being aligned flush right.

Formatting numbers:

Step 1. Select the range B6:C18.

To select the range B6:C18, move the mouse pointer to cell B6, and then press the mouse button down and drag across to cell C18.

Step 2. Select Number from the Format menu.

The Number Format dialog box appears.

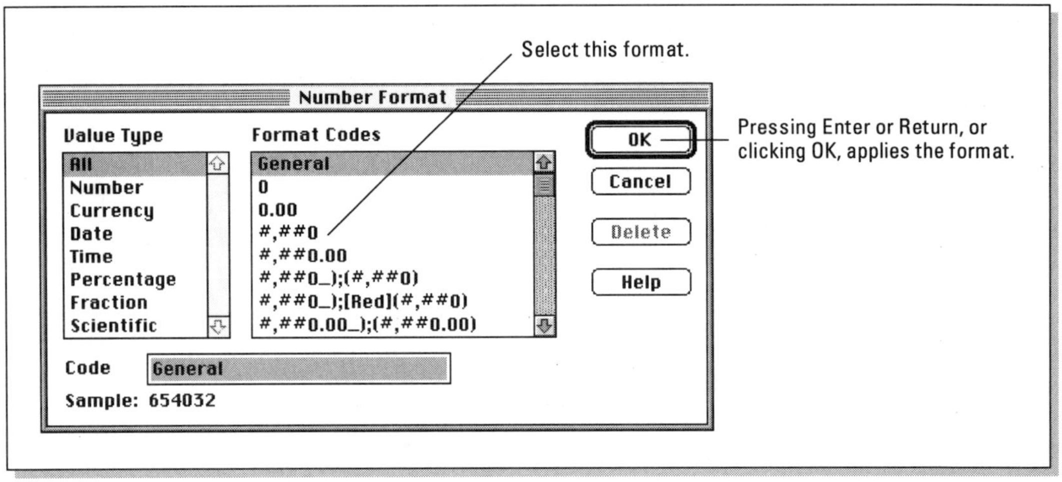

Figure 2-17: Using the Number Format dialog box to format numbers.

Step 3. Choose #,##0 from the Number Format dialog box (the fourth format in the Format Codes box); then click OK.

Excel formats the selected numbers by separating thousands with a comma with no decimal points (see Figure 2-18).

Step 4. Select Save As from the File menu, type the name TOPIC2 in the Save Worksheet as text box, and click Save or press Return.

Excel saves the changes you made to the worksheet to disk.

Changing column widths:

Step 1. Move the mouse pointer to the column headings area (the area along the top of the worksheet with the column letters). Place the mouse pointer on the line to the right of the column letter of the column whose width you want to change, as shown in Figure 2-19.

Step 2. Press and drag the mouse to the right to increase the width of the column; drag the mouse to the left to decrease the width of the column. Release the mouse when you reach the desired column width.

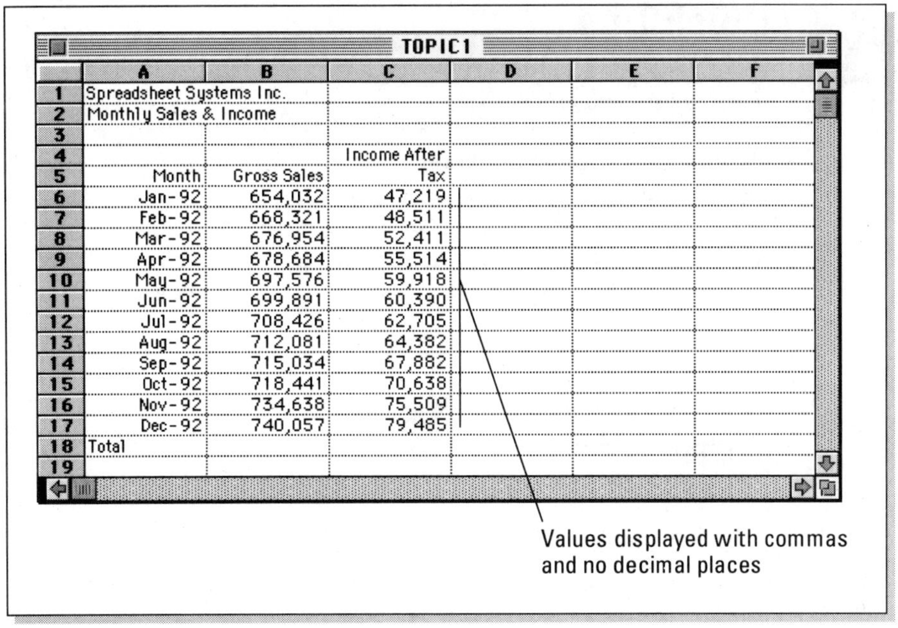

	A	B	C	D	E	F
1	Spreadsheet Systems Inc.					
2	Monthly Sales & Income					
3						
4			Income After			
5	Month	Gross Sales	Tax			
6	Jan-92	654,032	47,219			
7	Feb-92	668,321	48,511			
8	Mar-92	676,954	52,411			
9	Apr-92	678,684	55,514			
10	May-92	697,576	59,918			
11	Jun-92	699,891	60,390			
12	Jul-92	708,426	62,705			
13	Aug-92	712,081	64,382			
14	Sep-92	715,034	67,882			
15	Oct-92	718,441	70,638			
16	Nov-92	734,638	75,509			
17	Dec-92	740,057	79,485			
18	Total					
19						

Figure 2-18: Selecting the #,##0 format from the Number Format dialog box results in numbers with commas and no decimal points.

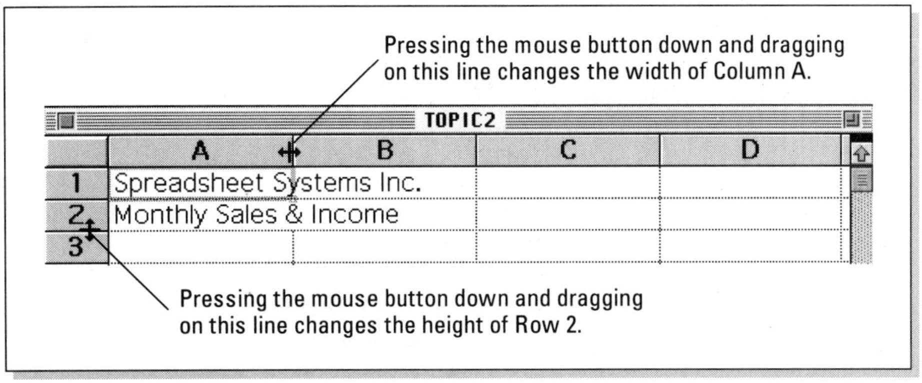

Figure 2-19: Changing the width of columns in a worksheet.

Changing row heights:

Step 1. Move the mouse pointer to the row headings area (the area along the left of the worksheet with the row numbers). Place the mouse pointer on the line below the row number of the row whose height you want to change.

Step 2. Press and drag the mouse down to increase the height of the row; drag the mouse up to decrease the height of the row. Release the mouse button when you reach the desired row height.

Quick Tips

This section provides you with tips on how to change the display of your worksheets to suit your likes and needs.

Using Excel's shortcut menu

Changing the display of data provides many opportunities to use Excel's shortcut menu. After you select a cell or range, place the pointer in the selected cell or range, and then press Command-Option and the mouse button. The menu shown in Figure 2-20 appears over the worksheet (the specific location will depend on the location of the selected range).

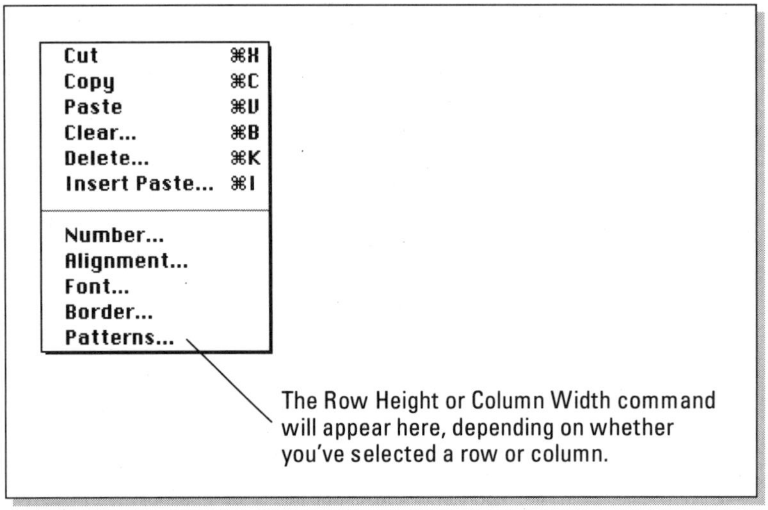

Figure 2-20: Using a shortcut menu to change the display of data.

Commands on the shortcut menu

If you've selected a row or column, Row Height or Column Width appear at the bottom of the menu after Patterns. Using a shortcut menu gives you access to dialog boxes of commonly used commands without having to use the menu bar.

Formatting large numbers

Format large numbers (greater than 999) with a comma to make them easier to read and understand.

Selecting an entire worksheet

Click the rectangle at the intersection of the column and row borders (or press Command-A) to select the entire worksheet for formatting, changing column widths or row heights, or to perform other worksheet tasks.

Applying fonts in a row

If you apply a font to a cell or range that has a larger point size than the height of the row, Excel automatically adjusts the height of the row to accommodate the font.

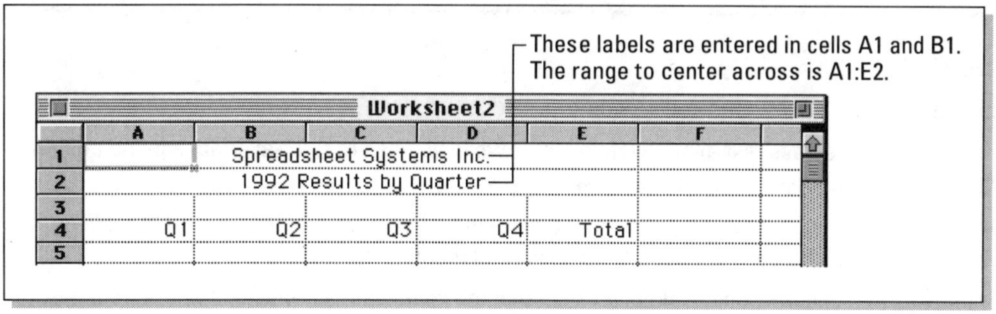

Figure 2-21: Selecting "Center across selection" from the Alignment dialog box results in labels being centered over multiple columns.

Adjusting column widths automatically

The Best Fit option on the Column Width dialog box automatically adjusts column width based on the contents of the active cell. Use Best Fit with the widest cell entry in the column. Double-clicking on a column letter's right line in the column headings area results in the best fit for that column.

Selecting noncontiguous rows and columns

To select rows or columns that aren't contiguous, click on the first row number or column letter. Then press Control and click on each row or column you want selected. You may want to select noncontiguous rows or columns if you've used rows or columns for spacing between data and want to adjust the spacing in one step.

- ✦ To center text across several columns of data, use the "Center across selection" option on the Alignment dialog box (Format menu), as shown in Figure 2-21.

  Select the range of cells you want to center text over (include blank cells), and make sure the text is in the far left cell of the range.

- ✦ To return one or more rows or columns to their default heights and widths, use the Standard Height and Standard Width options in the Row Height and Column Width dialog boxes, respectively.

Summary

- Formatting your data enhances and customizes its display.
- By default, Excel displays text aligned left in a cell, while values are right-aligned, with no commas or currency signs (for example, dollar signs).
- Change alignment of text and values by selecting them and using one of the alignment tools on the toolbar, or by choosing Alignment from the Format menu.
- Add commas and dollar signs to values by selecting the values and choosing Number from the Format menu, a style from the Style pull-down menu, or a shortcut key combination.
- Change the width of a column by pressing and dragging on the line to the right of the column whose width you want to change in the column headings area, or by choosing Column Width from the Format menu.
- Change the height of a row by clicking and dragging on the line below the row whose height you want to change in the row headings area, or by choosing Row Height from the Format menu.
- Select every cell in the active worksheet by clicking the rectangle at the intersection to the left of column heading A and above row heading 1, or press Command-A.
- You can bypass the command menu bar and access commonly used commands by pressing the Command, Option, and mouse button while the mouse pointer is positioned in a selected cell or range of cells.

Topic 3
Printing Your Worksheets

Overview

Printing your worksheet is the last step in the worksheet creation cycle. Displaying your worksheet on paper enables you to share your analysis and reports with your colleagues and superiors. You can also create a hard copy of your work for backup purposes in case you encounter a disk problem, power interruption, or other computer-related misfortune.

The first step to guaranteeing a successful printing session is to ensure that your Macintosh's hardware and software is properly set up for printing, the subject of the following discussion.

Setting up your hardware

Hardware considerations seem pretty logical to many people, yet they can trip up even the most experienced Macintosh veterans. First and foremost, you need a printer connected to your Macintosh to print a worksheet on paper. The printer can be for your exclusive use, or one shared with other users on a computer network. Either way, the printer should be turned on and should have an adequate supply of paper. In addition, the printer's ribbon should be in good shape if you use a dot-matrix printer, or the printer should have sufficient toner if you use a laser printer. Finally, the cable to the printer (or network) should be firmly and properly connected to your Macintosh, so that the print data can be sent from your Macintosh to the printer accurately and without interruption.

Setting up your software

Successful printing also includes letting your Macintosh know what type of printer you intend to use. If your Macintosh is connected to a network, or was set up by a technician, you can skip this step. If your Macintosh and printer have never been used, or you use more than one printer, you need to tell your Macintosh which printer you intend to use. Select Chooser from the Apple menu. Chooser, as the name implies, lets you choose the type of printer you'll be using with your Macintosh. Figure 3-1 shows a Chooser dialog box, which appears when you select Chooser.

The icon representing the printer and the printer port (the location on the back of your Macintosh where the printer cable is plugged in) should be highlighted. If the printer's icon doesn't appear in the left side of the window, you need to copy the appropriate printer program or driver (software that enables the Macintosh to communicate with your printer) from a disk to the System Folder, and then select the icon.

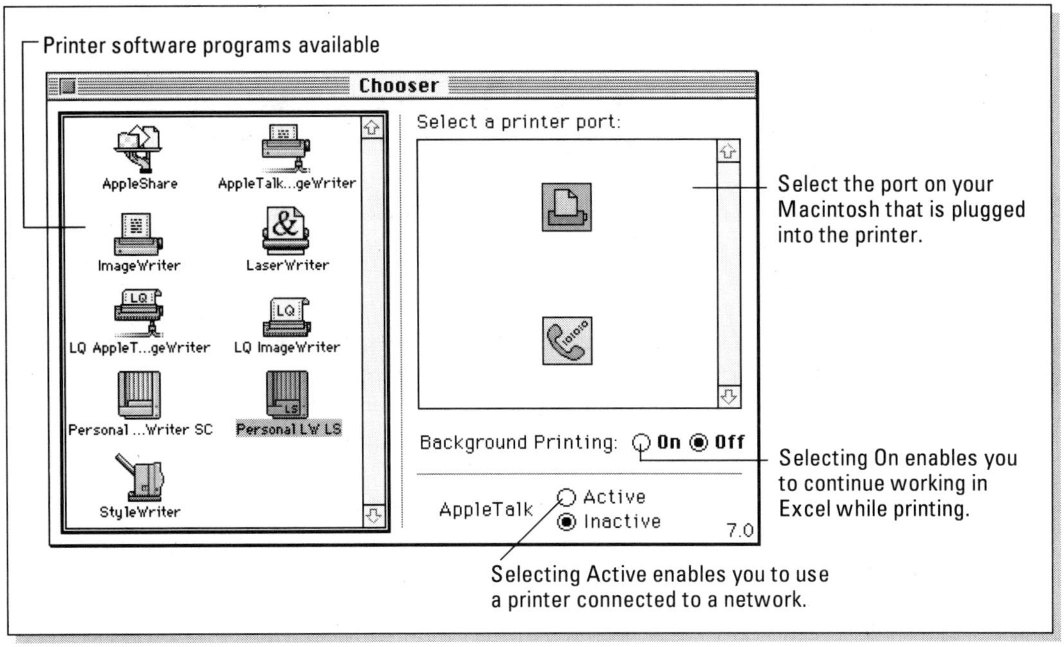

Figure 3-1: Setting up the printing software using the Chooser dialog box.

If your Macintosh is connected to a network, click the Active button located to the right of AppleTalk, and then click OK when the dialog box appears. Finally, if your network contains zones, you need to select the zone of the printer you'll be using (your network administrator can help you with all this, or your local Macintosh guru).

Close the Chooser window by clicking the close box. If you'd like to learn more about the Chooser, read Jim Heid's *Macworld Complete Mac Handbook* (IDG Books Worldwide, 1991). In any event, your Macintosh is now ready to print worksheets.

Printing standard worksheets

Printing a basic worksheet is an easy process with Excel. If your printer is properly connected, set up for your computer, and turned on with an adequate supply of paper and toner (or ribbon), you're ready to go. Follow these three steps:

1. Make the worksheet you want to print the active worksheet.
2. Select Print from the File menu or press Command-P.
3. When the dialog box in Figure 3-2 appears, click Print or press Return.

Excel will print all the data in the worksheet, the name of the worksheet centered at the top of the paper, and Page *x* centered at the bottom of the paper, where *x* is the number of the printed page.

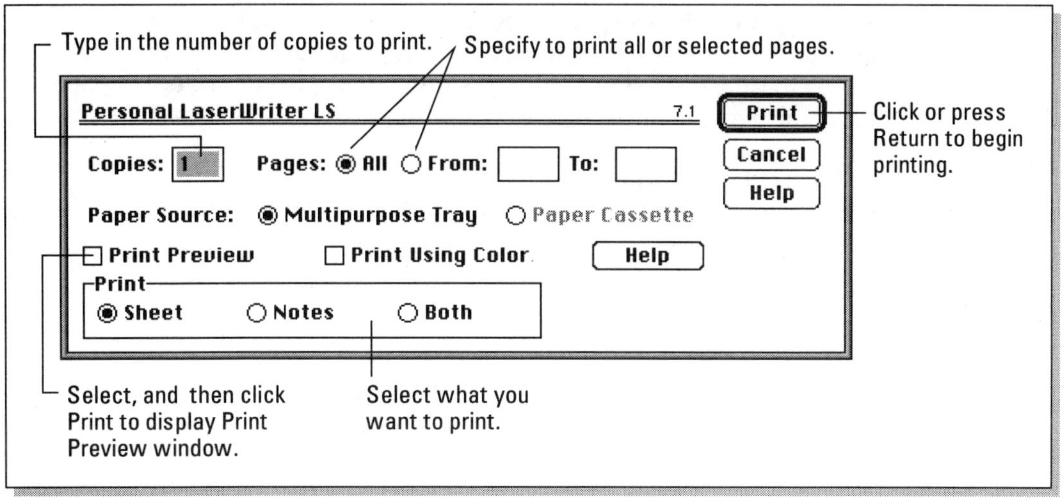

Figure 3-2: Setting your printing options with the Print dialog box.

If you need a little more than a basic printout, Excel provides you with a wide variety of print options, as you'll see in the following discussion.

Customizing your printouts

You may find after you print a worksheet that you may not need to print the entire worksheet. Or maybe your worksheet could use some improvements, such as smaller (or larger) margins, sideways (horizontal) printing, and so on. Customizing basic printouts in Excel is a snap. Two commands on the File menu, Print and Page Setup, provide you with all the printing horsepower you'll ever need.

Choosing print quantities and location

As you saw in Figure 3-2, the Print dialog box lets you specify print quantities and other aspects of the printed worksheet. The options that appear in the Print dialog box will depend on the type of printer you use, but all Print dialog boxes have some options in common (see Table 3-1.)

Table 3-1: Basic printing options

Option	*Purpose*
Copies	Assigns number of copies to be printed.
Pages	Prints all pages of a worksheet, or a range of pages you specify.
Paper Source	Specifies location of the paper in the printer to be used for printing.
Print Preview	Displays a window showing how the worksheet will look as printed.
Print Using Color	Prints worksheet in color when using a color printer.
Print	Specifies whether worksheet, cell notes, or both, are printed.

Type the number of printed copies you need into the Copies text box, or select the print options you want. If you only want a range of pages printed from the worksheet, type the page numbers in the From and To text boxes. Clicking Print or pressing Return prints the worksheet with the options you selected.

Selecting a range to print

In some cases you'll only need a portion of an active worksheet printed. You may only need to print, for example, a financial statement from a range in the worksheet. To print a range of cells rather than the entire worksheet, do the following:

1. Select the range you want to print.
2. Select Set Print Area from the Options menu.
3. Select Print from the File menu or press Command-P.
4. Click Print or press Return.

A dashed line appears around the selected area on the worksheet display, as shown in Figure 3-3, to remind you of what you've selected for printing, and to inform you where printing on the following page will occur. The dashed line is displayed on-screen only and will not print.

If you want to print a different range, select the range, and then select Set Print Area from the Options menu again. If you want to print the entire worksheet but have used Set Print Area with a previously selected range, select the entire worksheet by clicking on the

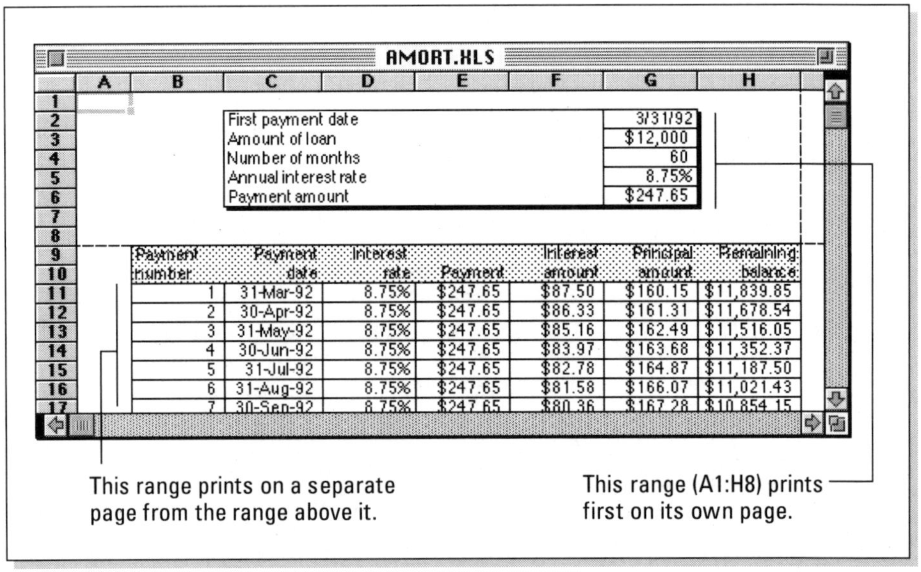

Figure 3-3: Selecting a portion of a worksheet to print using the Set Print command from the Options menu.

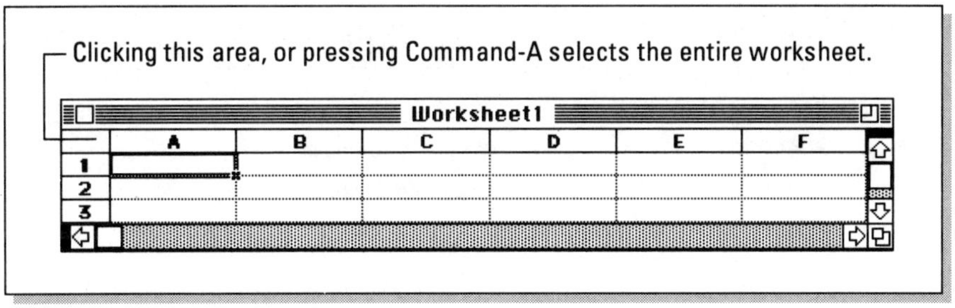

Figure 3-4: Selecting an entire worksheet to print by clicking on the upper-left rectangle.

rectangle at the upper-left corner of the worksheet window located at the left of Column A and above Row 1, as shown in Figure 3-4. Then select Remove Print Area from the Options menu. The dashed lines are no longer displayed, and you can now print the entire worksheet by selecting Print from the File menu or by pressing Command-P.

Enhancing worksheet printouts

The Page Setup command on the File menu is the key to enhancing your printouts. Figure 3-5 shows you a Page Setup dialog box.

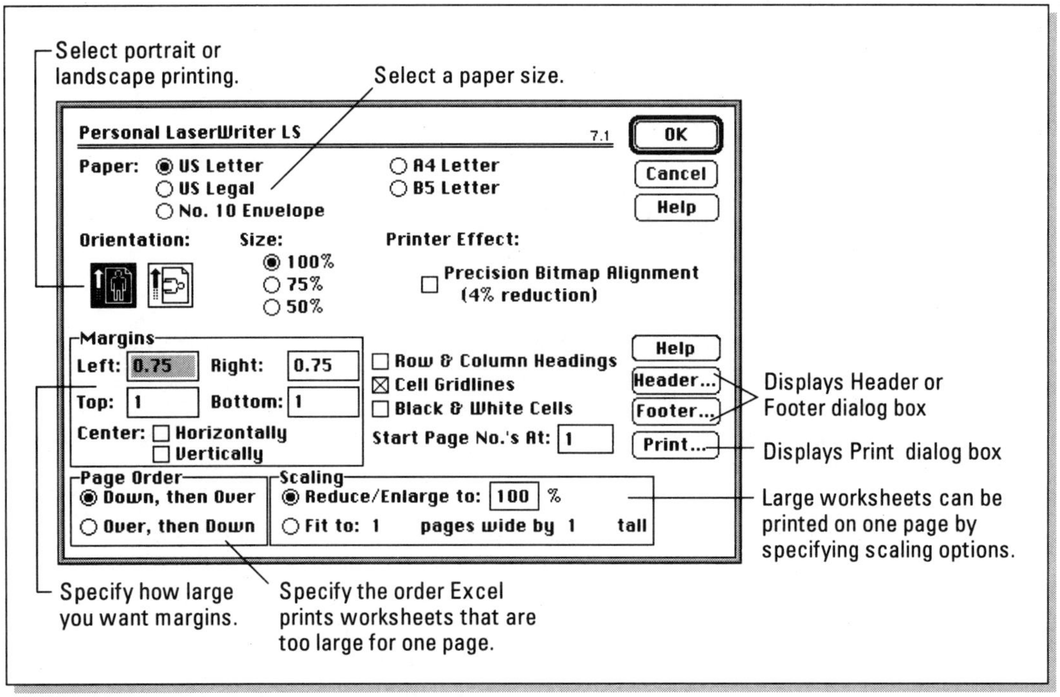

Figure 3-5: Enhancing worksheet printouts by using the Page Setup dialog box.

Table 3-2:	Basic Page Setup options
Option	***Purpose***
Paper	Assigns size of paper to print on.
Orientation	Prints in portrait (vertically) or landscape (horizontally).
Size	Prints worksheet as a percent of displayed worksheet.
Margins	Assigns amount of margin space (in inches); centers worksheet horizontally and/or vertically on the page.
Page Order	Sets the order pages will be printed in: from top to bottom, or from left to right.
Scaling	Sizes printout by a specified percentage, or fits printout into a specified number of pages.
Miscellaneous options	
Option	***Purpose***
Row & Column Headings	Prints or suppresses printing of row numbers and column letters.
Cell Gridlines	Prints or suppresses printing of worksheet gridlines.
Black & White Cells	Prints text formatted with color in black and white.
Start Page No.'s At:	Specifies the value to begin page numbering.
Header	Prints information that appears at the top of each printed page.
Footer	Prints information that appears at the bottom of each printed page.

The Page Setup dialog box may appear different from the one shown in Figure 3-5, depending on the printer you use. Table 3-2 shows the options that all Page Setup dialog boxes have in common.

To enhance a printout, simply choose the options you want from the Page Setup dialog box and click OK or press Return. When you print the worksheet again, the enhancements will be included in the printout. Select Save from the File menu or press Command-S to use the Page Setup options again with the worksheet in your next Excel session.

The Print tool

Once you have the worksheet set up for printing the way you want, you can use the Print tool to print the worksheet. The Print tool, the fourth tool on the Standard toolbar, resembles a printer. Clicking the Print tool bypasses all of the print-related dialog boxes and tells Excel to immediately begin printing the worksheet. You can use the Print tool at any time, but because the Print tool will start printing the worksheet immediately, consider setting your print options first.

Previewing a worksheet

As you add more printing enhancements to worksheets, you may want to preview the enhancements on-screen before printing. Previewing a worksheet saves you time and paper as you can see how your worksheet will look, and even adjust margins on-screen before printing a worksheet.

To see the worksheet on-screen as it will be printed, select Print Preview from the File menu, or press Shift and click the Print tool. Excel displays the worksheet in the Print Preview window, as shown in Figure 3-6.

The worksheet is displayed in a reduced view, one page per screen. The buttons along the top of the screen enable you to work in the Print Preview window (see Table 3-3 for the purpose of the Print Preview buttons).

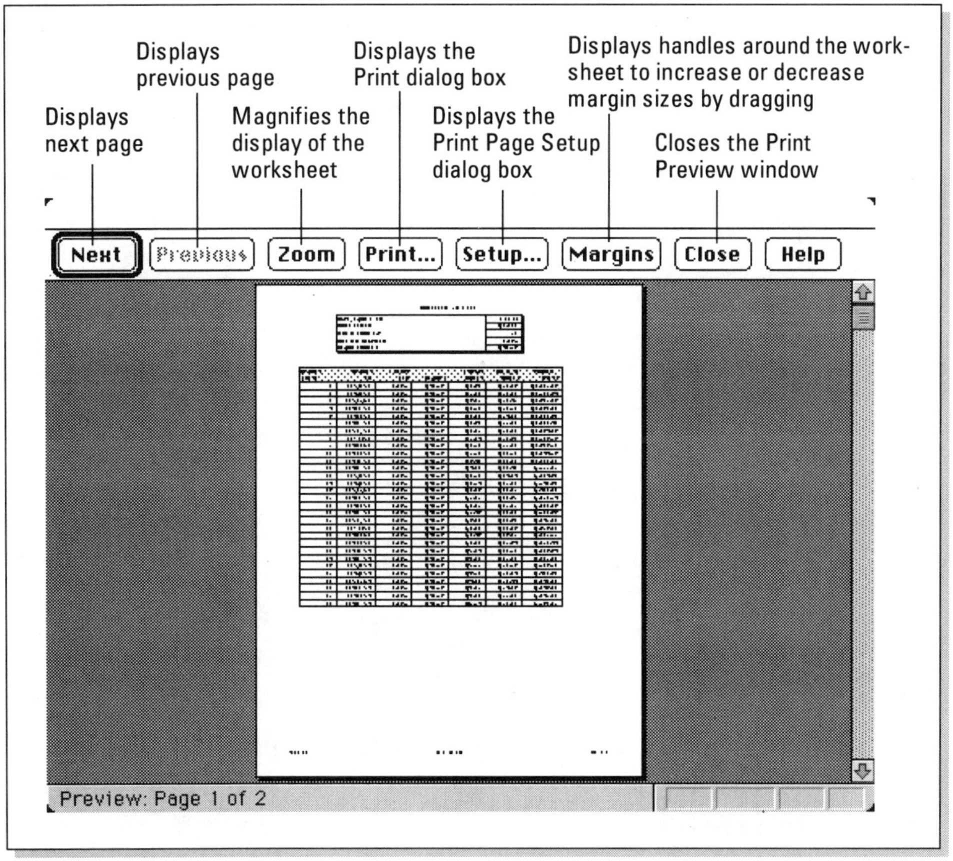

Figure 3-6: Viewing a worksheet as it will print using the Print Preview window.

Table 3-3: Print Preview buttons

Button	*Purpose*
Next	Displays the next page, if there is one. Same as pressing the down arrow key or the Page Down key.
Previous	Displays the previous page, if there is one. Same as pressing the up arrow key or the Page Up key.
Zoom	Toggles previewed worksheet between an enlarged or normal display. Also available by clicking on the previewed page when the mouse pointer resembles a magnifying glass.
Print	Displays Print dialog box for printing.
Setup	Displays Page Setup dialog box for print enhancements.
Margins	Toggles between displaying lines and markers to change margin or column widths.
Close	Closes the Print Preview window and displays the worksheet.

Clicking Margins in the Print Preview window displays the previewed worksheet with the margin handles and column handles, as shown in Figure 3-7. Clicking and then dragging on the handle changes the width directly without having to return to the worksheet. To remove the lines and handles from the Preview display, click the Margins button again.

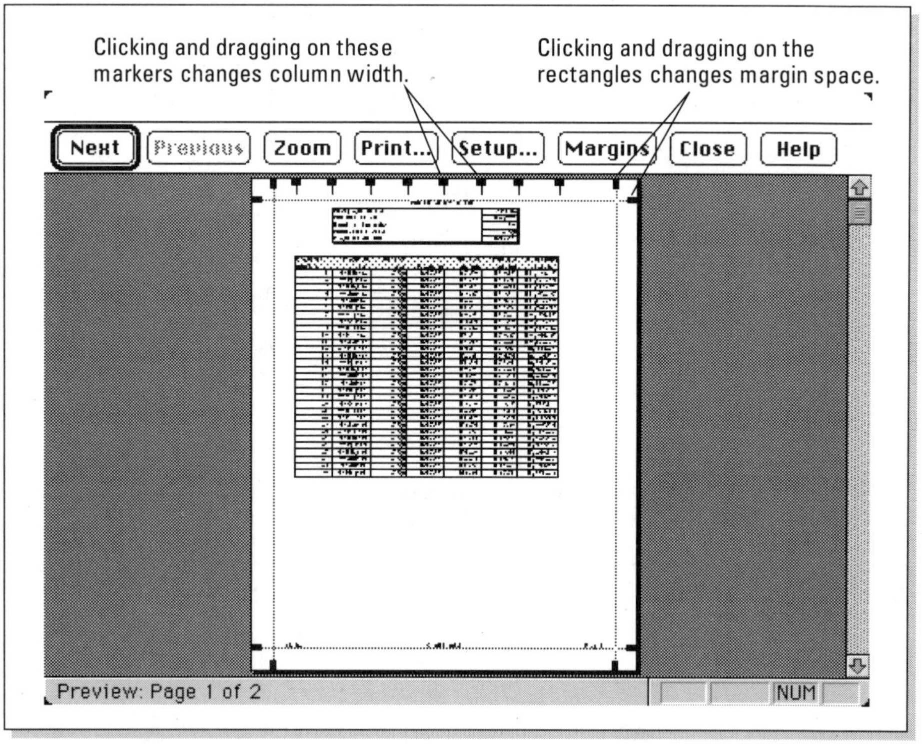

Figure 3-7: Adjusting a worksheet's margins in the Print Preview window using the Margins option.

Advanced printing techniques

As you accelerate up the Excel learning curve, you may want to customize your printed worksheets even further. You may, for example, want to have fairly detailed information in headers or footers, specify where you want Excel to begin printing on a new page, or print several rows and columns on every page. The following section covers these concepts.

Displaying information with headers and footers

Header and footer information appears at the top and bottom, respectively, of each printed page (but not on screen). Some of the more common information that appears in headers and footers includes: page numbers, company title, dates, and the type of file (for example, income statement).

Headers and footers have their own window, as shown in Figure 3-8, which you display by clicking the appropriate button on the Page Setup dialog box.

The Header and Footer dialog boxes each contain three text boxes that let you enter as much information as you want printed — you can have Excel print any combination of text or numbers. To enter the information, click the desired section (one of the three text boxes along the bottom of the window) to move the blinking cursor; then begin typing. The three sections will print the information on the worksheet as follows on the next page.

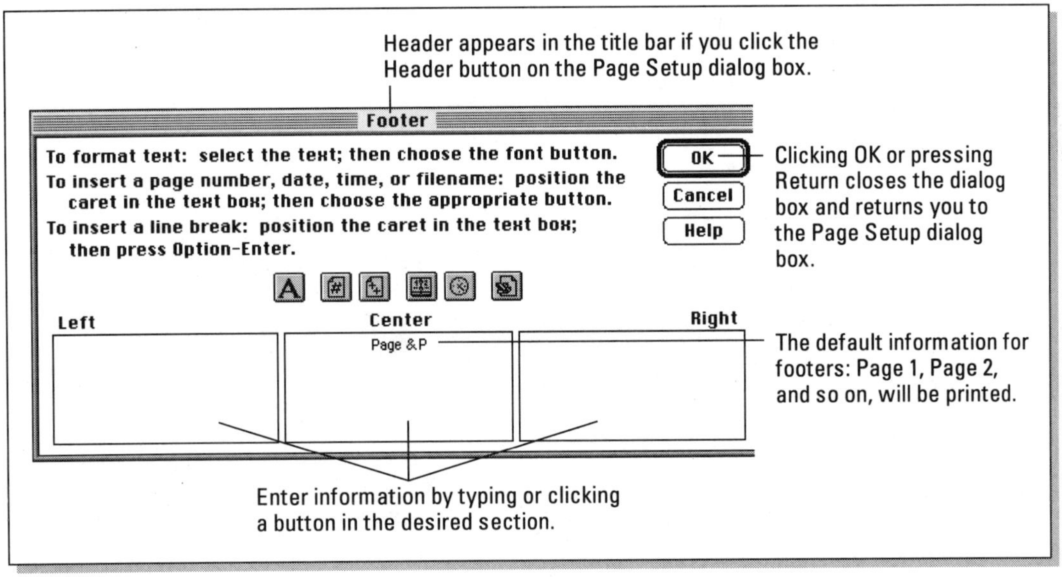

Figure 3-8: Clicking the Footer option in the Page Setup dialog box displays the Footer window.

Section	*Printed on worksheet*
Left section	Flush-left
Center section	Centered between left and right margins
Right section	Flush-right

You can quickly include the page number, total number of pages, date, time, and filename as part of a header or footer by clicking the desired Header or Footer section, and then clicking on the appropriate button above the sections (see Figure 3-9).

Excel displays the code for that information, such as &F for the name of the file. By default, Excel prints the name of the worksheet file as a centered header and the page number as a centered footer.

You can enhance the display of header and footer information by changing the font size or type, bolding, underlining, and so on, using the following steps:

1. Click the section containing the information you want to enhance.
2. Select the characters you want to enhance.
3. Click the Font button.
4. When the Font dialog box appears, select the options you want and click OK or press Return.

Closing the Font dialog box returns you to the Header or Footer dialog box.

To delete a header or footer, click the desired section, select the characters, and press Delete or Backspace.

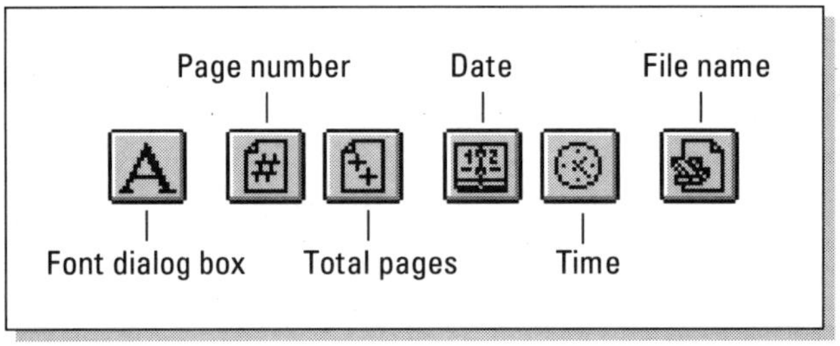

Figure 3-9: The options available in the Header and Footer dialog boxes enable you to include the page number, total number of pages, date, time, and filename in a header or footer.

Specifying page breaks

As you saw earlier, Excel uses many automatic settings when you select a range to print, preview a worksheet before printing, or print an entire worksheet. Excel automatically determines where to begin printing on a new page and indicates this by displaying dashed lines, or page break symbols, on worksheets that are too large to be printed on one page. Page break symbols help you see how your worksheet will print, and are especially useful if you insert rows or columns into a worksheet (which enlarge a worksheet).

You can specify where Excel begins printing on a new page. To manually set page breaks, first decide what type of page break you want: row, column, or both. Then position your cell pointer as follows:

Page break	***Cell pointer location***
Row	Column A and one row below desired page break
Column	One column to the right of desired page break
Both	Cell one row below and to the right of desired page break

Figure 3-10 shows where page breaks occur for various cell pointer locations.

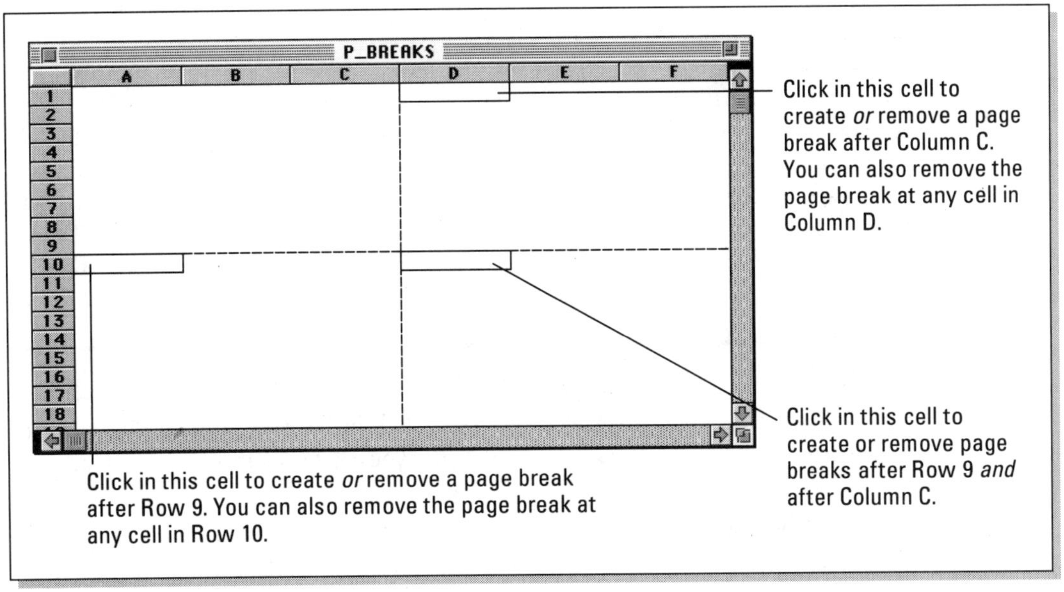

Figure 3-10: Cell pointer locations and their corresponding page breaks.

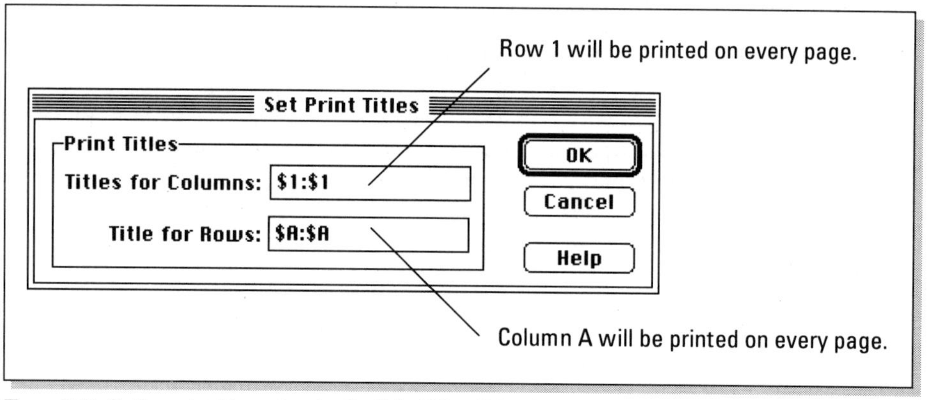

Figure 3-11: Setting print titles using the Set Print Titles dialog box.

Next, select Set Page Break from the Options menu. Excel displays page break lines and prints the row and/or column on a new page the next time you print the worksheet. Page breaks stay in effect until you remove them, which you can do by selecting any cell below or to the right of the page break, and then selecting Remove Page Break from the Options menu.

All page breaks can be removed simultaneously by selecting the entire worksheet and then choosing Remove Page Break from the Options menu.

Setting print titles

If you have a worksheet that contains many rows of data (such as an annual budget), you'll want to see the first few rows printed on every page to keep your place. For example, in a budget worksheet you'll want the months of the year printed at the top of each page. Setting print titles (rows or columns that contain text and print on every page) enables you to quickly identify each value in lengthy worksheets. To set a print title, select Set Print Titles from the Options menu. When the Set Print Titles dialog box appears, as shown in Figure 3-11, select one or both of these print title types:

Print title type	***Click***	***Select***
Row titles	Upper text box	Rows you want to appear on each page
Column titles	Lower text box	Columns you want to appear on each page

Next, manually select a range to print, and then select Set Print Area from the Options menu. Make sure you don't select a print area that overlaps the print title rows or columns, or the print titles will be printed twice on each page. For example, if you plan on printing row 1 and column A on every page, the upper-left cell in the print range should be B2.

Print titles vs. column text

Generally, this choice will depend on the nature of your worksheet. Using a header to display the title of a report makes several extra rows available for data to be displayed on screen. A header, however, cannot be used to describe the data in your columns. In most cases, use a header (or footer) to display information about your printouts — date, time, page numbers, and so on.

When you select columns or rows for print titles, notice that only row numbers and column letters appear in the Set Print Titles dialog box. Print titles must be an entire row and column rather than a single cell or range address.

Print titles can be completely removed by selecting the entire worksheet and then selecting Remove Print Titles from the Options menu. Or you can change or remove print titles by selecting Set Print Titles from the Options menu and editing or deleting the selection in one or both text boxes when the dialog box appears.

Step-by-Step

In this section, you'll practice printing a basic worksheet, enhancing the worksheet with a footer, previewing the worksheet, and then printing the enhanced worksheet. You'll use the worksheet from Topic 2 or a worksheet you create yourself. If you make a mistake, close the file by selecting Close from the File menu or by pressing Command-W; then without saving any changes, open the Topic 2 worksheet again.

1. If you haven't already, start Excel, or make Excel the active application.

   The Worksheet1 window appears.

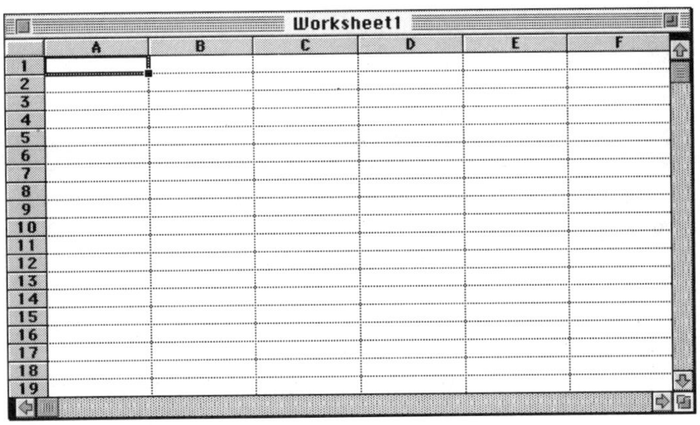

Figure 3-12: Starting Excel, or making Excel the active program, displays the Worksheet1 window.

2. Select Open from the File menu or press Command-O.

   The Open dialog box appears.

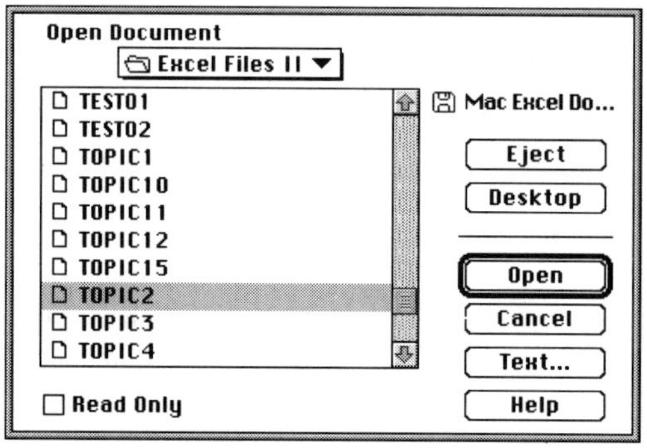

Figure 3-13: Selecting Open from the File menu displays the Open dialog box.

3. Select TOPIC2 and click Open or press Return.

   The TOPIC2 worksheet appears.

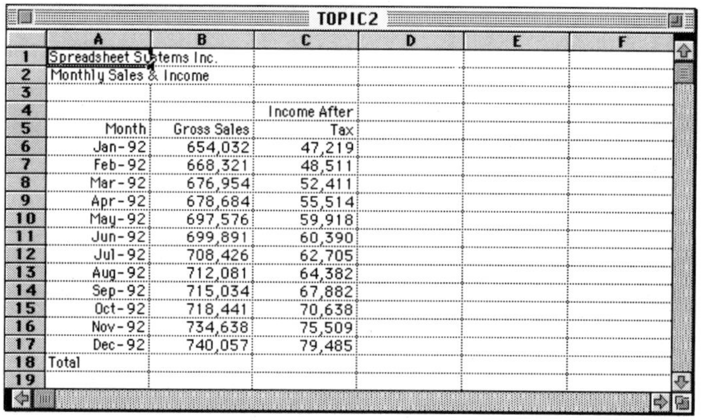
TOPIC2

	A	B	C	D	E	F
1	Spreadsheet Systems Inc.					
2	Monthly Sales & Income					
3						
4			Income After			
5	Month	Gross Sales	Tax			
6	Jan-92	654,032	47,219			
7	Feb-92	668,321	48,511			
8	Mar-92	676,954	52,411			
9	Apr-92	678,684	55,514			
10	May-92	697,576	59,918			
11	Jun-92	699,891	60,390			
12	Jul-92	708,426	62,705			
13	Aug-92	712,081	64,382			
14	Sep-92	715,034	67,882			
15	Oct-92	718,441	70,638			
16	Nov-92	734,638	75,509			
17	Dec-92	740,057	79,485			
18	Total					
19						

Figure 3-14: Selecting TOPIC2 from the Open dialog box displays the TOPIC2 worksheet.

Printing a basic report:

Step 1. Select Print from the File menu or press Command-P.

The Print dialog box appears.

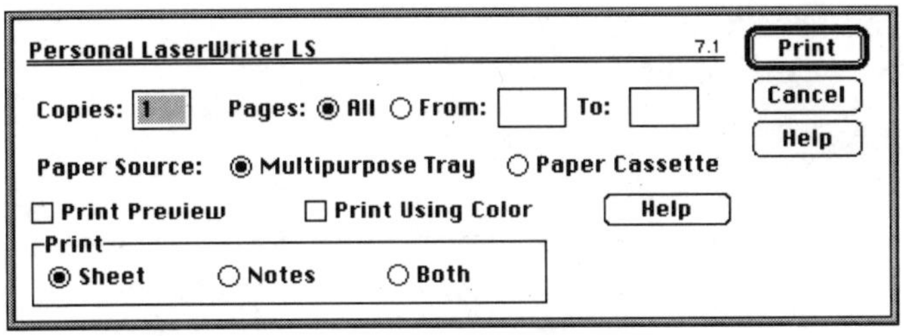

Figure 3-15: Choosing Print from the File menu displays the Print dialog box.

Step 2. Click Print or press Return.

Excel prints the worksheet.

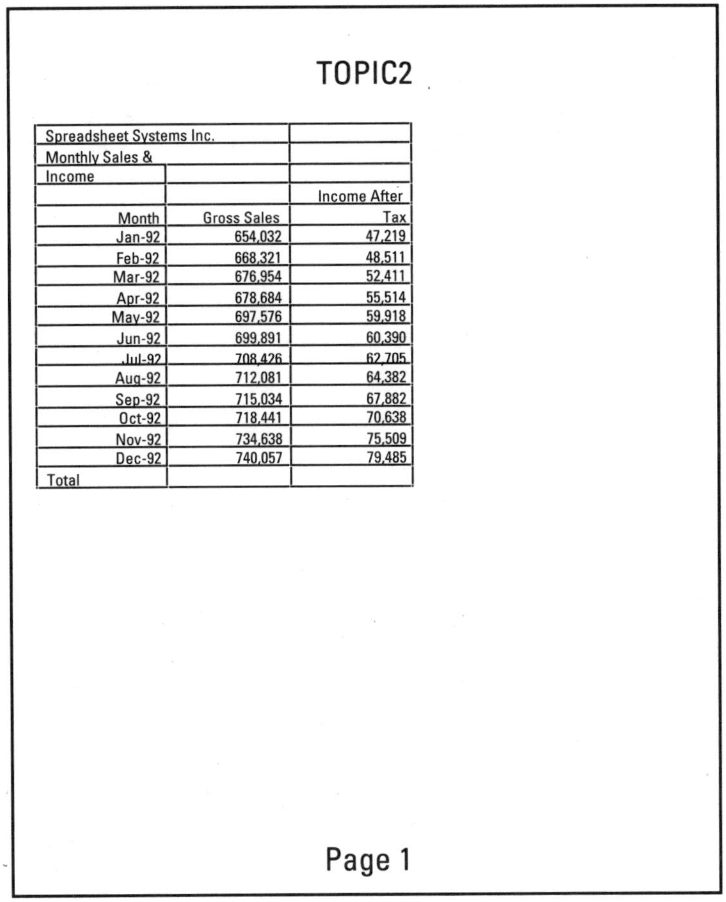

TOPIC2

Spreadsheet Systems Inc.		
Monthly Sales &		
Income		
		Income After
Month	Gross Sales	Tax
Jan-92	654,032	47,219
Feb-92	668,321	48,511
Mar-92	676,954	52,411
Apr-92	678,684	55,514
May-92	697,576	59,918
Jun-92	699,891	60,390
Jul-92	708,426	62,705
Aug-92	712,081	64,382
Sep-92	715,034	67,882
Oct-92	718,441	70,638
Nov-92	734,638	75,509
Dec-92	740,057	79,485
Total		

Page 1

Figure 3-16: The TOPIC2 worksheet as it looks when printed out.

Adding a footer to a worksheet:

Step 1. Select Page Setup from the File menu.

The Page Setup dialog box appears.

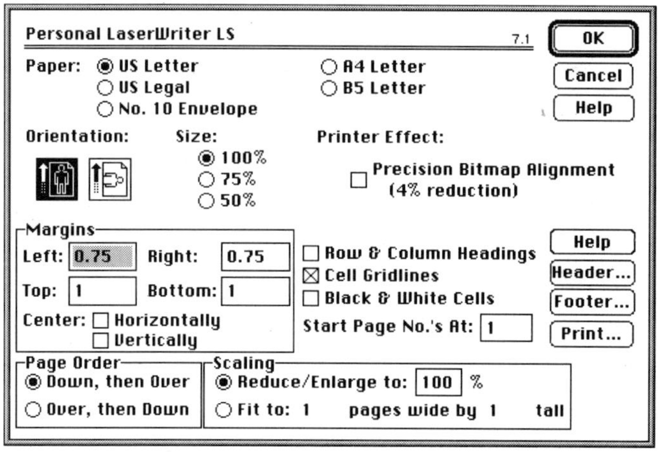

Figure 3-17: Choosing Page Setup from the File menu displays the Page Setup dialog box.

Step 2. Click Footer.

The Footer dialog box appears.

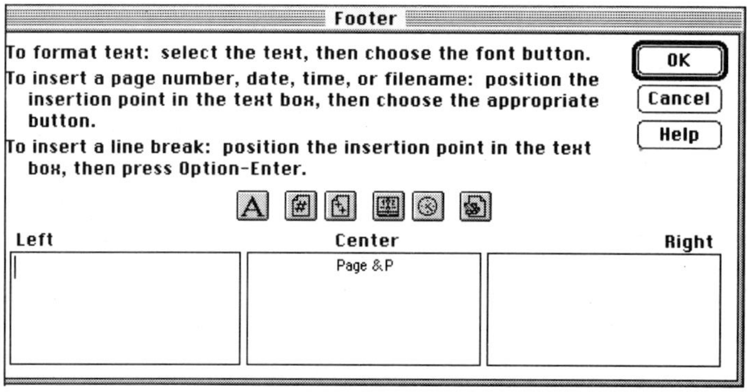

Figure 3-18: Adding a footer to a worksheet using the Footer dialog box.

Step 3. Click the Date tool, and then click the Center section. Select the Page &P characters, and press Delete or Backspace. Next type Monthly Earnings, and then click the Right section; type Page, a space, and then click the Page Number tool. Click the OK button.

Step 4. Click OK or press Return.

Excel displays the active worksheet.

Previewing the worksheet:

Step 1. Choose Print Preview from the File menu.

Excel displays the worksheet in the Print Preview window.

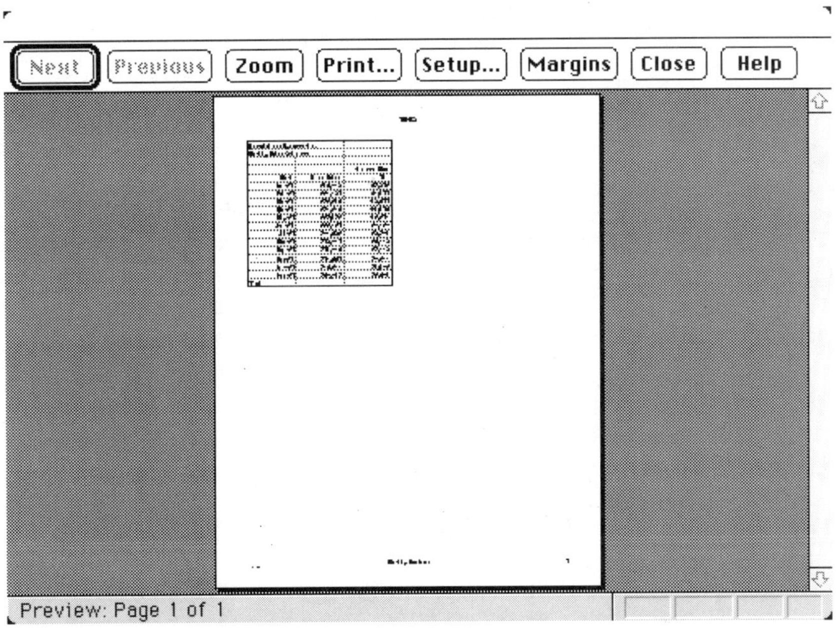

Figure 3-19: Previewing a worksheet as it will print using the Print Preview window.

Printing from the Print Preview window:

Step 1. Click the Print button.

Excel displays the Print dialog box.

Step 2. Click Print or press Return.

Excel prints the enhanced printout.

Saving the print settings with the worksheet:

Select Save As from the File menu, type `TOPIC3` in the Save As text box, and then click the Save button or press Return. This new file will have all of the print settings that you have just set.

Quick Tips

This section provides you with tips on how to print your worksheets efficiently.

Resetting your print settings

To reset the print settings of a worksheet, select the entire worksheet, and then use the following commands:

To reset . . .	*Use this option . . .*
Print area	Remove Print Area
Print titles	Remove Print Titles
All page breaks	Remove Page Break

Mixing and matching header and footer codes

Don't be shy about mixing and matching header and footer codes (that you enter by clicking a tool) with text or numbers. You can use any combination of both header and footer codes to display the information you need. For example, to print Page *x* of *y*, where *x* is the page number and *y* is the total number of pages, do the following:

1. Type Page and a space.
2. Click the Page Number tool.
3. Type a space, type of, and then type another space.
4. Click the Total Pages tool.

Page 1 of 3, Page 2 of 3, and so on, will be printed as a header or footer in a three-page printed worksheet.

Printing more columns per page

If you have difficulty printing all of a worksheet's columns on one page, try one or more of the following methods to print more columns per page:

- ✦ Remove row titles.
- ✦ Reduce left and right margin widths.
- ✦ Reduce the width of columns where possible.
- ✦ Print in landscape mode.

Printing efficiently with Print Preview

Selecting the Print Preview checkbox on the Print dialog box displays the worksheet in the Print Preview window, and clicking the Print or Setup buttons displays the corresponding dialog box. This operation makes the Print command your one-stop printing command enabling you to avoid going back to the menu bar to set print options.

Printing better black and white

Select Black & White Cells from the Page Setup dialog box if you've added colors to a worksheet, you have a black-and-white printer, or your printout looks muddied.

Summary

- To print a worksheet, you need to first ensure that your printer is properly connected to your computer, is turned on, and contains adequate printing supplies. You also need to tell your Macintosh, through the Chooser on the Apple menu, which printer you'll be using.
- To print a basic report, make the worksheet you want to print the active worksheet, and select Print from the File menu or press Command-P. Clicking Print or pressing Return starts the printing process.
- To print a specified range of cells in a worksheet, select the cells, select Print Area from the Options menu, and then select Print from the File menu.
- The Print dialog box contains options that enable you to specify print quantities and other aspects of the printed worksheet.
- Basic printouts can be enhanced through the Page Setup command on the File menu. Page Setup enables you to specify print orientation, select paper sizes, set margin widths, create headers and footers, and determine other attributes.
- The Print Preview command on the File menu enables you to see how a worksheet will appear on paper when it is printed.
- Headers and footers print at the top and bottom, respectively, on each page of a printed worksheet. Headers and footers can contain the date, page number, filename, and any other information you want to include. You can change the appearance of header and footer information so that the information appears bold, in a different-size font, italicized, and so on.
- You can specify where Excel begins printing on a new page using the Set Page Break command from the Options menu.
- Print titles are rows and/or columns that appear on every page of a printout. Print titles are specified by selecting Set Print Titles from the Options menu, and then selecting the row(s) and/or column(s) you want to appear on every page. You must also manually select a range of cells to print that excludes the print title row(s) or column(s).

Part II:

Worksheet Data Manipulation

Topic 4

Making Changes To Your Worksheets

Overview

Now that you've been through the complete worksheet cycle, there's a good chance you'll want or need to make changes to your worksheets. You can enter a completely new cell entry, edit, or erase the contents of a cell. If you've forgotten something you wanted to include in the worksheet, you can add a row or column to include it. If you change your mind later, you can delete the row or column.

Changing the contents of cells or the number of rows or columns in a worksheet enables you to correct errors or update your worksheets. As you make changes to the contents of cells, remember that you can choose Undo from the Edit menu (or press F1, or Command-Z) to undo the change. You should also save copies of your worksheets to disk at frequent intervals to avoid those Maalox® moments.

Erasing cell contents

Removing the contents of a cell is similar to erasing a number on accounting paper with a pencil's eraser. In Excel's electronic worksheet, you simply place the cell pointer on the cell whose contents you want to erase. Then you have a few ways to erase the data within the cell (see "Editing cell contents" in the Step-by-Step section in this Topic).

With the cell pointer in the cell whose contents you want to erase, you can permanently erase the contents of the cell by selecting the cell, and then doing one of the following:

- ✦ Click and drag on the fill handle
- ✦ Press Command-B
- ✦ Press Delete
- ✦ Select Clear from the Edit menu or the shortcut menu

VERSION 4 Microsoft

If you want to use the fill handle to erase the contents of a cell, place the pointer over the cell's fill handle, the small square in the lower-right corner of the cell. When the pointer appears as a black cross, click and then drag the mouse toward the upper-left corner of the cell. Finally, when the cell turns gray, releasing the mouse button erases the cell contents.

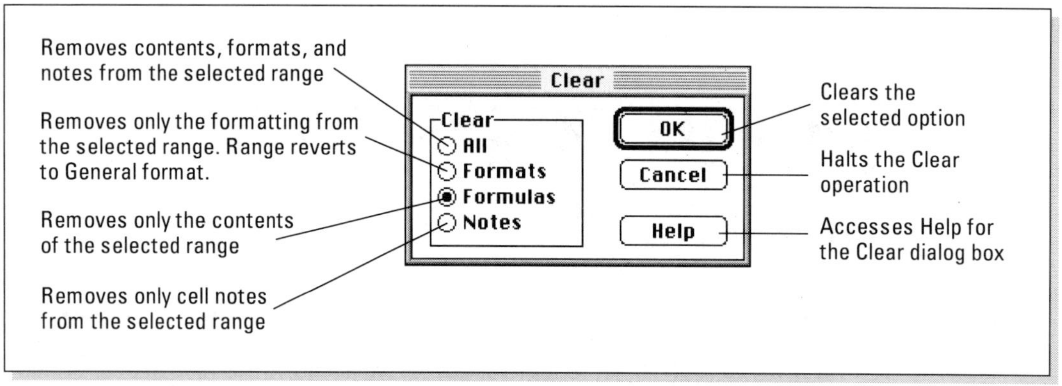

Figure 4-1: Removing attributes from a cell using the Clear dialog box.

Pressing Delete or choosing Clear from the Edit menu displays the dialog box shown in Figure 4-1. The Clear dialog box enables you to choose the attributes you want removed from a cell. (Note that the Formulas option removes all cell contents except formats and cell notes.) Clicking OK completes the erase operation.

You can also erase a range of cells or the contents of the entire worksheet. To do so, you follow the same procedure when erasing a single cell, except you select a range of cells or all of the cells in the entire worksheet. Remember, to select all of the cells in the worksheet, point and click on the rectangle located directly above row 1 and to the left of column A, or press Command-A.

Recycling cell contents

There may be times when you'd like to delete a cell's contents but keep the data for future use. In this case, use the Cut command from the Edit menu. The Cut command copies the contents of the selected cells to your Macintosh's Clipboard. When you select another cell and paste the contents, the contents are removed from the cell you originally cut the contents from. To cut a cell entry from your worksheet, select it, and then do one of the following:

✦ Press F2

✦ Press Command-X

✦ Choose Cut from the Edit menu or shortcut menu

To complete deletion of a cell's contents using the Cut command, paste the contents to another cell or range of cells. Select the cell (or the upper-left cell in a range of cells) that will hold the cut cell contents, and then do one of the following:

✦ Press F4

✦ Press Command-V

- ✦ Choose Paste from the Edit menu or shortcut menus
- ✦ Press Enter

Cutting and pasting are discussed in Topic 5.

Editing cell contents

Instead of erasing, cutting, or replacing cell contents, most of the time it's faster to change, or edit, the contents you already have in a cell. To edit the contents of a cell, move the cell pointer to the cell with the contents you want to change. You can edit cell contents with the mouse, keyboard, or a combination of the two.

To edit a cell's contents using the mouse, click on the formula bar, or better yet, click at the point where you want to make the change in the formula bar. Excel displays the flashing insertion point in the formula bar and *Edit* is displayed on the Status bar. Type new characters using the alphanumeric keys, and remove unwanted characters by selecting them and choosing Clear from the Edit menu. When you're finished editing, click the Enter box, as shown in Figure 4-2 . Excel returns to ready status and accepts the cell entry. If you have a change of heart and want to cancel editing the cell entry, click the cancel box.

To edit a cell's contents using the keyboard, activate the formula bar by pressing Command-U. Then move the insertion point to add or delete characters using the keys in Table 4-1.

Press Enter or click the Enter box to implement the edited cell contents, or press Return to accept the entry and make the next cell below the active cell. If you change your mind about what you've edited, click Cancel, or press Esc or Command-period to return to the ready status and cancel the edit operation, which will leave the original cell contents unscathed.

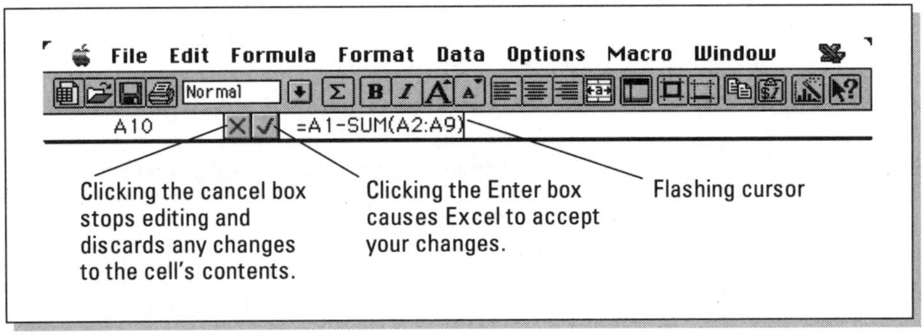

Figure 4-2: Editing a cell's contents using the formula bar.

Table 4-1:	Editing with the keyboard
To move insertion point . . .	***Use . . .***
One character	Left or right arrow key
One word	Command-arrow key
To beginning of data in formula bar	Home or up arrow key
To end of data in formula bar	End or down arrow key
Delete character to left of cursor	Delete or Backspace
Delete character to right of cursor	Forward Delete (extended keyboard only)

Overwriting existing cell contents

You may have some cell entries that need so many revisions that typing a new entry would be the easiest solution. To enter a new cell entry into a cell with existing cell contents, simply move the cell pointer to the cell you want to change. Then type a new entry and click the Enter box or press Return. The new entry replaces the original one in the active cell. As when you erase cell contents, you can use Undo from the Edit menu to retain the original cell entry if you change your mind.

Inserting and deleting rows and columns

After you've created a worksheet, you may find that you need a blank row or column in between rows or columns that contain data. For example, you've wisely included *Telephone* as part of a company budget. Your supervisor, however, wants to keep an eye on fax-related telephone expenses next year. Instead of recreating the budget worksheet, you can insert a row directly beneath *Telephone* to accommodate the new budget item.

When you insert a row or column in a worksheet, you're not enlarging Excel's 16,384-row-by-256-column worksheet with another new row or column. Rather, you're making a row or column blank by moving your data within the existing worksheet, as shown in Table 4-2 and Figure 4-3.

Table 4-2:	Row and column manipulation
Action	***Result***
Insert a row	Data beneath the cell pointer moves down one row.
Insert a column	Data to the right of the cell pointer moves right one column.
Delete a row	Data beneath the cell pointer moves up one row.
Delete a column	Data to the right of the cell pointer moves left one column.

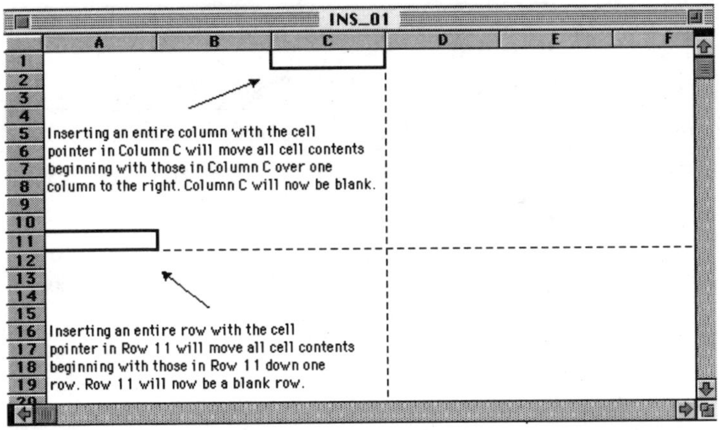

Figure 4-3: The effect inserting rows and columns has on the cell contents.

Excel provides you with two ways to insert and delete rows and columns. You can insert or delete partial rows or columns. Or you can insert or delete rows and columns the entire width and length of the Excel worksheet, respectively. The technique you use depends on the worksheet and your needs.

Use partial rows and columns when you know the position of adjacent data, and don't need an entire blank row or column. Use entire rows and columns when you need a full row or column, and data in other areas of your worksheet won't be affected by an insert or delete operation.

In either case, inserting and deleting is a potentially destructive operation, so be sure to save the worksheet to disk before proceeding, or use Undo from the Edit menu, if necessary.

After you've decided what insert or delete operation you need, position the cell pointer appropriately, as shown in Tables 4-3 and 4-4.

Table 4-3: Partial row and cell manipulation

To . . .	***Position the cell pointer at . . .***
Insert a partial row	The first cell where you need blank space, and then select any additional cells across the row you want as blank space.
Insert a partial column	The first cell where you need blank space, and then select any additional cells down the column you want as blank space.
Delete a partial row	The first cell whose contents you want to remove, and then select any additional cells across the row you want to remove.
Delete a partial column	The first cell whose contents you want to remove, and then select any additional cells down the column you want to remove.

Table 4-4: Row and column manipulation

To . . .	*Position the cell pointer at . . .*
Insert an entire row	Any cell in the row you want as a blank row.
Insert an entire column	Any cell in the column you want as a blank column.
Delete an entire row	Any cell in the row you want to remove the contents of from the worksheet.
Delete an entire column	Any cell in the column you want to remove the contents of from the worksheet.

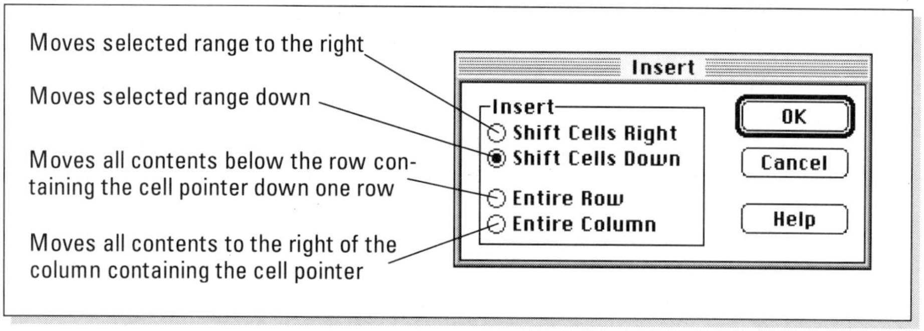

Figure 4-4: Inserting rows and columns using the Insert dialog box.

Next, choose Insert from the Edit menu or shortcut menu or press Command-I. For delete operations, choose Delete from the Edit menu or shortcut menu or press Command-K. These commands display the dialog boxes shown in Figures 4-4 and 4-5. Choose the option that's appropriate to your needs, and then click OK.

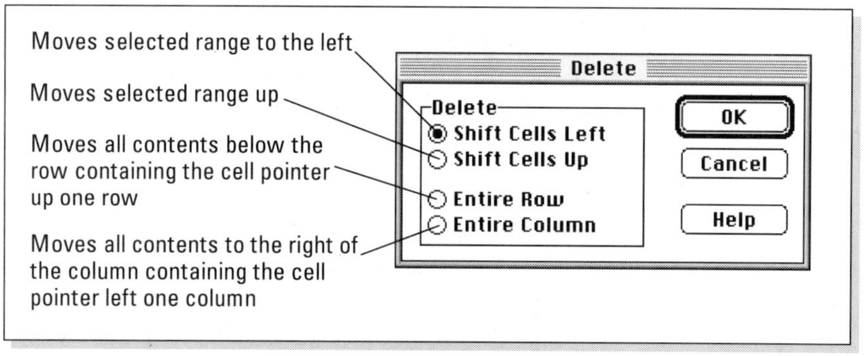

Figure 4-5: Deleting rows and columns using the Delete dialog box.

Choosing the correct eraser

If you want to remove the contents of cells only, use Clear from the Edit menu. If you want to remove cell(s) completely from the worksheet, use Delete from the Edit menu. These two commands produce very different results. Using Delete removes a cell's contents and moves the rest of the worksheet's cell contents to take the place of the vacant space. The Clear command, on the other hand, leaves the worksheet undisturbed except for the selected cells whose contents you want to erase, or clear. Therefore, if you're looking for an eraser for your electronic worksheet, use the Clear command.

You can also insert and delete more than one row in a single step. Position the cell pointer on the cell of the first row or column you want to insert or delete, and then select as many adjacent rows or columns as you need. You use Insert and Delete from the Edit menu the same way with single rows and columns as you do when working with multiple rows and columns. That way, you'll be ready when your supervisor wants *Telephone* separated into voice, facsimile, and data transmission telephone expenses.

Step-by-Step

In this section, you'll practice changing the contents of cells and inserting a partial column. You can also practice modifying other worksheets by placing random numbers in cells and seeing the effect of inserting and deleting single, multiple, partial, and entire rows and columns.

Editing cell contents:

Step 1. Start Excel if you haven't already.

The Worksheet1 window appears.

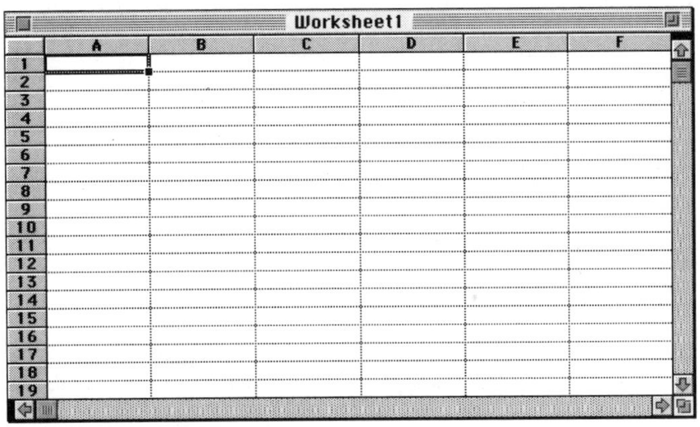

Figure 4-6: Starting up Excel displays the Worksheet1 window.

Step 2. Enter the labels in range A1:A4 exactly as shown in Figure 4-7, and then make cell A1 the active cell.

The cells are ready for editing.

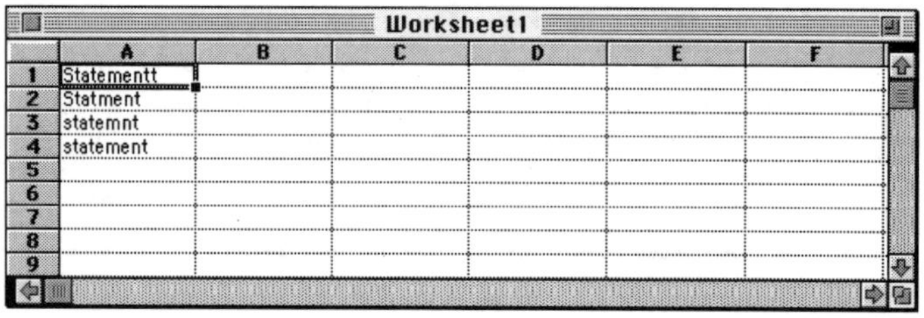

Figure 4-7: Sample labels in range A1:A4 ready to be edited.

Step 3. Click after the second *t* in *Statementt* in the formula bar.

The formula bar becomes active.

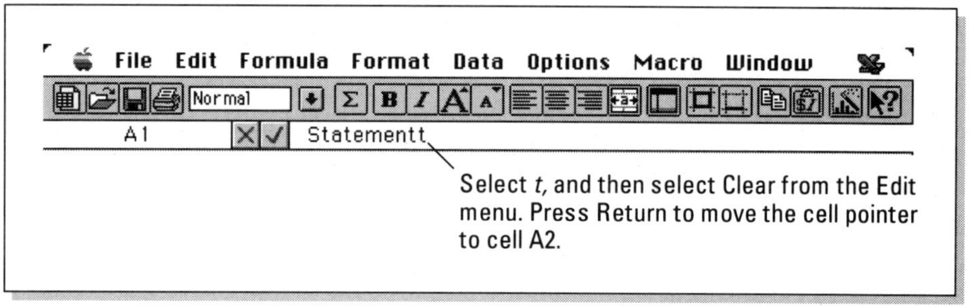

Figure 4-8: Editing text in a cell using the formula bar.

Step 4. Select the second *t*, select Clear from the Edit menu, and then press Return.

Excel accepts the correction and moves the cell pointer to cell A2.

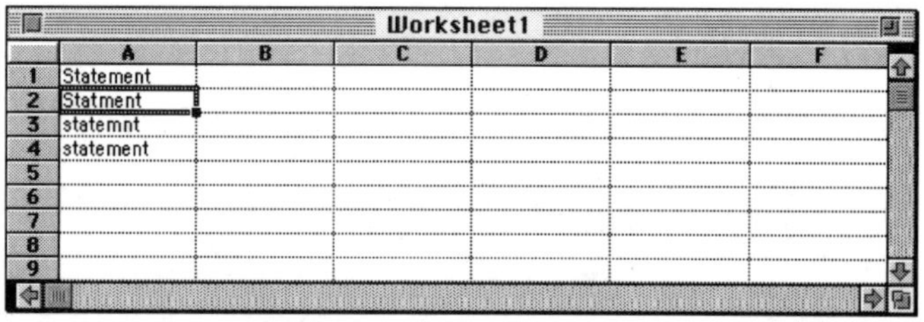

Figure 4-9: Pressing Return after editing cell A1 moves the cell pointer down to cell A2, making it the active cell ready for editing.

Step 5. Modify the contents of cells A2 and A3 so that they resemble the word *Statement* in cell A1. Press Return each time you finish editing the cell contents. Remember to use the mouse pointer to place the insertion point as close as possible to the section of the word you want to change.

Step 6. Erase the contents of cell A4 by moving the cell pointer to the fill handle. When the pointer resembles a black cross, drag to the upper-left corner of the cell. When the cell is completely shaded in gray, release the mouse button.

Now, undo the deletion by choosing Undo Clear from the Edit menu, pressing Command-Z, or by pressing F1.

Inserting a partial column:

Step 1. Close Worksheet1 by clicking the close box, pressing Command-W, or by selecting Close from the File menu. When the dialog box asking you if you want to save changes to the worksheet appears, select No. Next, open TOPIC3, the worksheet you saved to disk in Topic 3, by clicking the File Open tool, by pressing Command-O, or by selecting Open from the File menu.

TOPIC3 is displayed on screen.

Step 2. Select the range C4:C18, and choose the Insert command from the Edit menu.

The Insert dialog box appears.

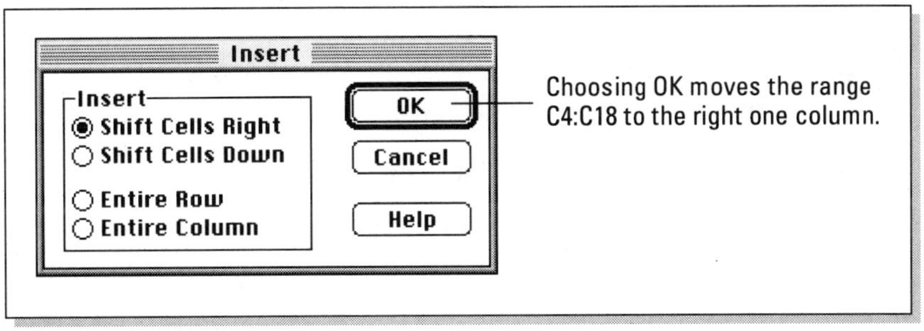

Figure 4-10: Choosing Insert from the Edit menu displays the Insert dialog box.

Step 3. Click OK.

Excel shifts the cell entries in Column C to Column D (see Figure 4-11 on next page).

Step 4. Select Save As from the File menu and type the name TOPIC4 in the Save Filename as text box. Click Save or press Return to save the worksheet to disk.

Excel saves the worksheet to disk.

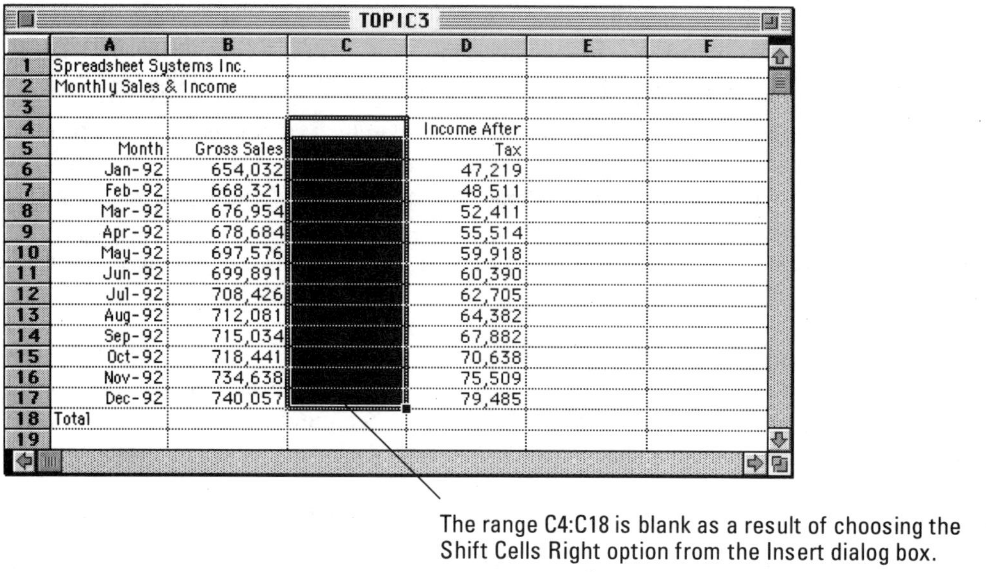

Figure 4-11: Inserting a partial column by choosing the Shift Cells Right option from the Insert dialog box.

Quick Tips

The following section provides tips on how to effectively make changes to your worksheets.

Using Insert and Delete commands with caution

CAUTION!

Use extreme care when making a change to a worksheet using any of the Insert or Delete commands. If you don't remember to use Undo from the Edit menu or have a copy of the worksheet saved to disk, your changes are irreversible and permanent.

Using partial or entire rows and columns

Whether you should use partial or entire rows and columns during an insert and delete operation depends on the Excel worksheet and what you're attempting to accomplish. If you're confident that inserting or deleting an entire row or column won't affect other areas of the worksheet, use the Entire Row and Entire Column options. If using an entire row or column would be destructive, and you know the precise range of cells to select, use the Shift Cells Right and Shift Cells Down options.

Lining up cell entries

If you use partial rows or columns, and your rows or columns have cell entries that correspond to each other, make sure you select the entire range of blank and nonblank cells before inserting or deleting. Selecting the entire range ensures that the cell entries will continue to line up properly.

Selecting rows and columns

You can quickly select an entire row or column to insert or delete by clicking on its row number or column letter. To select multiple rows or columns, click the first row number or column letter where you want to begin an insert or delete operation, and then drag across the subsequent row or column letters to complete the selection.

CAUTION!

When you select multiple rows or columns in this manner for inserting and deleting, Excel carries out an entire row or column insert or delete without displaying a dialog box or warning message. Be careful.

Selecting noncontiguous rows and columns

You can select multiple noncontiguous rows or columns by clicking on the first row number or column letter, and then pressing Control and clicking on subsequent row numbers or column letters.

Using blank cells

If you need blank cells, think carefully about what would be more appropriate for your worksheet: erasing the contents of cells or deleting them. If the worksheet contains formulas that depend on cells you've deleted, your formulas will display the #REF! error message. Use Undo from the Edit menu to return the cells to the worksheet.

Creating a backup worksheet

Instead of erasing all values, text, formulas, notes, and formatting from a worksheet, copy the range containing the cell contents to a new worksheet. When you copy the range in this manner, you have the original, unmodified worksheet available as a backup worksheet, and can modify the data in the new worksheet.

Summary

- To completely erase the contents of a cell or range of cells, select the cells, and then click and drag on the fill handle, press Command-B, press Delete, or select Clear from the Edit menu or shortcut menu.
- To erase and reuse cell contents, select the cell or range of cells you want to erase, and then press F2, Command-X, or select Cut from the Edit menu or shortcut menu. Select another cell, and then press F4, Command-V, or select Paste from the Edit menu or shortcut menu to complete the operation.
- You edit contents of cells in the formula bar. You can edit cell contents using the mouse, the keyboard, or a combination of both.
- Existing cell contents can be replaced by selecting the cell, typing the new entry, and then clicking the Enter box or pressing Return.
- Blank rows and/or columns can be inserted between cells with contents by selecting a cell above where you want the blank row, or to the right of where you want a blank column, and then by selecting Insert from the Edit menu or shortcut menu or pressing Command-I. You can insert entire or partial blank rows or columns.
- Remove rows or columns from the worksheet by selecting a cell in the row or column, and then selecting Delete from the Edit menu or shortcut menu or by pressing Command-K. You can delete entire or partial rows or columns.
- Use the Clear command from the Edit menu to erase the contents of cells, and use the Delete command to remove entire rows or columns from the worksheet.

Topic 5
Cutting, Copying, and Pasting Data

Overview

In the not-too-distant past, if you wanted to move the contents of one row from one location on your accounting ledger paper to another, you opened your desk drawer and got out your scissors and glue (or tape). Moving rows or columns meant cutting the cells out of the worksheet and then gluing them in the new location — a messy and time-consuming task.

The Macintosh and Excel have changed the way that you move contents in a worksheet. You now have a variety of software tools available to you for moving and copying data in a worksheet. You can copy cell entries from one location to another with or without the use of the Macintosh's Clipboard. If you do use the Clipboard, you can duplicate the contents of the Clipboard as many times as you need.

This Topic shows you how to use the mouse or Excel's edit commands to move and copy data from one location to another in your worksheet. You'll learn all of the copying and moving techniques that are available to you, and in the process, understand why the Macintosh and Excel have made the paper ledger a dinosaur.

Moving cell contents

In Topic 4, you learned how to move ranges of data by specifying one or more rows or columns you wanted blank, and then using Insert from the Edit menu to move the data to the right or down. You may, however, have cell entries in the worksheet that you'd like to move, but for one reason or another, don't want or need to do an insert operation. For example, you might want to move a cell entry down one cell. In this case, you have two easy-to-use options. To move cell contents, you can use the mouse, or the Cut and Paste commands from the Edit menu.

Moving cell contents with the mouse

VERSION 4 Microsoft

For fast and simple moving of cell contents, nothing beats using the mouse. Select the cell or range you want to move, and then point the mouse at one edge of the selection. When the pointer appears as a black arrow (similar to when you choose a command), click and drag on the edge of the selection. A gray outline of the selection will follow the mouse pointer as you drag, as shown in Figure 5-1. When the selected cells are at the desired location, release the mouse button. The cell contents move to the area of the worksheet where the outline was located when you released the mouse button, and will remain selected if you want to move them again or choose a command. What could be easier?

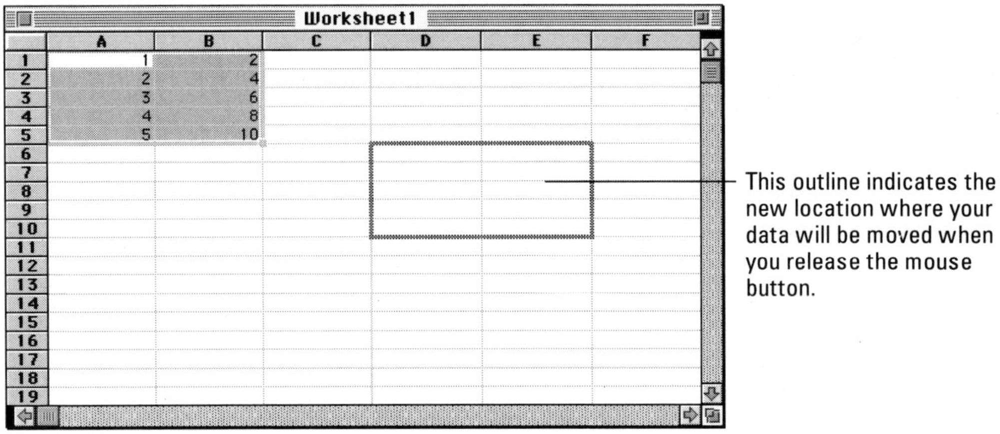

Figure 5-1: Moving cell contents with the mouse.

Moving cell contents using commands

Another way to move data in Excel is to "cut and paste" it just as you would with a paper worksheet (except without all the extra office supplies). The first step is to select the cell or range you want to move. Next, do one of the following:

- ✦ Choose Cut from the Edit menu or shortcut menu
- ✦ Press F2
- ✦ Press Command-X

When you use a cut command, the contents of the cell or range you selected to be cut are enclosed by dashed lines moving clockwise, called a *marquee* (looks similar to the marquee lights above theaters or around some homes during the holidays). A marquee helps you see the cell or range you selected. The marquee remains around the contents of the cell you selected to be cut until you choose another command, activate Excel's formula bar, or press Command-period.

The second step of the cutting operation is to select a destination for the selected cells. You can select a single cell or multiple cell range, but you must at least select the upper-left corner in a multiple cell range. After you select the destination cell or multiple cell range, do one of the following:

- ✦ Press the Enter key
- ✦ Choose Paste from the Edit menu or the shortcut menu
- ✦ Press F4
- ✦ Press Command-V

Excel moves the cells to their new location.

In summary, using Cut and Paste is like "picking up" the cell contents of a selected cell or range and "putting them down again" in one or more destination cells.

The cell or range you choose as the destination for the selected cells is important for several reasons. First, choose the destinations carefully. After you choose Paste from the Edit menu or press Enter, Excel cuts and then pastes the selected data to the destination cell or range. If you have existing cell entries in the destination range, they are overwritten without prior confirmation from Excel. As always, however, you can use Undo from the Edit menu to undo the cut and paste operation if it isn't what you had in mind.

Second, you must specify a destination for the cells that is either a single cell or the cell that is the upper-left corner of the multiple cell range, or a range that is the same size as the range to be cut. For example, if you want to move the contents of the cells in range A1:B5 (5 rows by 2 columns) in Figure 5-1, your destination range should also be 5 rows by 2 columns. If the destination cell or range size is not the same size as the cut cell or range, Excel can't paste the cut cell contents and displays the warning message shown in Figure 5-2.

Copying the contents of cells

Copying the contents of cells in a worksheet from one location to another is similar to moving cell contents. Instead of moving data, however, copying makes at least one duplicate of the selected cell or range and leaves the original data unchanged. The following discussion covers different ways to copy the contents of a cell.

Copying cell contents with the mouse

Copying cell contents with a mouse is virtually identical to moving cell contents with a mouse. First, select the cell or range of cells whose contents you want to copy. Second, press the Option key, and then point the mouse pointer at one of the selection's borders. The mouse pointer appears as a black arrow with a small plus sign (+) to the right of the arrow indicating that Excel is ready to copy. Click and drag the mouse to the area where you want the duplicate range, and then release the mouse button. Two identical sets of data appear with the second set now the selected range, as shown in Figure 5-3. That's all there is to it.

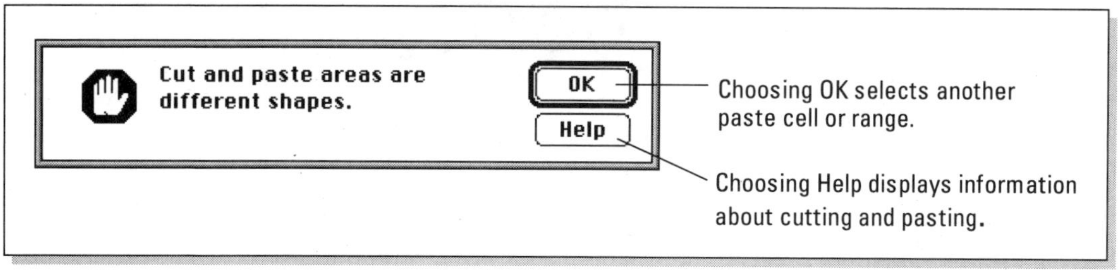

Figure 5-2: Moving cell or range contents into a destination cell or range of a different size displays this warning message.

What and where is the Clipboard?

If you're new to the Macintosh, you may have heard about the Clipboard, and are wondering just exactly what it is. The Clipboard isn't a separate program that you have to start up like Excel. Rather, when you power up your Macintosh, the Clipboard is active and ready to go with no intervention on your part.

The Clipboard is actually random-access memory (RAM) that your Macintosh's system software sets aside to hold whatever you cut or copy to it: text, numbers, or graphics. Although there's no program icon or other indicator of the Clipboard's presence, you can access the current contents of the Clipboard by choosing Show Clipboard from the Window menu. When you do, a window similar to the one in the following figure appears.

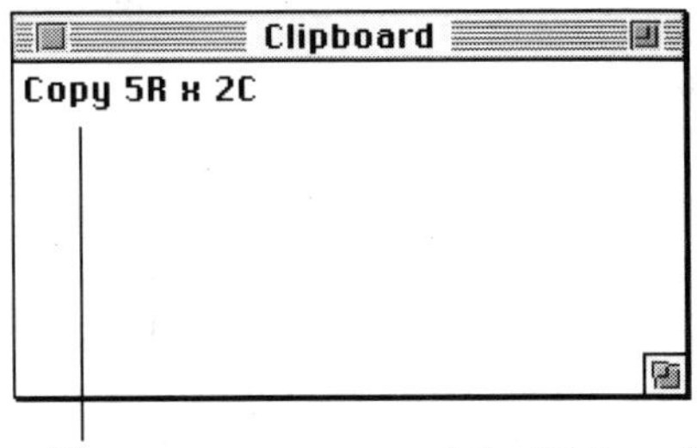

Because the Clipboard is random-access memory, it is similar in one respect to a new unsaved worksheet file. If you turn off your Macintosh, all Clipboard contents disappear into thin air forever (if the data is large, however, your Macintosh will display a warning message). If you feel you'll need the Clipboard's contents for a future Excel (or other application) session, paste the contents into a new worksheet file, and choose Save from the File menu. Or paste the contents to the Scrapbook (from the Apple menu). Either way, think of the Clipboard as one of your silent spreadsheet partners.

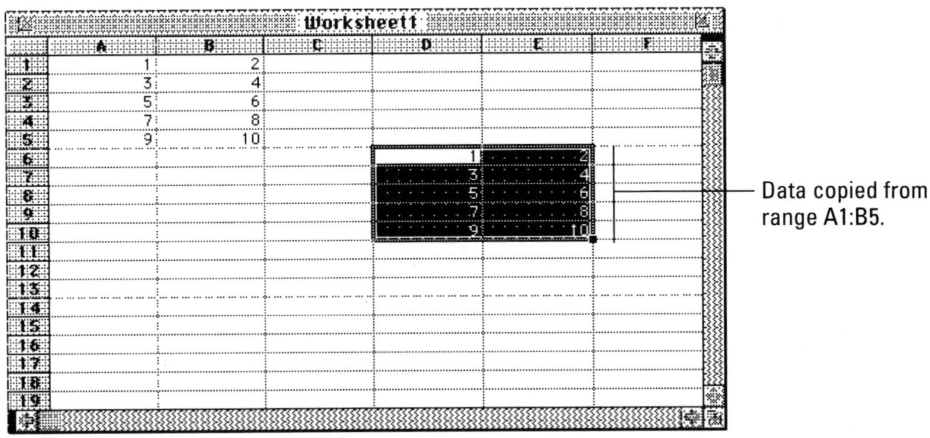

Figure 5-3: Copying cell contents with the mouse.

Copying cell contents using commands

The major difference between moving and copying data is the command you use from the Edit menu; to copy data, you use the Copy command, whereas in moving data, you use the Cut command. But the same rules and cautions apply to copying data as with moving data. Make sure the paste range is the single cell of the upper-left corner of your paste range, or the same size as the selected range.

As with moving cell contents, copying cell contents overwrites any existing cell entries in the paste range. Remember, however, you can always fall back on the Undo command from the Edit menu if the result of the copy operation is an unpleasant surprise.

To copy cell contents using commands, select the cell or range you want to copy, and then do one of the following:

- ✦ Choose Copy from the Edit menu or shortcut menu
- ✦ Press F3
- ✦ Press Command-C

The cell or range becomes surrounded by the marquee. Next, select the cell or range to hold the duplicate cell contents, and then do one of the following:

- ✦ Choose Paste from the Edit menu or the shortcut menu
- ✦ Press F4
- ✦ Press Command-V
- ✦ Press Enter

If you press Enter, the marquee disappears and the selected range is copied to the specified worksheet location, as you saw in Figure 5-3. If you choose Paste, press F4, or press Command-V, the marquee remains around the original cell contents, letting you paste as many times as you need. When you're finished copying, press Command-period, or choose another command to turn off the marquee. When you stop the copying operation, the last duplicate you created becomes the selected cell or range.

One-stop copying

If you want to simply copy a selected cell or range across a row of cells or down a column of cells, as you would, for example, in a budget worksheet, there are a few methods available to you. To copy a selected cell or range in this way, you can use the mouse, or choose Fill Right or Fill Down from the Edit menu. For example, in Figure 5-4, you need enter only the SUM function in cell C6 by clicking the SUM tool, and then click the Enter box. Entering totals for the other quarters is easy, either way you choose to copy them.

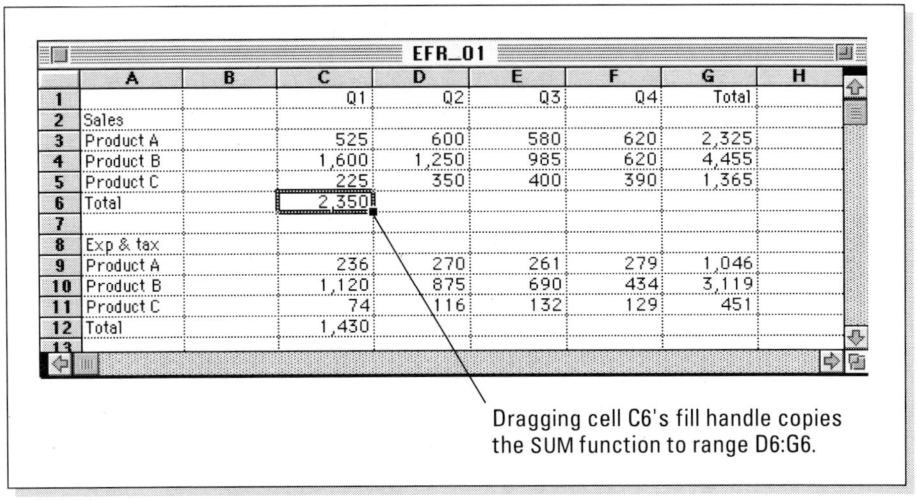

Figure 5-4: Copying a selected cell or range across a row of cells or down a column of cells.

VERSION 4 Microsoft

To use the mouse to copy the contents in Figure 5-4, you'd place the mouse pointer over cell C6's fill handle. When the mouse pointer appears as a black cross, drag across the row for each column's total, and then release the mouse button. The SUM function will be entered in each cell in Row 6.

To use Fill Right to copy the contents in Figure 5-4, select the range C6:F6, and choose Fill Right from the Edit menu. Excel enters the SUM function in range D6:G6, as shown in Figure 5-5. You use the mouse or choose Fill Right from the Edit menu in a similar fashion to copy the SUM function in cell C12 to range D12:G12.

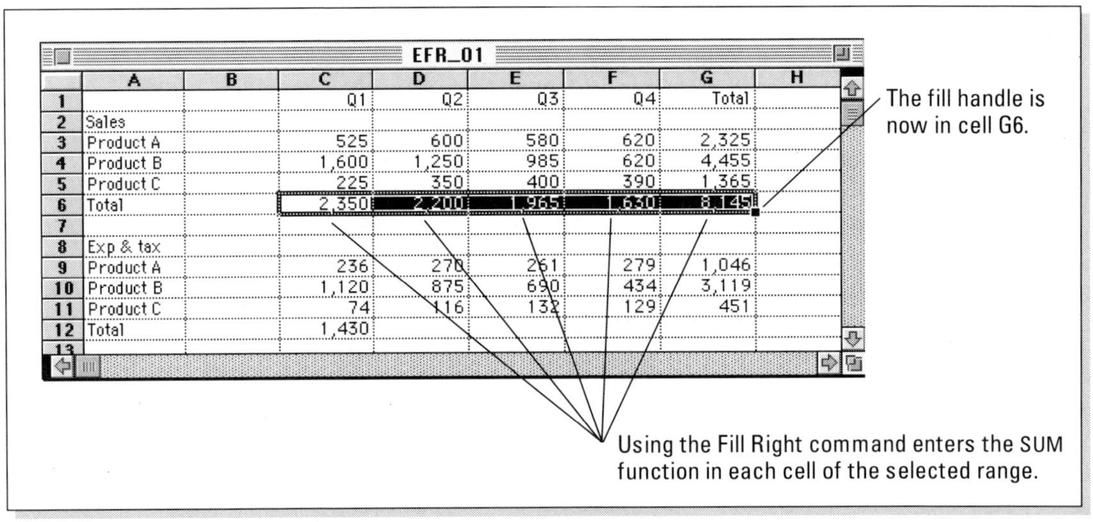

Figure 5-5: Using the Fill Right command to copy cell contents.

Copying data into existing cell contents

You may encounter a situation where you'd like to place a range of data into another range of existing data. Instead of inserting blank cells at the location and then pasting the data there, you can use the mouse, or the Cut, Copy, and Insert Paste commands from the Edit menu to move the data into a range containing existing cell contents. Excel automatically moves the existing data so it isn't overwritten when accommodating the new data. (Excel also adjusts any ranges in SUM functions to include the new data in the totals.)

Inserting data using the mouse

Excel enables you to insert data into a range that already contains data. To insert copied or cut data in a range using the mouse (see Figure 5-6), do the following:

1. Select the cells in range B4:B18.
2. To cut and insert the data, press Shift. To copy and insert the data, press Shift-Option.
3. Drag the selection. The selection collapses horizontally over a row gridline, vertically over a column gridline.
4. When the vertical outline is on the gridline between Columns D and E in range E4:E18, release the mouse button.

Excel moves and inserts the new data without overwriting any existing data.

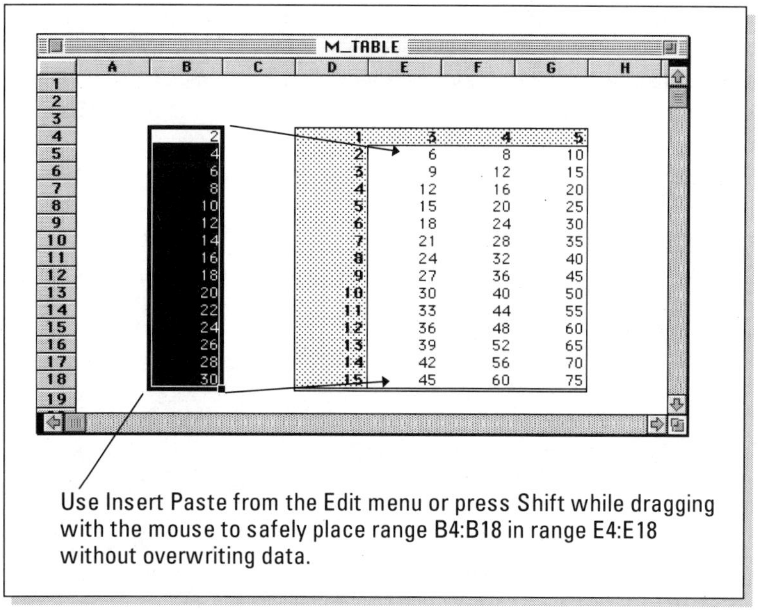

Figure 5-6: Inserting data into a range using the mouse.

Inserting data using menu commands

Data can be inserted into cells using Cut and Paste from the Edit menu. To insert data, do the following:

1. Select the cells whose contents you want to insert.
2. Choose Cut from the Edit menu.
3. Select the cell or range you want to be the destination.
4. Choose Insert Paste from the Edit menu.
5. When the Insert Paste dialog box appears, as shown in Figure 5-7, choose whether you want existing data to move to the right across columns (Shift Cells Right), or down rows (Shift Cells Down) if the data you want to insert has different dimensions from the existing data.

Advanced copying techniques

So far you've learned the basics of moving and copying data using the mouse and the Cut, Copy, and Paste commands. For most of the work you'll do, these methods will meet your copying needs. But you should be aware of some more specialized copying techniques. Excel's Paste Special command on the Edit menu opens up a whole new world in paste capabilities that you may not use that often, but are good to keep in your hip pocket. Keep in mind as you explore the Paste Special command that it only works in conjunction with the Copy command on the Edit menu.

To use Paste Special, select a cell or range to copy, choose Copy from the Edit menu, and then choose Paste Special. The Paste Special dialog box appears, as shown in Figure 5-8.

Excel's default Paste Special options (the All and None buttons in the Paste and Operation boxes) provide the same results as using Paste from the Edit menu. The Paste options, however, enable you to select one cell or range attribute you want to copy. You can copy a cell or range's formulas, values, formats, or cell notes.

Recall with the Paste command that the cell or range you selected to move or copy overwrites any existing cell entries in the destination, or paste range. The Operation box, however, gives you the opportunity to perform basic arithmetic tasks (add, subtract,

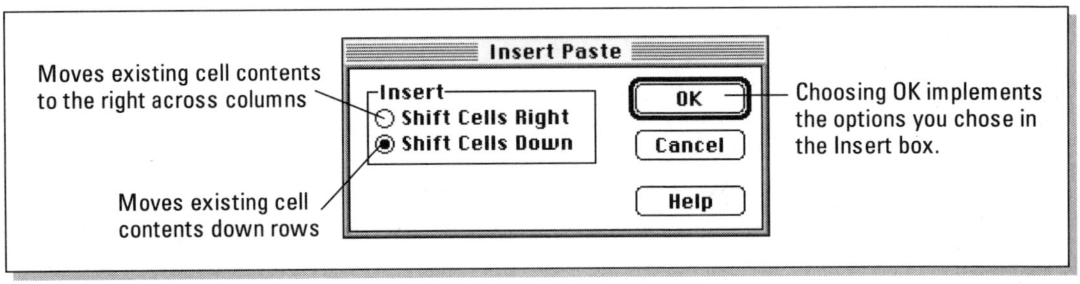

Figure 5-7: Inserting data using the Insert Paste dialog box.

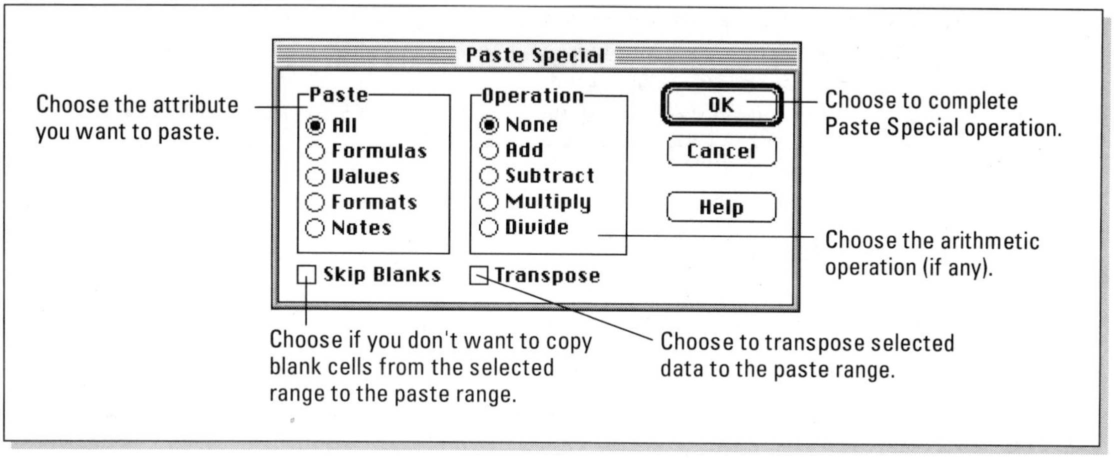

Figure 5-8: Using the Paste Special dialog box to copy specific cell and range attributes.

multiply, or divide) on the cells in your paste range. The cells you select to copy aren't just copied to your paste range, rather they can be added, subtracted, multiplied, or divided with, to, or by the existing cell contents. For example, if you've select *2* from cell A1 and use Paste Special from the Edit menu to add it to cell B1 (which currently contains *2*), B1 will contain *4* after the operation.

The Transpose option in the Paste Special dialog box provides you with an opportunity to view data from another perspective. Transpose pastes and shifts your selected data from rows to columns or columns to rows. For example, look at the worksheet in Figure 5-9.

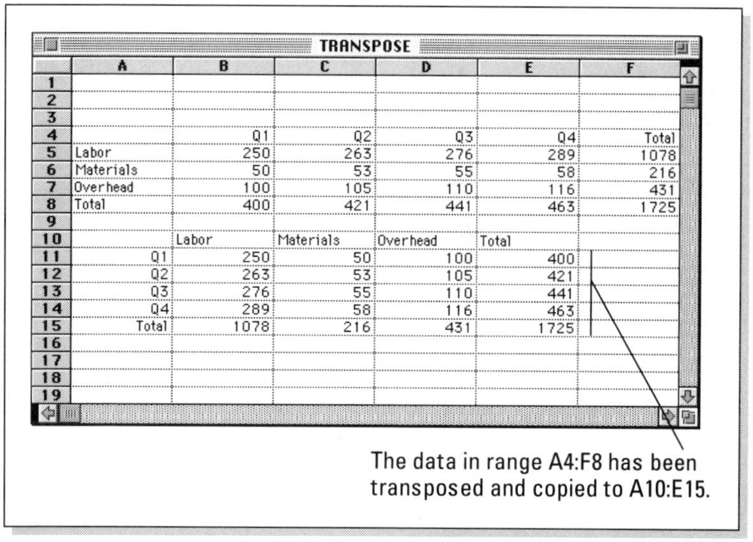

Figure 5-9: Using the Transpose option from the Paste Special dialog box enables you to view a worksheet in different ways.

The data in range A4:F8 has been transposed and copied to the range A10:E15 in the figure, with cell A10 as the paste range. When you transpose a range that contains functions or formulas, Excel adjusts the ranges in the formulas automatically. For example, Excel changed the SUM function's range in cell F5 (B5:E5) to (B11:B14) in cell B15. You can cut and paste the transposed data to another open worksheet as part of your analysis.

Step-by-Step

In this section, you'll practice moving, copying, and transposing cell contents. You'll be using the worksheet you created in Topic 2, and since the changes won't be necessary for a future Topic, you don't need to save your worksheet to disk.

Remember to use Undo from the Edit menu if you make a mistake. Or you can close the worksheet without saving it and then open it again to start over by choosing Close and then Open from the File menu.

1. Start Excel, or make it the active application.
2. Choose Open from the File menu.

   The Open dialog box appears.

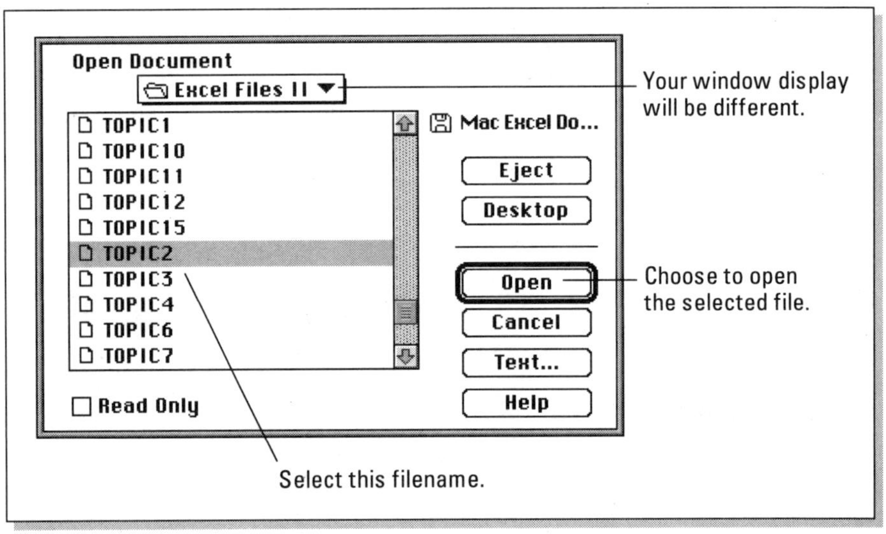

Figure 5-10: Choosing Open from the File menu displays the Open dialog box.

3. Select TOPIC2 and press Return, or choose Open from the File menu.

   The TOPIC2 worksheet appears.

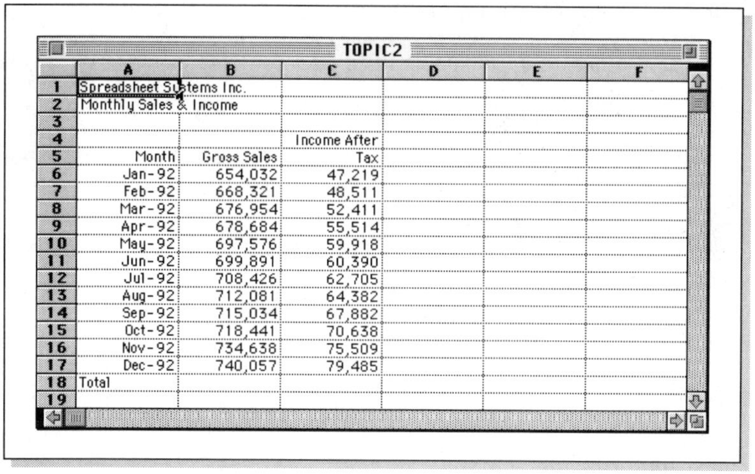

	A	B	C
1	Spreadsheet Systems Inc.		
2	Monthly Sales & Income		
3			
4			Income After
5	Month	Gross Sales	Tax
6	Jan-92	654,032	47,219
7	Feb-92	668,321	48,511
8	Mar-92	676,954	52,411
9	Apr-92	678,684	55,514
10	May-92	697,576	59,918
11	Jun-92	699,891	60,390
12	Jul-92	708,426	62,705
13	Aug-92	712,081	64,382
14	Sep-92	715,034	67,882
15	Oct-92	718,441	70,638
16	Nov-92	734,638	75,509
17	Dec-92	740,057	79,485
18	Total		
19			

Figure 5-11: Opening TOPIC2 from the Open dialog box displays the worksheet.

Moving cell contents with the mouse:

Step 1. Select the range A1:A2, and then place the mouse pointer on the right border of the selection until it appears as a black arrow.

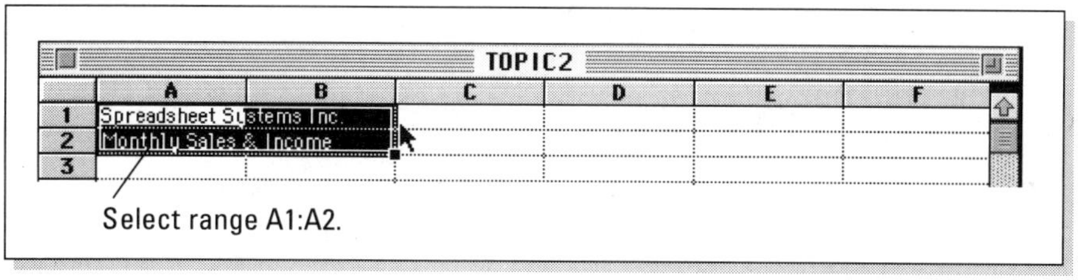

Figure 5-12: Selecting the contents of a range of cells to be moved using the mouse.

Step 2. Drag the selected range to B1:B2.

A gray outline appears around range B1:B2.

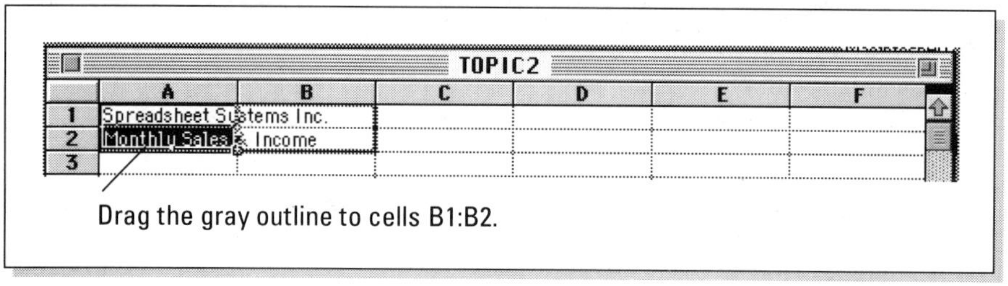

Figure 5-13: Using the mouse to move a selected range's contents.

Step 3. Release the mouse button.

Excel moves the worksheet titles (the contents in range A1:A2) to range B1:B2.

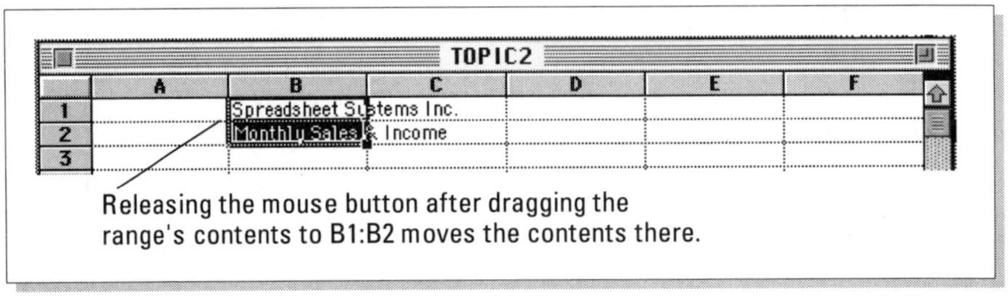

Figure 5-14: Range A1:A2 becomes range B1:B2 after it is moved using the mouse.

Moving cell contents using commands:

Step 1. Choose Cut from the Edit menu.

Range B1:B2 is selected and outlined by a marquee.

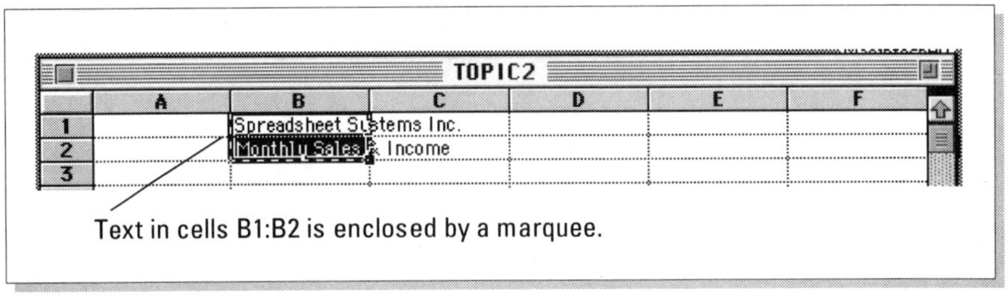

Figure 5-15: Choosing Cut from the Edit menu outlines the contents of a cell or range with the marquee.

Step 2. Click on cell A1.

Cell A1 becomes the active cell.

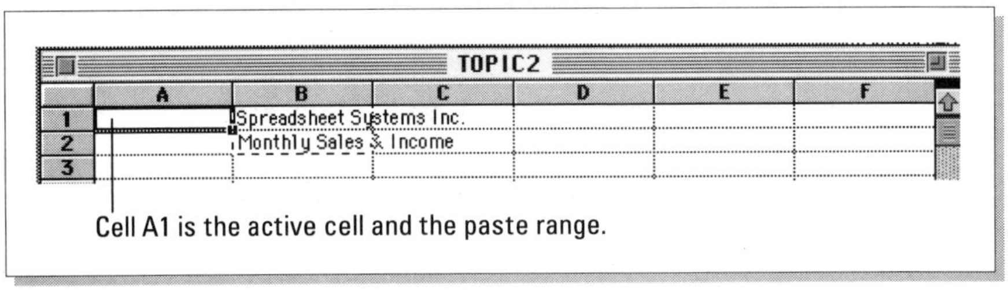

Figure 5-16: Selecting a paste range to move the contents of B1:B2 into.

Step 3. Choose Paste from the Edit menu.

Excel moves the worksheet titles (the contents in range B1:B2) to range A1:A2.

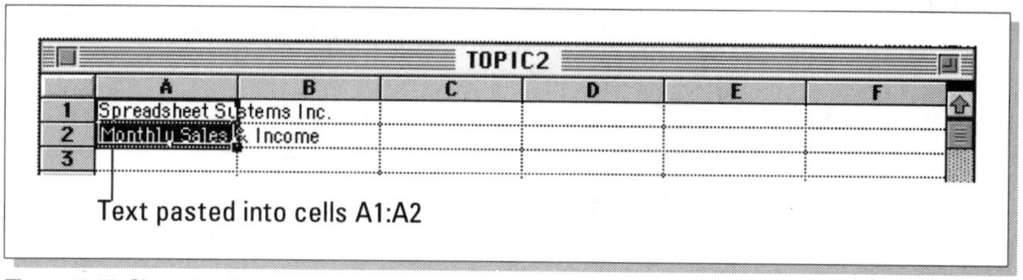

Figure 5-17: Choosing Paste from the Edit menu results in the range B1:B2 being moved to cells A1 and A2.

Copying cell contents with the mouse:

Step 1. Select the range A5:A18, press Option, and then place the mouse pointer anywhere along the right border of the selected range until the mouse pointer appears as a black arrow with a plus sign.

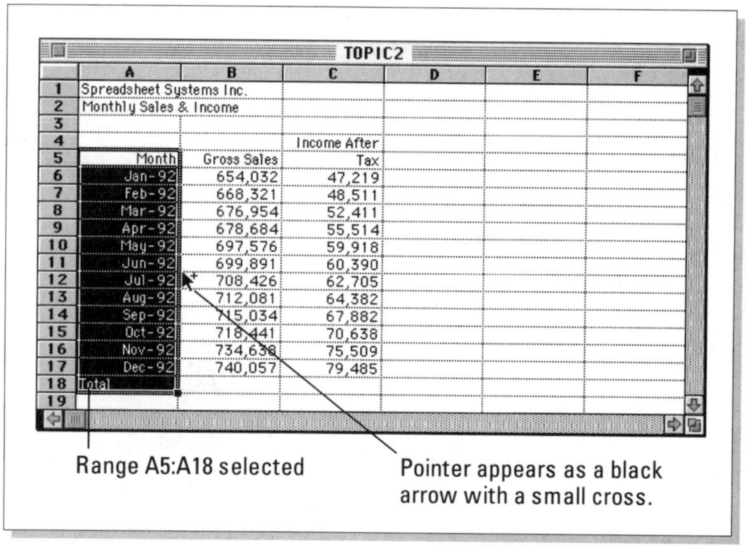

Figure 5-18: Selecting cell contents for copying using the mouse.

Step 2. Drag the mouse so the gray outline is displayed over D5:D18.

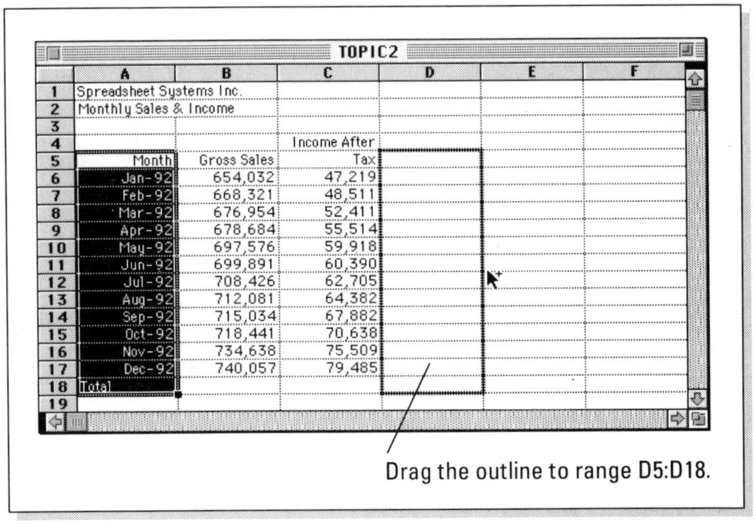

Figure 5-19: Using the mouse to move a copy of the contents of range A5:A18.

Step 3. Release the mouse button.

Excel duplicates the contents in range A5:A18 and places the copy beginning in cell D5.

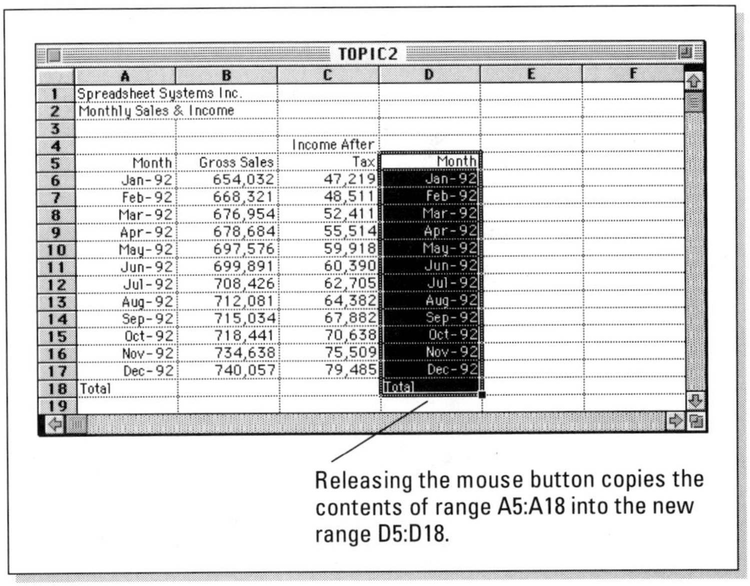

Figure 5-20: The result of copying the contents of range A5:A18 to range D5:D18.

Copying and pasting with menu commands:

Step 1. Choose Copy from the Edit menu.

The range D5:D18 is selected and is outlined by a marquee.

Step 2. Click on cell E5.

Cell E5 becomes the active cell.

Step 3. Choose Paste from the Edit menu.

Excel duplicates the contents in range D5:D18 and places the copy beginning in cell E5.

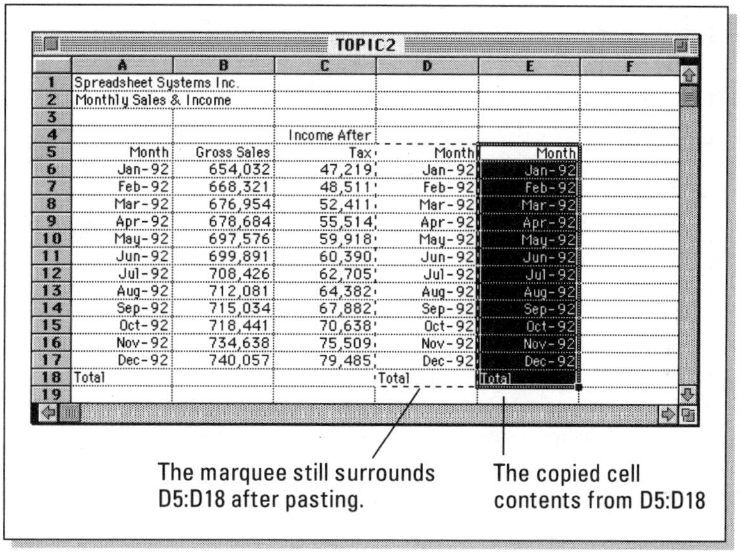

Figure 5-21: The result of copying the contents of range D5:D18 to cell E5 using the Copy and Paste commands.

Step 4. Press Command-period to turn off the marquee.

Transposing data:

Step 1. Select range A6:A17, and then choose Copy from the Edit menu.

Range A6:A17 is selected and outlined by a marquee.

Step 2. Make cell A20 the active cell, and choose Paste Special from the Edit menu.

The Paste Special dialog box appears.

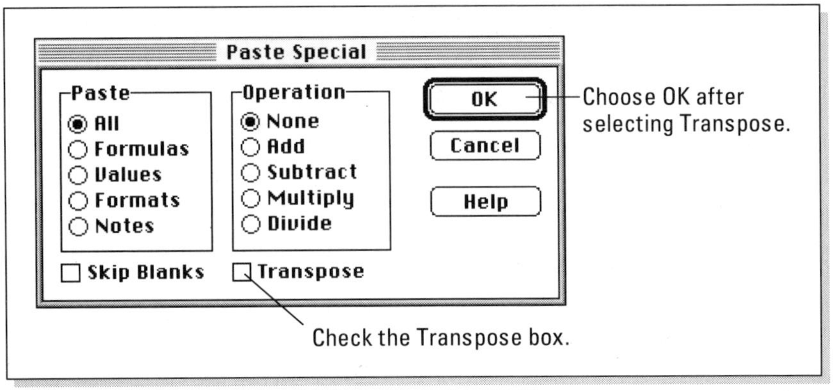

Figure 5-22: Transposing data in a cell using the Paste Special dialog box.

Step 3. Check the Transpose box and press Enter or choose OK.

Excel transposes the data.

Step 4. Close the worksheet by clicking the close box, pressing Command-W, or by choosing Close from the File menu. When the dialog box appears asking if you want to save changes, choose No.

Quick Tips

The following section provides you with tips on how to move and manipulate the data in your worksheets quickly and easily.

Moving and copying with consistency

This Topic has shown you several methods to move and copy data. Choose a method (mouse, function keys, shortcut keys, or commands) that is best for you. If you don't use the mouse to move or copy, however, you may find it easiest to use the same technique to begin and end an operation — using F2 and F4 together, or Cut and Paste together, for example.

Canceling the marquee

If you have an extended keyboard, you can cancel the marquee by pressing Esc.

Using caution when moving and copying

Move or copy cell contents to other worksheet locations with caution: Excel will not warn you if you are about to overwrite existing cell contents with the new entries. The exception to this rule is moving cell contents with a mouse. If the move operation will overwrite nonblank cells, a warning message appears, as shown in Figure 5-23.

Choose Undo from the Edit menu, press F1, or close the file without saving it and open it again, if you don't like the resulting moved data.

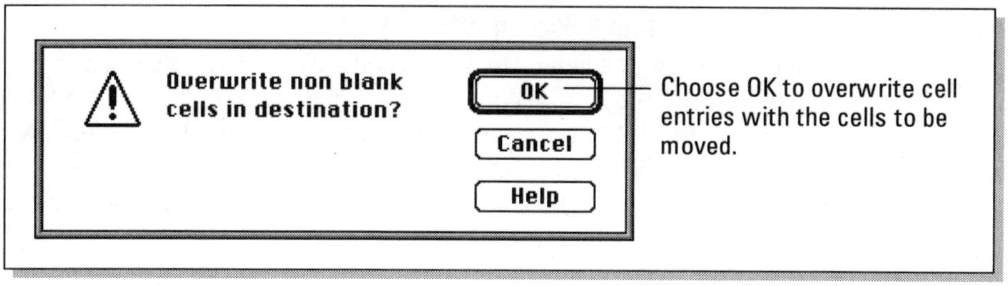

Figure 5-23: Overwriting nonblank cells during a move operation results in this warning message.

Changing Fill commands

Pressing Shift before pulling down the Edit menu changes the Fill Right and Fill Down commands to Fill Left and Fill Up, respectively.

Copying with the marquee

As long as the marquee is active after choosing the Copy command, you can paste as many times as needed.

Pasting an item only once

If you want to paste only once, press Enter after selecting the destination cell during a copy operation.

Reusing the Insert Paste command

The Insert Paste command is available from the Edit menu only *once* after using the Cut or Copy commands from the Edit menu. You must select a range and choose Cut or Copy from the Edit menu to use Insert Paste again.

Using gridlines to insert cut data

Using the mouse to insert cut data is easiest with the worksheet gridlines displayed. Gridlines help you position the Insert Paste outline in the correct paste range.

Pasting data and blank cells

The Skip Blanks option on the Paste Special dialog box enables you to paste a selection that contains data as well as blank cells without overwriting data in the paste area with the blank cells.

Cutting, copying, and pasting with the formula bar

In addition to cutting and pasting in the worksheet, you can cut and paste in the formula bar. You can cut, copy, and paste to the formula bar from the worksheet, and vice versa, using the same rules for cutting and pasting in the worksheet as you do in the formula bar. Note, however, that when you cut from the formula bar, the selection is completely removed from the formula bar and is placed on the Clipboard. You can paste the contents of the Clipboard using Paste from the Edit menu as many times as you need as long as a single cell is selected.

Cutting and pasting between worksheets

Remember, you're not limited to cutting and pasting in a single open worksheet. You're also able to cut or copy from one open worksheet to another open worksheet. To do so, simply select the cell or range you want to cut or copy from your source worksheet. Then select the open worksheet you want to move or copy the data to using the Window menu, or by clicking on the worksheet, if it's visible. Select the cell or range, and then use Paste or Paste Special from the Edit menu.

Summary

- To move cell contents with the mouse, select the data, and then drag the gray outline of the range to a new location.
- To move cell contents by cutting and pasting: Select the data; cut the selection by selecting Cut from the Edit menu or shortcut menu, pressing F2, or by pressing Command-X; select the destination cell or range to paste the contents into; then paste the selection by selecting Paste from the Edit menu or shortcut menu, pressing F4, or by pressing Command-V.
- To copy cell contents with the mouse, select the data you want copied, press Option, and then drag the gray outline of the range to the desired location.
- To copy cell contents using commands or the keyboard: Select the data; copy the selection by selecting Copy from the Edit menu or shortcut menu, or by pressing F3 or Command-C; select the cell or range to paste to; then paste the selection by selecting Paste from the Edit menu or shorcut menu, pressing F4, or by pressing Command-V.
- To use the mouse to cut or copy a selection to a range that contains data without overwriting it, first select the data. Press Shift for a cut operation, or press Shift-Option to copy the data. Drag the collapsed gray outline to the desired location, and then release the mouse button.
- To use commands to insert a cut selection into a range of data without overwriting the data, Choose Cut from the Edit menu or shortcut menu, select the new location for the data, and choose Insert Paste from the Edit menu.
- The Paste Special command on the Edit menu enables you to specify cell attributes you want moved or copied; it also enables you to perform arithmetic operations between the selected data and existing data, as well as transpose selected data.

Part III: Intermediate Excel

Topic 6

Putting Formulas and Functions to Work

Overview

Formulas are the engines of Excel worksheets. Formulas enable you to change the data in a worksheet, producing updated results instantly. As a result, formulas enable you to produce accurate calculations quickly and are another reason yesterday's analysis tools — pencil, ledger paper, and an adding machine — have ended up on the scrap heap.

This Topic introduces you to formulas — what they are, how to create and document them, and how to troubleshoot them. You'll also learn about functions — formulas that are built into Excel. Finally, you'll learn how copying and moving cell contents affect formulas, and how using names can help you create and understand formulas easily.

Introducing formulas

A formula is a mathematical relationship among the cells in an Excel worksheet. On a basic level, you perform arithmetic on your worksheet's values (add, subtract, multiply, or divide), much like you did in grade school. On a more advanced level, you can combine functions and values in your formulas to arrive at results, and even have Excel take a specific action based on a calculation. One of the most important steps in creating a formula is the first step: defining your problem or need so you can express it mathematically as an Excel formula.

For example, do you need to total a range of sales values? Or do you need to subtract total expenses from total sales? Or perhaps you'd like to know how much that shiny new red $30,000 sports coupe will set you back monthly at 9 percent interest over five years.

In any case, after you've defined your needs, entering a formula into Excel that calculates what you need to know is easy. To enter a formula into a cell, do the following:

1. Make the cell you want to hold the formula the active cell.
2. Type an equal sign (=).

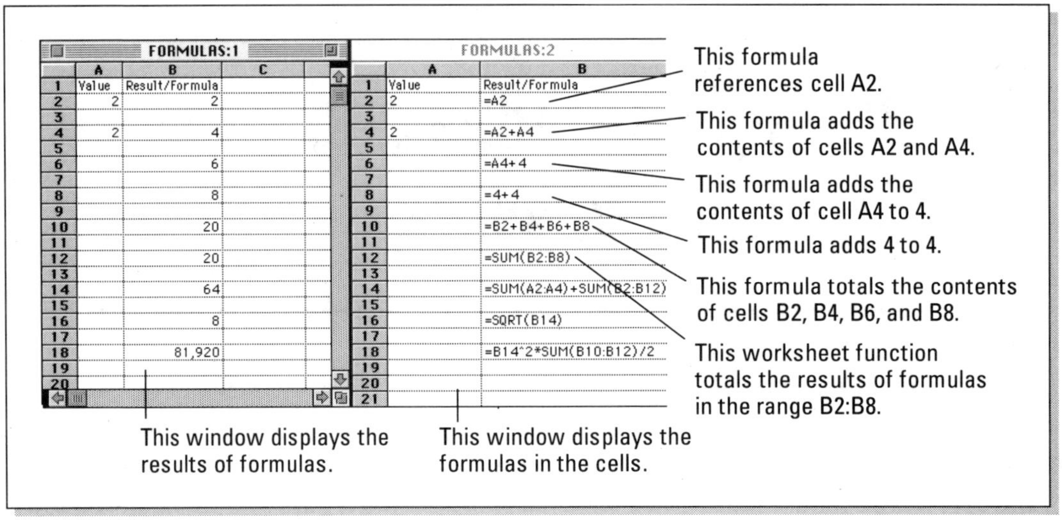

Figure 6-1: Sample formulas in an Excel worksheet.

3. Enter a value by doing one of the following:
   - ✦ Typing
   - ✦ Clicking the cell that contains the value
   - ✦ Typing the address of the cell containing the data
4. Type an operator (+, -, *, /).
5. Repeat steps 3 and 4 until you've completed the formula, but don't end your formula with an operator.
6. Click on the Enter box in the formula bar, press Return, or press an arrow key.

That's all there is to it. Figure 6-1 displays several types of simple formulas.

Note in Figure 6-1 that your formulas can have one or a combination of values, cell references, and worksheet functions. If you want to reference a cell in a formula, use the mouse or the arrow keys to select the cell containing the value you need, and then continue building the formula by entering the next operator. If you try to combine values and text, however, Excel displays the #VALUE? error message in the cell.

Creating advanced formulas

Two options on the Formula menu are available to help you create more advanced formulas. Paste Name and Paste Function let you quickly use names and worksheet functions in your formulas. These options save you time because you avoid having to correct typographical errors, and you can access names you've created and the worksheet functions that come with Excel. You can begin a formula with a worksheet function or range, or include them anywhere in the formula.

To use a named cell, range, or value in a formula, select the cell that will hold the formula, and type an equal sign. Choose Paste Name from the Formula menu, and select a name from the list in the Paste Name dialog box. Clicking OK pastes a copy of the name in the formula bar, so you can continue pasting names or building the formula, or clicking the Enter box to complete the formula (names and worksheet functions are discussed in detail later in this Topic).

Entering a worksheet function in a formula is similar to entering a name. Select the cell for the formula, choose Paste Function from the Formula menu, and select the name of the function you want from the list in the Paste Function dialog box. Excel will paste a copy of the function in the formula bar, but you'll need to furnish the function's arguments. Continue pasting names or functions, or entering values or operators, and click the Enter box or press Return when you're finished.

Correcting errors in a formula

If you make a mistake entering a formula (or function), Excel beeps and displays the message box shown in Figure 6-2.

Most errors are the result of mistyping, or having missing arguments or mismatched parentheses within a formula, such as those errors shown in the following table:

Formula	*Reason for error*
A1+B1	Missing equal sign
=((A1+B1)*(C1+D1)	Extra (left) parenthesis
=RAND	Missing argument (left and right parentheses)

After you click OK or press Return, Excel highlights a possible cause for the error in the formula bar.

You can then repair the formula. Excel switches to Edit mode so you can add or delete operators, parentheses, values, or in the case of functions, arguments. If you still have trouble finding the error in the function or formula, delete the equal sign while still in Edit mode and Excel will accept the function or formula as text. When you do this, you won't have to reenter the formula, and you can correct the formula after you've had an opportunity to mull it over. Clicking the cancel box or pressing Esc clears the formula bar so you can start over from square one.

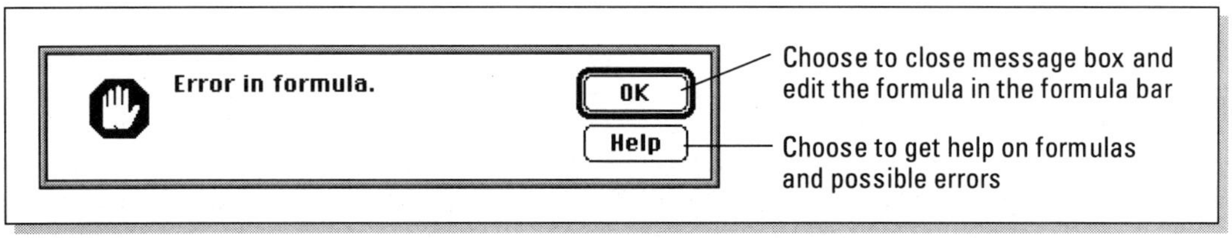

Figure 6-2: This message box alerts you to errors you have made when entering a formula or function.

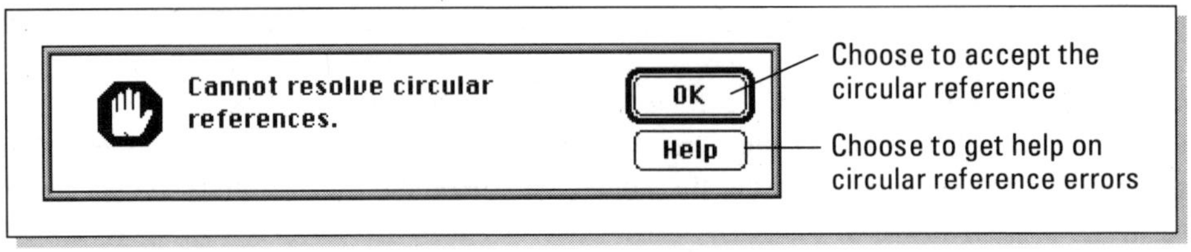

Figure 6-3: This message box alerts you when you make a circular reference error when creating a formula.

Understanding circular reference errors

A special type of error you may come across when creating a formula is when a formula refers to its own cell address. For example, entering the following formula:

=A1+A2+A3

into cell A3 displays the message box shown in Figure 6-3. Excel displays the message box in Figure 6-3 and displays *Circular:A3* on the status bar after you click the Enter box or press Return.

Excel won't be able to calculate an accurate result because the formula refers to itself, much like a dog chasing its tail. To untangle the formula, select the cell and activate the formula bar. Delete or change the cell address of the selected cell that appears in the formula bar; click the Enter box or press Enter, and you're back in business.

Calculating with formulas

If you have a formula that uses one type of operator, such as the plus sign (+), Excel calculates the formula beginning with the far left value and proceeds right to the last value — just as you would with manual arithmetic. Using other operators, however, alters the order in which values are calculated. In addition to the four basic arithmetic operators, you can use the operators listed in Table 6-1 in your formulas.

The operators calculate the formula's values in the order listed in Table 6-1. For example, multiplication and division are performed before addition and subtraction. You can, however, tell Excel which parts of a formula you want calculated first by enclosing the components of the formula in parentheses. For example, the following formulas use the same values and operators, but because of the parentheses, they produce different results:

Formula	*Result*
=2+3*4/2	8
=(2+3)*(4/2)	10

If you have more than one set of parentheses in the formula, Excel first calculates the results of each enclosed arithmetic expression, and then uses the normal order of precedence to complete the calculation.

Operator	Symbol	Order of calculation
–	negation	1
%	percentage	2
^	exponentiation	3
*	multiplication	4
/	division	4
+	addition	5
–	subtraction	5
&	concatenation	6
=	equal to	7
<	less than	7
>	greater than	7
<=	less than or equal to	7
>=	greater than or equal to	7
<>	not equal to	7

Table 6-1: Formula operators

Choosing when to calculate

Excel normally calculates the formulas in a worksheet when a value, function, or other formula it depends on changes. Excel also begins calculating at the bottom of a worksheet's formula hierarchy. That is, the less a formula depends on other cells for information, the sooner it's calculated. That way, all formulas reflect the most current results. And last but not least, Excel temporarily suspends calculation if you're busy with another worksheet task, and resumes when you're finished.

If creating a single monster worksheet is unavoidable (as opposed to a set of smaller, linked worksheets), you may want to change to manual calculation. Manual calculation enables you to choose when you want the worksheet updated, which is useful if you have a lot of data to enter or complex open charts that depend on new or edited data.

To change to manual calculation, choose Calculation from the Options menu. When the Calculate Options dialog box appears, as shown in the following figure, choose Manual. Manual calculation will be in effect until you either change back to Automatic, or close the worksheet without saving it to disk.

To calculate a worksheet in Manual calculation mode, press F9, or choose Calc Now from the Calculate Options dialog box. Be sure the worksheet is calculated before you print it so it will reflect the most current information.

Clicking OK changes the worksheet to manual calculation

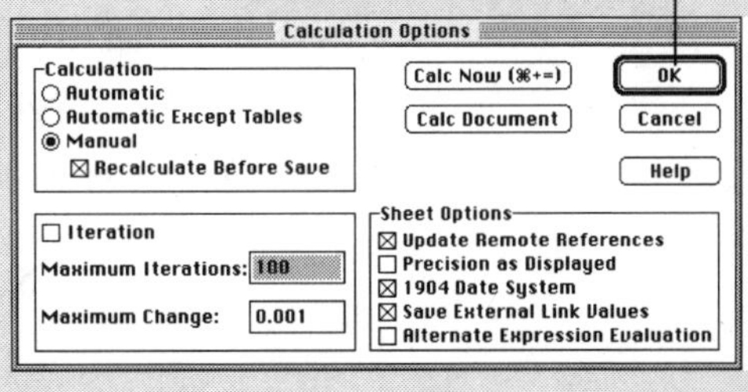

Understanding worksheet functions

Worksheet functions are built-in formulas Excel provides. As you saw in Figure 6-1, functions can be less tedious than entering their formula equivalents. For example, notice in Figure 6-1 the formula and the SUM function in cells B10 and B12. The formula and the function calculate the same result, using the same cell references. But the SUM function in cell B12 calculates totals more quickly and accurately while using less memory (Excel has less expressions to evaluate) than the formula in cell B10. The SUM function eliminates having to type or point to cell references, reducing the chance of error. Worksheet functions can be entered in one of two ways: manually, by typing, or by choosing Paste Function from the Formula menu.

To enter a function manually, follow these steps:

1. Select the cell you want to hold the function.
2. Type an equal sign (=).
3. Type the name of the function, followed by a left parenthesis.

   Next, you have to provide some information for the function to operate properly. Excel refers to these as *arguments*. Some functions, such as SUM, require only one piece of information, which is the address or name of the range to total. Other functions, such as PMT, which calculates the payment on a loan or annuity, needs at least the interest rate, total number of payments, and the present value (principal) of the amount. You supply these arguments by entering a value or cell reference, which you can type in or point to, or by entering a name (names are discussed later in this Topic). If you use a function that uses multiple arguments, you separate the arguments with commas.

4. Type a right parenthesis.
5. Click the Enter box, or press Return.

   Excel enters the function in the selected cell and calculates a result.

   If you change your mind, you can stop entering the function by pressing Esc or by clicking the cancel box. Excel will clear the formula bar so you can start over.

The Paste Function option helps you enter functions more quickly and accurately than typing them yourself. To enter a function with the Paste Function do the following:

1. Select the cell you want to hold the function.
2. Choose Paste Function from the Formula menu or press Shift-F3.

   The Paste Function dialog box appears, as shown in Figure 6-4.

3. Select the function you need and click OK or press Return.
4. Select an argument name in the formula bar, and then replace the argument name by clicking a cell containing the value, or by typing the cell address or value.

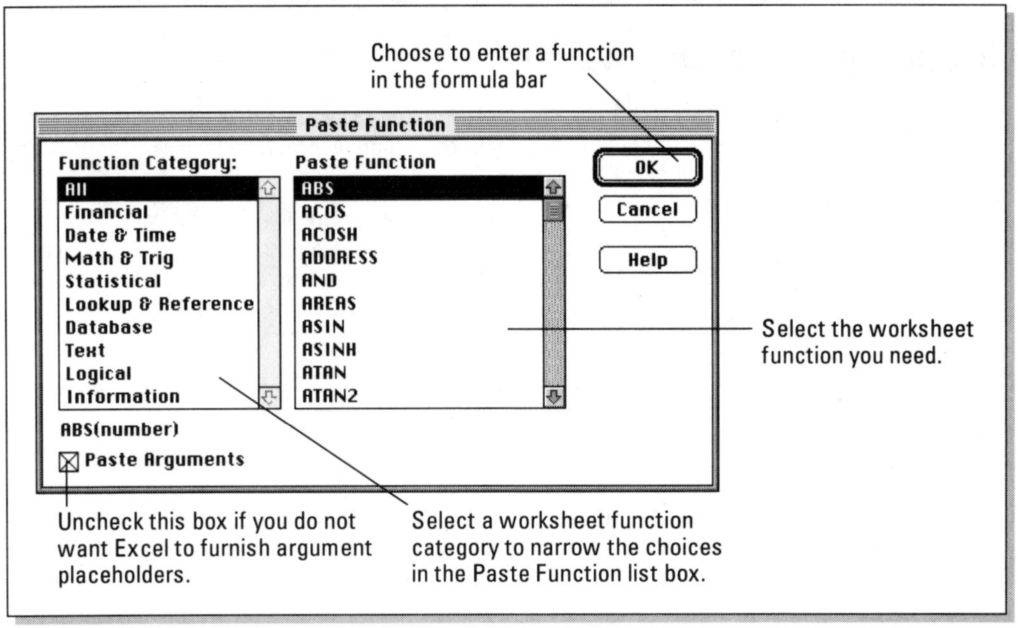

Figure 6-4: Entering a function with the Paste Function dialog box.

5. Repeat Step 4 for each argument.
6. Click the Enter box or press Return.

Excel has well over 100 functions. Figure 6-5 shows you some of the functions you're likely to use most often in your Excel sessions.

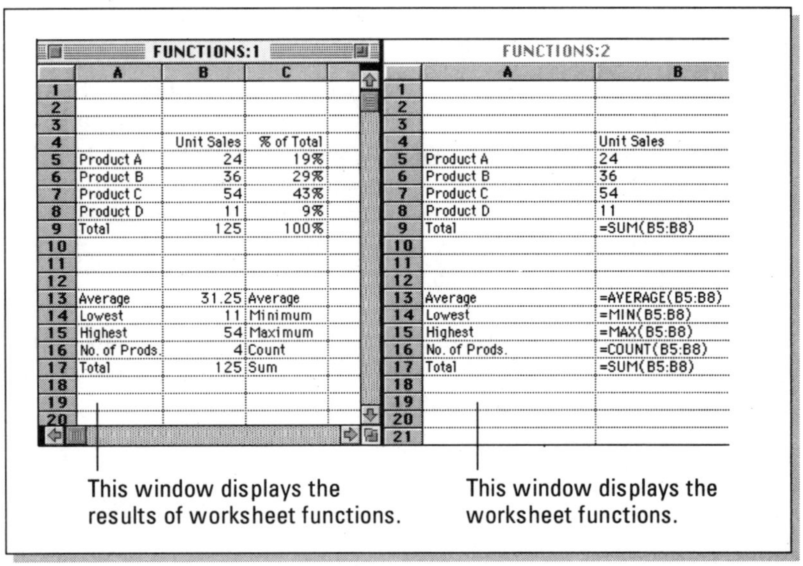

Figure 6-5: The most commonly used functions in Excel.

Calculating without a calculator

If you find yourself digging through a desk drawer for your calculator to calculate a number to use in your worksheet, or to do a quick calculation, help is only an Excel keystroke away. Make Excel the active application, type an equal sign, and then type the operators and values. Press the F9 key (or Command-=), and Excel performs the calculation in the formula bar, which you can enter into the selected cell or clear by clicking Enter or the cancel box, respectively.

You can also calculate a portion of a formula by selecting the part of the formula you want to calculate and pressing F9. Selecting the part of a formula that you want to calculate is also a way you can determine which part of a complex formula is *not* causing an error.

Σ

Autosum tool

Remember, you can total a column or row of values quickly by selecting the cell immediately below the column or to the right of the row of values, respectively clicking the Autosum tool on the Standard toolbar, and then clicking the Enter box.

Copying and pasting formulas and functions

In Topic 5 you learned how to cut, copy, and paste cell contents. As with any other cell entry, you can save time by copying and pasting functions and formulas.

What happens when you copy and paste functions and formulas that reference other cells? The cell address of the function or formula and the range of cells it references both change to reflect the new location of the formula or function. Consequently, you can move a function or formula from one cell to another and still obtain the same result.

Similarly, you can copy a function or formula in one cell to the rest of any selected cells, and in the process duplicate the function or formula in each cell. Excel automatically adjusts the range argument and cell references (if any) in your function or formula. This is known as *relative* cell addressing, because Excel modifies cell references relative to the location of the function or formula as shown in Figure 6-6. For example, if you want to total values in columns B through F in a worksheet, you need enter only the SUM function below the last cell in column B that contains a value. As you copy the SUM function across columns C through F, Excel will use each column's values to arrive at a total for that column. You don't need to manually adjust the range reference for each SUM function.

At times, however, you may need an *absolute* cell reference in a formula — a reference that you absolutely do not want to change when you copy a formula. You may encounter a situation similar to the one shown in Figure 6-7.

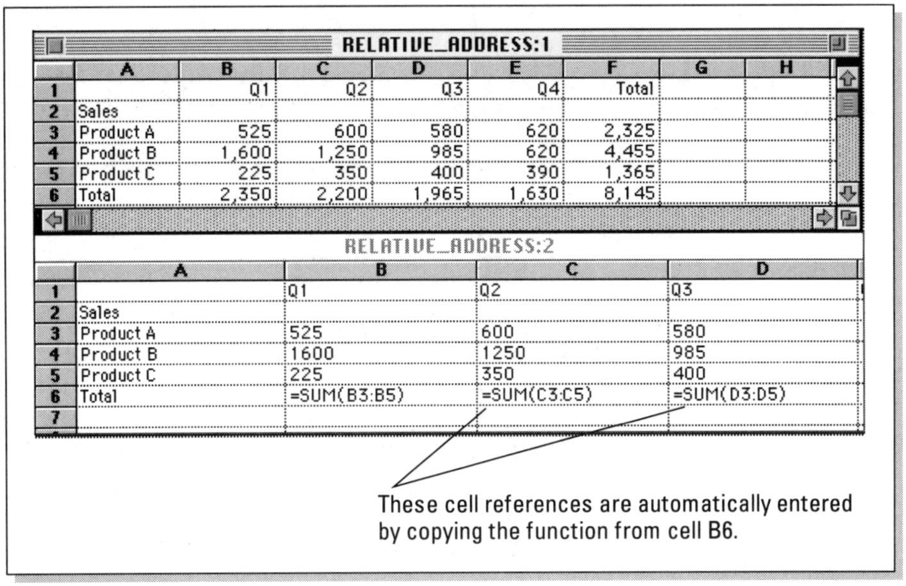

Figure 6-6: An example of relative cell referencing.

Look at the formula in cell C5. The dollar signs in the reference to cell B9 make cell B9 absolute — cell B9 will be in each formula in Column C. If cell B9 wasn't absolute, the divisor in the formulas in range C5:C9 would be B9, B10, B11, and so on.

You may also need to use a *mixed* cell reference — one in which either the column letter or the row number of the cell stays fixed as you copy, as shown in Figure 6-8. In this case, a dollar sign precedes only the column letter ($A4) and row number (B$4) in the PMT function in cell B5.

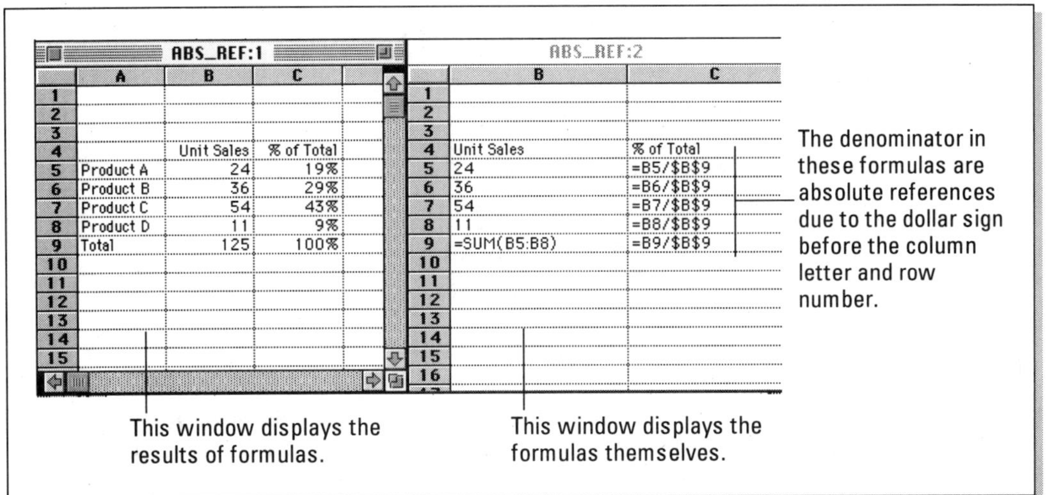

Figure 6-7: An example of absolute cell referencing.

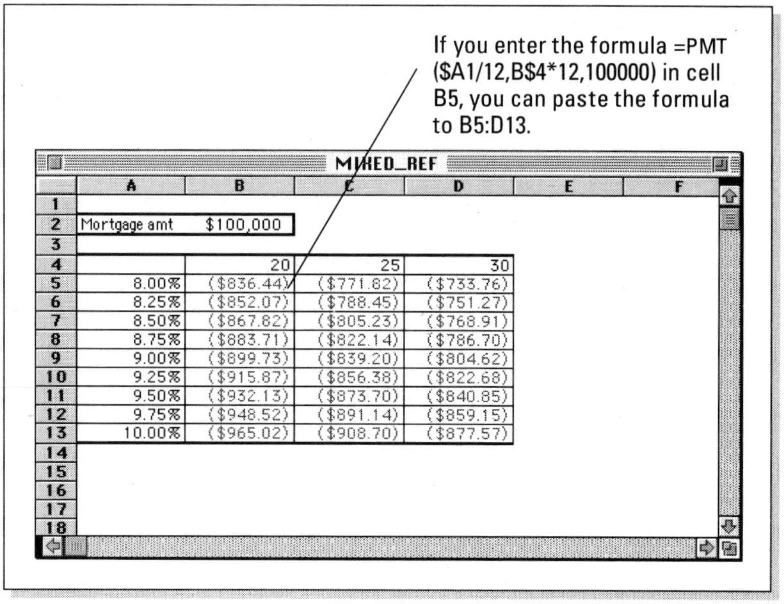

Figure 6-8: An example of mixed cell referencing.

You can change a cell reference in several ways. As you enter a formula, you can type the dollar sign(s) yourself. Or you can select the cell containing the formula; activate the formula bar; place the blinking cursor next to the cell address; and then choose Reference from the Formula menu, or press Command-T. Repeat the Reference command or press Command-T to cycle through the four available reference types, as shown in Table 6-2.

Table 6-2: Available cell reference types

Cycle	*Current*	*New*	*New type*
First	B9	$B$9	Absolute
Second	$B$9	B$9	Mixed
Third	B$9	$B9	Mixed
Fourth	$B9	B9	Relative

Naming cells, ranges, values, and formulas

So far, you've seen how to reference cells by clicking a cell or typing the cell's address. You can also name a cell, range, value, or formula with descriptive text, much like naming Excel worksheet files. Naming has many advantages. For example, it's much easier to understand sales as:

=sum(sales)

rather than:

=sum(A1:A20)

especially if a cell in the formula is in a location far from the selected cell. With names, you increase the accuracy and reduce the creation time of formulas because you aren't required to type cell addresses or point to cells.

Creating names is easy. To name a cell or range, select it, and then choose Define Name from the Formula menu. The Define Name dialog box appears, as shown in Figure 6-9.

Enter a name in the Name text box that has meaning to you, such as SALES or TOTAL. The name can contain up to 255 characters without spaces; use an underscore (_) if you want to separate words. Click OK when you're through creating names, or click Add if you want to create more names. If you make a mistake or change your mind, you can edit a name by selecting it from the Name list box, selecting the Name text box, and then making your changes.

You can save memory and make your worksheets easier to understand by naming a value or formula once and then using the name in other areas of the worksheet. For example, in the Define Name dialog box, type `TOTAL`, and in the Refers to box, type the SUM function with the range of cells you want to total as the argument, such as A3:A10, for January's budget total. You then type or paste the name =TOTAL for each of the other eleven months of the year.

You can also create names using the text entries in the worksheet if the text is adjacent to the cells you want to name. For example, the simple worksheet shown in Figure 6-10 calculates loan payment information. You can use the text in Column A to name the cells in Column B.

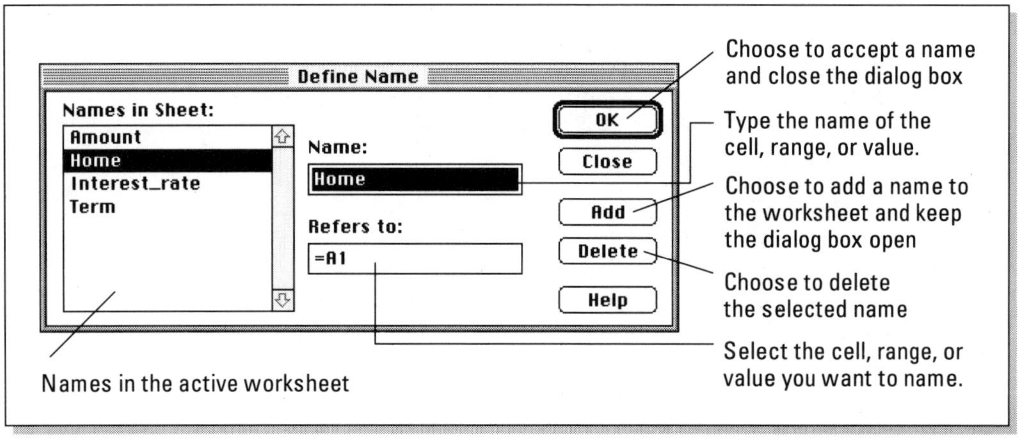

Figure 6-9: Naming a cell or range with the Define Name dialog box.

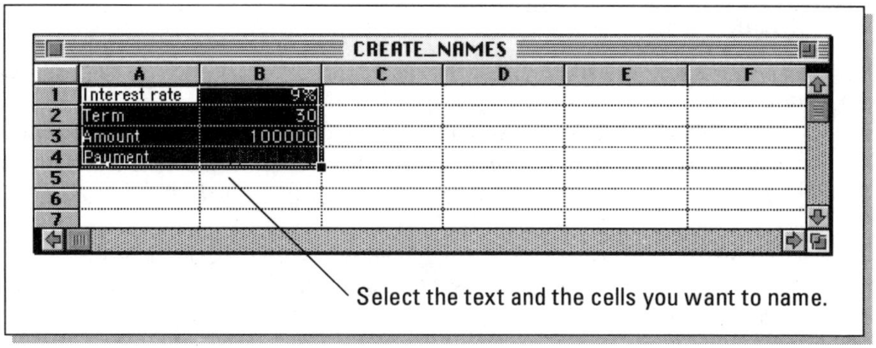

Figure 6-10: Creating names using the text entries in a worksheet.

To use the text in Column A to name cells in Column B, select the range containing the text and the cells you want named (range A1:B4 in Figure 6-10), and choose Create Names from the Formula menu; the Create Names dialog box appears, as shown in Figure 6-11. Excel selects an option that creates the name. You can change the option, or accept it by clicking OK.

Names provide you with another way to quickly move around a worksheet. If a worksheet contains named ranges, you can use Goto from the Formula menu (or press F5) to quickly move the cell pointer to the named cell or range. After you choose Goto, the Goto dialog box shown in Figure 6-12 appears. Simply select the name you need, click OK, and Excel will make the cell you selected the active cell (if you selected a name that represents a multiple cell range, the upper-left corner of the range will be the active cell).

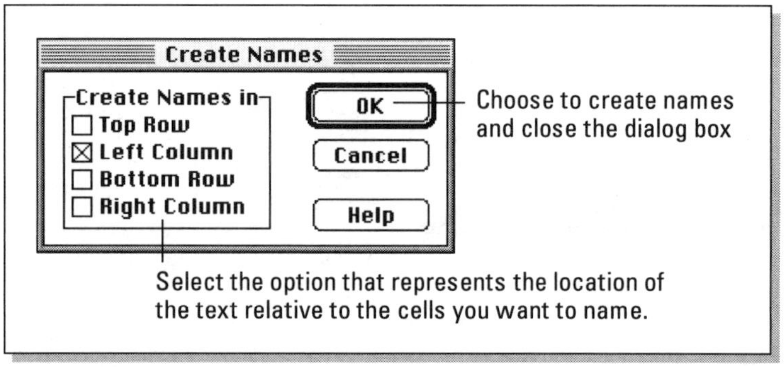

Figure 6-11: Creating cell, range, value, and formula names with the Create Names dialog box.

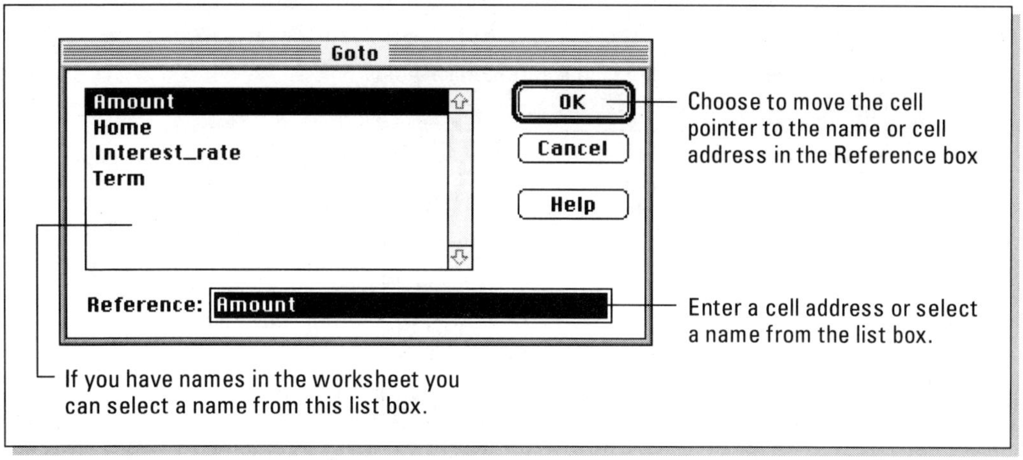

Figure 6-12: Moving around in a worksheet using the Goto dialog box.

Finally, names enable you to create formulas quickly. Choosing Paste Name from the Formula menu displays the Paste Name dialog box shown in Figure 6-13, which lets you select the name you want in the formula. When you click OK, the name will be pasted into the formula bar, and you can continue building the formula or click the Enter box to complete it.

Leaving an electronic (rather than paper) trail

As you learn to create more advanced worksheets, you'll want to document your formulas. Adding notes to your formulas is a good habit to acquire as you may have trouble remembering that, for example, last month you felt next year's supplies expense would increase 7 percent from this year. In addition to jogging your memory, cell notes are helpful to those who use or inherit your worksheets.

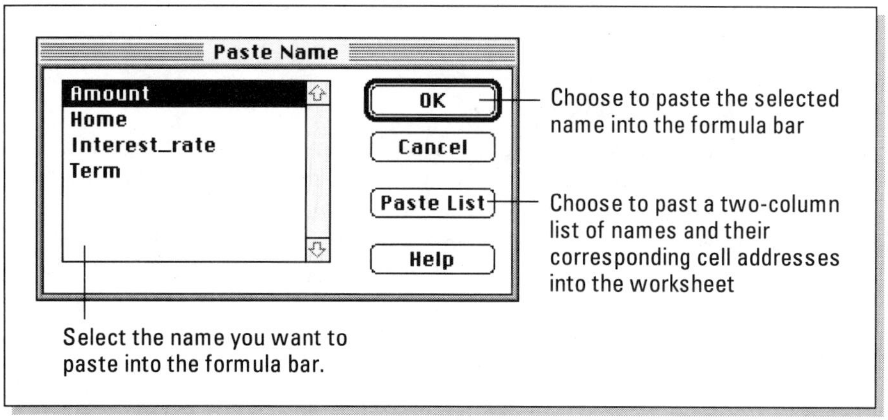

Figure 6-13: Pasting formula names into the formula bar using the Paste Name dialog box.

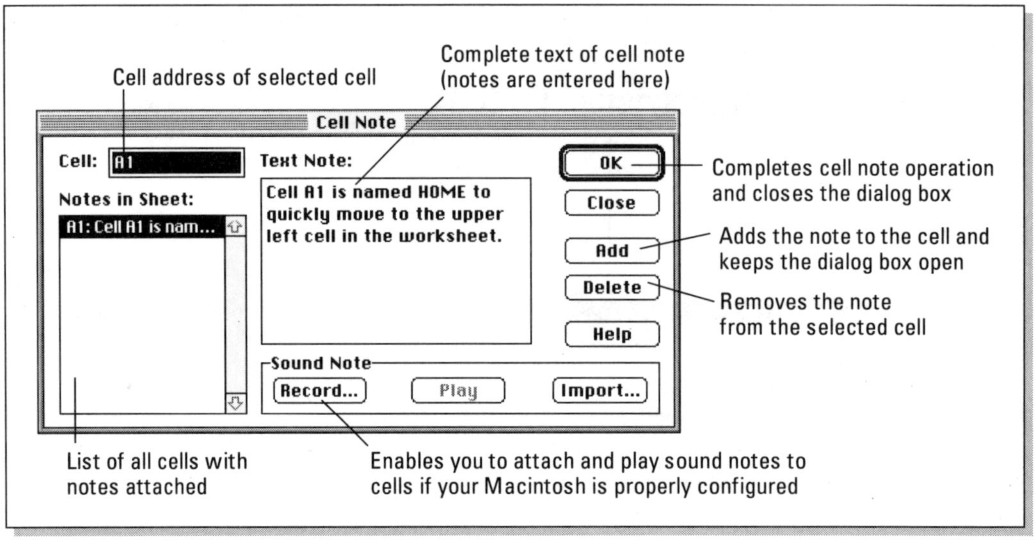

Figure 6-14: Documenting formulas using the Cell Note dialog box.

To document formulas, select the cell whose contents you want to note, and then choose Note from the Formula menu. The Cell Note dialog box appears, as shown in Figure 6-14.

Type your documentation in the Text Note text box, and then click OK. If you select Add, the Cell Note dialog box remains open so you can view, edit, and delete notes. Using the Note command provides you with documentation in an organized manner without having to clutter your worksheet with text in adjoining cells.

Reading notes attached to cells

Once you've added a note to a cell, that cell displays a dot in the upper-right corner of the cell. You can view a cell's note by selecting the cell and then double-clicking on the cell, which will open the Formula Note dialog box, or by selecting Note from the Formula menu.

Step-by-Step

In this section, you'll practice entering a formula and a function into a worksheet. For purposes of this practice session, you can use the worksheet you saved during Topic 4. Of course, you can apply the following concepts to any worksheet. As always, if you make a mistake or want to start over, choose Undo from the Edit menu, or close the worksheet without saving it and open it again with the Close and Open commands, respectively, from the File menu.

To open the TOPIC4 worksheet, do the following:

1. Start Excel, if you haven't already.

   The Worksheet1 worksheet appears.

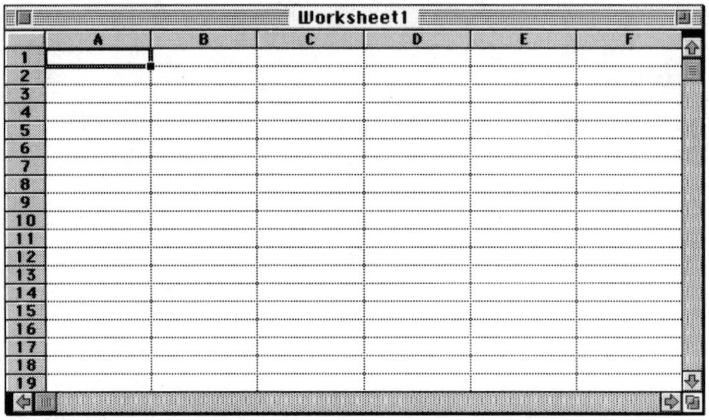

Figure 6-15: Starting up Excel displays the Worksheet1 worksheet.

2. Choose Open from the File menu, or click the File Open tool.

   The Open dialog box appears.

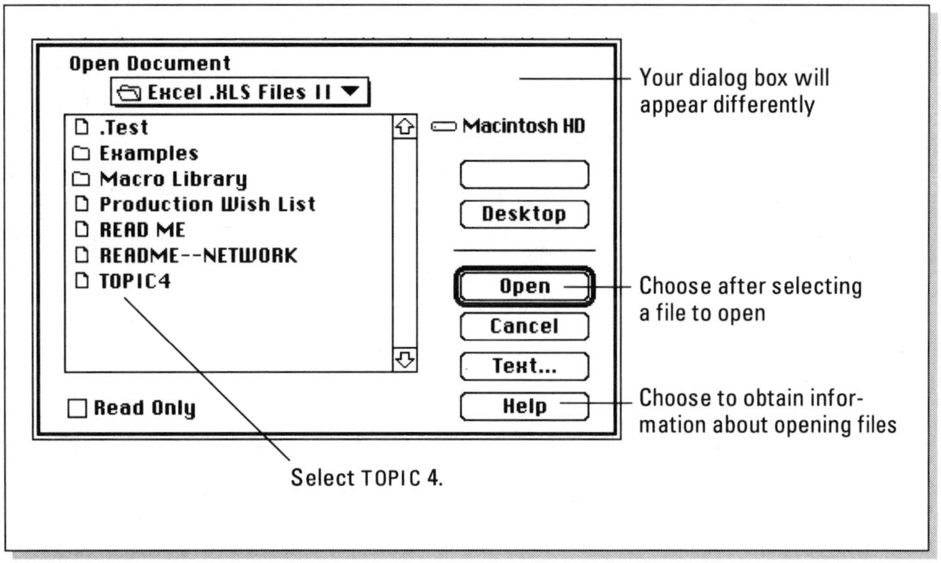

Figure 6-16: Opening the file TOPIC4 from the Open dialog box.

3. Select TOPIC4, and press Return or choose Open.

   The TOPIC4 worksheet appears.

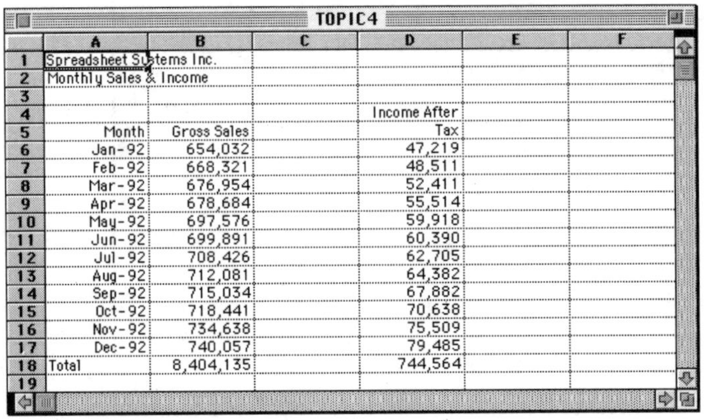

	A	B	C	D	E	F
1	Spreadsheet Systems Inc.					
2	Monthly Sales & Income					
3						
4				Income After		
5	Month	Gross Sales		Tax		
6	Jan-92	654,032		47,219		
7	Feb-92	668,321		48,511		
8	Mar-92	676,954		52,411		
9	Apr-92	678,684		55,514		
10	May-92	697,576		59,918		
11	Jun-92	699,891		60,390		
12	Jul-92	708,426		62,705		
13	Aug-92	712,081		64,382		
14	Sep-92	715,034		67,882		
15	Oct-92	718,441		70,638		
16	Nov-92	734,638		75,509		
17	Dec-92	740,057		79,485		
18	Total	8,404,135		744,564		
19						

Figure 6-17: The TOPIC4 worksheet.

4. Select cell C4, type `Expenses`, and press Enter; then type `And Taxes`, and press Enter.

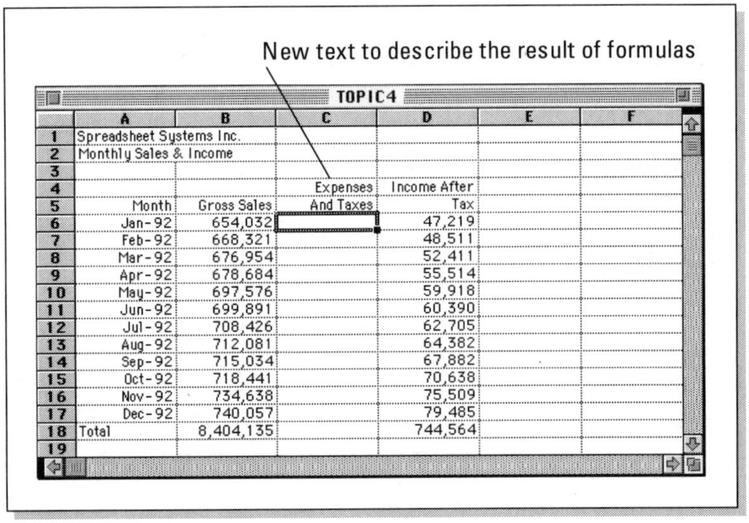

	A	B	C	D	E	F
1	Spreadsheet Systems Inc.					
2	Monthly Sales & Income					
3						
4			Expenses	Income After		
5	Month	Gross Sales	And Taxes	Tax		
6	Jan-92	654,032		47,219		
7	Feb-92	668,321		48,511		
8	Mar-92	676,954		52,411		
9	Apr-92	678,684		55,514		
10	May-92	697,576		59,918		
11	Jun-92	699,891		60,390		
12	Jul-92	708,426		62,705		
13	Aug-92	712,081		64,382		
14	Sep-92	715,034		67,882		
15	Oct-92	718,441		70,638		
16	Nov-92	734,638		75,509		
17	Dec-92	740,057		79,485		
18	Total	8,404,135		744,564		
19						

Figure 6-18: The TOPIC4 worksheet with new text added.

Entering a formula into a worksheet:

Step 1. Select cell C6.

Step 2. Type the equal sign (=).

Step 3. Select cell B6.

Step 4. Type the minus sign (-).

Step 5. Select cell D6, and click the Enter box.

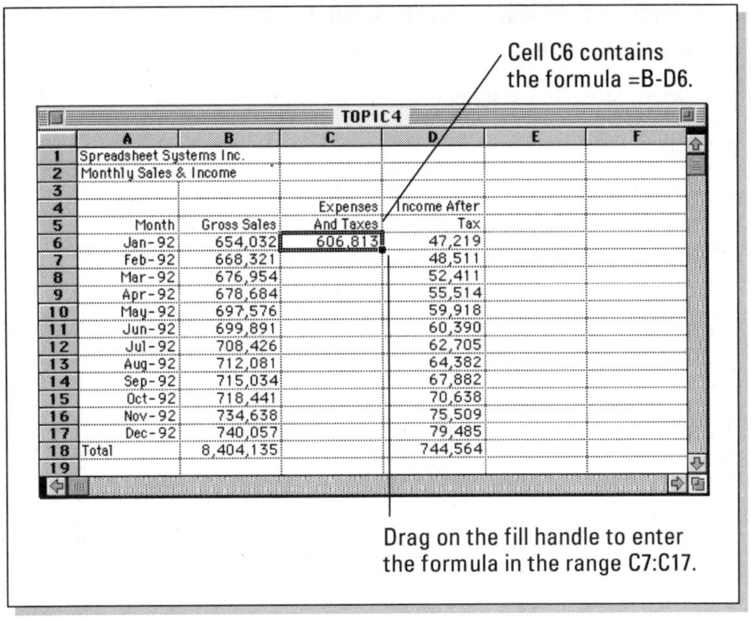

Figure 6-19: Entering a formula to calculate expenses and taxes.

Copying a formula:

Step 1. Move the mouse pointer to cell C6's fill handle.

Step 2. When the pointer appears as a black cross, click and drag down through the range C7:C17.

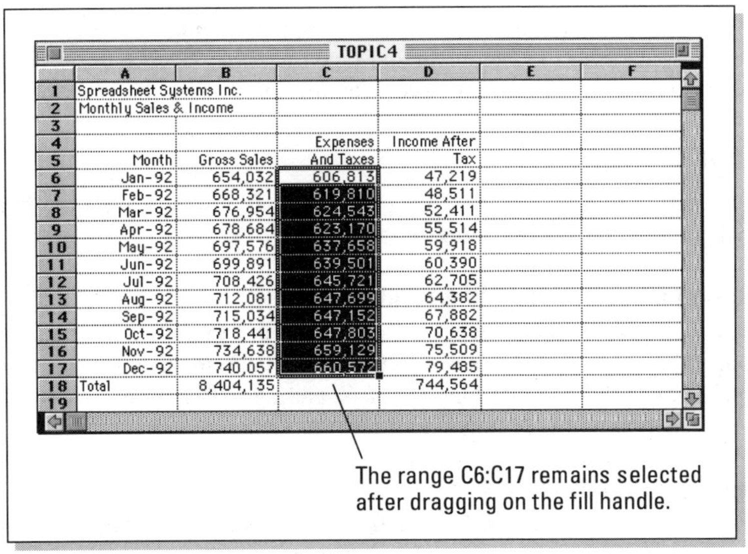

Figure 6-20: Copying a formula in a worksheet.

Entering a function into a worksheet:

Step 1. Select cell C18.

Step 2. Select SUM, and uncheck the Paste Arguments box.

Step 3. Click OK.

Step 4. Select the range C6:C17, and click the Enter box.

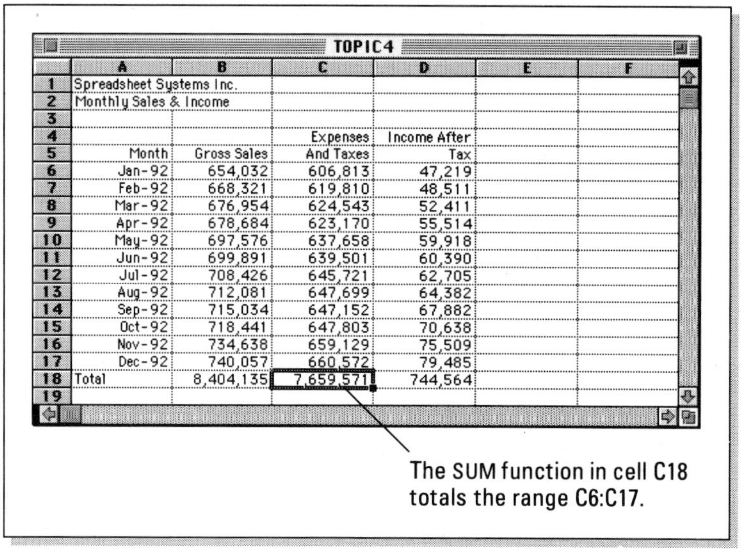

	A	B	C	D	E	F
1	Spreadsheet Systems Inc.					
2	Monthly Sales & Income					
3						
4			Expenses	Income After		
5	Month	Gross Sales	And Taxes	Tax		
6	Jan-92	654,032	606,813	47,219		
7	Feb-92	668,321	619,810	48,511		
8	Mar-92	676,954	624,543	52,411		
9	Apr-92	678,684	623,170	55,514		
10	May-92	697,576	637,658	59,918		
11	Jun-92	699,891	639,501	60,390		
12	Jul-92	708,426	645,721	62,705		
13	Aug-92	712,081	647,699	64,382		
14	Sep-92	715,034	647,152	67,882		
15	Oct-92	718,441	647,803	70,638		
16	Nov-92	734,638	659,129	75,509		
17	Dec-92	740,057	660,572	79,485		
18	Total	8,404,135	7,659,571	744,564		
19						

Figure 6-21: Entering the SUM function in a worksheet.

To save the formulas and functions you have entered into the TOPIC4 worksheet, select Save As from the File menu and type the name TOPIC6 in the "Save Filename as" text box; then click Save or press Return. Excel saves the worksheet to disk.

Quick Tips

This section provides you with tips on how to get the most from the formulas and functions you use in your worksheets.

Matching parentheses in a formula

Excel helps you match left and right parentheses in a formula when Excel is in Edit mode. When you move the blinking cursor across a formula in the formula bar, Excel momentarily bolds the matching set of parentheses. This is also the case if you add a missing parenthesis in response to a formula error.

Entering cell addresses

When you supply arguments to functions, reference a cell address or name rather than a value. For example, instead of entering values for rate, nper, and pv in the PMT function, enter cell addresses that contain values, such as B1, B2, and B3. By entering

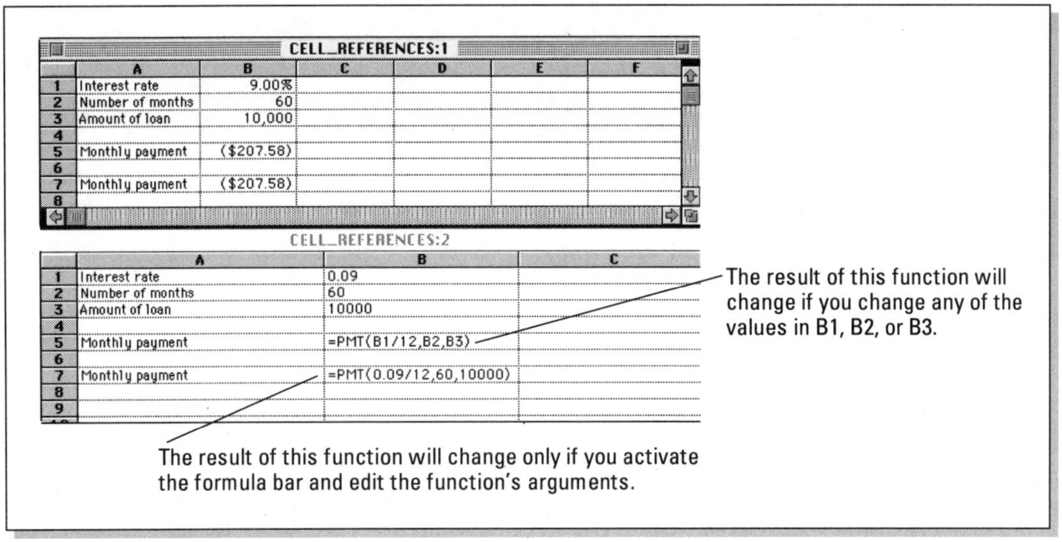

Figure 6-22: Entering cell addresses that contain values.

cell addresses, you can quickly change a value by changing the value in the cell rather than editing the formula. Also, place descriptive text in adjoining cells to document the arguments, as shown in Figure 6-22.

Pasting functions into the formula bar

As you become more familiar with Excel worksheet functions, and if you use Paste Name from the Formula menu, consider turning off the Paste Arguments box. You may find it faster to paste the function into the formula bar and then enter the arguments directly without Excel's argument placeholders.

Using formulas and functions creatively

Be creative when you create formulas and use functions. Depending on the worksheet, you can use formulas as arguments in functions, and you can use more than one function in formulas. Remember that a function (such as SUM) will calculate more quickly with less memory than a formula equivalent.

Using the DAVERAGE function

The AVERAGE function will not return accurate results if there are blank or empty cells in your argument. If this is the case, use DAVERAGE as shown in Figure 6-23.

Make sure you use the same text in cells A1 and B1, use the formula in B2, and include these cells in DAVERAGE's cell range arguments as shown in the right window in Figure 6-23.

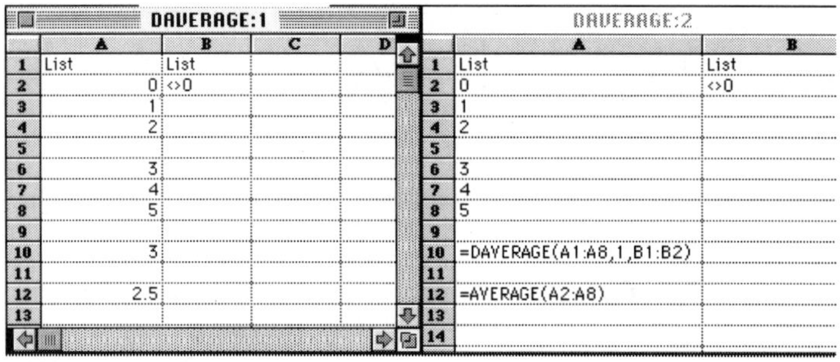

Figure 6-23: Using the DAVERAGE function to average arguments with blank cells in them.

Finding logical errors in formulas

The Worksheet Auditor macro add-in can help you find logic errors in formulas and provide you with information about a worksheet. See Topic 15 for information about the Worksheet Auditor.

Duplicating a formula and its results

Press Command-' and Command-" in the cell immediately below a cell containing a formula to duplicate the formula and the result of the formula, respectively. Note that if you use this method to copy a formula, the cell references do not change.

Exchanging cell references in formulas and functions

New single or multiple cell names won't automatically appear in formulas and functions currently in the worksheet. To make the new names appear, choose Apply Names from the Formula menu to exchange cell references with the corresponding range names. When the Apply Names dialog box shown in Figure 6-24 appears, uncheck the "Ignore Relative/Absolute" and "Use Row and Column Names" boxes, and click OK or press Enter.

Deleting names in formulas and functions

Clicking Delete from the Define Name dialog box removes the selected name from the worksheet. You can also delete names, or substitute one name for another in all functions and formulas that use the name, with the Name Changer add-in macro, discussed in Topic 15. The Rename a Name dialog box shown in Figure 6-25 shows the Name Changer options.

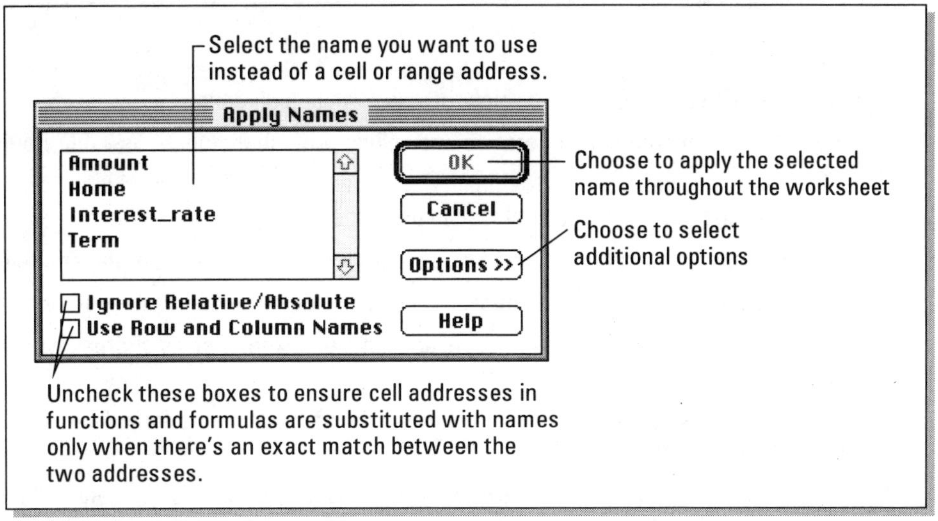

Figure 6-24: Exchanging cell references in formulas and functions using the Apply Names dialog box.

Using cell notes

Use the Cell Note command often. You can note everything on your worksheet, including macro statements, worksheet design, and data, in addition to functions and formulas. You'll do yourself and your worksheet users a favor by having properly documented worksheets. To print cell notes, select Notes or Both from the Print dialog box.

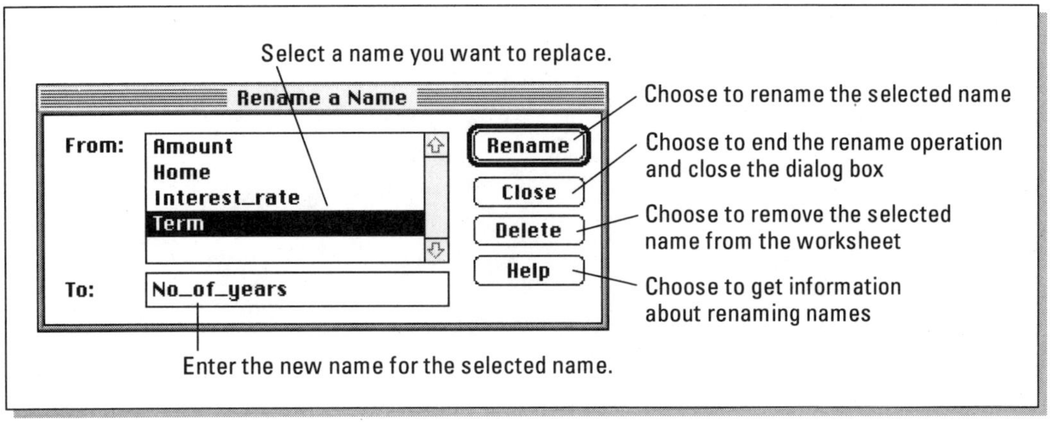

Figure 6-25: Deleting names in formulas and functions using the Rename a Name dialog box.

Summary

- Formulas are entered into cells in which they perform calculations.
- Formulas consist of arithmetic operators and values, worksheet functions, and/or other formulas.
- Excel calculates values from left to right in a cell, unless the cell has more than one type of operator, or values and operators are enclosed in parentheses.
- Excel follows a calculation order when calculating a formula similar to arithmetic rules.
- You can change the order of calculation in a cell by using parentheses in your formulas.
- Cell addresses in formulas can be relative, absolute, or mixed. A cell's address type affects the copies of a formula.
- Circular references occur when a formula refers to itself. Editing the formula enables Excel to calculate an accurate result.
- The Define Name command from the Formula menu enables you to create and delete names for single and multiple cell ranges, values, or formulas. The Create Names command from the Formula menu enables you to create names from text in the worksheet.
- The Paste Name command from the Formula menu enables you to paste a name into the formula bar. The Paste Function command from the Formula menu enables you to paste a worksheet function into the formula bar.
- The Note command from the Formula menu helps you understand or describe your worksheet by enabling you to attach descriptive text to a cell.

Topic 7
Adding Style To Your Worksheets

Overview

In Topic 2, you learned how to make some simple changes to the way text and values were displayed that made your worksheet easier to read and understand. You found in Topic 3 that printing your worksheet after making format changes produced a clear, crisp copy of your worksheet on paper.

You may be perfectly happy with your results from Excel so far, but in this Topic, I'm going to introduce you to another powerful Excel feature: the ability to add or change font sizes and type, draw lines around cells or ranges, and add shading to important areas of a worksheet. Combining the graphical capability of your Macintosh with Excel's presentation tools is like leaving the black-and-white world of Kansas and opening the door to the Land of Oz.

This Topic provides you with an overview of enhancing worksheets with fonts, borders, and shading; it discusses style strategies and techniques; and it gives you some background on the style attributes you'll be using.

Introducing your style options

Three formatting options are available to enhance the display and printouts of Excel worksheets: Font, Border, and Patterns. The Font option enables you to select the type and size of fonts you want to use to display the characters in text and values. The Border option enables you to add lines to the sides of a cell or range. And the Patterns option controls the way you want shading and colors applied to a cell or range. When you first begin adding snap and sizzle to a worksheet, you usually start by making changes to the font currently being used to display text and values.

Understanding fonts

If you've just arrived from the character-based computing world, you may be wondering what fonts are. A font is the shape, size, and weight of the characters you want to display. For example, telephone books commonly use a font similar to the font Lotica; newspapers use Times Roman. There are many shapes of fonts that you can choose from depending on the printer and software you use. Figure 7-1 shows Excel's Geneva font in 10- and 12-point with several different attributes, also known as a *font family*. If you'd like to know more about Macintosh fonts, read Chapter 3 of *Macworld Read Me First Book* by Erfert Fenton, IDG Books Worldwide, 1991.

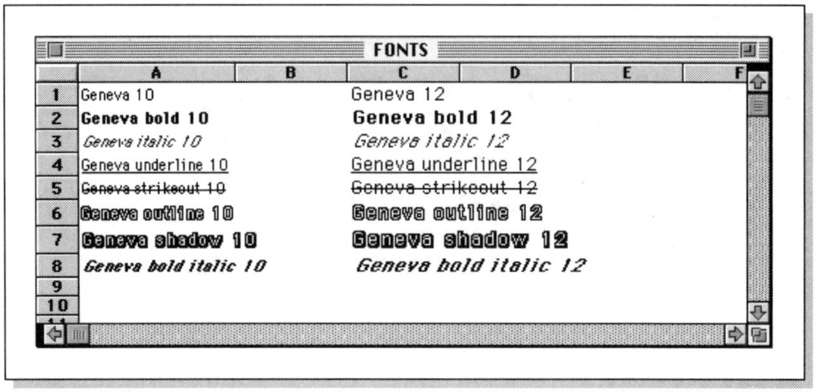

Figure 7-1: The Geneva font family displaying various attributes.

Choosing a font type or size

You can use a maximum of 256 fonts per worksheet in various sizes (if you really want to use that many). Changing the font type or size, or adding an attribute, is no different from other Excel worksheet operations; simply do the following:

1. Select the cell or range containing the characters with the font you want to change.
2. Do one of the following:
   - ✦ Choose Font from the Format menu or shortcut menu.
   - ✦ Click the appropriate tool on the Standard toolbar.
   - ✦ Press a shortcut key.
   - ✦ Choose a style from the Style box (discussed later in this topic).

If you choose Font from the Format menu or shortcut menu to change fonts or add attributes, the Font dialog box shown in Figure 7-2 appears. Select the font or at-

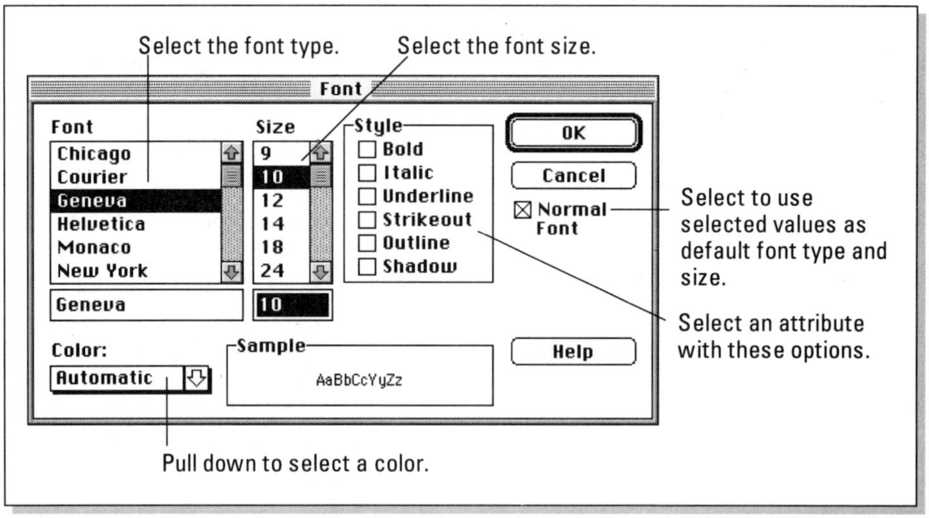

Figure 7-2: Changing fonts and adding attributes using the Font dialog box.

tribute you want, and as you do, watch the Sample box. Excel displays how the characters will appear. This gives you the opportunity to view and change the font or attribute you've selected before clicking OK or pressing Return.

You can click on several of the tools on the Standard toolbar to quickly change font size and attributes, as shown in Figure 7-3. The Formatting toolbar (displayed by choosing Toolbars Show from the Options menu) enables you to add underlining, strikeout, and font type and size, as shown in Figure 7-4.

Finally, the shortcut keys listed in Table 7-1 are available for making attribute changes:

Table 7-1: Shortcut key attribute changes

Attribute	***Shortcut keystroke***	***Example***
Plain	Command-Shift-P	Plain
Bold	Command-Shift-B	**Bold**
Italic	Command-Shift-I	*Italic*
Underline	Command-Shift-U	Underline
Strikeout	Command-Shift-_	~~Strikeout~~
Shadows	Command-Shift-W	Shadows

Note: Except for the plain format, these shortcut keys act as a toggle. For example, you can turn bolding on and off by pressing Command-Shift-B.

Heading for the border

When you start Excel, Worksheet1 displays with gridlines. As you learned in earlier Topics, gridlines help you keep your place on the worksheet as you enter data and perform worksheet operations, such as cutting and pasting. You can, however, draw a line with

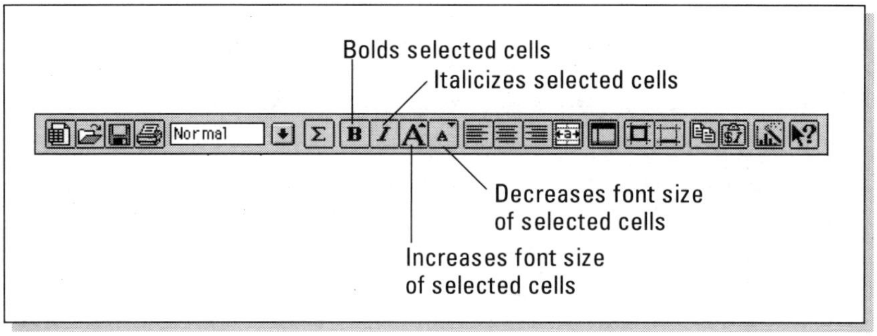

Figure 7-3: Changing fonts and adding attributes using the Standard toolbar.

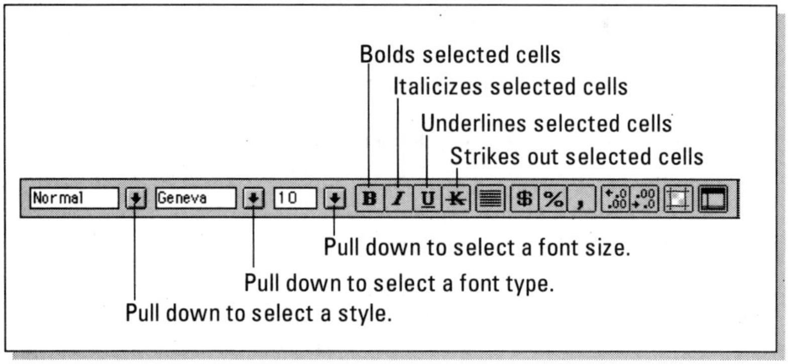

Figure 7-4: Formatting text using the Formatting toolbar.

various styles, such as a single and double line above and below a grand total. Excel's line styles are shown in Figure 7-5.

Drawing lines is similar to changing fonts. To draw a line (border) around a single cell or range, do the following:

1. Select the cell or range to which you want to add a border.
2. Do one of the following:
   - ✦ Choose Border from the Format menu or shortcut menu.
   - ✦ Click the appropriate tool on the toolbar.
   - ✦ Press a shortcut key.
   - ✦ Choose a style from the Style box (again, discussed later in this Topic).

The Border command displays the Border dialog box shown in Figure 7-6. Select the border style by clicking on a style in the Style box, and then select a border by clicking on a border in the Border box.

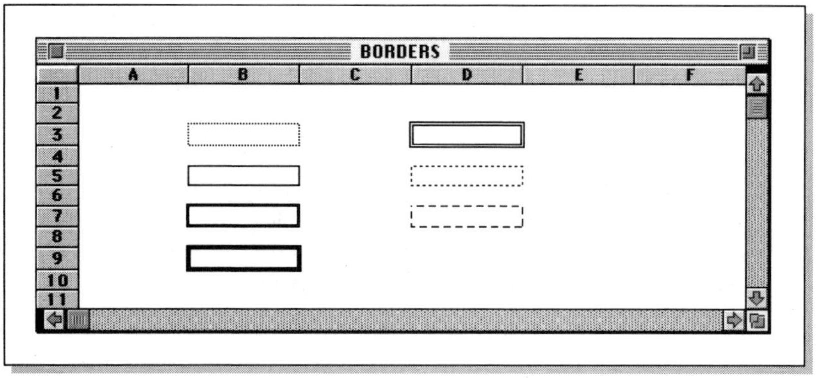

Figure 7-5: The line styles available in Excel.

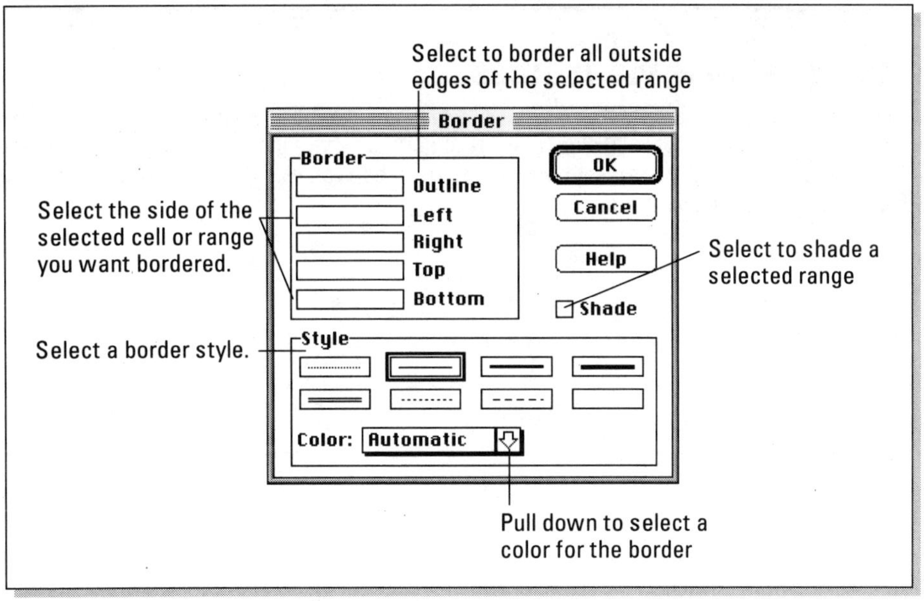

Figure 7-6: Specifying border attributes using the Border dialog box.

When you click OK or press Return, Excel draws the line using the style you specified. You can also select a color for the border by selecting the Color pull-down menu, or shade the selected cell or range by checking the Shade box.

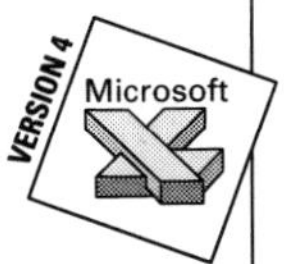

The Standard toolbar has tools that enable you to apply an outline or border around a selected cell or range; the Formatting toolbar has a tool for applying a light shade.

You can use the following shortcut keys listed in Table 7-2 for applying borders:

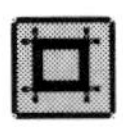

Outline tool

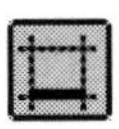

Bottom border tool

Table 7-2: Shortcut keys for adding borders

Border/action	*Shortcut keystroke*
Outline	Command-Option-0 (zero)
Left	Command-Option-left arrow
Right	Command-Option-right arrow
Top	Command-Option-up arrow
Bottom	Command-Option-down arrow
Remove borders	Command-Option-minus sign

All but the last border option (Remove borders) act like a toggle, similar to the Font short-cut keys.

Using borders vs. outlines

Adding a line around a selected cell or range can be confusing — do you use a border or an outline? An easy way to choose which line to use is to determine whether you want a line around *every* side of a cell or range, or around just the outside sides. When you've determined where you want the lines, use the following guidelines:

Selection	***Action***	***Format Border option***
Single cell	Draw a line around all edges.	Outline
Multiple cells	Draw a line around the edges of each cell.	Left, Right, Top, Bottom
Multiple cells	Draw a line around outside edge only.	Outline

Selecting a Shade

To add shading to a cell or range, check the Shade box in the Border dialog box. If you prefer to change the shading pattern, or use more than one shading pattern in the worksheet, use the Patterns option from the Format menu or shortcut menu to select a shade. The Pattern pull-down menu lets you choose solid to light shading, and horizontal, vertical, and diagonal lines. The Foreground and Background pull-down menus enable you to apply colors to the pattern. Figure 7-7 shows the available patterns.

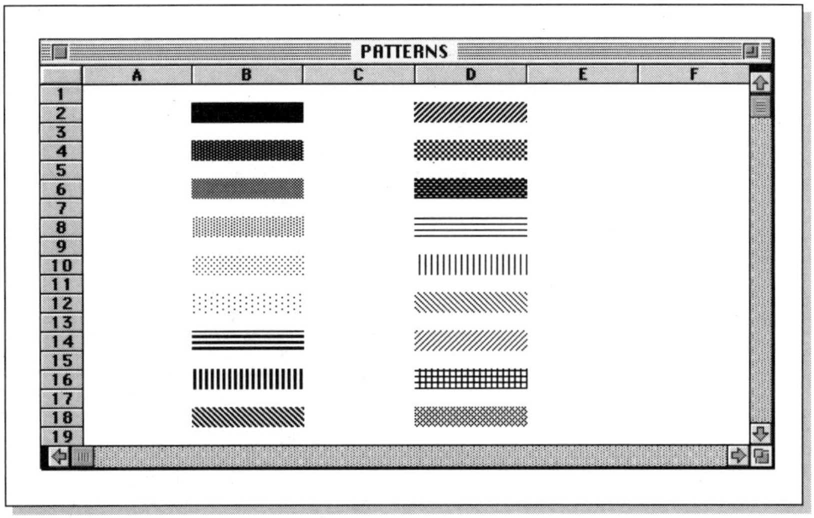

Figure 7-7: The available shading patterns in Excel.

Choose a pattern appropriate for the job at hand. For example, if you shade a range with cell contents, use a very light shade and consider making the data boldface. On the other hand, solid-shading a range with a small row height or narrow column width can be an effective way to create a prominent separator line. As you experiment with patterns and colors, keep an eye on the Sample box to help you get the combination you want before clicking OK or pressing Return.

Dropping shadows

Drop shadows enable you to highlight worksheet titles or other selected ranges in a dramatic way, as shown in Figure 7-8.

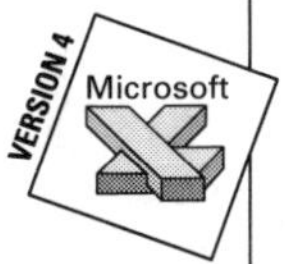

You can use several methods to create drop shadows: with the Drop Shadow tool (on the Drawing toolbar), or by adding solid shading to the height of a row and to the width of a column. If you use the Drop Shadow tool, select the range you want drop-shadowed and click on the tool — that's all there is to it.

Drop Shadow tool

The second way to create a drop shadow is to change the height of a row, the width of a column, and use solid shading, as shown in Figure 7-9. In this figure, notice the reduced width of Columns B and G, and the reduced height of row 7.

To add a drop shadow quickly to the worksheet, use the Drop Shadow tool. Use solid shading if you want to adjust the size of the shadow.

Adding styles with style

If you find yourself repeatedly using a combination of fonts, lines, and shading, you can assign a name to them, known as a *style*. A style can contain up to six attributes:

- ✦ Number format
- ✦ Border
- ✦ Font (type and size)

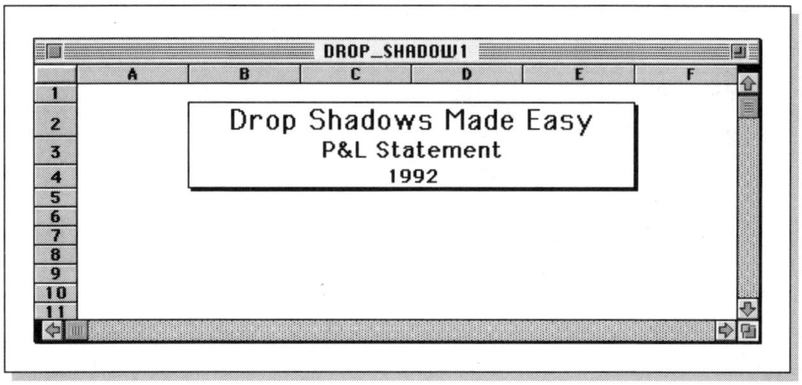

Figure 7-8: An example a of drop shadow used to highlight a worksheet's title.

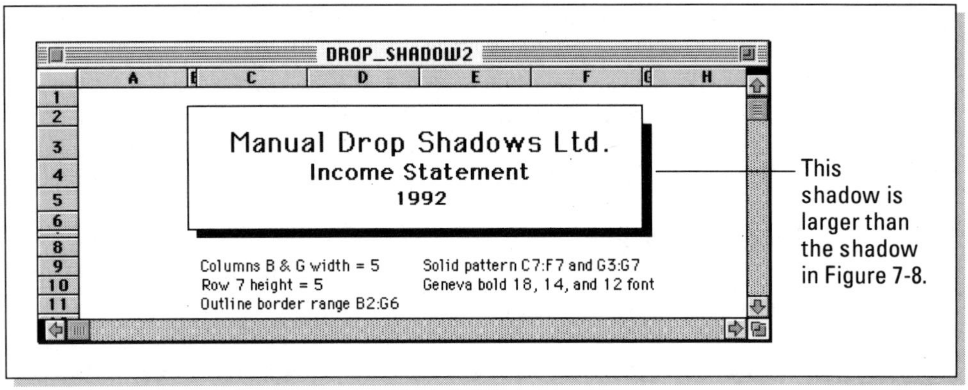

Figure 7-9: Creating a drop shadow by changing the height and width of a row and column, and then adding solid shading.

- ✦ Pattern
- ✦ Alignment
- ✦ Protection

To use a style, select the cell or range to which you want to apply the style, and then select the name of the style. The attributes that comprise the style will be applied automatically to the range. Think of these named styles as one-stop worksheet enhancements.

Excel comes with the following six styles that you can quickly apply from the Style box on the Standard toolbar:

Style	***Example***
Normal	2500
Comma	2,500.00
Comma [0]	2,500
Currency	$2,500.00
Currency [0]	$2,500
Percent	250000%

Excel's default style is Normal, and is made up of the following attributes:

Attribute	***Description***
Number format	General (numbers left-aligned; no currency sign, punctuation, or decimal places)
Font	Geneva 10 (will depend on your printer type and software)
Alignment	General, Bottom Aligned
Border	No borders
Pattern	No shading
Protection	Locked

The other five styles are defined with only a number format, including the following:

Style	***Number format***
Comma	#,##0_);[Red](#,##0)
Comma [0]	#,##0.00_);[Red](#,##0.00)
Currency	$#,##0_);[Red]($#,##0)
Currency [0]	$#,##0.00_);[Red]($#,##0.00)
Percent	0%

Apply a style to a selected cell or range by selecting a style from the list on the Style box's pull-down menu. Or you can choose Style from the Format menu. The Style dialog box furnishes you with additional information about the style, as shown in Figure 7-10.

You may want to modify or add a style to suit your particular needs. To do so, click the Define button on the Style dialog box; additional options appear, as shown in Figure 7-11.

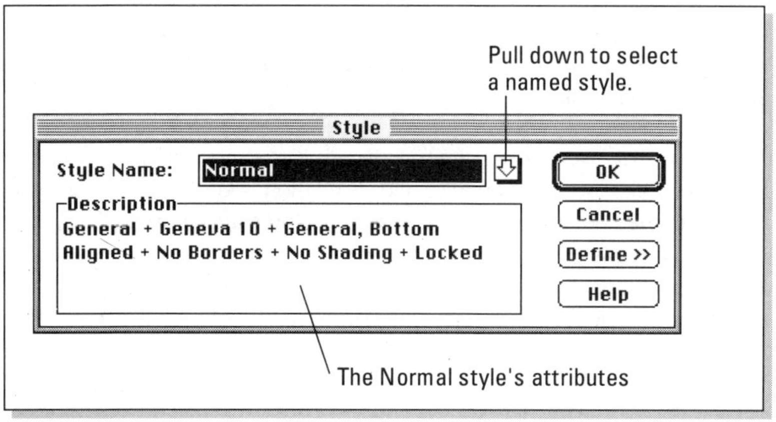

Figure 7-10: Adding a style to a cell or cell range using the Style dialog box.

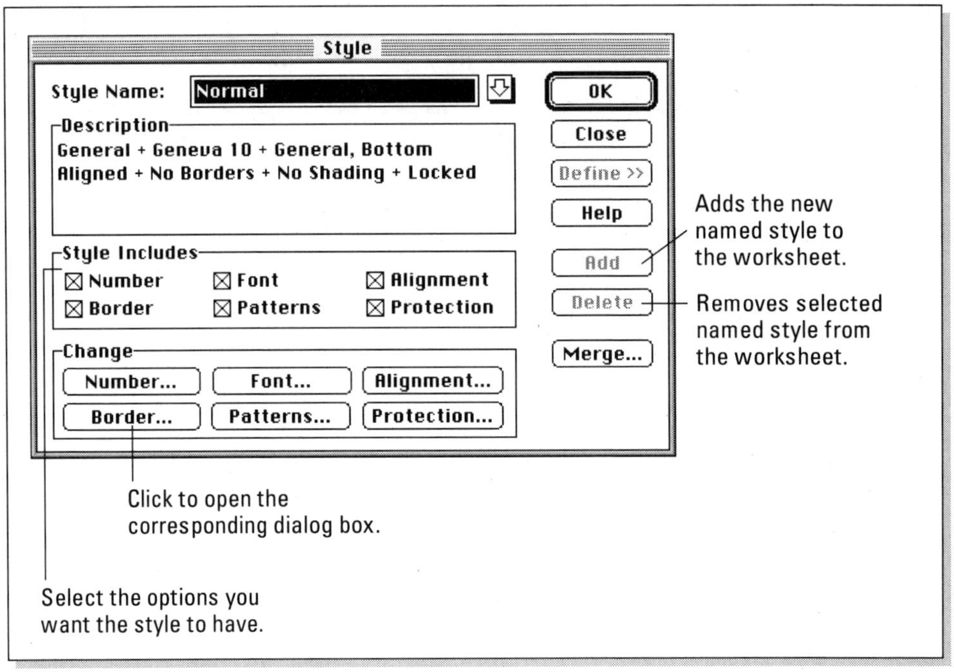

Figure 7-11: Modifying or adding a style using the Define button in the Style dialog box.

Check the appropriate check box in the Style Includes box to include or exclude the listed cell attributes. If you want to change an attribute, click the appropriate button in the Change box. The dialog box for that option appears, so you can make the changes. For example, clicking the Font button displays the Format Font dialog box. After you select OK, you're returned to the Style dialog box. Click OK to accept the style.

You create a new style in a similar manner. After choosing Style from the Format menu, and then Define from the Style dialog box, enter a new name in the Style Name text box.

Select the attributes you want by clicking the appropriate check boxes on and off, and choosing the corresponding options as needed. Click OK or press Return to create your new named style. Your new style name appears on the Style box pull-down menu on the Standard toolbar, which you can use to format selected cells.

A quick way to change or create style names is to use a cell or range that already has the attributes you want as a named style (this method is known as *by example*). Choose Style from the Format menu, select the name you want to modify, or enter a new name in the Style Name text box. The attributes you've selected appear in the Description (By Example) box. At this time you can select other attributes you do or do not want the style to have. Clicking OK assigns the specified attributes to the style.

Applying formatting automatically

If you're in a hurry to create an attractive report, you can have Excel format selected cells for you. Automatic formats are a turbocharged version of named styles. Figure 7-12 shows you a worksheet before and after automatic formatting has been applied.

Applying an automatic format is similar to applying a style, font, border, or shade. To have Excel format the worksheet for you, do the following:

1. Select the cell or range you want formatted.
2. Choose AutoFormat from the Format menu.
3. Select a format from the Table Format list box and choose OK.

As shown in Figure 7-13, the Sample box in the AutoFormat dialog box lets you window-shop automatic formats before you choose OK.

Although you can't modify automatic formats (something new for Excel 5.0?), you can mix and match automatic formats or combine an automatic format with a style or format you've already applied to a cell or range.

To do so, apply the format or style you want to a selected cell or range; then choose AutoFormat from the Format menu. When the AutoFormat dialog box appears, choose Options. The AutoFormat dialog box expands to display the automatic format options, as shown in Figure 7-14.

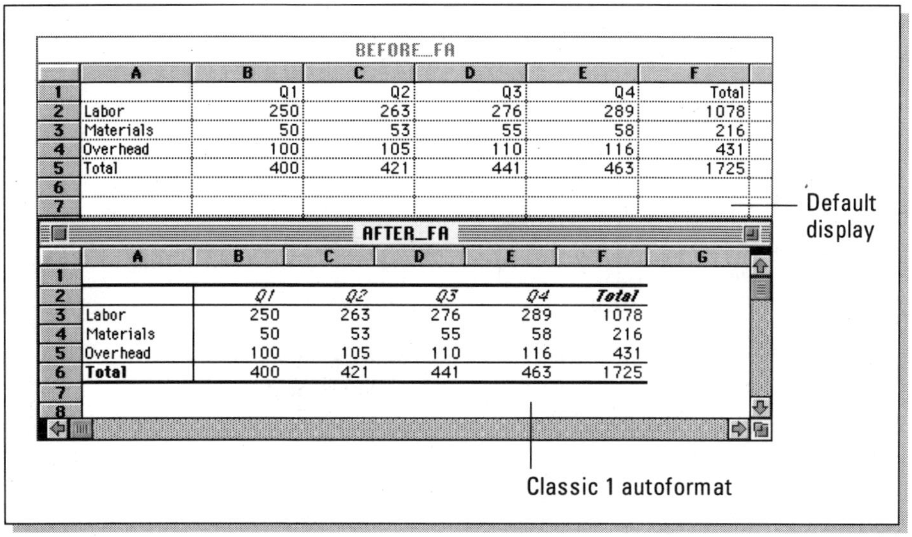

Figure 7-12: A worksheet before automatic formatting has been applied (top), and the same worksheet after automatic formatting has been applied.

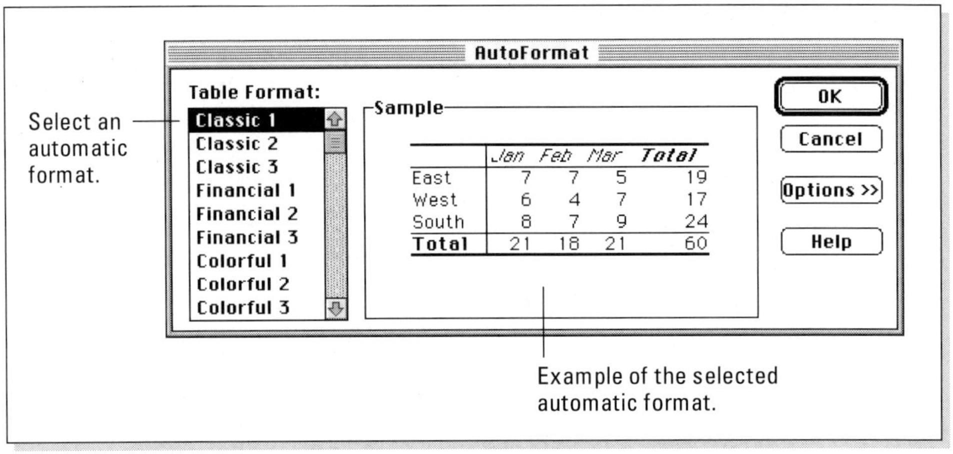

Figure 7-13: Previewing automatic formats using the Sample box in the AutoFormat dialog box.

Uncheck the boxes in the Formats to Apply box that represent the automatic format attributes you *don't* want Excel to apply. For example, if you've already applied a desired font to the selected cell or range, uncheck the Font box. When you click OK, only the checked attributes of the automatic format will be applied, leaving any previously applied formatting unchanged.

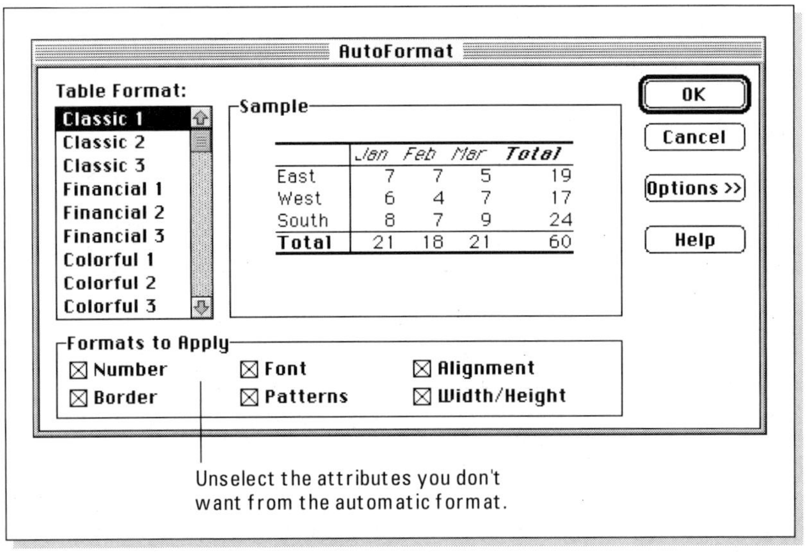

Figure 7-14: Setting the autoformat attributes using the Options button in the AutoFormat dialog box.

Step-by-Step

In this section you'll enhance the worksheet from Topic 6 with some of the attributes you learned about in this Topic (you can also use any worksheet of your choice). Remember, if you make a mistake or want to start over, choose Undo from the Edit menu, or close the worksheet without saving it and open it again with the Close and Open commands from the File menu, respectively.

To open the worksheet from Topic 6, do the following:

1. Start Excel if you haven't already, or make Excel the active application.

   The Worksheet1 worksheet appears.

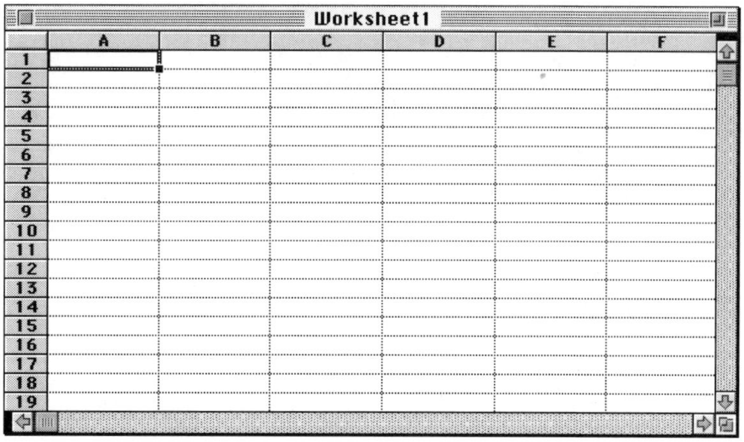

Figure 7-15: Starting up Excel displays the Worksheet1 worksheet.

2. Select the Open command from the File menu.

   The Open dialog box appears.

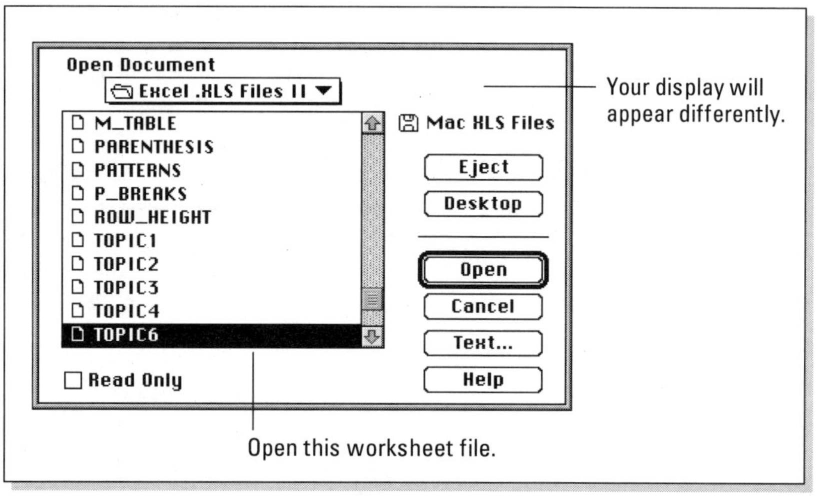

Figure 7-16: Choosing Open from the File menu displays the Open dialog box.

3. Select TOPIC6 and press Return or choose Open.

   The TOPIC6 worksheet appears.

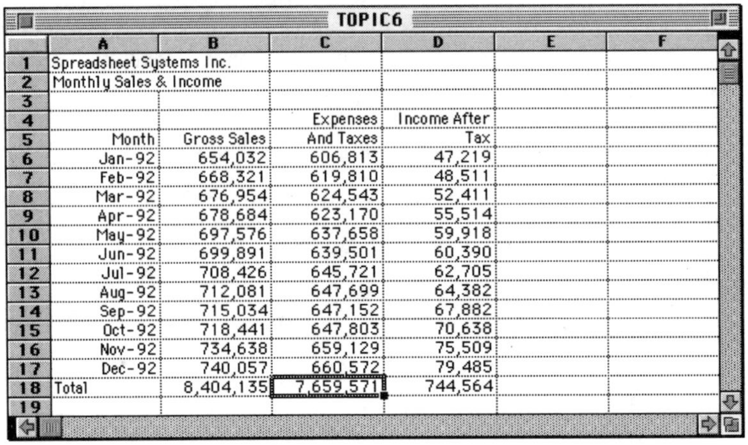
TOPIC6

	A	B	C	D	E	F
1	Spreadsheet Systems Inc.					
2	Monthly Sales & Income					
3						
4			Expenses	Income After		
5	Month	Gross Sales	And Taxes	Tax		
6	Jan-92	654,032	606,813	47,219		
7	Feb-92	668,321	619,810	48,511		
8	Mar-92	676,954	624,543	52,411		
9	Apr-92	678,684	623,170	55,514		
10	May-92	697,576	637,658	59,918		
11	Jun-92	699,891	639,501	60,390		
12	Jul-92	708,426	645,721	62,705		
13	Aug-92	712,081	647,699	64,382		
14	Sep-92	715,034	647,152	67,882		
15	Oct-92	718,441	647,803	70,638		
16	Nov-92	734,638	659,129	75,509		
17	Dec-92	740,057	660,572	79,485		
18	Total	8,404,135	7,659,571	744,564		
19						

Figure 7-17: Selecting TOPIC6 from the Open dialog box displays the TOPIC6 worksheet.

To turn off the gridlines, do the following:

4. Choose Display from the Options menu.

   The Display Options dialog box appears.

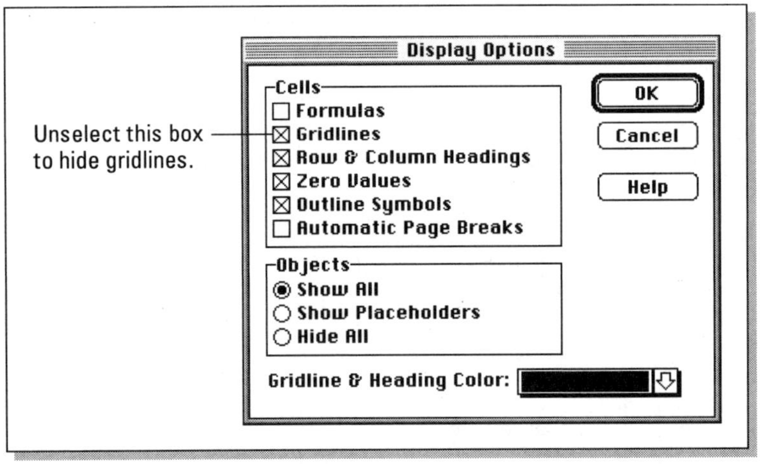

Figure 7-18: Turning off a cell's gridlines using the Display Options dialog box.

5. Turn off the Gridlines check box, and choose OK.

   Excel displays the worksheet without gridlines.

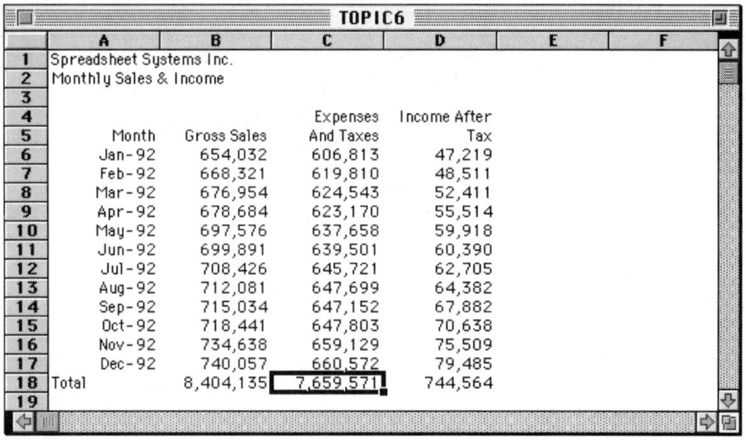
TOPIC6

	A	B	C	D	E	F
1	Spreadsheet Systems Inc.					
2	Monthly Sales & Income					
3						
4			Expenses	Income After		
5	Month	Gross Sales	And Taxes	Tax		
6	Jan-92	654,032	606,813	47,219		
7	Feb-92	668,321	619,810	48,511		
8	Mar-92	676,954	624,543	52,411		
9	Apr-92	678,684	623,170	55,514		
10	May-92	697,576	637,658	59,918		
11	Jun-92	699,891	639,501	60,390		
12	Jul-92	708,426	645,721	62,705		
13	Aug-92	712,081	647,699	64,382		
14	Sep-92	715,034	647,152	67,882		
15	Oct-92	718,441	647,803	70,638		
16	Nov-92	734,638	659,129	75,509		
17	Dec-92	740,057	660,572	79,485		
18	Total	8,404,135	7,659,571	744,564		
19						

Figure 7-19: The TOPIC6 worksheet without gridlines.

Outlining a range:

Step 1. Select the range A4:D5, and then choose Border from the Format menu or shortcut menu.

The Border dialog box appears.

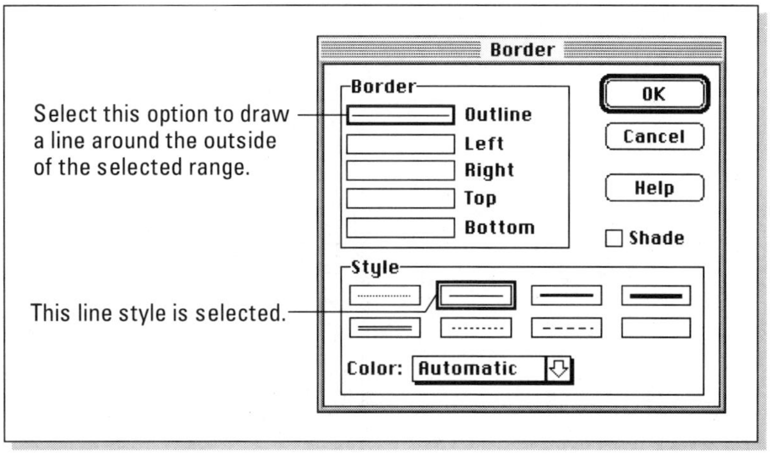

Figure 7-20: Choosing Border from the Format menu or shortcut menu displays the Border dialog box.

Step 2. Select Outline; then choose OK.

Excel outlines the selected range.

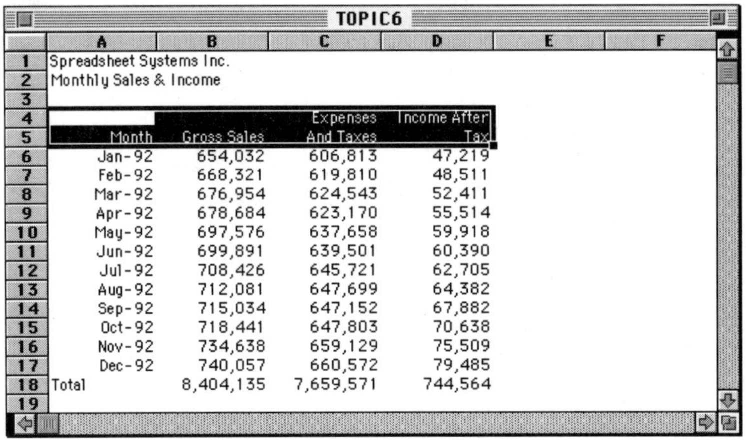

TOPIC6

	A	B	C	D
1	Spreadsheet Systems Inc.			
2	Monthly Sales & Income			
3				
4			Expenses	Income After
5	Month	Gross Sales	And Taxes	Tax
6	Jan-92	654,032	606,813	47,219
7	Feb-92	668,321	619,810	48,511
8	Mar-92	676,954	624,543	52,411
9	Apr-92	678,684	623,170	55,514
10	May-92	697,576	637,658	59,918
11	Jun-92	699,891	639,501	60,390
12	Jul-92	708,426	645,721	62,705
13	Aug-92	712,081	647,699	64,382
14	Sep-92	715,034	647,152	67,882
15	Oct-92	718,441	647,803	70,638
16	Nov-92	734,638	659,129	75,509
17	Dec-92	740,057	660,572	79,485
18	Total	8,404,135	7,659,571	744,564
19				

Figure 7-21: Outlining a selected range using the Outline option in the Border dialog box.

Adding borders to all sides of the cells in a range:

Step 1. Select the range A6:D18, and then choose Border from the Format menu or shortcut menu.

The Border dialog box appears.

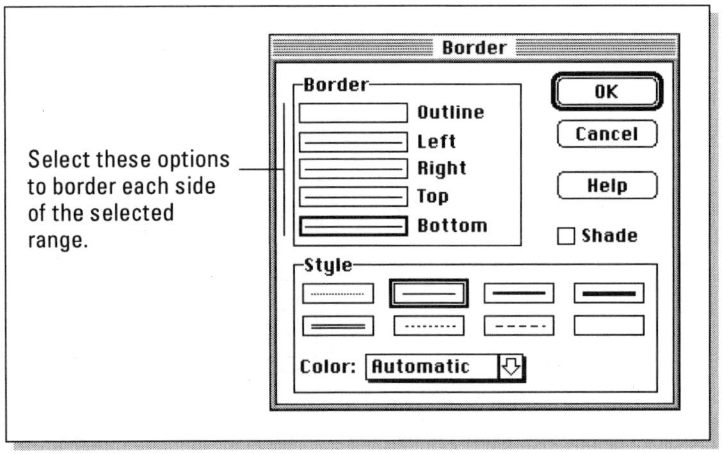

Figure 7-22: Choosing Border from the Format menu or shortcut menu displays the Border dialog box.

Step 2. Select Left, Right, Top, and Bottom, and then choose OK.

Excel draws the lines.

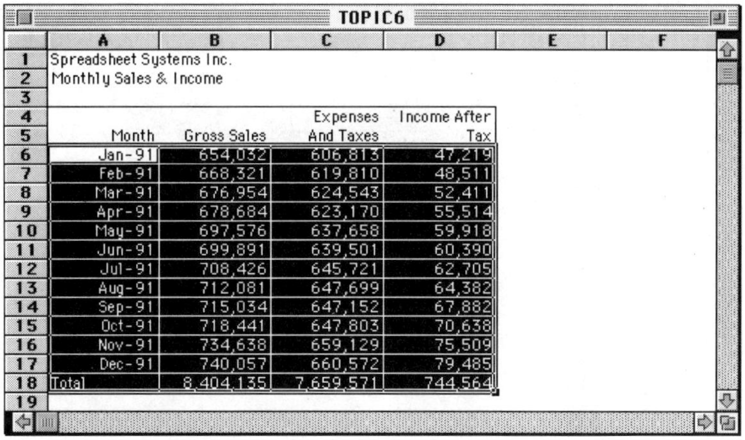

Month	Gross Sales	Expenses And Taxes	Income After Tax
Jan-91	654,032	606,813	47,219
Feb-91	668,321	619,810	48,511
Mar-91	676,954	624,543	52,411
Apr-91	678,684	623,170	55,514
May-91	697,576	637,658	59,918
Jun-91	699,891	639,501	60,390
Jul-91	708,426	645,721	62,705
Aug-91	712,081	647,699	64,382
Sep-91	715,034	647,152	67,882
Oct-91	718,441	647,803	70,638
Nov-91	734,638	659,129	75,509
Dec-91	740,057	660,572	79,485
Total	8,404,135	7,659,571	744,564

Figure 7-23: Outlining a range of cells using the Left, Right, Top, and Bottom options in the Border dialog box.

Adding shading to ranges:

Step 1. Select the range A4:D5, and then choose Border from the Format menu or shortcut menu.

The Border dialog box appears.

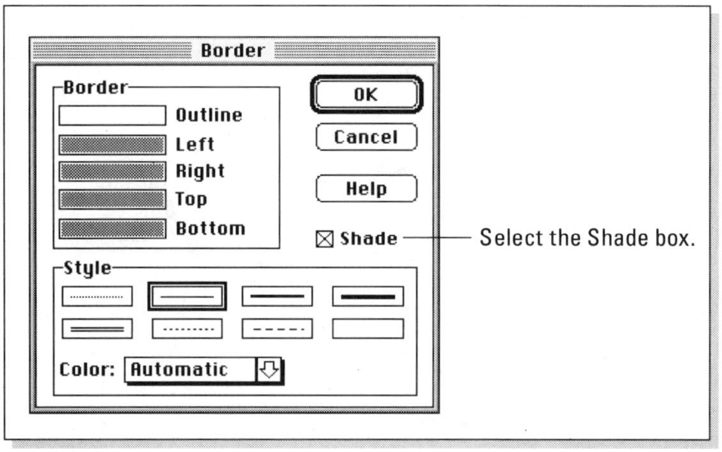

Figure 7-24: Choosing Border from the Format menu or shortcut menu displays the Border dialog box.

Step 2. Select the Shade box, and then choose OK.

Excel shades the range. Repeat shading for range A18:D18.

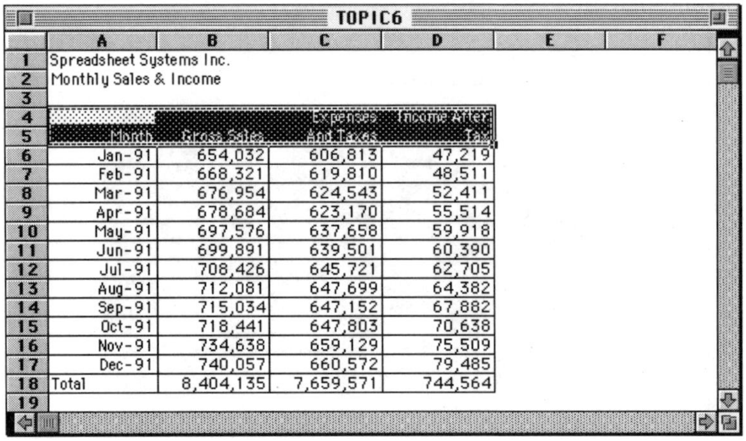

TOPIC6

	A	B	C	D	E	F
1	Spreadsheet Systems Inc.					
2	Monthly Sales & Income					
3						
4			Expenses	Income After		
5	Month	Gross Sales	And Taxes	Tax		
6	Jan-91	654,032	606,813	47,219		
7	Feb-91	668,321	619,810	48,511		
8	Mar-91	676,954	624,543	52,411		
9	Apr-91	678,684	623,170	55,514		
10	May-91	697,576	637,658	59,918		
11	Jun-91	699,891	639,501	60,390		
12	Jul-91	708,426	645,721	62,705		
13	Aug-91	712,081	647,699	64,382		
14	Sep-91	715,034	647,152	67,882		
15	Oct-91	718,441	647,803	70,638		
16	Nov-91	734,638	659,129	75,509		
17	Dec-91	740,057	660,572	79,485		
18	Total	8,404,135	7,659,571	744,564		
19						

Figure 7-25: Shading a range of cells by checking the Shade box in the Border dialog box.

Changing font size and attributes:

Step 1. Select cell A1, and then choose Font from the Format menu or shortcut menu.

The Font dialog box appears.

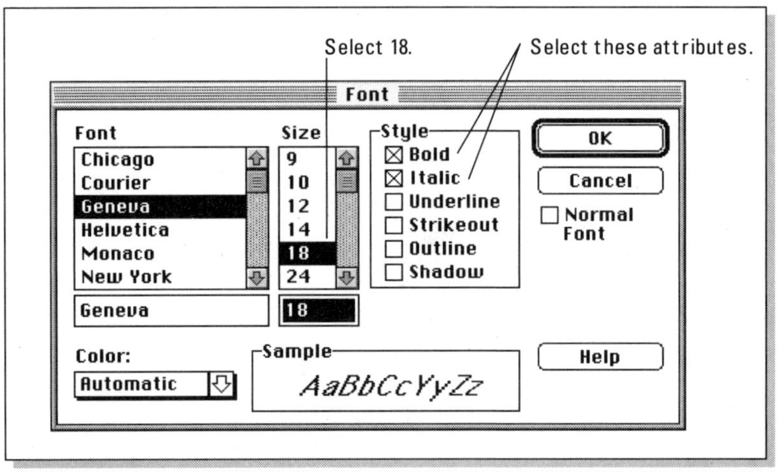

Figure 7-26: Choosing Font from the Format menu or shortcut menu displays the Font dialog box.

Step 2. Select 18 from the size list, turn on Bold and Italics, and then choose OK.

Excel makes the change to the font. Repeat for cell A2 using the 14-point Geneva font.

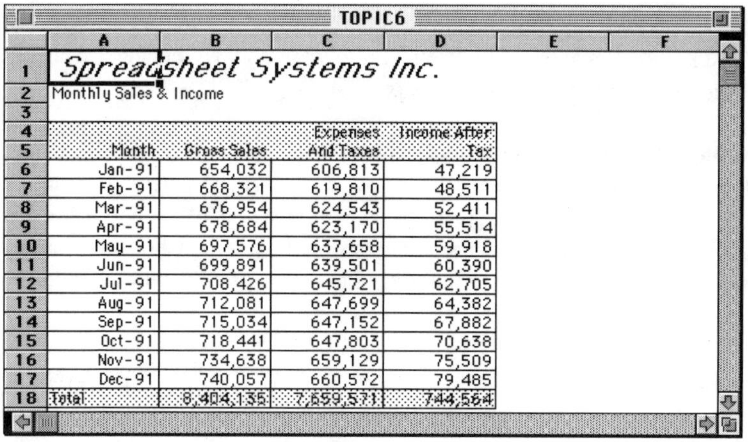

TOPIC6

	A	B	C	D
1	Spreadsheet Systems Inc.			
2	Monthly Sales & Income			
3				
4			Expenses	Income After
5	Month	Gross Sales	And Taxes	Tax
6	Jan-91	654,032	606,813	47,219
7	Feb-91	668,321	619,810	48,511
8	Mar-91	676,954	624,543	52,411
9	Apr-91	678,684	623,170	55,514
10	May-91	697,576	637,658	59,918
11	Jun-91	699,891	639,501	60,390
12	Jul-91	708,426	645,721	62,705
13	Aug-91	712,081	647,699	64,382
14	Sep-91	715,034	647,152	67,882
15	Oct-91	718,441	647,803	70,638
16	Nov-91	734,638	659,129	75,509
17	Dec-91	740,057	660,572	79,485
18	Total	8,404,135	7,659,571	744,564

Figure 7-27: Changing the font size and attributes of text in a cell.

To save your formatting select Save As from the File menu and use the name TOPIC7; Excel saves the worksheet to disk.

Quick Tips

This section provides you with tips on how to make your worksheets look professional using the available styles in Excel.

Avoiding a cluttered worksheet

Don't go overboard with the number of style attributes you apply to a worksheet. Too many fonts, lines, and shades can produce a cluttered and confusing worksheet display. A rule of thumb is to limit yourself to no more than two font types per worksheet. Remember, you want your worksheets to sizzle, but it's their substance that counts.

Displaying gridlines

Display worksheet gridlines or lines drawn with Format Border, not both. Using gridlines obscures drawn lines and results in an unattractive display.

Using shading with borders

For best shading effect, surround shaded ranges with a border. Emphasize important ranges, such as totals or text above columns of values, with a light shade and a border.

Formatting text for clarity

Text and values that are located in a shaded range will stand out better if they're bolded.

Use the same font type, but in progressively smaller sizes, for a worksheet's titles and subtitles.

Previewing your worksheet

Choose Print Preview from the File menu to view how a worksheet will appear with fonts and other attributes before it is printed.

Clearing up your printout

Colors added to a worksheet print as patterns on black-and-white printers. To avoid having these patterns show up in the cells in a worksheet, choose the Black and White Cells check box from the Page Setup dialog box. Choosing this option results in text printed in black-and-white and text boxes printed with a white background.

Deleting and modifying styles

If you delete a named style, any cell or range with the deleted style reverts to Normal style.

If you create and then modify a style, any cells with the style are updated with the modified style. Also, if you've applied a different attribute (font, border, or shade) to a cell or range since using the original style, the cell or range won't be updated with the modified style. Apply the modified style to those cells if you want.

Summary

- Fonts are typefaces and come in different styles, shapes, and sizes.
- You can apply attributes to fonts such as underlining, bold, and italics.
- You can apply font choices to selected cells by choosing Font from the Format menu or shortcut menu.
- You can add Lines (borders) to selected cells by choosing Border from the Format menu or shortcut menu.
- You can add shading to selected cells by selecting the Shade box from the Border dialog box, or by choosing Patterns from the Format menu.
- You can add drop shadows to a worksheet using the Drop Shadow tool on the Drawing toolbar, or by using solid shading.
- Named styles enable you to apply predefined formatting options to selected cells.
- You can create styles by choosing Style from the Format menu or by example. Creating styles by example creates a style from formatting applied to a cell or range.
- You can automatically format a range with an established set of style attributes by choosing AutoFormat from the Format menu.

Topic 8
Creating Basic Charts

Overview

Thus far, you've learned how to create and use an Excel worksheet. You've learned how to move around the worksheet, enter text, values, functions, and formulas. And you know how to save and print your worksheet. For some Excel users, this is all that is needed to operate Excel successfully. There is another feature of Excel, however, that you'll want to check into: charting.

Charting enables you to see your data in a picture format. When you see your data pictorially, you can easily recognize trends and better understand your data. You create a chart from the data in your worksheet, and you can place the chart near the data in your worksheet. Or it can be linked to the data in the worksheet and be a separate document in its own window.

Excel has eight two-dimensional and six three-dimensional chart types to choose from, and many variations on these individual types. In addition, Excel enables you to combine chart types (a Combination chart) and enables you to create your own. Table 8-1 lists the chart types available to you.

Table 8-1: Excel chart types

Chart type	***Dimension***	***Displays . . .***
Area	2,3	Data and the magnitude of data over time
Bar	2,3	Data over time using horizontal bars
Column	2,3	Data over time using vertical bars
Line	2,3	Data over time using horizontal lines
Pie	2,3	Data as a proportion of a total
Radar	2	Data relative to a center point and other data
XY	2	The relationship of one set of data to another with lines, markers, or both
Combination	2	Data with differing magnitudes or different chart types
Surface	3*	The relationships between large amounts of data that would otherwise be difficult to detect

*2-D type available as a format.

The data you chart is only one part of your chart. Excel charts can contain other items of information to help you describe your data, as listed and shown in Table 8-2 and Figure 8-1, respectively.

Table 8-2: Chart elements

Element	*Description*
Axis	In 2-D charts, the horizontal line (x-axis) that displays categories of data; the vertical line (y-axis) that displays the range and increments of data
	In 3-D charts, the x-axis displays categories of data, the y-axis displays data series names, and the z-axis displays the range and increments of data.
Chart	All items in the chart window, including the chart, axes, legend, and titles
Chart text	Labels that identify items in a chart. Text can be unattached (movable) or attached (unmovable) to an object in a chart.
Data marker	The symbol that represents a value in a worksheet, such as a bar, dot, or pie wedge
Data series	The symbols that represent the values of a row or column of data in a worksheet
Gridlines	Lines you display for easier identification of the values in a chart
Legend	Information that identifies a marker's data series
Menu bar	The pull-down menu bar that is available when a chart window is active
Plot area	The region of the chart that contains the axis lines and the data markers
Tick mark	The small lines on the axis lines that separate data categories or indicate value increments

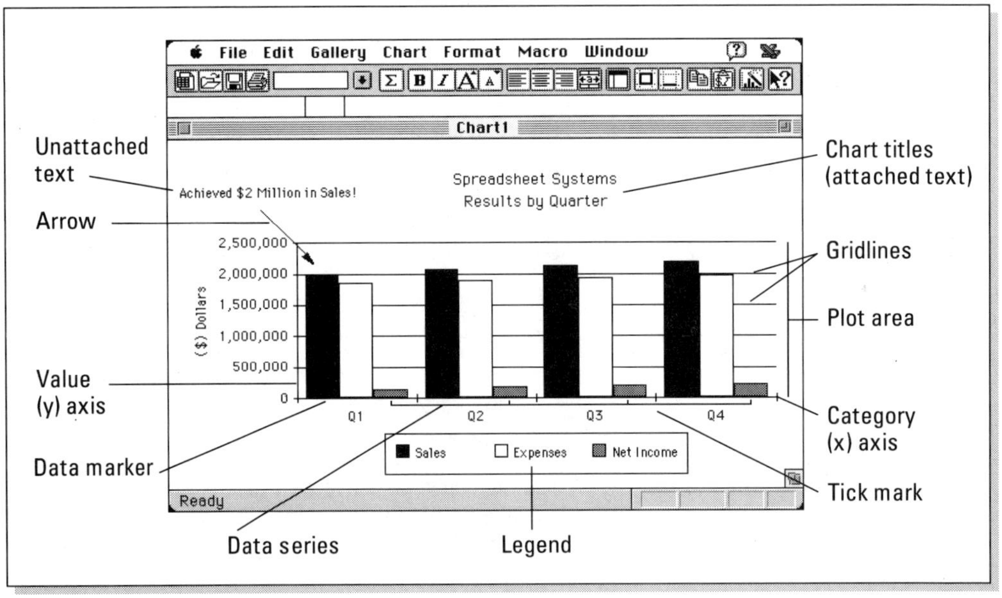

Figure 8-1: The elements of a chart that help describe the chart's data.

Charting your course with shortcut menus

Pressing Option, Command, and the mouse button when a chart is the active document displays the shortcut menu shown in the following figure.

The chart shortcut menu, like the worksheet shortcut menu, gives you fast access to commonly used chart commands. The chart shortcut menu, however, will contain different options, depending on the chart item selected. Selecting items in the chart is covered in Topic 9, though you can put the shortcut menu to work now.

Creating a chart with ChartWizard

Like most operations in Excel, creating a chart is easy. The first step is the most important. The data you want to chart should be located in contiguous cells (for example, B2, B3, B4, and so on) and preferably in adjacent rows or columns in the worksheet. For example, in Figure 8-2, you want to make sure you have data in each cell in rows 6, 7, and 8. In addition to your data, include row and column text, so the range you should select is A5:E8, as shown in Figure 8-2.

VERSION 4 Microsoft

Next, you should decide whether you want to use Excel's ChartWizard tool to create your chart. If you're new to Excel, ChartWizard steps you through the chart creation process via a series of dialog boxes and is the easiest way to create and place a chart on the worksheet. See the Step-by-Step section in this Topic for instructions on how to use ChartWizard.

If you prefer to create a chart directly in its own window, or if you prefer not to use ChartWizard, read on. You'll also want to read Topic 9 to learn how to add titles and a legend to your chart, something you have the opportunity to do while using ChartWizard.

Creating a chart without ChartWizard

If ChartWizard isn't for you, don't despair. Simply choose New from the File menu, and select Chart. After you click OK, Excel displays the chart shown in Figure 8-3.

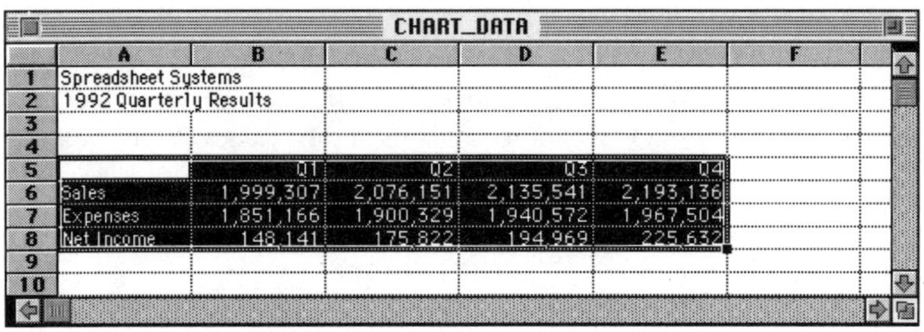
CHART_DATA

	A	B	C	D	E	F
1	Spreadsheet Systems					
2	1992 Quarterly Results					
3						
4						
5		Q1	Q2	Q3	Q4	
6	Sales	1,999,307	2,076,151	2,135,541	2,193,136	
7	Expenses	1,851,166	1,900,329	1,940,572	1,967,504	
8	Net Income	148,141	175,822	194,969	225,632	
9						
10						

Figure 8-2: Selecting a range of cells that includes row and column text to create a chart.

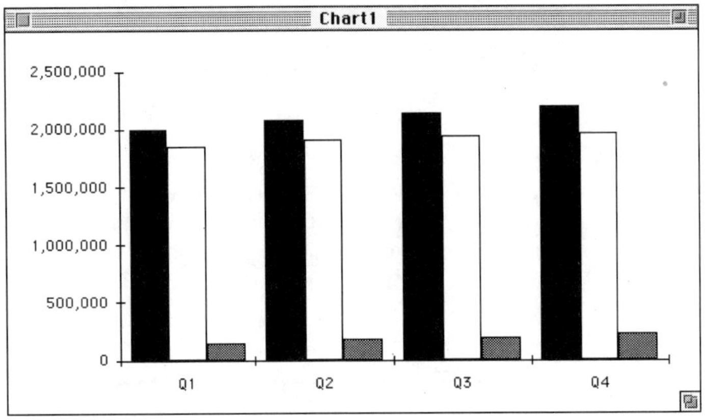

Figure 8-3: Choosing New from the File menu and selecting Chart creates a chart without using the ChartWizard.

That's all there is to creating a chart. Excel displays the quarter of the year along the x-axis, dollar amounts along the y-axis, and the sales, expenses, and net income data as vertical bars. A vertical bar chart, known as a column chart, is Excel's default chart type.

Changing a chart's data categories

When Excel created a chart from the range of data you highlighted in the worksheet, Excel made a few assumptions. Excel used the range B1:E1 (quarters) as the data categories (x-axis labels) because there were more labels in rows than columns. If you create a chart where there are more labels in columns than rows, Excel uses the labels in the far right column as the data categories to create the chart.

Note, however, that you can easily use column labels instead of row labels for data categories, or vice versa. To do this, close the chart window after Excel creates the chart by choosing Close from the File menu, pressing Command-W, or by clicking the close box. Click the No button when the dialog box appears asking you whether you want to save the chart to disk. Next, select the range of data and choose Copy from the Edit menu. After the marquee appears, create a new chart by choosing New from the File menu. Select Chart and click OK or press Return. Next, choose Paste Special from the Edit menu in the Chart menu bar. When you do, the Paste Special dialog box shown in Figure 8-4 appears.

Check Rows or Columns in the "Values (Y) in" box to tell Excel which labels to use as your data categories. If you choose Columns in the "Values (Y) in" box for Figure 8-3, Excel creates the chart shown in Figure 8-5.

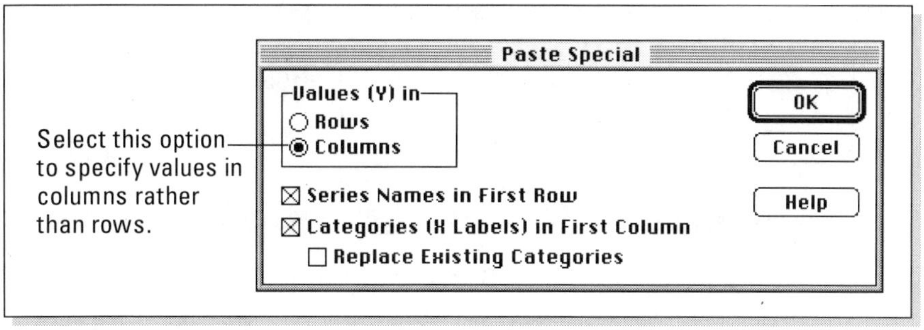

Figure 8-4: Choosing Paste Special from the Edit menu displays the Paste Special dialog box.

Changing chart types

If you prefer a different chart type than the column chart, you have a few options to choose from. You can select another chart type from the Chart toolbar, or you can use the Gallery pull-down menu. The Chart toolbar is a bit faster, although the Gallery commands enable you to select a chart format.

If you've used the ChartWizard, the Chart toolbar will be visible. If it's not visible, choose Toolbars from the Options menu, select Chart, and then click Show or press Return. Next, simply click the tool that corresponds to the chart type you want, as shown in Figure 8-6.

Excel displays the chart using the chart type you selected.

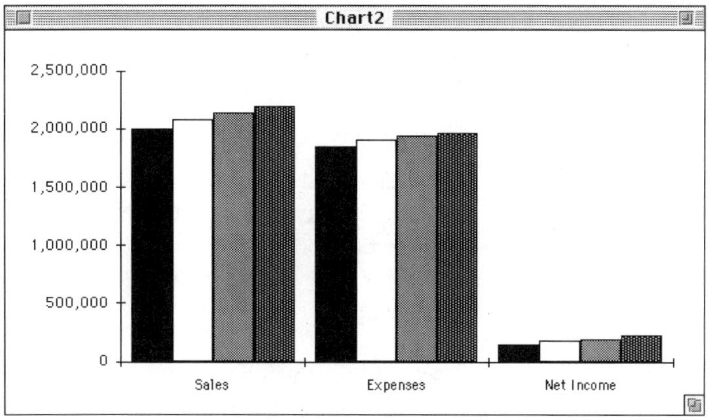

Figure 8-5: Choosing the Columns option from the "Values (Y) in" box gives the data categories shown in this chart.

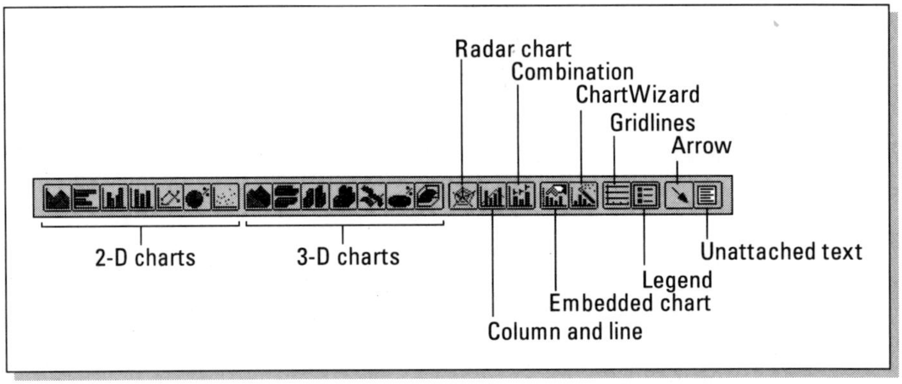

Figure 8-6: Choosing Toolbars from the Options menu and selecting Chart displays the Chart toolbar.

To change chart types and formats, make sure the chart is in its own window. Then pull down the Gallery menu as shown in Figure 8-7.

A check mark appears to the left of the currently selected chart type. To change chart types, select the type of chart you want with the mouse or the keyboard. After you select a new chart type, a gallery appears with the format available for that chart, as shown in Figure 8-8.

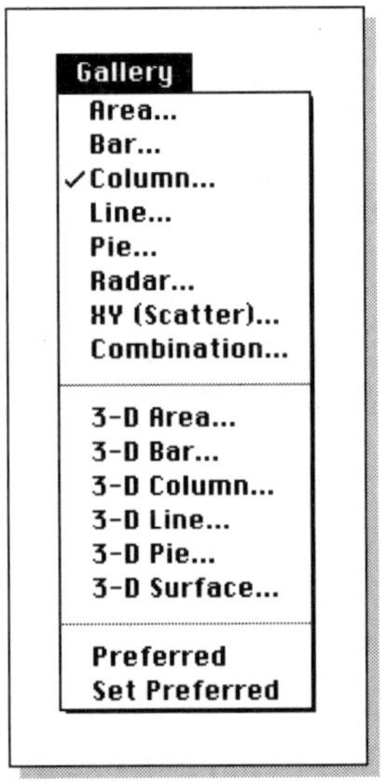

Figure 8-7: The Gallery menu can be used to change chart types and formats.

Select the format you want and choose OK. Excel then redraws the chart using the new chart type. Remember, however, that some chart types are more appropriate for the data than others. The following section shows you an example of Excel's chart types, and unless noted otherwise, the section uses chart format 1, the default format type.

Bar charts

Bar charts are the horizontal version of column charts: The data markers in a bar chart have a horizontal, rather than vertical, orientation, as shown in Figure 8-9. Note that the x- and y-axes are reversed from the column chart in Figure 8-3.

Use a bar chart when you want to show how your data changes over time, and compare data points, such as product sales by month.

Line charts

Line charts use lines only, markers only, or both, to display data over time, as shown in Figure 8-10.

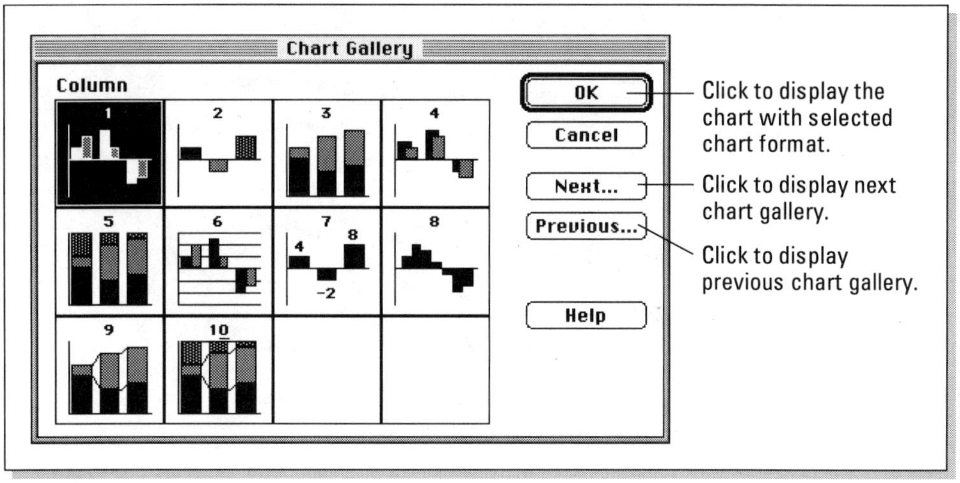

Figure 8-8: Choosing a new chart type from the Gallery menu displays a gallery with available chart formats.

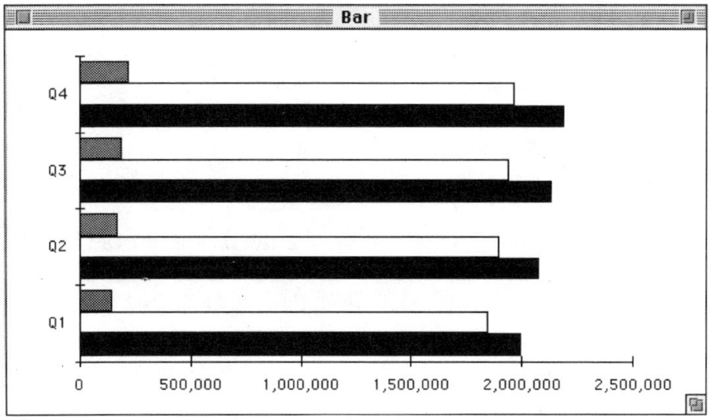

Figure 8-9: The data markers in a bar chart are horizontally oriented.

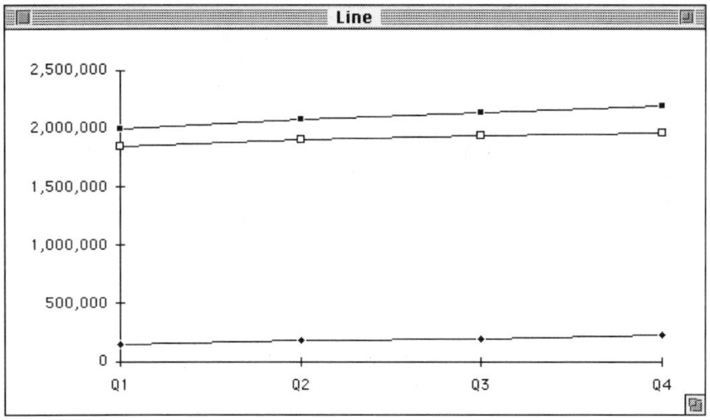

Figure 8-10: An example of a line chart.

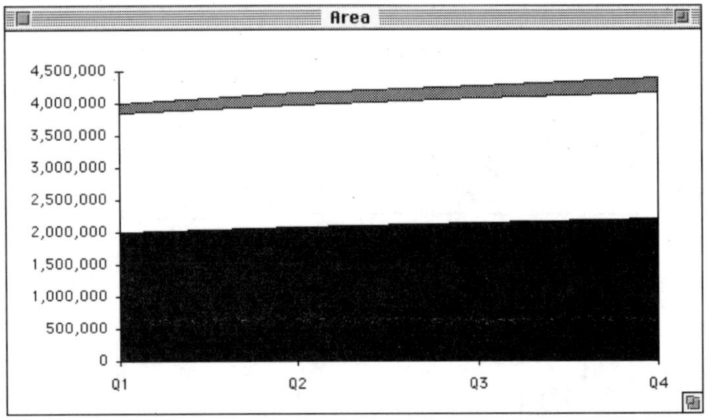

Figure 8-11: An example of an area chart.

Use a line chart when you want to spot trends easily — data points are not compared with one another in line charts, such as multiple product sales by month.

Area charts

Area charts display the total of data points for a specific period of time, as shown in Figure 8-11. Area charts are similar to line charts in that they display data over time using lines. But with area charts, the area below the lines is filled in representing totals, much like a stacked column chart (format 3).

Use an area chart when you're more interested in the magnitude of change rather than the rate of change, such as the amount of difference between sales of two products by month. Area charts are most useful when each successive line is different (using higher or lower values) than the other.

Pie charts

Pie charts display each data point as a pie wedge representing a proportion of the total of one data series. See Figure 8-12.

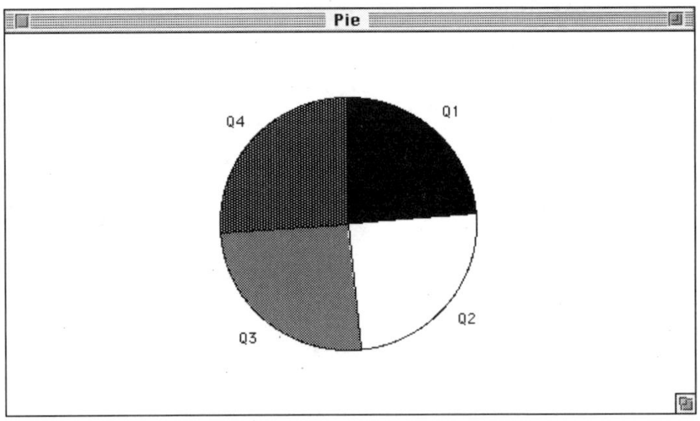

Figure 8-12: An example of a pie chart.

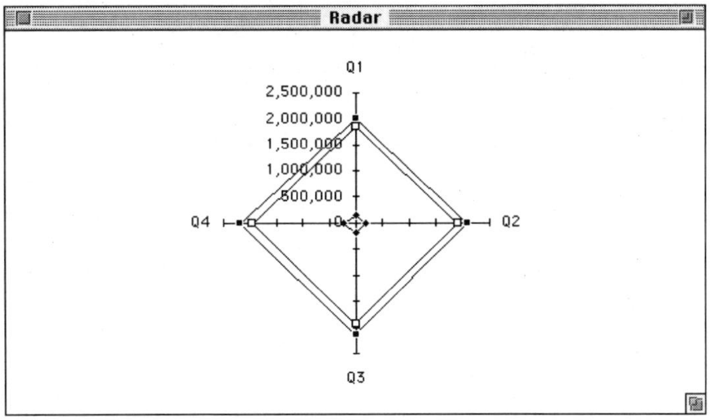

Figure 8-13: An example of a radar chart.

A pie chart is useful when you want to compare how each data point contributes to a total, such as the percent each product's sales contributes to total sales.

Radar charts

Radar charts display the relationship of data points to the chart's center point and among the other data points. Note that lines connect the data markers in the same data series, as shown in Figure 8-13.

Use a radar chart, for example, when you want to be able to visually compare sales of products between each other and a center point. In Figure 8-13, the center point is zero because the chart data are positive values.

XY (scatter) charts

XY charts are a different breed of chart. XY charts display the relationship between two series of values over time, and therefore, values make up both the x- and y-axes. Figure 8-14 is an XY chart using format 2.

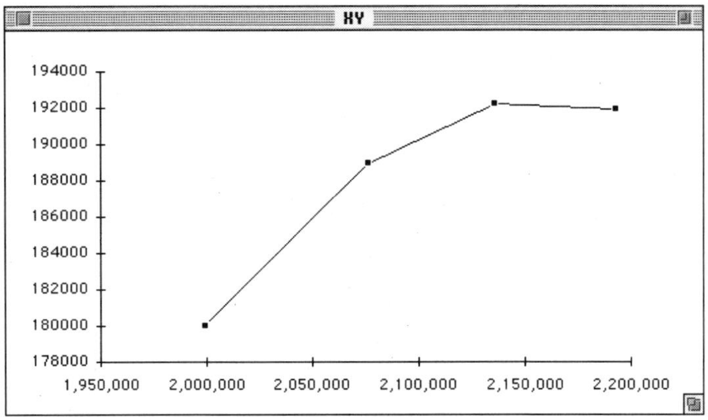

Figure 8-14: An example of an XY (scatter) chart.

Use an XY chart to determine whether one set of data depends on another, such as mortgage interest rates and unit sales of homes.

Combination charts

A combination chart, as its name implies, is a combination of two chart types. A combination chart begins as a column chart. Then Excel places, or overlays, another chart over the column chart, but without obscuring it. Combination charts are particularly useful when you need a second y-axis because of the disparity in the magnitude between individual data series.

When you select Combination from the Gallery menu, you're presented with the five combination chart formats as listed in Table 8-3.

Table 8-3: Combination chart formats

Format	*Combination chart*
1	Column and line
2	Column and line with a second y-axis
3	Two-line chart with a second y-axis
4	Column and area
5	Column and high-low-close with a second y-axis

To create a combination chart, Excel divides the data series into two camps: the main and overlay chart groups. The main chart group is assigned the first half of the data, while the overlay chart gets the second half. If you're charting an odd numbered data series, the main chart group displays the extra series. Figure 8-15 shows a combination chart using format 2.

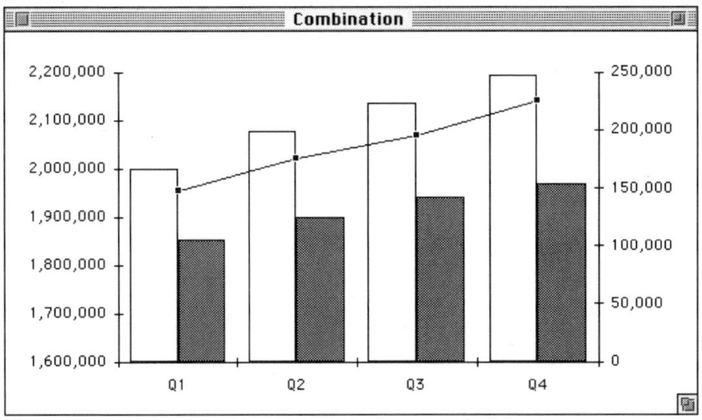

Figure 8-15: An example of a combination chart.

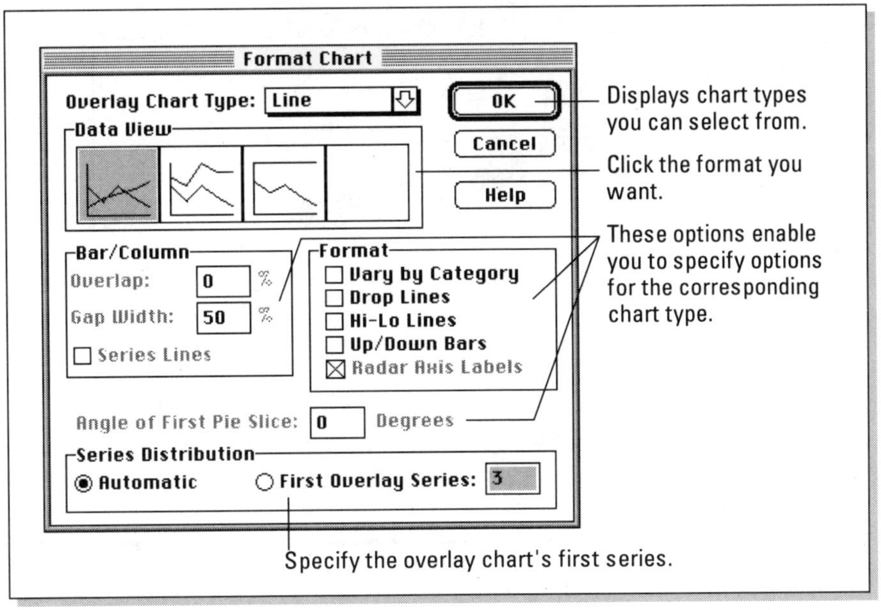

Figure 8-16: Customizing the overlay portion of a combination chart using the Format Chart dialog box.

After you've selected Combination, you can customize the overlay portion of your chart by choosing Overlay from the Format menu. The Format Chart dialog box shown in Figure 8-16 provides numerous chart format options, depending on the type of chart you've selected.

For example, pulling down the Overlay Chart Type menu in the Overlay dialog box enables you to select another chart type for the overlay chart. You can also control which data series Excel first uses to create the overlay chart. Choose First Overlay Series from the Overlay dialog box and enter the number of the data series that you want Excel to use as the first data series for the overlay chart. For example, suppose you want to create a combination chart based on five data series. By default, Excel will place the first three series in the main chart. But you want the third through fifth data series displayed in the overlay chart. To do so, you enter 3 in the First Overlay Series box.

3-D charts

In addition to the 2-D chart types, Excel provides six 3-D chart types: area, bar, column, line, pie, and surface. You cannot overlay another chart type with 3-D charts. Figure 8-17 shows you a surface chart (with gridlines) — Excel's (only) 3-D chart type.

3-D charts are a bit different than their 2-D brothers. The following table lists how chart axes are used in 2-D and 3-D charts.

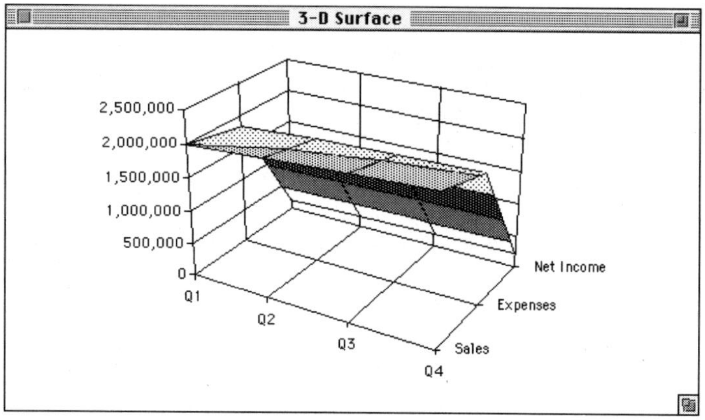

Figure 8-17: An example of a 3-D surface chart.

Axis	*2-D*	*3-D*
X	Data categories	Category names
Y	Data values	Data series names
Z	N/A	Data values

The z-axis is known as the depth axis, which is what gives 3-D charts their 3-D appearance. The third axis enables you to see differences in the magnitude among the data series more clearly.

As with combination charts, Excel provides several commands to customize the appearance of 3-D charts. Choosing 3-D View from the Format menu, for example, provides the customization options listed in Table 8-4.

Table 8-4: Customizing options for 3-D charts

Option	*Purpose*
Elevation	Selects the height of the chart. Enter a value in the Elevation box or click the up and down arrows to increase or decrease the height incrementally.
Rotation	Rotates the display of the chart. Enter a value in the Rotation box or click the left or right arrows to rotate the chart incrementally.
Height	Percentage of the height of the chart to the x-axis or base. Enter a value in the Height box. The default, 100%, indicates that the height of the chart equals its width.
Right Angle Axes	All axes are displayed at right angles to each other. When checked, this option disables the Perspective option.
Perspective	Increases or decreases the size of the data markers. Enter a value in the Perspective box or click the up and down arrows to change the chart's perspective incrementally. Not available when Right Angle Axes is checked.

Use the Apply button to see the changes you've made to your chart without closing the 3-D View dialog box. If you have a change of heart about your modifications, you can start over by clicking the Default button.

Finally, choosing Main Chart from the Format menu provides you with several options that help you fine-tune the appearance of 3-D charts. In addition to being able to change to another chart type, you can adjust the distance between bars (Gap Depth) and the distance between a bar and the one immediately behind it (Chart Depth).

Using chart file operations

Similar to Excel worksheet files, you use the File menu to perform file operations for charts. For example, you saw earlier in this Topic that to create a chart in its own window you use the New command from the File menu. Also, since a chart and the worksheet that the chart is based on are separate documents, you need to save the chart as a separate file using the Save or Save As command from the File menu. You open previously saved charts by choosing Open from the File menu, and put the chart away using Close from the File menu. Finally, choose Print from the File menu to print your chart.

Moving and sizing charts

File operations aren't the only similarities between charts and worksheets. Because a chart is in its own window, you can move and size a chart window. First change the size of the window by pressing and dragging on the resize box. Then move the modified chart window to the desired on-screen location by clicking and dragging the chart's title bar. You also can move charts on a worksheet by clicking and dragging on an edge of the chart.

Resize box

You can use this moving technique to place a chart next to the worksheet that supports it. When you display the chart and the worksheet on-screen simultaneously, as shown in Figure 8-18, you need not flip back and forth between the two windows.

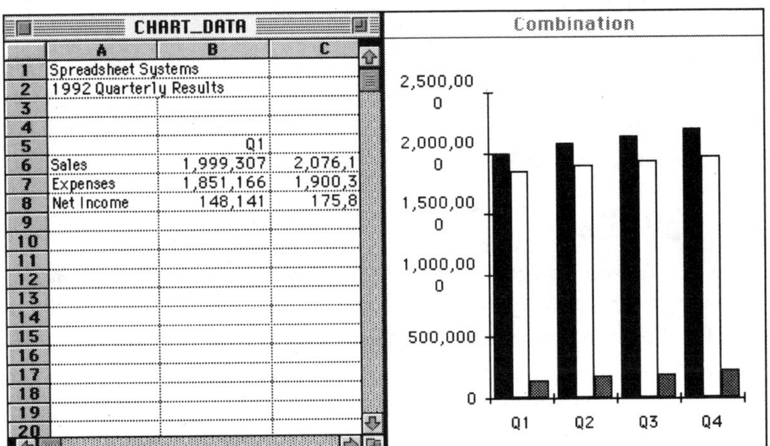

Figure 8-18: Displaying a chart and a worksheet on-screen simultaneously.

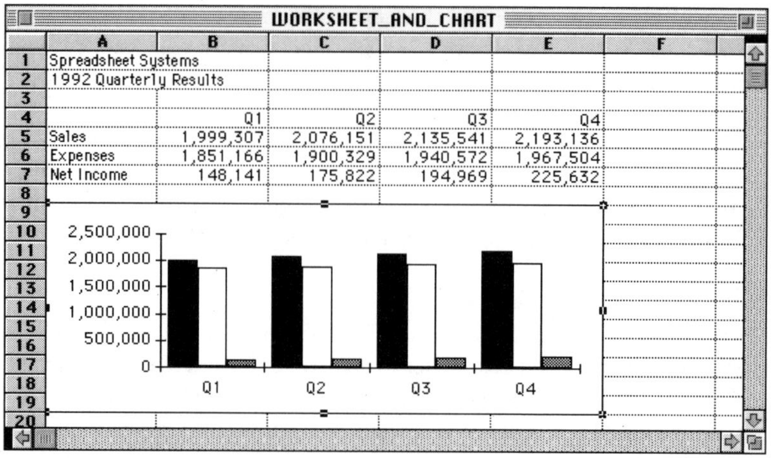

Figure 8-19: Attaching a chart to a worksheet using the Select Chart command from the Chart menu.

Note, however, one important difference between worksheet and chart windows: A reduced worksheet window displays fewer cells of the worksheet, while a chart window continues to display the entire chart, though smaller in size.

Attaching a chart to a worksheet

If you would like to see the worksheet and chart together, but separate windows aren't your cup of tea, and you didn't use ChartWizard, you can still place a copy of the chart on the worksheet. To do so, make the chart the active window and resize it as desired. Next, select the chart by choosing Select Chart from the Chart menu, or by clicking on it. Choose Copy from the Edit menu, make the worksheet the active window, and select the cell that represents the upper-left corner where you want the chart to appear on the worksheet. After you select Paste from the Edit menu or press Return, Excel places a copy of the chart on the worksheet, as shown in Figure 8-19.

The copy of the chart on the worksheet is separate from the chart in the chart window. That is, any changes you make to either chart won't affect the other. If you want to make changes to the chart on the worksheet, double-click the chart to invoke the Chart menu bar. Any changes you make in the worksheet data, however, affect both charts.

Step-by-Step

In this section you'll practice creating a chart. First, you'll create and place a column chart on the worksheet using ChartWizard. Second, you'll save the chart to disk as a separate chart file. You'll use the worksheet you saved in Topic 7 (or one of your own choosing).

Remember, if you make a mistake, choose Undo from the Edit menu or press F1. If you want to start over, close the TOPIC7 worksheet by clicking the close box. When the alert box appears, click the No button. Then choose Open from the File menu, select TOPIC7, and click Open or press Return. To open the TOPIC7 worksheet, do the following:

1. Select the Open command from the File menu.

   The Open dialog box appears.

2. Select TOPIC7 and press Return or choose Open.

   The TOPIC7 worksheet appears.

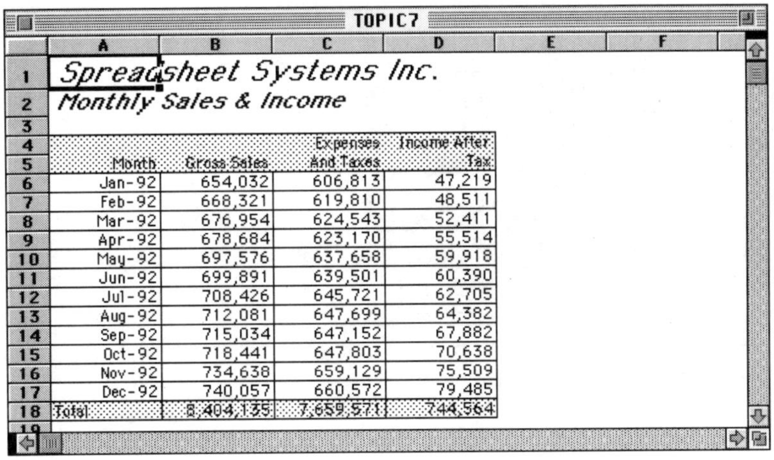

	Month	Gross Sales	Expenses And Taxes	Income After Tax
6	Jan-92	654,032	606,813	47,219
7	Feb-92	668,321	619,810	48,511
8	Mar-92	676,954	624,543	52,411
9	Apr-92	678,684	623,170	55,514
10	May-92	697,576	637,658	59,918
11	Jun-92	699,891	639,501	60,390
12	Jul-92	708,426	645,721	62,705
13	Aug-92	712,081	647,699	64,382
14	Sep-92	715,034	647,152	67,882
15	Oct-92	718,441	647,803	70,638
16	Nov-92	734,638	659,129	75,509
17	Dec-92	740,057	660,572	79,485
18	Total	8,404,135	7,659,571	744,564

Figure 8-20: Choosing TOPIC7 from the Open dialog box opens the TOPIC7 worksheet.

Edit the column text by doing the following:

3. Select cells C4 and D4.

4. Place the pointer over the fill handle in cell D4, drag left until the cells are completely grayed, and then release the mouse button.

5. Type `Exp & Tax` into cell C5, and type `Inc After Tax` in cell D5.

6. Change the width of the following columns with the mouse by choosing Column Width from the Format menu or shortcut menu and by typing the following width values:

Column	*Width*
A	7
B and C	8
D	9

Creating a chart:

Step 1. Select range B5:D17.

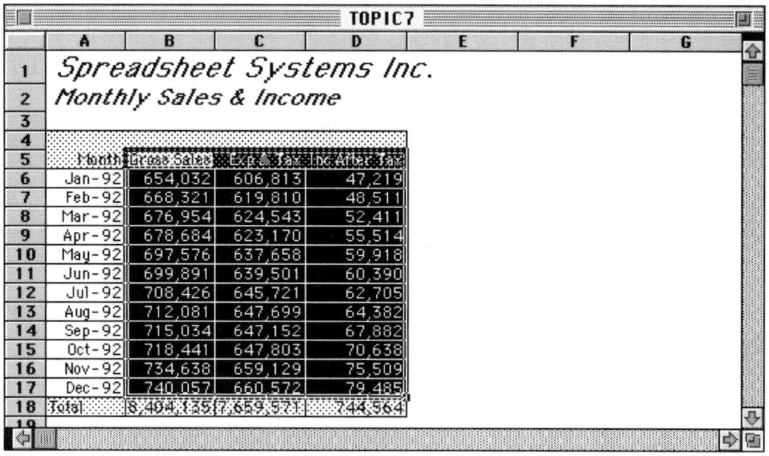

Figure 8-21: Selecting range B5:D17.

Step 2. Click the ChartWizard tool, hold down the Control key, and drag the mouse over range E4:G18.

The first ChartWizard window appears.

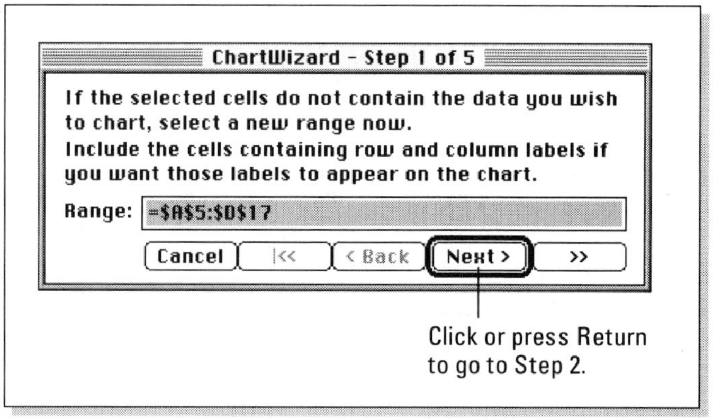

Figure 8-22: Clicking the ChartWizard tool displays the first ChartWizard window.

Step 3. Press Return or click Next.

The second ChartWizard window appears.

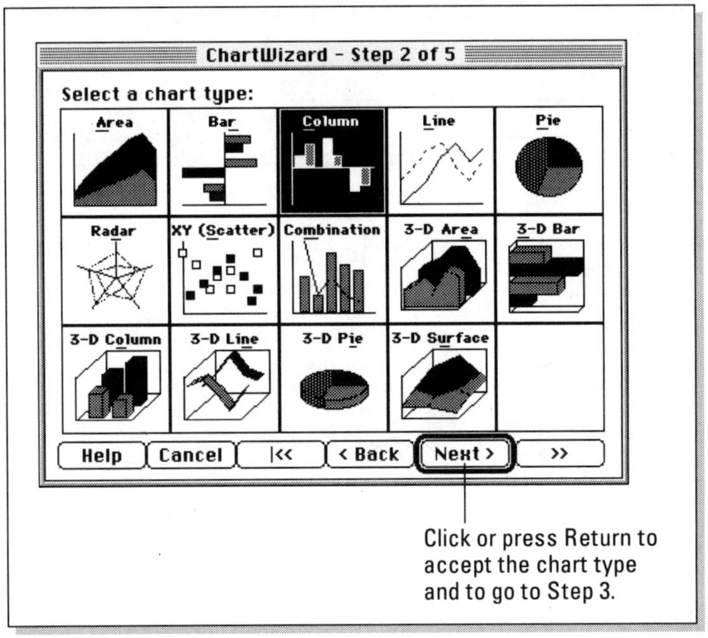

Figure 8-23: Clicking Next or Pressing Return on the first ChartWizard window displays the second ChartWizard window.

Step 4. Accept Column as the chart type by pressing Return or clicking Next.

The third ChartWizard window appears.

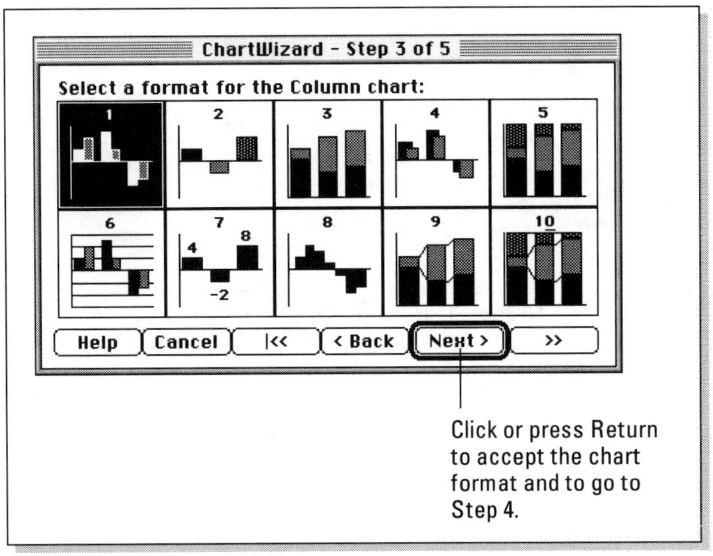

Figure 8-24: Clicking Next or pressing Return on the second ChartWizard window accepts the selected chart format and displays the third ChartWizard window.

Step 5. Accept the first format for the chart format by pressing Return or clicking Next.

The fourth ChartWizard window appears.

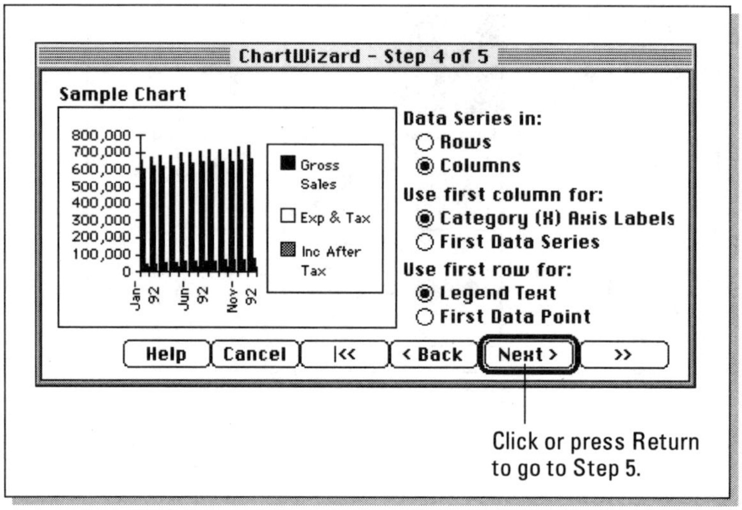

Figure 8-25: Clicking Next or pressing Return on the third ChartWizard window accepts the selected format for the column chart and displays the fourth ChartWizard window.

Step 6. Press Return or click Next.

The fifth ChartWizard window appears.

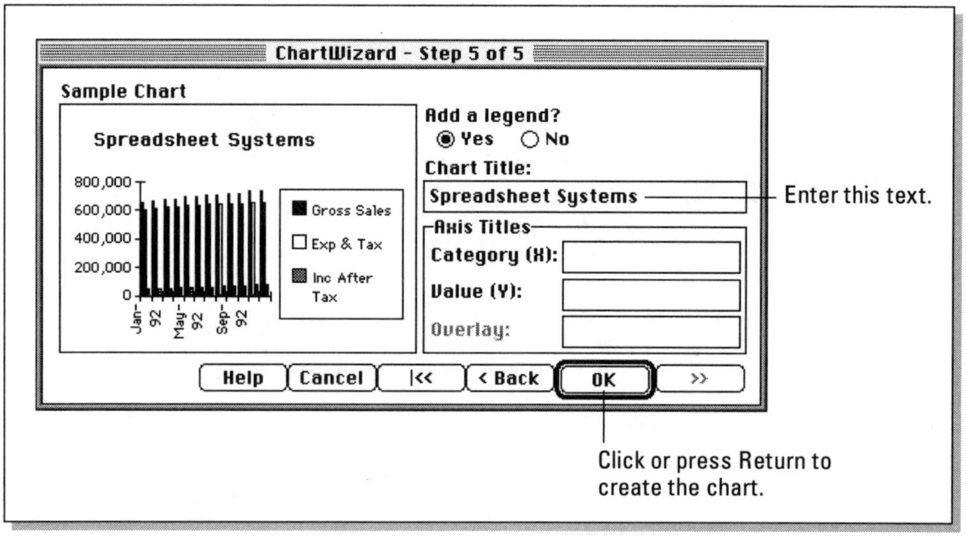

Figure 8-26: Clicking Next or pressing Return on the fourth ChartWizard window displays the fifth ChartWizard window.

Step 7. Click Yes to add a legend, type `Spreadsheet Systems` in the Chart Title text box. Press Return or click OK.

The chart appears on the worksheet.

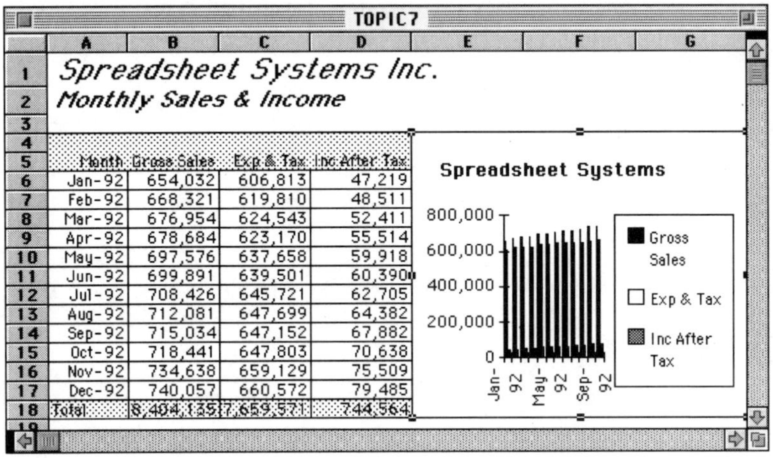

Figure 8-27: An example of a chart created using the ChartWizard tool.

Creating a chart in its own window:

Step 1. Double-click on the chart.

The chart appears in its own window.

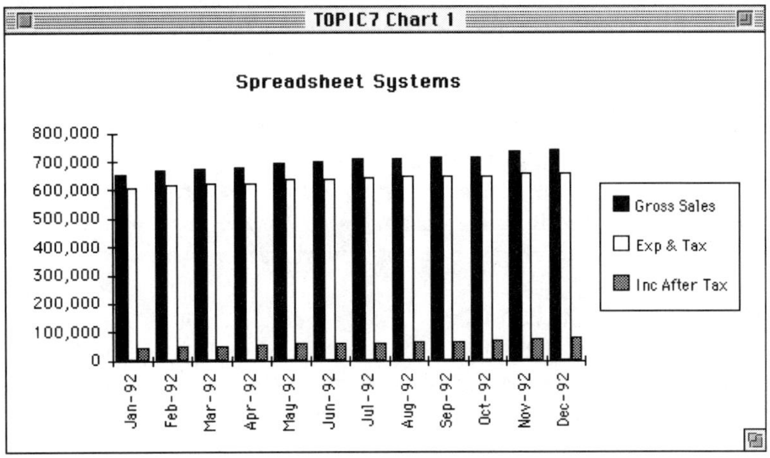

Figure 8-28: Double-clicking a chart displays the chart in its own window.

Saving a chart to disk:

Step 1. Choose Save from the File menu.

The Save dialog box appears.

Step 2. Select the 7 in TOPIC7 CHART1 in the Save Chart as text box, type 8, and then press Return or click the Save button.

Excel saves the chart file to disk.

Saving a chart with a worksheet:

Step 1. Make the worksheet the active window, select Save As from the File menu, type the name TOPIC8 in the Save Worksheet As text box, and press Return or click the Save button.

Excel saves the worksheet and embedded chart to disk.

Quick Tips

This section provides you with tips on how to get the most from the charts you create in Excel.

Using function keys to create charts

You can quickly create a chart as a separate document by selecting the range of data and pressing F11 if you have an extended keyboard.

Charting with data in noncontiguous ranges

You can use data in noncontiguous ranges for charting. Begin by selecting the cells in the worksheet as the first data series. Then press Command and select the next group of cells. You can continue selecting as many contiguous or noncontiguous ranges as you want as long as you press Command before selecting.

Using the double arrow buttons

Pressing the double right arrow button (>>) in any ChartWizard window tells Excel to accept the default settings in the remaining ChartWizard windows and display the chart on the worksheet. The double left arrow button (<<) returns you to the first ChartWizard window; the Back button returns you to the previous ChartWizard window. Use these buttons to change a setting you've made previously.

Setting the default chart type

If you want the currently displayed chart type to be Excel's default chart type, choose Set Preferred from the Gallery menu. Conversely, to change the chart type that is currently displayed on the screen to the default chart type, choose Preferred from the Gallery menu.

Creating charts for investment data

Use line chart format 8 (high-low-close) for creating charts for investment data. Use column format 5 (100% stacked) when you want to display percentages of more than one data series.

Updating chart values

If you open a chart without opening the worksheet the chart depends on for data, and Excel cannot find the worksheet to update the values that the chart is based on, Excel displays the dialog box shown in Figure 8-29. Use the dialog box to tell Excel where the worksheet is located (in another folder and/or disk).

Representing the first row of a chart

If you select a range to chart where the top row and the far-left column do not contain text or dates, Excel displays the New Chart dialog box shown in Figure 8-30 after you select Chart from the File New dialog box. Choose the option you want for the chart (x-values for an XY chart, for example) and click OK. Excel displays the chart as a separate file.

3-D default options

The Default option on the 3-D View command from the Format menu does not reset chart settings to their default if you've used a Gallery option since creating the chart. Close the chart without saving it and reopen it if you need to start over from the beginning.

Removing a chart on a worksheet

You can remove a chart on a worksheet by clicking on it, and then pressing Delete or choosing Clear from the Edit menu.

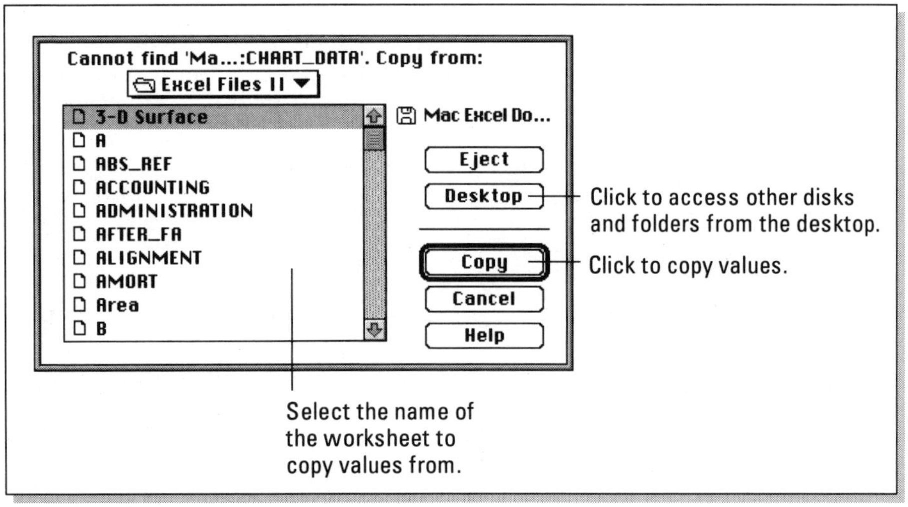

Figure 8-29: Finding a worksheet to update the values a chart is based on.

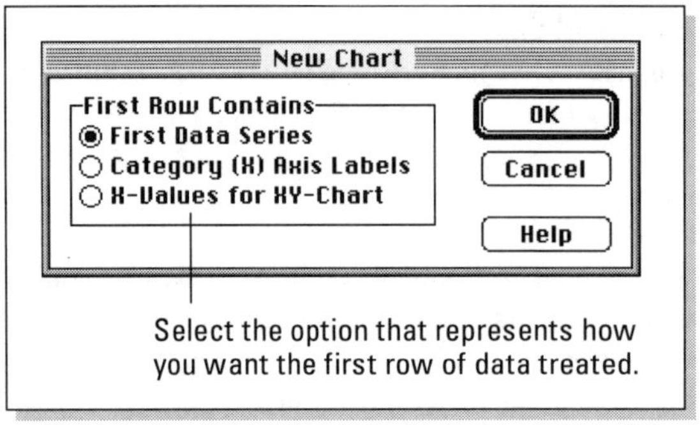

Figure 8-30: Choosing how to represent the first row of a range in a chart using the New Chart dialog box.

Selecting chart types quickly

You can quickly select other chart types without using the Gallery menu by selecting the Next and Previous buttons on any of the chart type dialog boxes. The Next and Previous buttons display the gallery of formats for the chart type in the order they appear on the Gallery menu.

Aligning charts with gridlines

Displaying gridlines helps you align a chart on your worksheet. In addition, holding down Command as you drag the mouse aligns the chart to the worksheet gridlines.

Adding and deleting an overlay chart

You can add and delete an overlay chart to a preexisting chart by choosing Add Overlay and Delete Overlay from the Chart menu, respectively.

Viewing all worksheets and charts simultaneously

Choosing Arrange from the Window menu quickly enables you to view all currently open worksheets and charts on-screen simultaneously.

Summary

- You can use charts to display data in a picture format and see relationships among data that you ordinarily could not identify.
- Charts are based on the data in the worksheet.
- You can place charts on a worksheet or in their own window as a separate file.
- You can create charts by selecting data in a worksheet and using ChartWizard, or by selecting New from the File menu, and then choosing the Chart option.
- Excel has eight 2-D and six 3-D chart types. A column chart is Excel's default chart type.
- Combination charts combine two chart types: a main chart and an overlay chart.
- Within chart types there are formats for the chart that appear in a gallery you choose from.
- You can quickly rotate a 3-D chart by selecting it, and then clicking and dragging on a black selection handle.
- You can change the values a chart is based on by using the ChartWizard tool or by selecting Edit Series from the Chart menu.

Topic 9
Customizing Your Charts

Overview

If you've read Topic 8, you're probably pretty excited about charting because you can see the value of creating charts from your data. You understand that displaying your data graphically helps you and your audience gain additional insight into your analyses and reports. But you may also be scratching your head. If you inherit a worksheet and chart without explanatory text, or didn't add text to your chart as you were creating it, you may be somewhat in the dark.

Well, don't panic — you have a chance to rebound. This Topic shows you how to add explanatory text to your charts if you didn't do so while you were creating them initially. In addition, you'll learn how to change the appearance of your basic charts so they'll contain even more snap and sizzle. But first a little background.

There are a few general guidelines to keep in mind as you customize your charts. If you've created charts or graphs in the past with paper and pencil, you know how valuable a title and legend are to a chart. You can add those items and more to a chart in Excel. You can add text anywhere on your chart, plus lines and arrows, as you saw in Figure 8-1 in the previous Topic. Text added anywhere on your chart is called *unattached* (which is movable), and *attached* text (connected, for example, to an object such as a data marker) is not so movable (it moves with the object, if at all).

Before you can customize an element of your chart, you must first select the chart, just like selecting cells for a worksheet operation. With charts, you select an item or object by clicking on it. You can select an item (for example, a chart title), data series, gridline, axis, the plot area, or the entire chart. Items that are selected are identified by the small squares that enclose them. If the squares are black, they're known as *handles,* because you can move and size the selected item with your mouse. If the squares are white, you can't move or size your selection directly.

Finally, Excel provides you with its usual array of formatting options. You can choose the color, font, and pattern of most chart elements, including text, which can also be aligned in various ways.

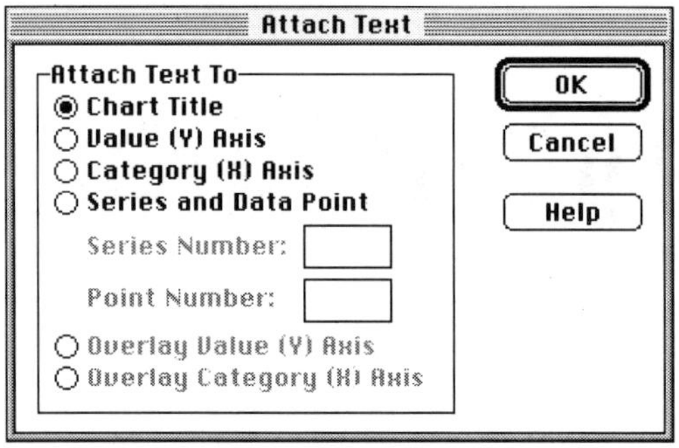

Figure 9-1: Choosing Attach Text from the Chart menu displays the Attach Text dialog box.

Adding titles

Everyone has a title, and so should your charts. Titles identify the subject matter of your chart. To add a title, make the chart you want to add a title to the active window. Then choose the Attach Text command from the Chart menu. When you choose Attach Text, the Attach Text dialog box appears, as shown in Figure 9-1.

While the Attach Text dialog box is open, notice that you use the Attach Text command to add text to other selected chart objects, such as the category (x) and value (y) axes, data series, or a data marker.

Select Title from the Chart menu and then choose OK. Excel displays white selection squares on the chart. Enter the title you want for the chart using the keyboard. If you want a subtitle, press the Command-Option-Enter keys simultaneously, and then type your subtitle. If you make a mistake, edit either title from the keyboard, or in conjunction with the mouse. When you're satisfied with your title(s), click your formula bar's Enter box or press Return, and Excel adds the titles to the chart. Notice that the text is selected, so you can format it at this time if you want.

Adding a legend

A legend provides a bridge between the data in your worksheet and your chart's data series. A legend identifies a range of data and its corresponding data series, so in most cases it's a good idea to include one in your chart.

Adding a legend to a chart is a two-step process and is as easy as adding titles. First, select Add Legend from the Chart menu. Excel then adds a legend to your chart along its right side. Second, select Legend from the Format menu. When you do, the Legend dialog box in Figure 9-2 appears.

The Legend command from the Format menu enables you to change the position of the legend if you want. Most legends appear along the bottom or right side of a chart, but you

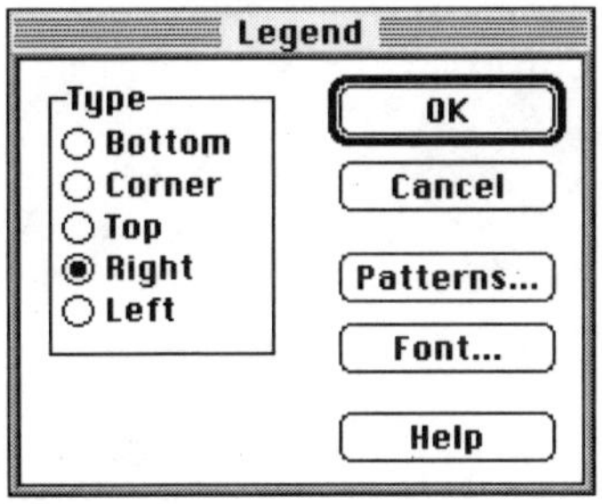

Figure 9-2: Selecting Legend from the Format menu displays the Legend dialog box.

may have a situation where you need a legend located elsewhere. A legend contains handles, so you can move it with the mouse.

Choose the position for your legend by selecting one of the location options in the Legend dialog box. After you select OK, Excel moves and sizes the legend appropriately for its new location. You can also move the legend by clicking and dragging on it with the mouse, but it will remain the same size.

Adding arrows

Another way you can draw attention to a data series (or any other chart element) is to add an arrow to it. To add an arrow to your chart, simply choose Add Arrow from the Chart menu. Excel adds an arrow as a selected object to your chart, with solid handles as shown in Figure 9-3. It's likely that you'll need to move and size the arrow because Excel has a way of simply plopping them down with abandon on your chart.

Move the arrow by clicking and dragging on the shaft of the arrow. When you have the arrow properly positioned, you can rotate it so that it points in another direction by clicking and then dragging on one of the handles in a circular direction. You can also

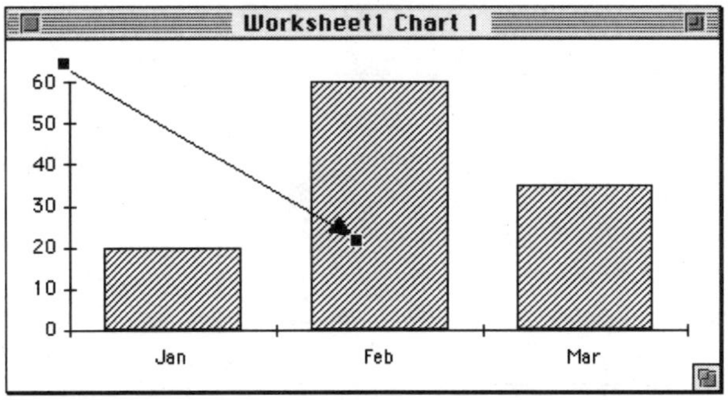

Figure 9-3: Adding an arrow to a chart using Add Arrow from the Chart menu.

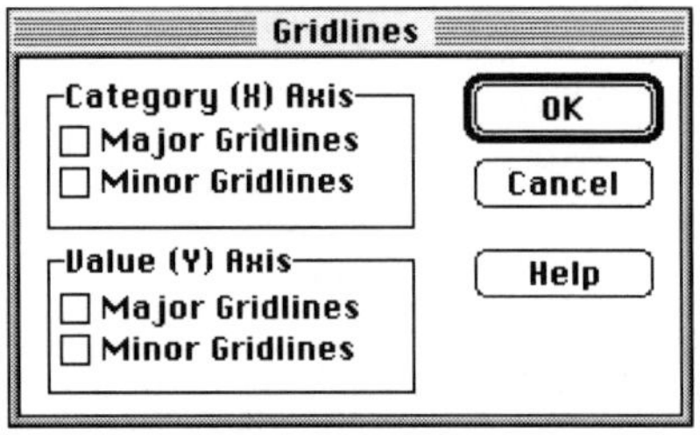

Figure 9-4: Choosing gridlines from the Chart menu displays the Gridlines dialog box.

change the arrow's size by clicking and dragging on a handle. Dragging toward the center of the arrow decreases its length; dragging away from the arrow increases its length.

Adding gridlines

With some charts it's sometimes challenging to determine the value a data marker represents, or which category label goes with which data marker. If you choose Gridlines from the Chart menu, the Gridlines dialog box shown in Figure 9-4 appears. Horizontal gridlines are displayed if you make a choice from the Value (Y) Axis box; vertical gridlines are displayed if you make a choice from the Category (X) Axis box.

You can add any number of gridlines to your chart depending on the level of detail you want to show. If your charts are relatively simple, Major Units is probably sufficient, as shown in Figure 9-5. More complex charts may need Major and Minor Units. Choosing OK adds the gridlines to the chart; you can format the gridlines, as discussed later in this Topic.

Describing data series

You may want to explain a data series if its magnitude differs greatly from other data series. You can display attached text or the underlying value near a data point. To do so, choose Attach Text from the Chart menu, and then choose "Series and Data Point."

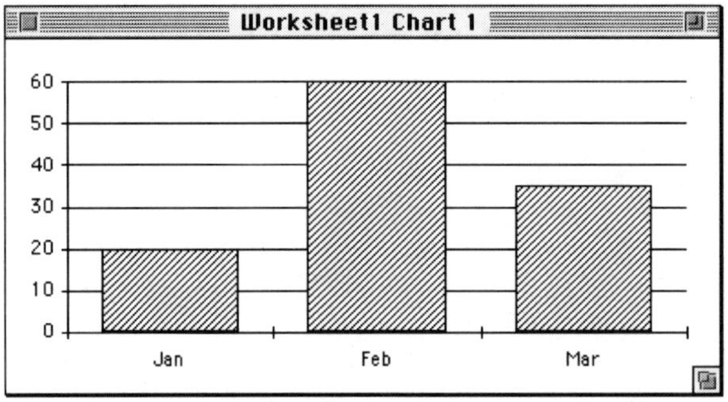

Figure 9-5: Displaying gridlines in Major Units using the Gridlines dialog box.

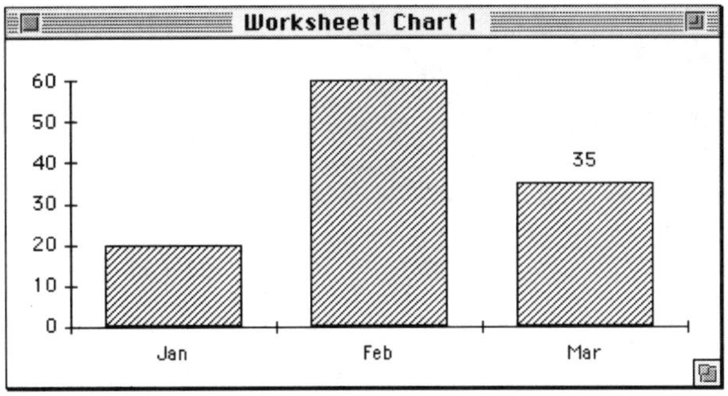

Figure 9-6: Displaying a value in a worksheet using the formula bar.

Specify the Series Number and Point Number in the respective text boxes. The Series Number refers to the data series in the worksheet used to create the chart. The Point Number refers to the individual value in the data series. When you choose OK, Excel displays the underlying value near the data series (where the value is displayed depends on the chart type) which is selected. You can display the value or use text (as shown in Figure 9-6) by activating the formula bar, deleting the value, and entering your text.

Changing axis settings

Recall from Topic 8 that Excel makes certain assumptions about data as it creates a chart — the number of columns vs. the number of rows to determine the range to use as the category labels, for example. Similarly, you've probably observed that Excel creates a range of values to use as the y-axis, based on the minimum and maximum values of the data. At times, however, you may want to specify the minimum and maximum y-axis values. For example, look at the chart in Figure 9-7.

By changing the range of values, or *scale*, of the y-axis, however, you can tweak the chart so the information it displays is a bit more meaningful.

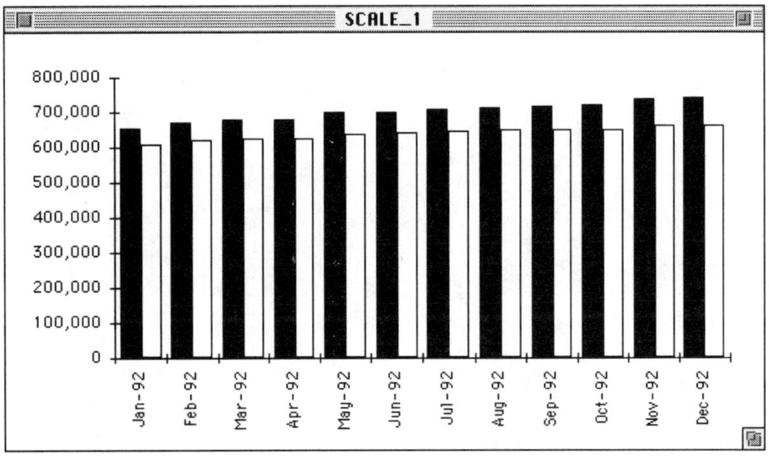

Figure 9-7: A chart whose y-axis settings have been changed.

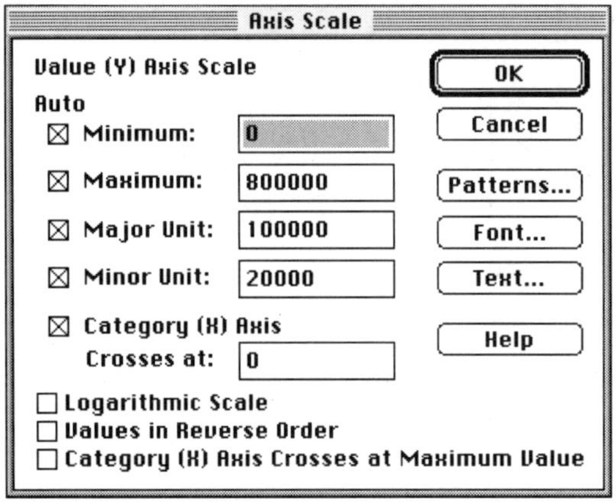

Figure 9-8: Choosing Scale from the Format menu displays the Axis Scale dialog box.

To change the scale of the y-axis, select the y-axis by clicking on it, and then choose Scale from the Format menu. The Axis Scale dialog box shown in Figure 9-8 appears. Notice that several types of chart attributes are automatically set for you — including the minimum and maximum values. To change the value Excel uses as its lower and upper chart values, uncheck the Minimum and the Maximum check boxes and enter a value in the appropriate text box (a check in the box tells Excel to determine the appropriate value for you). Be sure to use a number that makes sense. For example, if the smallest data point is 100, don't set a minimum value of 150, because if you do, 100 will not appear on the chart.

Setting a minimum value of 500,000 and choosing OK displays the chart in Figure 9-9. Notice how it's easier to see the month-to-month difference between the data points.

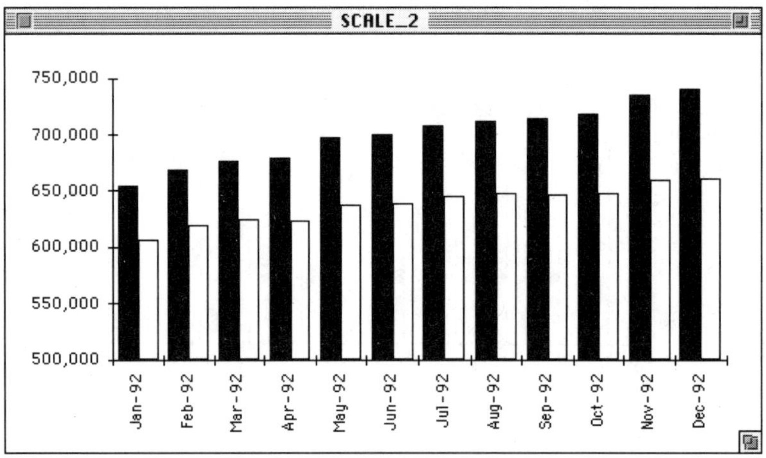

Figure 9-9: Using a minimum y-axis value of 500,000 displays this chart.

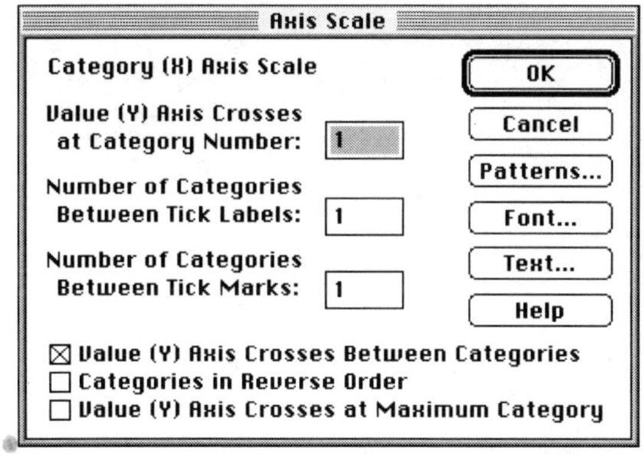

Figure 9-10: Choosing Scale from the Format menu with the x-axis selected displays these options in the Axis Scale dialog box.

You may have noticed the Major and Minor Units options in the Scale dialog box. These options allow you to specify how tick marks are displayed (the small horizontal lines on the y-axis). For Major Units, specify how much difference you want between the values on the y-axis. In Figure 9-9, this would be 50,000. Minor Units enables you to choose the number of tick marks between major units. The division of the major unit by the minor unit results in the number of tick marks displayed. Major and minor units are another chart feature that enables you to tailor the display of a chart so you can emphasize important points that might be missed using the automatic settings.

Similarly, you can choose which x-axis categories are labeled and the number of categories between each pair of tick marks, using "Number of categories between tick *labels*" and "Number of categories between tick *marks*," respectively. If you select the x-axis and choose Scale from the Format menu, these options appear in the Axis Scale dialog box shown in Figure 9-10. Most of the time, however, you'll want to keep the default setting of 1 for both options.

Formatting chart elements

The Format menu has a number of command options you can use to customize the display of your chart elements. Depending on the element and how you want it displayed, you can specify colors, font size and type, and weight, to name a few options.

You can format all the different chart elements using the same technique: You select the element you want to customize, and then choose the attribute and style from the corresponding dialog box. As you make your selections, watch the Sample box in the lower-right corner of the dialog box to get a sneak preview of how the chosen attribute will appear on the chart. Table 9-1 shows you the available formatting choices.

Table 9-1: Chart formatting options	
Attribute	***Format menu command***
Style, color, weight, patterns	Patterns
Font size and type	Font
Text alignment and orientation	Text
Reposition legend	Legend
Set scaling*	Scale
Increment of tick marks and labels*	Scale
Placement and display of tick marks and labels*	Patterns

* X- and y-axis only.

Changing values

Now that you have your chart up and running, you may want to change the data it relies on. You may want to do something as simple as changing a data point, or add or delete a data series from the chart.

If you want to change a data point your chart depends on, make the worksheet that contains your data the active document. Select the cell that contains the value, edit or type a new value, then click Enter or press Return. When you make the chart the active document, your chart will reflect the changed data.

If you want to add or delete a data series, you have two ways to go: By using the ChartWizard tool, or by selecting Edit Series from the Chart menu. The easiest way to add or delete a data series, when the data is located in contiguous rows or columns, is to use ChartWizard, as follows:

1. Make sure the chart and the worksheet the chart is linked to are open.
2. From the chart window, click the ChartWizard tool.
3. When the first ChartWizard window appears (as shown in Figure 9-11), select the data, including the series of data you want to add or delete, in the worksheet. Alternatively, you can enter the range address or name of the data in the Range text box.

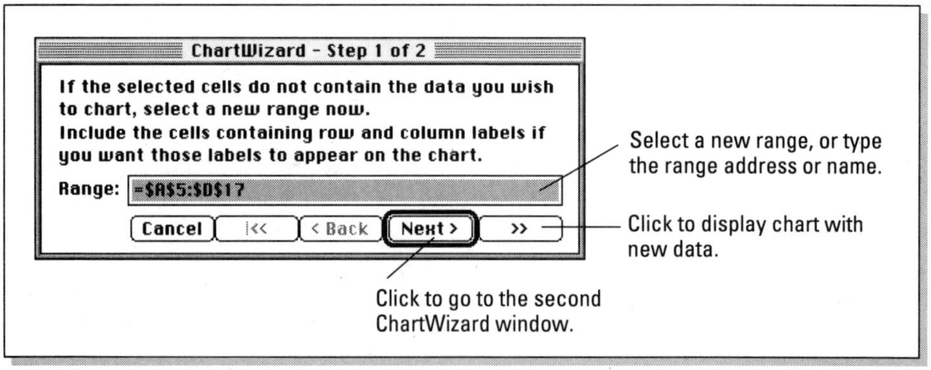

Figure 9-11: Clicking the ChartWizard tool displays the first ChartWizard window.

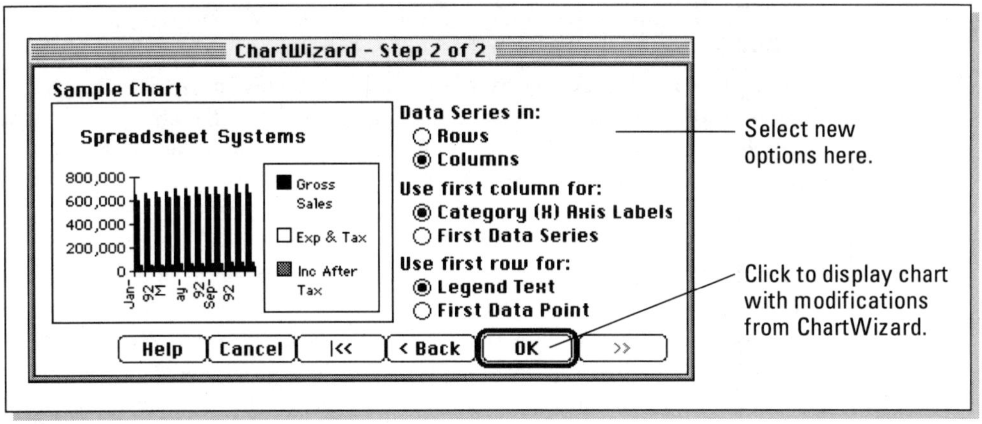

Figure 9-12: Clicking the Next button in the first ChartWizard window displays the second ChartWizard window.

4. If you only want to change the chart's data series, click the >> button. The chart appears with the new data series. If you want to specify how you'd like Excel to treat the data for charting purposes, click the Next button. The second of two ChartWizard windows appears, as shown in Figure 9-12.

5. Select the options you want then click OK. The chart appears with the new data series and the options (if any) you selected.

You may want to select the range of data from the worksheet before invoking Chart-Wizard. In this manner, you avoid having to move the first ChartWizard window to select the data with the mouse. This is especially useful when the chart was previously based on data in a contiguous range. Remember, however, to click the ChartWizard tool from the chart window when you finish selecting the data in the worksheet.

The other method is to select Edit Series from the Chart menu. The Edit Series option is more versatile than ChartWizard to change data series. Selecting Edit Series displays the dialog box in Figure 9-13.

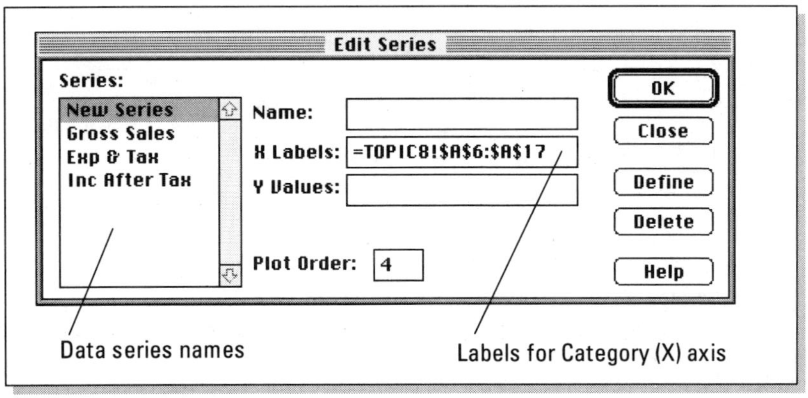

Figure 9-13: Choosing Edit Series from the Chart menu displays the Edit Series dialog box.

To change an existing data series, such as increasing or decreasing the number of data points in the series, select the series' name from the Series list box. Click the Y Values text box then select the values from the worksheet you want to use for that series (the worksheet will be displayed on screen). Clicking OK makes the change to the chart and closes the dialog box. If you want to make additional changes, click Define, and the Edit Series dialog box remains open.

To add a new series, select New Series from the Series box, then provide the Name, X Labels, and Y Values for the new series by clicking on the corresponding text box and selecting the cells in the worksheet. In addition, type a number in the Plot Order text box if you prefer one other than the one Excel suggests. Excel assigns plot order based on how the data is arranged on the worksheet: Data in rows is plotted and assigned a number beginning with the top row of values in the range; data in columns is plotted and assigned a number beginning with the far-left column. Click OK to add the series and close the dialog box, or Define to add the series and continue adding others. You can plot up to 255 data series on the chart.

To delete an existing data series, select the name of the series in the Series box then click Delete. Alternatively, click on one of the data series' elements — a bar, a column, or a point on a line. Select Clear from the Edit menu or press Delete. When the dialog box appears, select Series, then click OK.

Changing a value in the worksheet can affect the chart depending on whether or not it's open. If a worksheet and chart are open, and you change a value the chart is dependent on, Excel automatically updates your chart to reflect the change. If the chart is closed, and a value is changed, the chart is updated the next time you open it.

But what about the converse? What happens when you open a chart and not the worksheet the chart depends on? If you do, Excel displays an alert message, as shown in Figure 9-14, asking you if you want to update the chart with the most current data.

If you select Yes, Excel updates the chart using the most current data. If you select No, be careful because the chart continues to use the values it was originally based on, and may not reflect updated information.

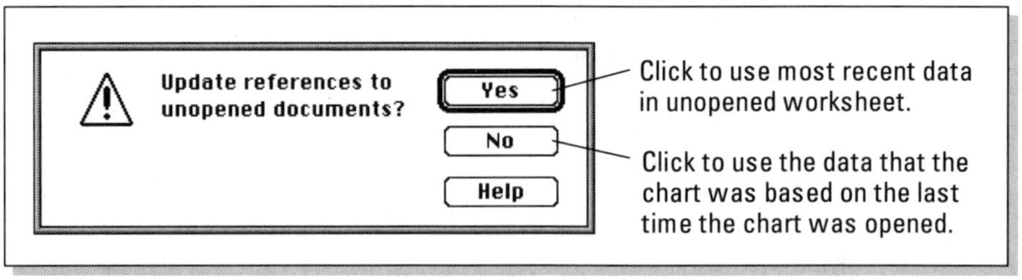

Figure 9-14: Opening a chart without opening the worksheet the chart depends on displays this alert message box.

Step-by-Step

In this section, you'll practice changing a chart type, adding a second title, changing the position of the legend, adding an arrow, adding text, and displaying gridlines to the chart you created in Topic 8. Remember, if you make a mistake, choose Undo from the Edit menu or close the worksheet without saving it by choosing the Close command from the File menu, and then open it again with the Open command from the File menu.

To open the TOPIC8 worksheet, do the following:

1. Start Excel, if you haven't already.

   The Worksheet1 worksheet appears.

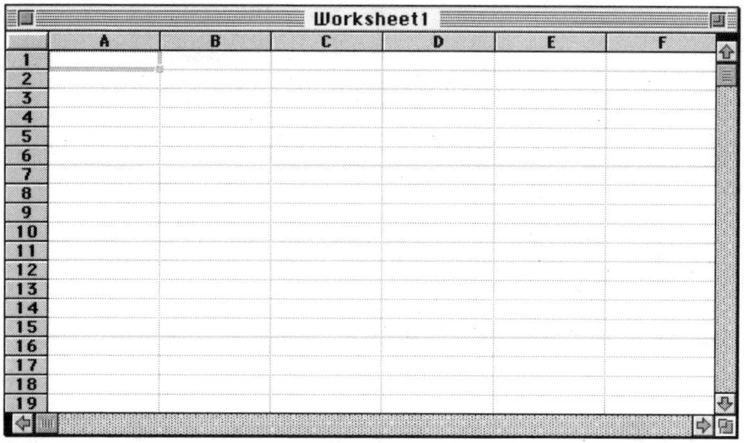

Figure 9-15: Starting Excel displays the Worksheet1 worksheet.

2. Choose the Open command from the File menu.

   The Open dialog box appears.

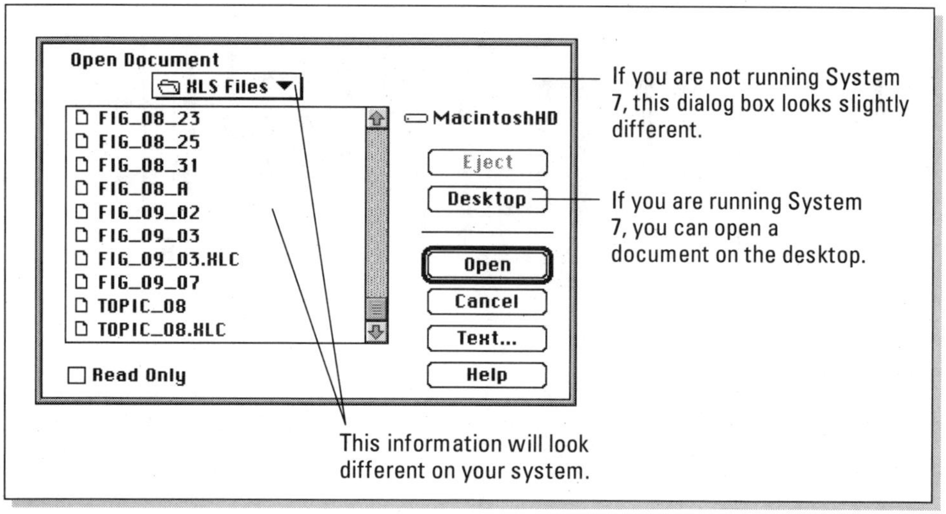

Figure 9-16: Choosing Open from the File menu displays the Open dialog box.

3. Select TOPIC8 and press Enter or choose Open.

   The TOPIC8 worksheet appears.

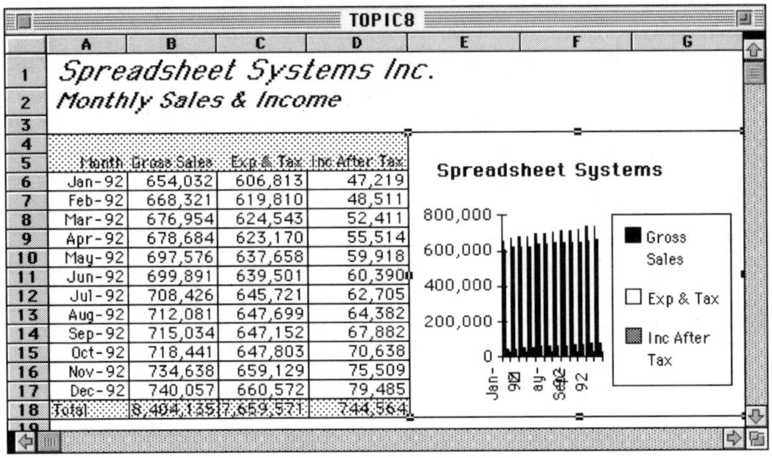

Figure 9-17: Selecting TOPIC8 from the Open dialog box displays the TOPIC8 worksheet.

4. Double-click the chart.

   The TOPIC8 CHART1 chart appears in its own window.

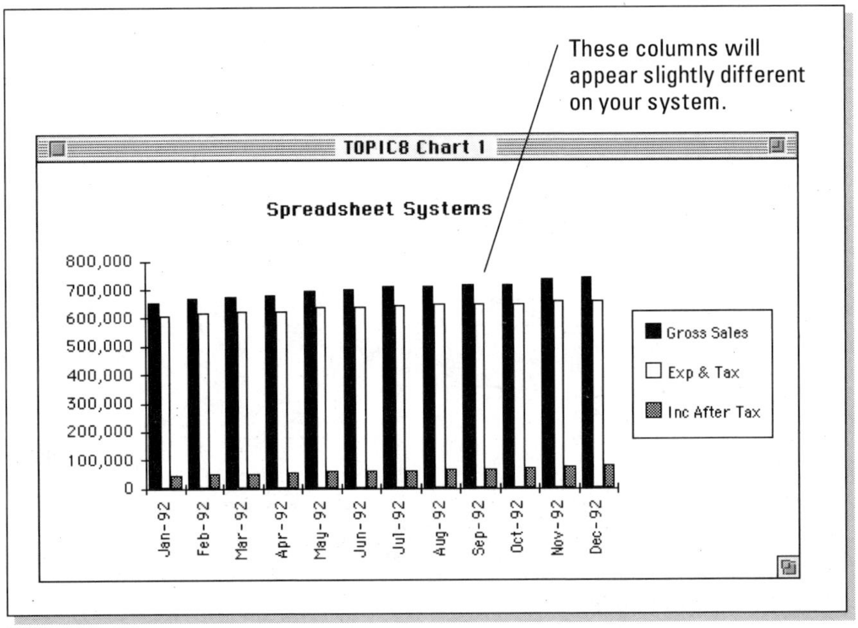

Figure 9-18: Double-clicking on the chart in the TOPIC8 worksheet displays the TOPIC8 CHART1 chart in its own window.

Changing chart type and format:

Step 1. Choose Combination from the Gallery menu.

The Chart Gallery dialog box appears.

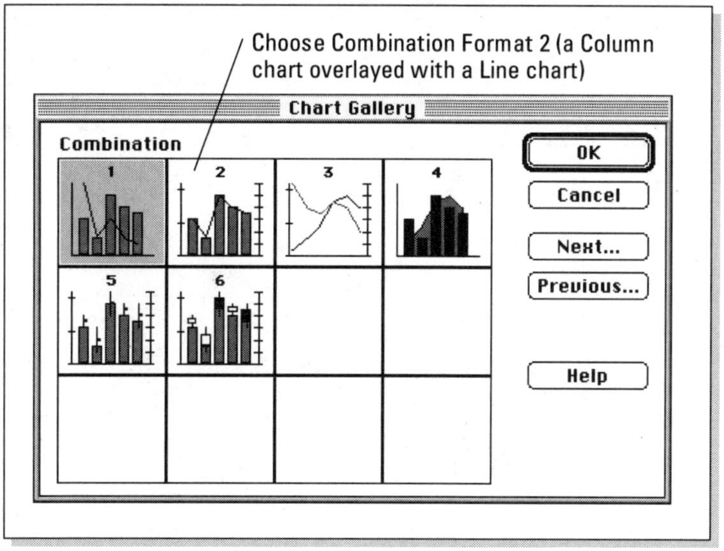

Figure 9-19: Choosing Combination from the Gallery menu displays the Chart Gallery dialog box.

Step 2. Select format 2 and choose OK.

Excel displays the chart with its new type and format.

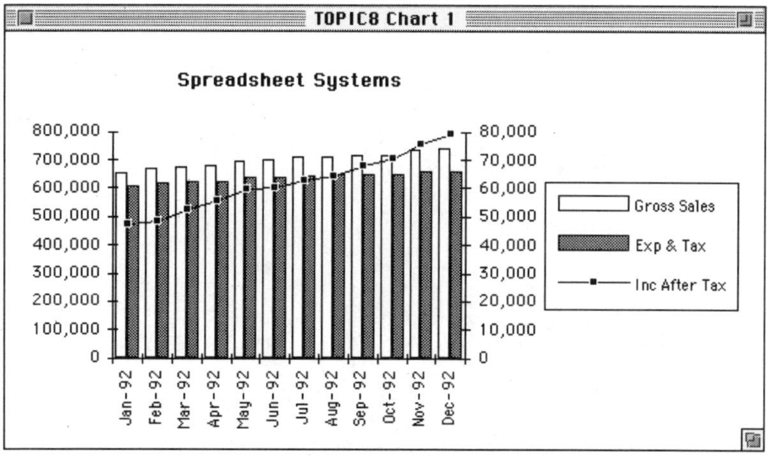

Figure 9-20: Choosing format 2 from the Combination Gallery dialog box results in a newly formatted TOPIC8 CHART1 chart.

Adding a subtitle to a chart:

Step 1. Select the chart's title.

The chart's title appears with handles.

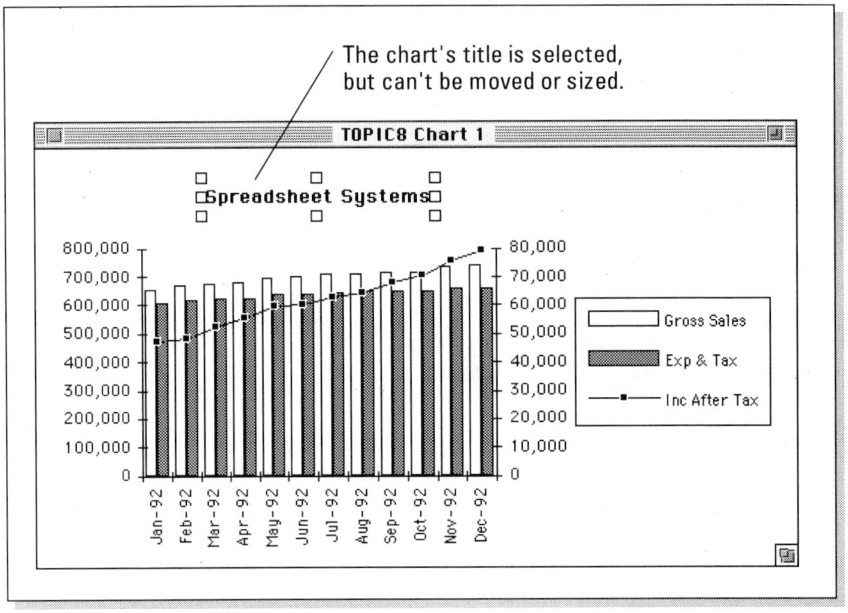

Figure 9-21: Selecting a chart's title displays handles around the text.

Step 2. Activate the formula bar (by clicking after the *s* in *Systems,* or by pressing Command-U), press Command-Option-Return, type `Results by Month`, and then click Enter or press Return.

The chart displays a title and a subtitle.

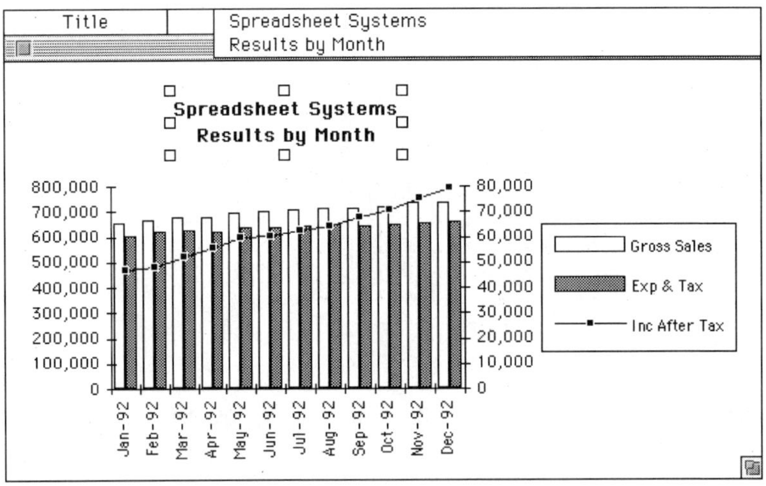

Figure 9-22: Adding a subtitle to a worksheet using the formula bar.

Relocating a chart's legend:

Step 1. Select the legend, and then choose Legend from the Format menu.

The Legend dialog box appears.

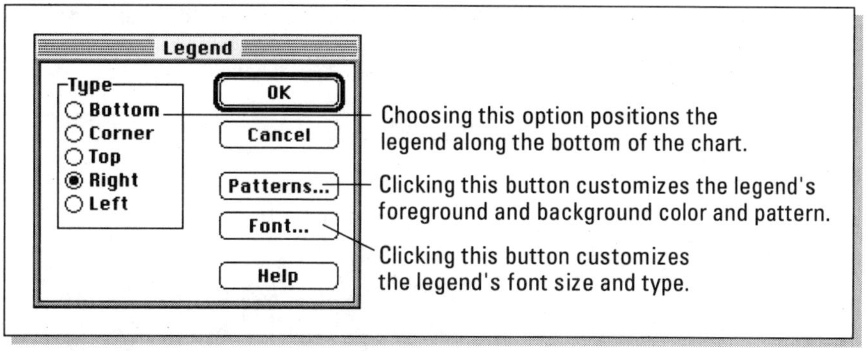

Figure 9-23: Selecting Legend from the Format menu displays the Legend dialog box.

Step 2. Select Bottom and then choose OK.

Excel displays the legend along the bottom of the chart.

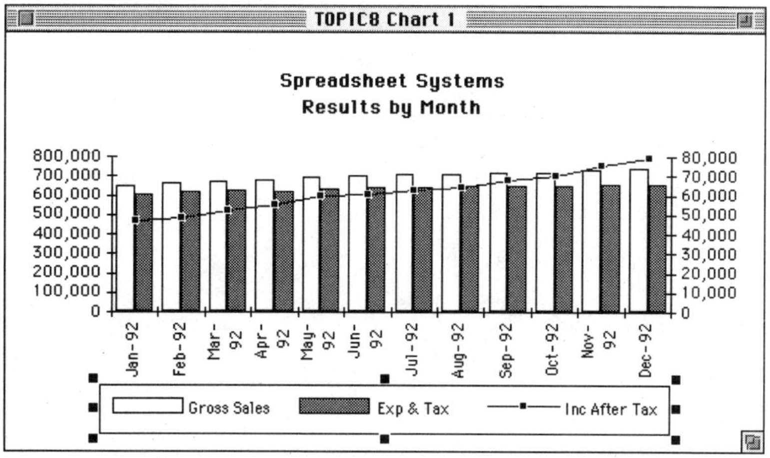

Figure 9-24: Relocating a chart's legend using the Bottom option from the Legend dialog box.

Adding arrows to a chart:

Step 1. Choose Add Arrow from the Chart menu.

Excel adds an arrow to the chart.

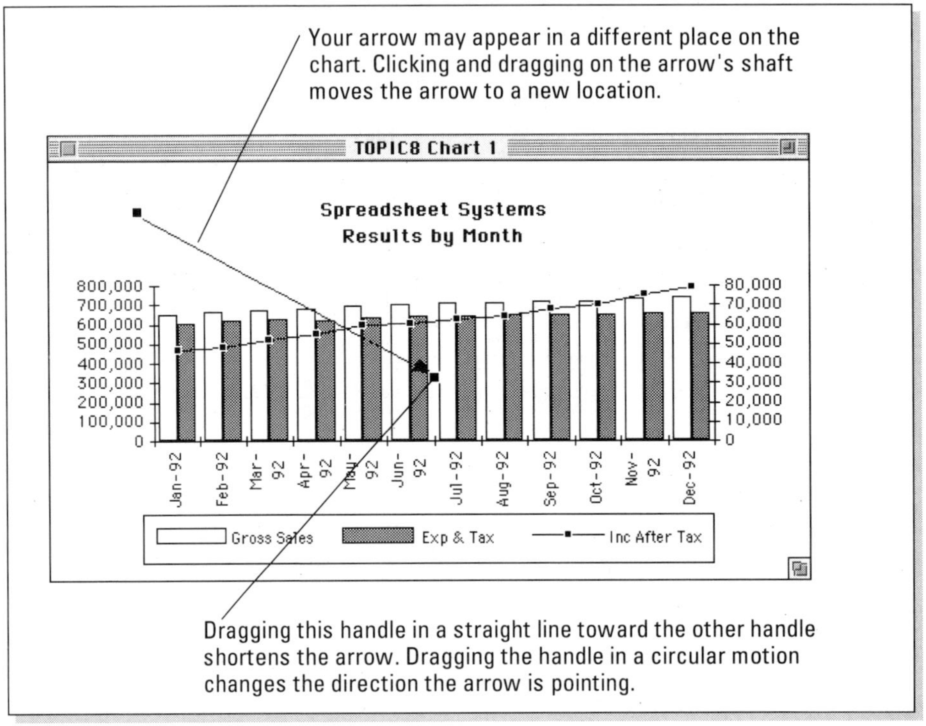

Figure 9-25: Choosing Add Arrow from the Chart menu displays an arrow on the chart.

Step 2. Move and size the arrow until it's positioned as shown in Figure 9-26 (click and drag on its shaft to move it; click and drag on a handle to change its size and the direction it's pointing).

The arrow appears in its new position.

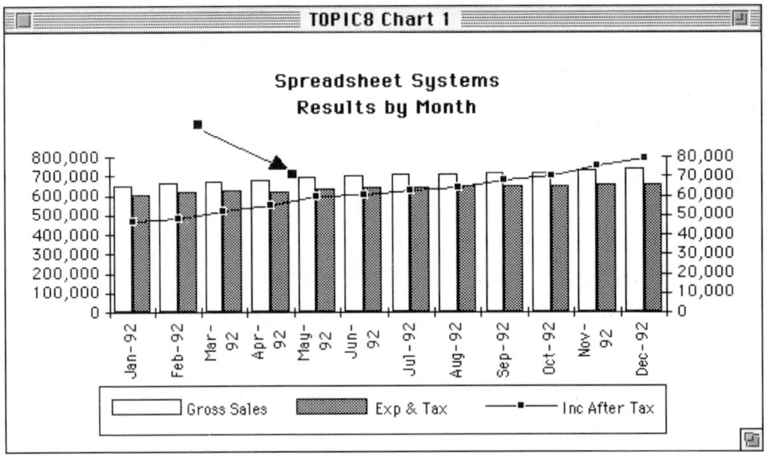

Figure 9-26: Clicking and dragging on an arrow's shaft and handles moves and sizes the arrow, respectively.

Part III
Intermediate Excel

Formatting arrows in a chart:

Step 1. Choose Patterns from the Format menu.

The Patterns dialog box appears.

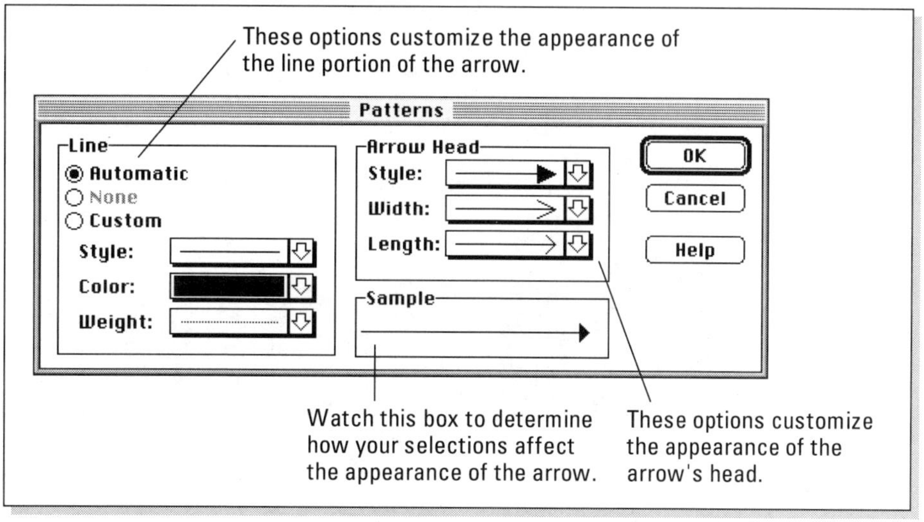

Figure 9-27: Choosing Patterns from the Format menu displays the Patterns dialog box.

Step 2. Change the Arrow Head format option from the Style pull-down menu in the Patterns dialog box (select the bottom option — the option with the solid arrow head), and then choose OK.

The arrow appears with its new formatting.

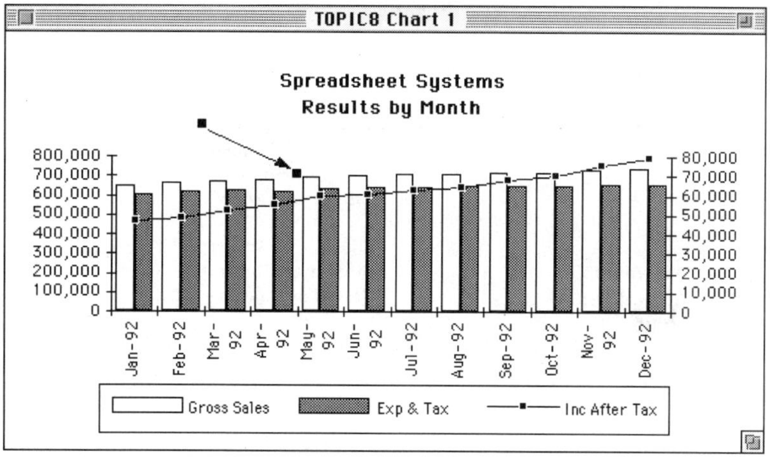

Figure 9-28: Formatting an arrow's head using the Arrow Head options in the Patterns dialog box.

Adding text to a chart:

Step 1. Type `$700K in Sales!` and then click Enter or press Return. Click and drag on the text (not on a handle) until it's near the arrow.

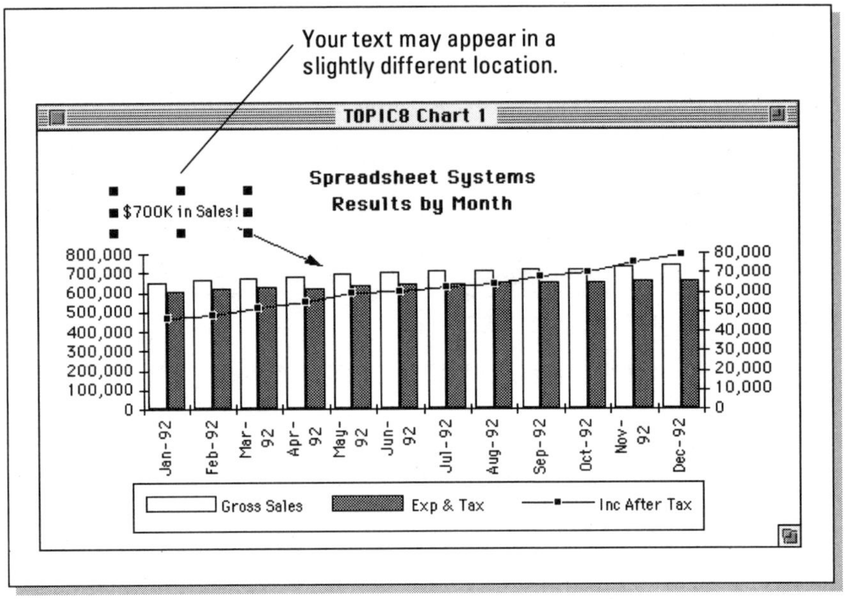

Figure 9-29: Adding text to a chart and moving it to a desired location.

Adding gridlines to a chart:

Step 1. Choose Gridlines from the Chart menu.

The Gridlines dialog box appears.

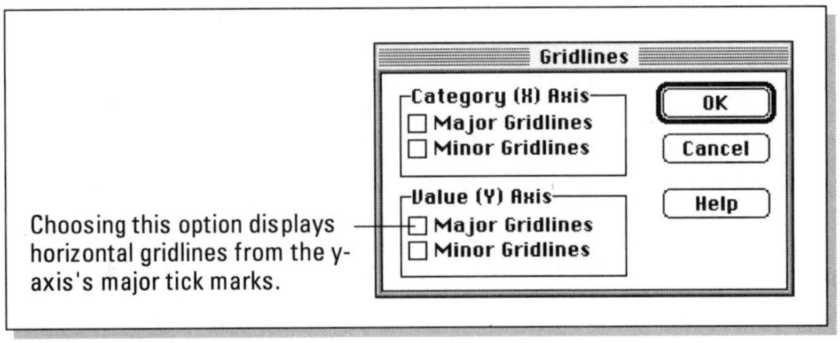

Figure 9-30: Choosing Gridlines from the Chart menu displays the Gridlines dialog box.

Step 2. Choose Major Gridlines from the Value (Y) Axis box, and then choose OK.

Excel displays the chart with a horizontal gridline from the major (y-axis) value's tick marks.

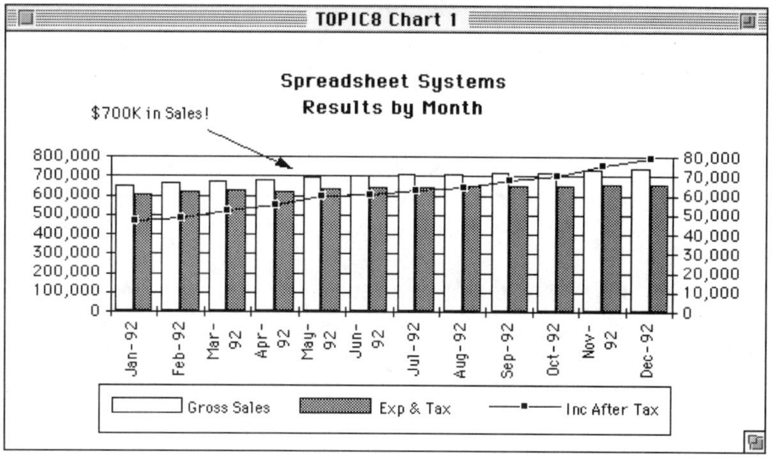

Figure 9-31: Adding Major Gridlines to a chart using the Gridlines dialog box.

Saving a customized chart:

Step 1. Choose Save As from the File menu, type TOPIC9 in the Save Chart as text box, and then click Save or press Return.

Excel saves the chart to disk.

Quick Tips

This section provides you with tips on how to customize the charts you create in Excel to your liking.

Selecting the chart and plot area

Use the Select Chart (or Command-A) and Plot Area commands to select the chart and plot area (the rectangular area containing the data markers of the chart), respectively, from the Chart menu.

Selecting a single data marker

To select a single data marker, press Command as you click the data marker.

Specifying Major and Minor Units

When using the Scale command from the Format menu, entering the same number as the Major Unit for the Minor Unit makes tick marks invisible. When specifying a Minor Unit, be sure to use a number that can divide the Major Unit evenly.

Text movement in data series

Though you can't move text that describes a data series, the text will move with the data series if the data itself moves or changes.

Attaching text to an axis or data point

If you plan on attaching text to an axis or data point, select the axis or data point first. Excel then automatically selects the corresponding option for you in the Attach Text dialog box.

Accessing Format menu dialog boxes

All Format commands except Patterns enable you to access other Format menu dialog boxes by choosing the appropriate button.

Accessing the Patterns dialog box quickly

Double-click a chart element to quickly access the Patterns dialog box.

Creating "what-if" scenarios

You can play "what-if" games by clicking and dragging on a data marker. The corresponding data in the worksheet will change accordingly.

Displaying major tick marks in combination charts

In combination charts with two y-axes, use the Patterns command from the Format menu to display major tick marks for the left y-axis, and minor tick marks for the right y-axis.

Previewing a chart

Select Print Preview from the File menu to determine how your chart will appear on paper before it is printed.

Summary

- Charts can be customized with titles, a legend, arrows, gridlines, and text.
- Text can be attached or unattached.
- Attached text is not movable while unattached text can appear anywhere on the chart and can be moved and sized.
- A chart element must be selected before you can customize it with formatting, such as adding or changing a color, its font, or a pattern.
- A chart legend identifies the worksheet data that appears as a data series in a chart.
- To change a value that appears as part of a data series in a chart, make the worksheet that contains the value the active document. Select the cell that contains the value, and enter a new value. When you make the chart the active document, the chart will display the new value.
- Data series can be added to or deleted from a chart using the ChartWizard tool or by selecting Edit Series from the Chart menu.

Topic 10
Adding Drawings To Your Worksheets

Overview

If you're a new Excel user and just completed Topic 9, you may be wanting to add lines and arrows to worksheets as you did with charts. On the other hand, if you're an Excel veteran, you may be wondering what Microsoft did with the drawing tools on the Standard toolbar.

Well, want or wonder no more. You can add all sorts of chart-like objects to a worksheet to get your reports noticed, such as lines, arrows, circles, and so on, as shown in Figure 10-1. And the drawing tools available in earlier versions of Excel have been expanded and moved to their own toolbar — the Drawing toolbar.

This Topic introduces you to drawing on a worksheet — how to create, format, move, size, and delete drawings, often called objects.

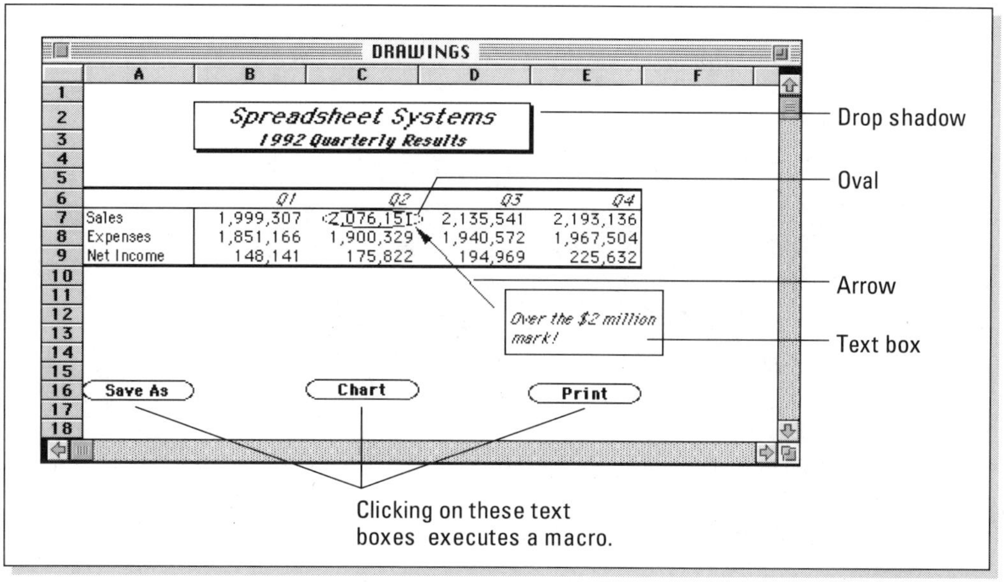

Figure 10-1: A example of objects you can add to an Excel chart.

Creating objects with the Drawing toolbar

The Drawing toolbar enables you to add drawings to a worksheet. You were introduced to the Drawing toolbar in Topic 7 as a way to add drop shadows to a worksheet.

If the Drawing toolbar isn't currently displayed on screen, choose Toolbars from the Options menu, and the Toolbars dialog box shown in Figure 10-2 appears.

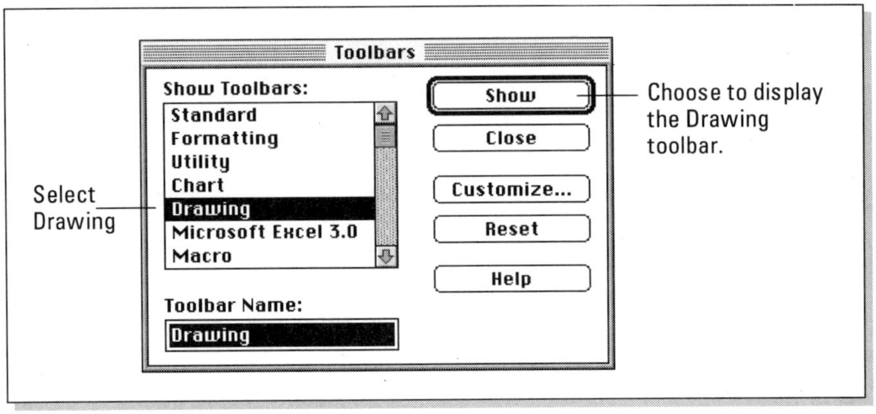

Figure 10-2: Choosing Toolbars from the Options menu displays the Toolbars dialog box.

Select Drawing from the Toolbars dialog box, and then choose Show, which displays the Drawing toolbar, as shown in Figure 10-3.

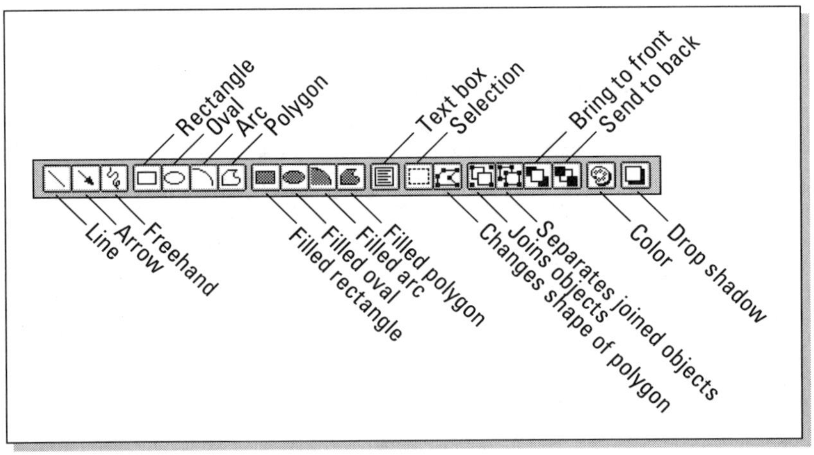

Figure 10-3: Choosing Show from the Toolbars dialog box displays the Drawing toolbar.

In addition to the drawings you can create with the Drawing tools shown in Figure 10-3, the following keys used with the mouse offer you further options:

Tool	***Shift key***	***Command key***
Line	Horizontal, vertical, or 45° angles	Aligns object to gridlines
Oval	Circle	Aligns object to gridlines
Rectangle	Square	Aligns object to gridlines

After you have the Drawing toolbar displayed, you can add drawings to the worksheet by doing the following:

1. Click the tool with the corresponding object that you want to draw. Click the tool twice if you want to add more than one object at the same time.

Cross-hair

2. When the mouse pointer changes to a cross-hair, position it at the point in the worksheet where you want to begin drawing.
3. Drag the mouse until the shape of the object is the size you want, and then release the mouse button. If you've created more than one object, click the tool to stop drawing.

When you release the mouse button, the object is placed on the worksheet. In the case of text boxes, a blinking cursor appears so you can enter your text. Text automatically wraps to the next line when the cursor reaches the right side of the box.

After you draw the object, the object is selected — it appears with selection handles. And as you may recall from Topic 9, because the handles are solid (black), you can delete, format, move, or size the object.

Selecting singular objects

Before you can manipulate an object in a worksheet, you must — that's right, you guessed it — select the object first. If you've just added an object to a worksheet, the object is already selected and ready to go. But if you want to go back to a previous object and change its size, for example, you'll need to select it.

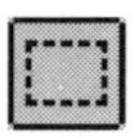
Selection tool

To select a single object, move the mouse pointer to any side of the object. When the mouse pointer changes to a black arrow, click the mouse button. Alternatively, you can use the Selection tool on the Drawing toolbar. To use the Selection tool, click it and position the mouse pointer on one corner of the area near the object. Click and drag the mouse until the selection rectangle encloses the object, and then release the mouse button. Either way you choose to select an object, the object appears with selection handles.

Selecting multiple objects

To select multiple objects, select the first object as you would normally. To select subsequent objects, press Shift and click on them if you're using the mouse, or drag if you're using the Selection tool. Each additional object that becomes selected displays black selection handles. Selecting multiple objects is an essential step when you want to group several objects, as discussed later.

If you want to remove an object from a selection, you need only reverse engines. Press Shift, and then click on the selected object you don't want selected. Or use Shift with the Selection tool and draw the selection rectangle around the objects you want deselected. Releasing the mouse button deselects the objects.

Now that you know how to select objects, you're ready to learn how to manipulate drawn objects.

Manipulating objects

After you've drawn an object in the worksheet, you may feel the object would look better moved over to the right a little. Or maybe you'd like to make the object a little larger. Fine-tuning drawings is a simple process and saves you time by not having to re-create the object from scratch.

Moving an object

There are two ways you can move an object in a worksheet. To move an object a short distance from its current location, follow these steps:

1. Select the object you want to move.
2. Place the mouse pointer on an edge of the object, but not on a selection handle.
3. Drag the object to its new location, and then release the mouse button.

Pressing Shift as you drag with the mouse limits movement of the object to horizontal and vertical directions, and pressing Command while you drag with the mouse aligns the object to the worksheet gridlines in its new position.

If you need to move an object a great distance from its current location, or to a different worksheet entirely, you can cut and paste the object just as you would a cell entry. To cut and paste an object, do the following:

1. Select the object you want to move.
2. Choose Cut from the Edit menu or shortcut menu, or press F2 or Command-X.

The drawing shortcut menu

When an object is selected, the shortcut menu contains several Edit and Format menu options, as well as several new options relative to drawings, as shown in the following figure. Remember, however, to display the shortcut menu by pressing Option-Command and clicking the mouse.

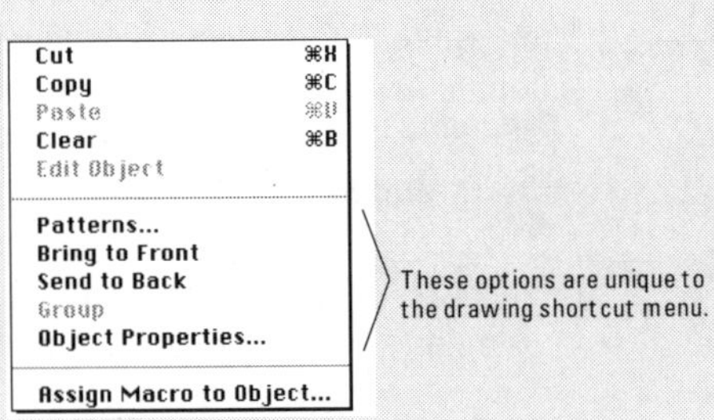

3. Make the worksheet you want the object pasted to the active worksheet.
4. Select the cell (or other object) you want to paste the object to.
5. Choose Paste from the Edit menu or shortcut menu, or press F4 or Command-V.

When you cut the object from a worksheet, the object disappears and is placed on the Clipboard. When you paste the object, the object's upper-left selection handle appears over the selected cell.

Changing an object's size

Changing an object's size is much like changing its position. The major difference is that you drag on a handle, instead of an edge. To change an object's size, do the following:

1. Select the object whose size you want to change.
2. Place the mouse pointer on a selection handle of the object — the mouse pointer changes to a line with an arrowhead on each end, or to a cross-hair for lines and arrows.
3. Drag the mouse away from the object to increase the object's size; drag toward the center of the object to decrease the object's size. Release the mouse button to stop sizing.

   Pressing Shift while dragging increases or decreases the size of the object proportionally. As before, pressing Command while dragging aligns the object to the worksheet gridlines.

Becoming too attached to your drawings?

When you add a drawing to a worksheet, it isn't entered into a cell like a value or text. In a manner of speaking, however, it's "attached" to the underlying cells, like a rubber band stretched between two or more nails. As a result, if you insert or delete cells, or change the height or width of rows or columns, the drawing will expand or contract. For example, a circle you drew may turn into an oval if you insert a row or two below the circle. The good news is that a drawing can also "float" unattached above the worksheet, remaining unharmed by any cell activity below the drawing.

You can choose the way drawings behave relative to row and column changes by choosing Object Properties from the Format menu. When you do, the Object Properties dialog box appears, as shown in the following figure.

By default, objects are attached to cells and change size and position as do their underlying cells. You may find this default setting beneficial if you have a line or an arrow pointing at a cell — the line increases or decreases in length while pointing in the right direction. In other cases, however, you may want a line or shape to move or stay put, but remain the same size in either case. Selecting the second and third options from the Object Properties dialog box gives you control over the moving and sizing of an object.

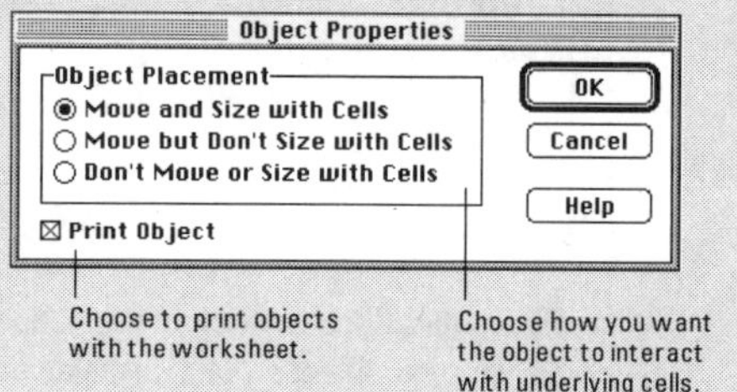

Formatting drawings

After you have the drawing at the location and in the size you want, you may want to format it. You can format objects in the same manner as formatting ranges, which you learned about in Topics 7 and 9. Depending on the object you want to format, you can change its border, color, and interior pattern if it's a shape, or its line and arrowhead style if it's a line or an arrow. Choosing Patterns from the Format menu or shortcut menu displays the appropriate dialog box for the object you want to format.

Selecting a text box to format gives you two more formatting options. You can select the font and alignment for the object's text by choosing Font and Text, respectively, from the Format menu or shortcut menu. Don't forget to select the object, and then the text, first.

Protecting an object

You spend a great deal of time getting your objects just right, and it's only natural to want to protect them. To protect your time investment, you can prevent unauthorized or accidental changes to your work of art. Choosing Object Protection from the Format menu displays the Object Protection dialog box shown in Figure 10-4.

The Locked option indicates the selected object is a candidate for protecting. The next step is to choose Protect Document from the Options menu, which displays the dialog box in Figure 10-5.

When the Objects box is selected, clicking OK protects the object from change by preventing the object from being selected. A password isn't necessary, but if you do use one, making changes to a locked object (or cell) requires that you reenter the password in the Options Unprotect Document dialog box exactly the way you typed it originally (including upper- and lowercase characters). If you forget the password and want to make changes to a protected object, you have to re-create the object from scratch or (preferably) copy it from another worksheet. Recording and storing passwords in a safe place is a good practice to acquire.

If you don't use a password, simply choosing Unprotect Document from the Options menu unprotects the object so you can make changes again.

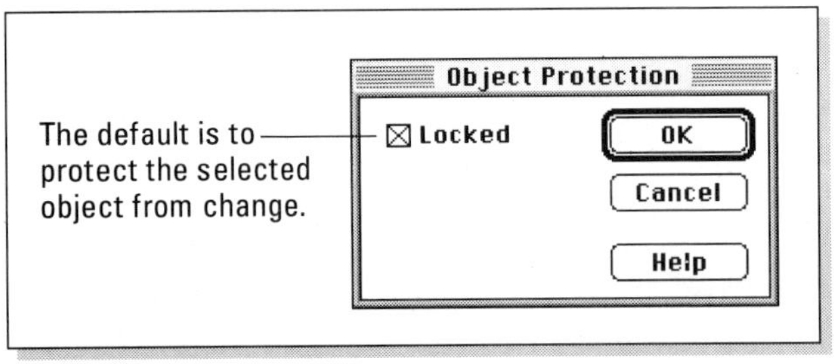

Figure 10-4: Choosing Object Protection from the Format menu displays the Object Protection dialog box.

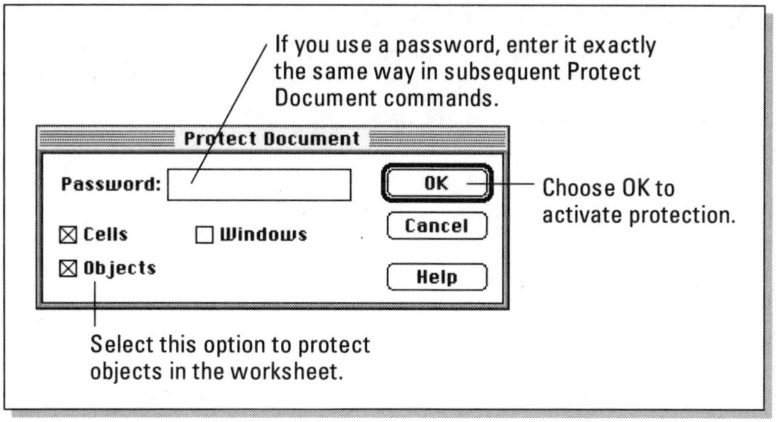

Figure 10-5: Choosing Protect Document from the Options menu displays the Protect Document dialog box.

Copying an object

Making copies of a line or shape is similar to moving an object. To duplicate an object near the original, use the following steps:

1. Select the object you want to copy.
2. Place the mouse pointer on an edge of the object, but not on a selection handle.
3. Press Option. The mouse pointer appears as a black arrow with a plus sign (+).

Arrow with plus sign

4. Drag the copy of the object to the desired location, and then release the mouse button.

As with moving, pressing Shift as you drag the object with the mouse limits movement to horizontal and vertical directions, and pressing Command while you drag the object aligns the copied object to the worksheet gridlines.

If you want the copied object in another area of the worksheet, dragging to the edge of the worksheet scrolls the screen so you can place the object accordingly. Or you can copy and paste by doing the following:

1. Select the object you want to copy.
2. Choose Copy from the Edit menu or shortcut menu.
3. Make the worksheet you want the copied object pasted to the active worksheet.
4. Select the cell (or other object) you want to paste the copied object to.
5. Choose Paste from the Edit menu or shortcut menu.

Rearranging overlapping objects

Catching object mania may lead to so many objects on the worksheet that they end up overlapping each other. Overlapping objects may partially or fully obscure other objects on the worksheet, making selection impossible.

Two commands on the Format menu solve this problem. The Send to Back and Bring to Front commands display the selected object under, and on top of, respectively, all other objects.

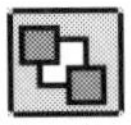

Send to Back tool

Bring to Front tool

To rearrange the display of overlapping objects, do the following:

1. Select the object you want to reorder within overlapping objects.
2. Choose Send to Back or Bring to Front from the Format menu or shortcut menu. Alternatively, click the Send to Back or Bring to Front tools on the Drawing toolbar.

And that's all there is to rearranging overlapping objects. You can continue rearranging the position of overlapping objects as many times as you need until you get the display you're looking for. You can also use overlapping objects to create custom objects, such as drop shadows. A drop shadow created in this manner enables you to control the amount of shadow.

To create a drop shadow using overlapping objects, place a text box in the worksheet. After you type the text, draw a filled rectangle on top of the text box. The filled rectangle should be about the same size as the text box, as shown in Figure 10-6. If you want, you can change the rectangle's fill pattern by using the Patterns option on the Format menu.

Placing the filled rectangle under the text box with Send to Back displays the objects shown in Figure 10-7. The width and length of the filled rectangle (the shadow) can be changed by selecting the filled rectangle and dragging on a handle. Finally, choose "Move

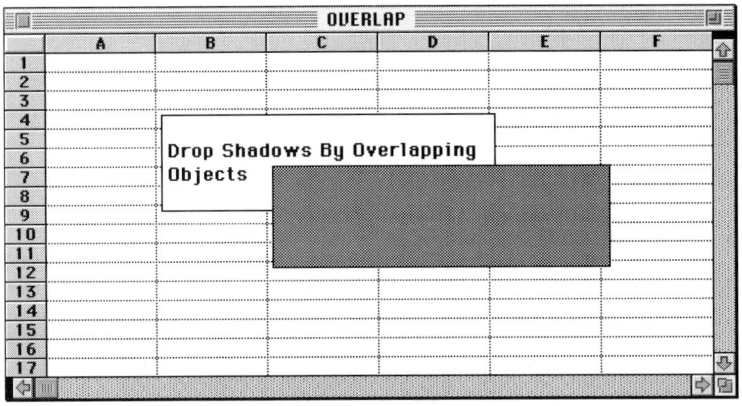

Figure 10-6: Creating a drop shadow using overlapping objects.

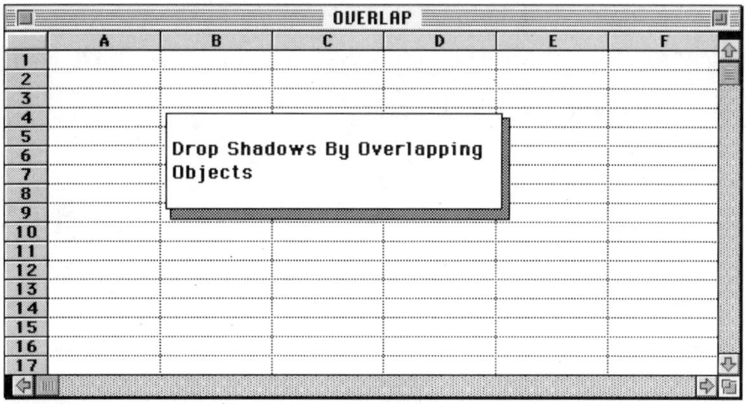

Figure 10-7: Placing a filled rectangle under a text box using Send to Back.

but Don't Size with Cells" from the Object Properties dialog box so the drop shadow is able to traverse the worksheet as needed, without causing unwanted changes in its dimensions.

If you're satisified with the drop shadow, you can also combine the objects into one to maintain their relative shape, size, and position to each other, as discussed in the next section.

Combining objects

Combining separate objects lets you move, size, and apply formats to a single object. To group multiple objects into one, use the following steps:

1. Click the Selection tool.
2. Select all of the objects you want to combine.
3. Choose Group from the Format menu or shortcut menu, or click the Group tool.

Group tool

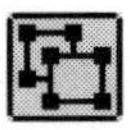

Ungroup tool

The objects are now one single object. If you want to format or perform another operation on a formerly individual object, you'll need to separate all the objects (at least temporarily). To separate all of the objects, follow the above steps, only use Ungroup from the Format menu or shortcut menu, or click the Ungroup tool.

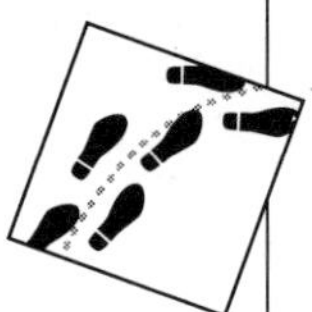

Step-by-Step

In this section, you'll practice drawing on the worksheet from Topic 7 (or a worksheet of your own choosing). Specifically, you'll add a drop shadow, draw an oval and an arrow, and add a text box. If you make a mistake or want to start over, choose Undo from the Edit menu or close the worksheet without saving it and open it again with the Close and Open commands from the File menu, respectively.

To open the Topic7 Worksheet, do the following:

1. Start Excel if you haven't already, or make Excel the active application.

   The Worksheet1 worksheet appears.

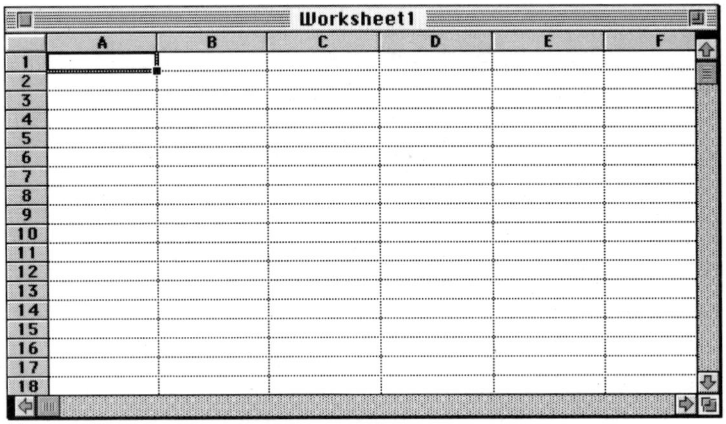

Figure 10-8: Starting up Excel displays the Worksheet1 worksheet.

2. Choose the Open command from the File menu.

   The Open dialog box appears.

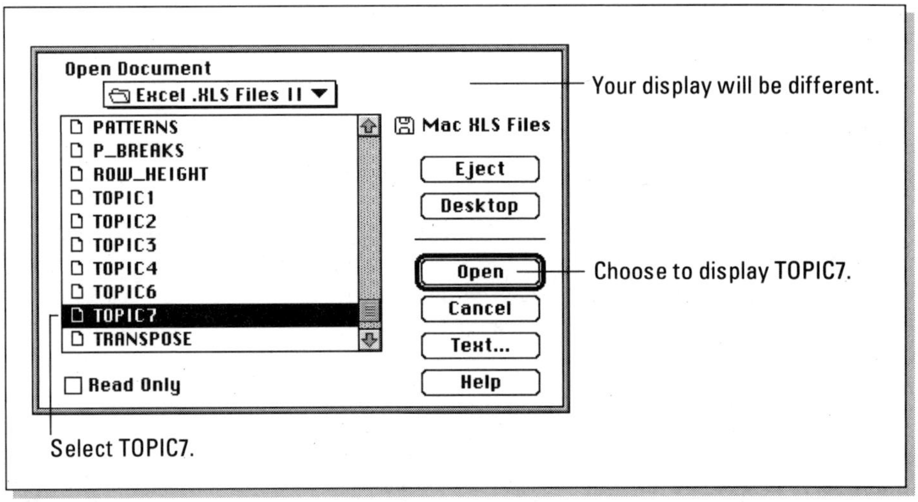

Figure 10-9: Choosing Open from the File menu displays the Open dialog box.

3. Select TOPIC7 and press Return or choose Open.

   The TOPIC7 worksheet appears.

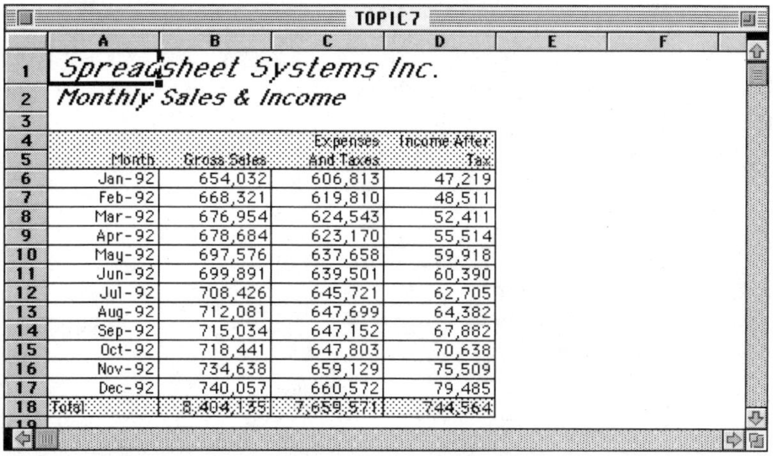

Month	Gross Sales	Expenses And Taxes	Income After Tax
Jan-92	654,032	606,813	47,219
Feb-92	668,321	619,810	48,511
Mar-92	676,954	624,543	52,411
Apr-92	678,684	623,170	55,514
May-92	697,576	637,658	59,918
Jun-92	699,891	639,501	60,390
Jul-92	708,426	645,721	62,705
Aug-92	712,081	647,699	64,382
Sep-92	715,034	647,152	67,882
Oct-92	718,441	647,803	70,638
Nov-92	734,638	659,129	75,509
Dec-92	740,057	660,572	79,485
Total	8,404,135	7,659,571	744,564

Figure 10-10: Selecting TOPIC7 from the Open dialog box displays the TOPIC7 worksheet.

Displaying the Drawing toolbar:

Step 1. Choose Toolbars from the Options menu, select Drawing, and press Return or choose Open.

Excel displays the Drawing toolbar.

Figure 10-11: Choosing Drawing from the Toolbars dialog box displays the Drawing toolbar.

Adding a drop shadow:

Step 1. Select the range A1:D2.

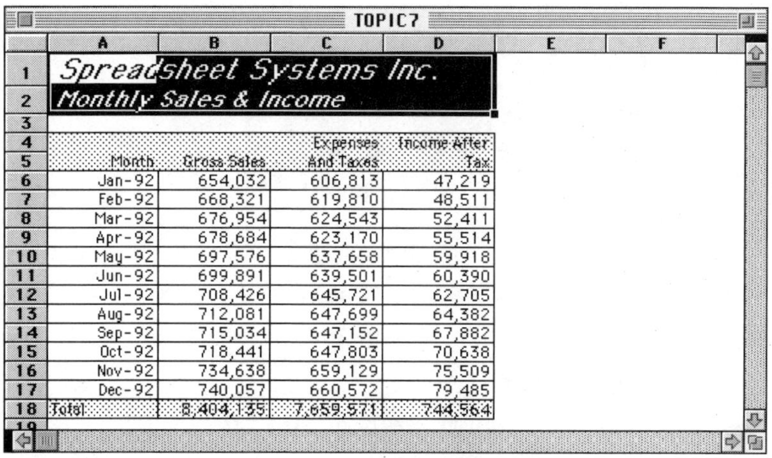

Month	Gross Sales	Expenses And Taxes	Income After Tax
Jan-92	654,032	606,813	47,219
Feb-92	668,321	619,810	48,511
Mar-92	676,954	624,543	52,411
Apr-92	678,684	623,170	55,514
May-92	697,576	637,658	59,918
Jun-92	699,891	639,501	60,390
Jul-92	708,426	645,721	62,705
Aug-92	712,081	647,699	64,382
Sep-92	715,034	647,152	67,882
Oct-92	718,441	647,803	70,638
Nov-92	734,638	659,129	75,509
Dec-92	740,057	660,572	79,485
Total	8,404,135	7,659,571	744,564

Figure 10-12: Selecting range A1:D2 in the TOPIC7 worksheet.

Step 2. Click the Drop shadow tool.

Range A1:D2 appears with a drop shadow.

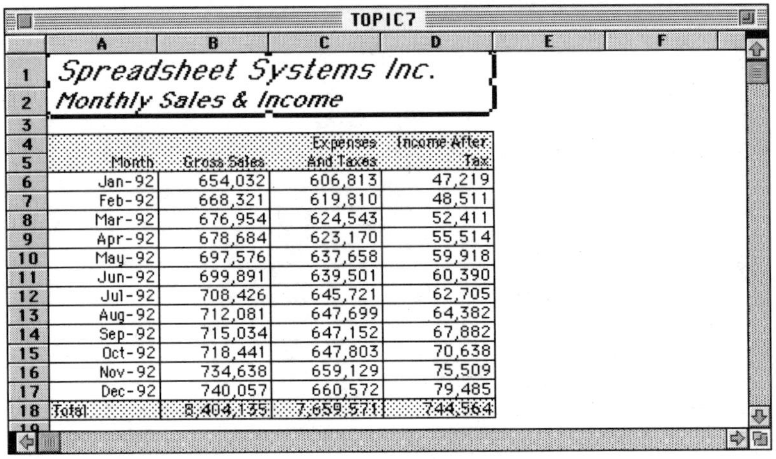

Month	Gross Sales	Expenses And Taxes	Income After Tax
Jan-92	654,032	606,813	47,219
Feb-92	668,321	619,810	48,511
Mar-92	676,954	624,543	52,411
Apr-92	678,684	623,170	55,514
May-92	697,576	637,658	59,918
Jun-92	699,891	639,501	60,390
Jul-92	708,426	645,721	62,705
Aug-92	712,081	647,699	64,382
Sep-92	715,034	647,152	67,882
Oct-92	718,441	647,803	70,638
Nov-92	734,638	659,129	75,509
Dec-92	740,057	660,572	79,485
Total	8,404,135	7,659,571	744,564

Figure 10-13: Adding a drop shadow to a worksheet using the Drop shadow tool.

Drawing an oval:

Step 1. Click the Oval tool, and then click the mouse button near the top of the 7 in cell B12. Drag the mouse to the right and then release the button.

Excel adds an oval over cell B12.

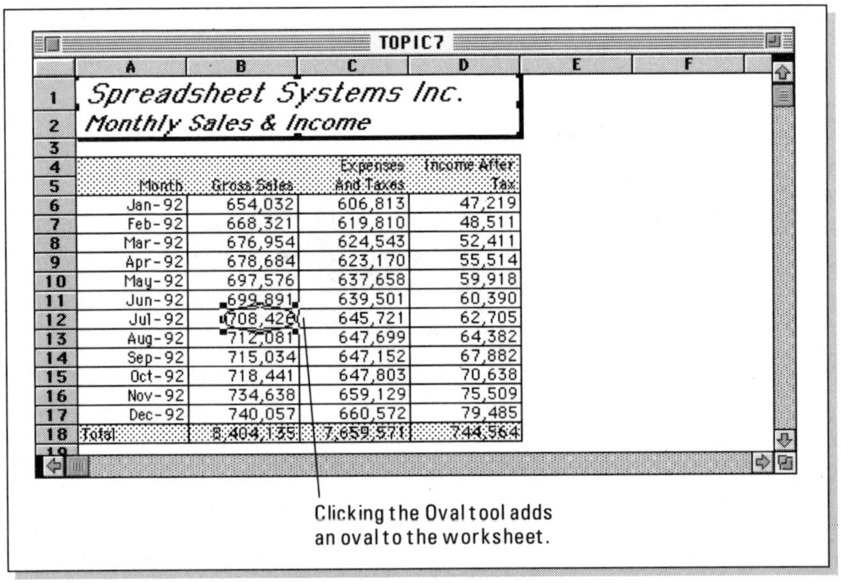

Month	Gross Sales	Expenses And Taxes	Income After Tax
Jan-92	654,032	606,813	47,219
Feb-92	668,321	619,810	48,511
Mar-92	676,954	624,543	52,411
Apr-92	678,684	623,170	55,514
May-92	697,576	637,658	59,918
Jun-92	699,891	639,501	60,390
Jul-92	708,426	645,721	62,705
Aug-92	712,081	647,699	64,382
Sep-92	715,034	647,152	67,882
Oct-92	718,441	647,803	70,638
Nov-92	734,638	659,129	75,509
Dec-92	740,057	660,572	79,485
Total	8,404,135	7,659,571	744,564

Figure 10-14: Adding an oval to a worksheet using the Oval tool.

Adding an arrow:

Step 1. Click the Arrow tool, drag the mouse from cell E8 to cell C12, and then release the mouse button.

Excel adds an arrow to the worksheet.

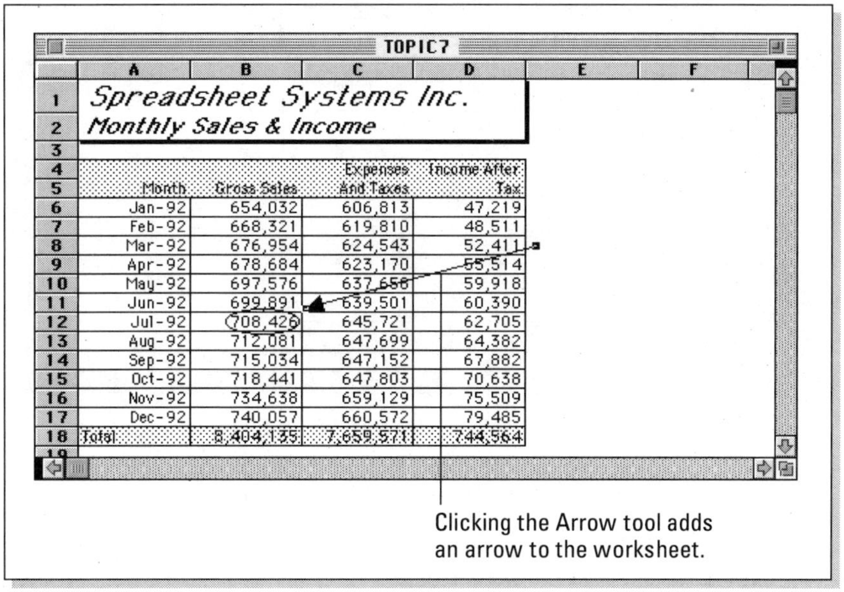

Figure 10-15: Adding an arrow to a worksheet using the Arrow tool.

Formatting an arrow:

Step 1. Choose Patterns from the Format menu or shortcut menu.

The Patterns dialog box is displayed.

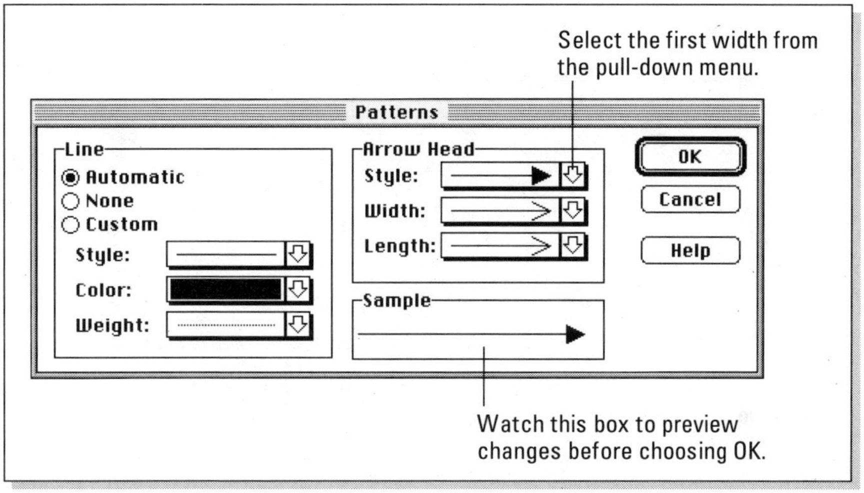

Figure 10-16: Choosing Patterns from the Format menu displays the Patterns dialog box.

Step 2. Pull down the Width menu, select the first pattern, and choose OK.

Excel displays the arrow with the new arrowhead.

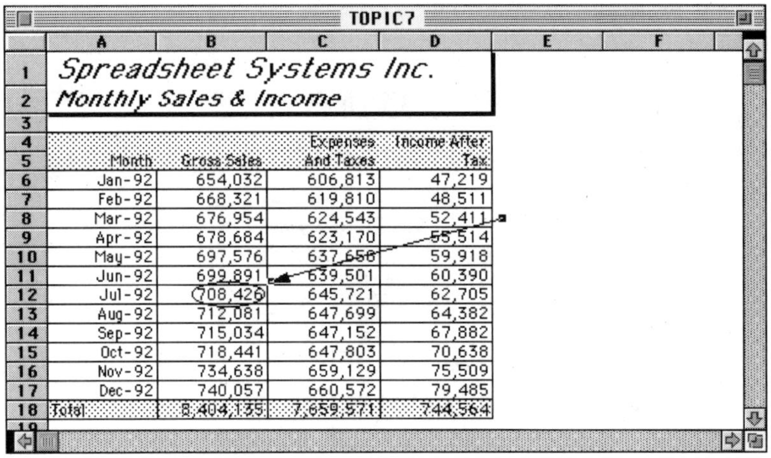

Month	Gross Sales	Expenses And Taxes	Income After Tax
Jan-92	654,032	606,813	47,219
Feb-92	668,321	619,810	48,511
Mar-92	676,954	624,543	52,411
Apr-92	678,684	623,170	55,514
May-92	697,576	637,656	59,918
Jun-92	699,891	639,501	60,390
Jul-92	708,426	645,721	62,705
Aug-92	712,081	647,699	64,382
Sep-92	715,034	647,152	67,882
Oct-92	718,441	647,803	70,638
Nov-92	734,638	659,129	75,509
Dec-92	740,057	660,572	79,485
Total	8,404,135	7,659,571	744,564

Figure 10-17: Formatting an arrow using the Patterns dialog box.

Adding a text box:

Step 1. Click the Text box tool, drag in the range E7:F11, and then release the mouse button.

Excel adds an empty text box to the worksheet.

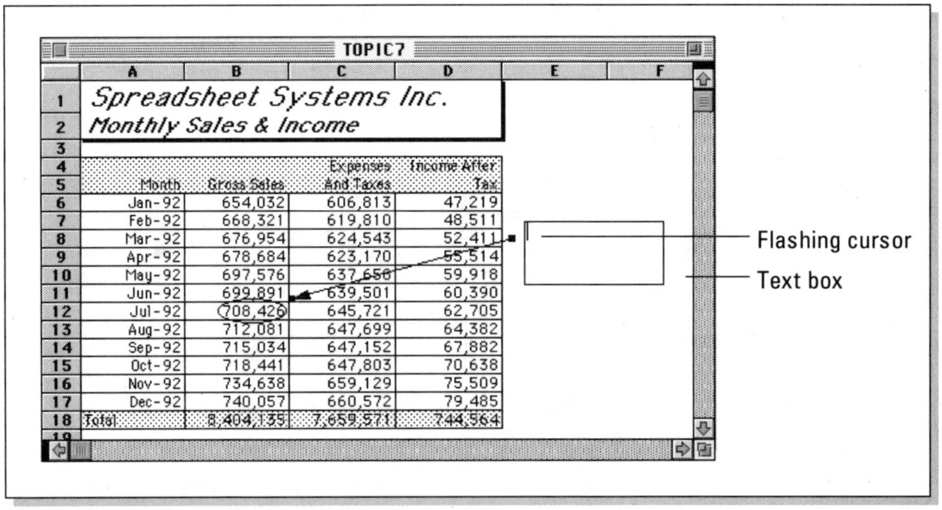

Month	Gross Sales	Expenses And Taxes	Income After Tax
Jan-92	654,032	606,813	47,219
Feb-92	668,321	619,810	48,511
Mar-92	676,954	624,543	52,411
Apr-92	678,684	623,170	55,514
May-92	697,576	637,656	59,918
Jun-92	699,891	639,501	60,390
Jul-92	708,426	645,721	62,705
Aug-92	712,081	647,699	64,382
Sep-92	715,034	647,152	67,882
Oct-92	718,441	647,803	70,638
Nov-92	734,638	659,129	75,509
Dec-92	740,057	660,572	79,485
Total	8,404,135	7,659,571	744,564

Figure 10-18: Adding a text box to a worksheet using the Text box tool.

Step 2. Type `Over $700K in sales!`

Excel displays the text in the text box.

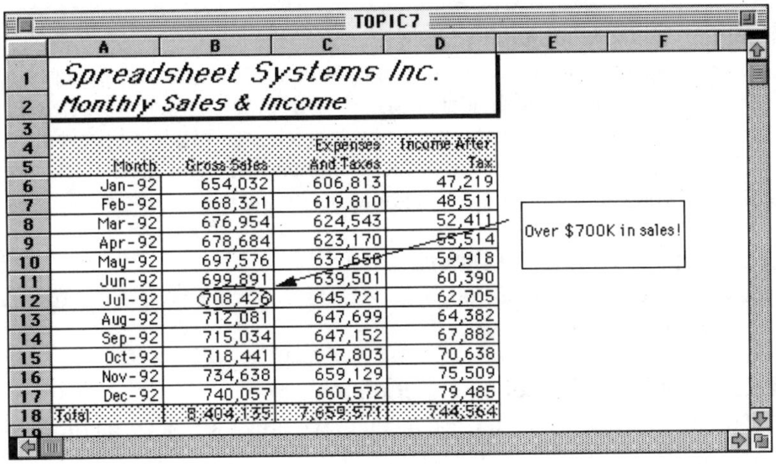

Month	Gross Sales	Expenses And Taxes	Income After Tax
Jan-92	654,032	606,813	47,219
Feb-92	668,321	619,810	48,511
Mar-92	676,954	624,543	52,411
Apr-92	678,684	623,170	55,514
May-92	697,576	637,658	59,918
Jun-92	699,891	639,501	60,390
Jul-92	708,426	645,721	62,705
Aug-92	712,081	647,699	64,382
Sep-92	715,034	647,152	67,882
Oct-92	718,441	647,803	70,638
Nov-92	734,638	659,129	75,509
Dec-92	740,057	660,572	79,485
Total	8,404,135	7,659,571	744,564

Figure 10-19: An example of how text is displayed in a text box.

Saving the drawing:

Step 1. Choose Save As from the File menu, type `TOPIC10`, and choose OK.

Excel saves the worksheet to disk.

Quick Tips

This section provides you with tips on how to help you add eye-catching drawings to your worksheets so your worksheets get the attention they deserve.

Selecting all objects quickly

To select all objects in a worksheet rapidly, choose Select Special from the Formula menu, select Objects, and then choose OK.

Selecting objects that contain macro assignments

To select a graphic object with a macro assigned to it (see Topic 14 for more on macros), press Command and then click the object. Clicking the object without pressing Command executes the macro, producing results that may not be intended.

Deleting objects from a worksheet

Objects can be deleted from a worksheet by selecting them and then choosing Clear from the Edit menu or pressing Delete.

Cataloging graphic objects

Keep a worksheet file that contains graphic objects you use frequently so you can copy them as needed.

Cycling through overlapping objects

Selecting each object and then choosing Send to Back from the Format menu or shortcut menu enables you to cycle through all overlapping objects.

Updating the screen quickly

If your worksheet contains several objects and Excel starts taking longer to update the display, choose Show Placeholders or Hide All from the Options Display menu. Show Placeholders displays shaded versions of the objects, and Hide All prevents objects from being displayed entirely. Use one of these options when you need quick screen updating and when you can temporarily do without displaying the objects themselves.

Displaying cell entries in shapes

Shapes with a Fill pattern of None will be blank and will enable cell entries underneath the shape to be displayed.

Previewing a worksheet before printing

Choose Print Preview from the File menu to see how the objects on the worksheet will be printed before actually printing the worksheet.

Using third-party art

You can use clip art (art created by other people) and drawings created by other programs such as MacDraw in a worksheet by selecting the drawing and choosing Copy from the other program's Edit menu. Make Excel the active application and choose Paste from Excel's Edit menu to place the copy in the worksheet.

Adding lines, arrows, and text to charts

The Drawing toolbar is for worksheets only. Add lines, arrows, and text to charts with the Add Arrow and Text commands from the Chart menu.

Summary

- You can add objects to a worksheet using the tools from the Drawing toolbar. Objects include lines, arrows, ovals, circles, squares, and rectangles, to name a few.
- You can move selected objects by dragging the object with the mouse.
- You can resize selected objects by dragging on an object's selection handle.
- You can protect objects from accidental change by locking them.
- You can group multiple objects to form a single object by selecting the objects and choosing Group from the Format menu.
- You can rearrange overlapping objects so a hidden object is displayed in its entirety.

Part IV: Advanced Excel

Topic 11

Linking and Consolidating Worksheets

Overview

You may have taken a look at the title of this Topic and immediately decided it's not for you. Knowing how to link and consolidate worksheets, however, is a good skill to have under your spreadsheet belt, because you never know when you'll be called upon to perform a task that uses more than one open worksheet at a time.

This Topic introduces you to the concept of multiple worksheets — what they are, why you should consider using them, and how to put them to work for you.

Using multiple worksheets simultaneously

With a 16,384 row by 256 column worksheet, you may be wondering why you would ever use more than one worksheet at a time, especially if you use Excel for quick and simple calculations, or printing a one-page report once a month. But what if you need to prepare your company's annual budget, which consists of five departments? You may have a worksheet like the one shown in Figure 11-1 to arrive at a company grand total.

A worksheet like the one in Figure 11-1 has a range for each department, using formulas to sum the total division. The worksheet gets the job done, but it takes the long way around. Due to its size, it's cumbersome to use, maintain, and enhance.

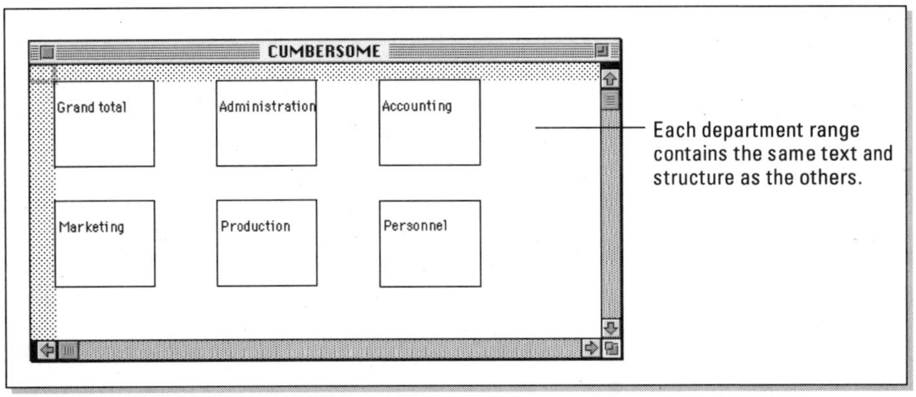

Figure 11-1: Calculating a company's annual budget with a single worksheet like this one is less efficient than using multiple worksheets.

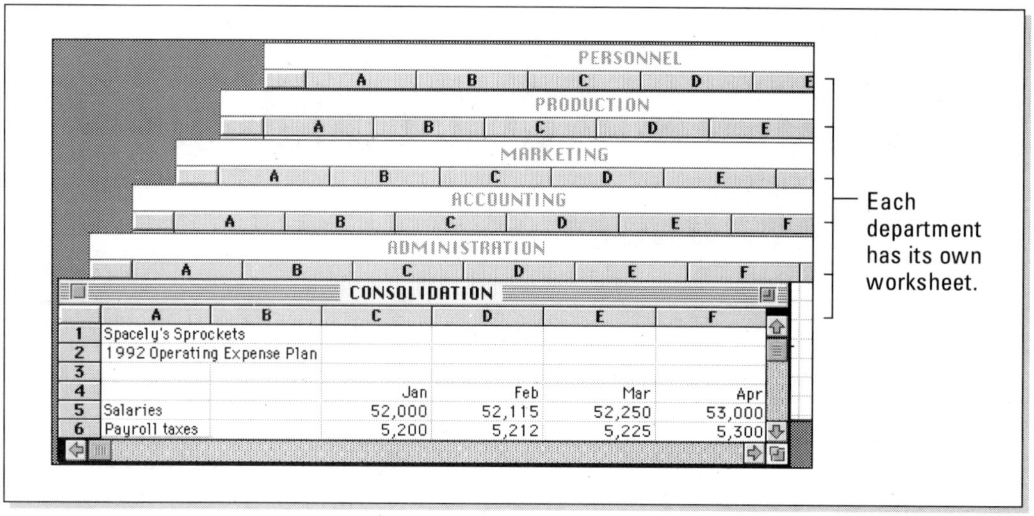

Figure 11-2: Calculating a company's annual budget using a system of multiple worksheets.

And a worksheet of that magnitude puts Excel through some (unnecessary) paces — it requires a lot of your Macintosh's memory, and screen scrolling and updating is sluggish.

Instead of using a worksheet the size of a football field, consider using a worksheet system similar to the one shown in Figure 11-2.

Each department has its own worksheet, so if you need to change something, you can go directly to that worksheet and do what needs to be done. No hunting all over one large worksheet for a specific area and cell address — something the people who cover for you (not to mention your supervisor) will appreciate when you're on vacation or out with the current season's flu.

Using multiple worksheets has the following advantages over using a single, large worksheet:

- ✦ Each worksheet has a specific purpose, and thus enables you to create worksheet systems that are easily understood, organized, and logical.
- ✦ Faster calculation, screen updating, and opening
- ✦ Uses less memory

There are many ways to use multiple worksheets, and the following discussion will help you choose the technique that's right for you and your situation.

Using the Clipboard to transfer data between worksheets

On a basic level, you can use the Clipboard to transfer data from one open worksheet to another. As you know from Topic 5, you select the cell or range of cells you want to cut or copy, and then choose Cut or Copy from the Edit menu. Next, you make another worksheet the active worksheet, select the cell or range you want to hold the data, and then choose Paste, again from the Edit menu. The data is copied to the second worksheet, and as long as you don't use Cut or Copy again, you can paste the current contents of the Clipboard as many times as you want.

This easy-to-use method is great for simple tasks that occur during a current Excel session. This method is a little limited, however, particularly when you need to copy from the first worksheet and paste to the second any time there's a change to the data in the worksheet you're copying from.

What you need is a turbo-charged version of copying and pasting, known as *linking*.

Linking worksheets

You can create a dynamic link between two worksheets. A worksheet that is linked to another will always reflect the most current data — when you change the data in the first worksheet, it will also change in the second worksheet. You can create a link to another worksheet's cell, range, or name, while the worksheet supplying the data is open or closed.

One of the more useful applications of linking is a report worksheet that depends on other worksheets for totals. For example, each item in an income statement worksheet could depend on other worksheets that calculate totals. In this situation, there'd be a worksheet that lists assets and calculates depreciation, and another worksheet that calculates taxes, and so on.

In the world of linking, you should understand the following key terms:

- *Dependent worksheet*: A worksheet that depends on another (source) worksheet for its data. The dependent worksheet has at least one cell linked to another worksheet through an external reference formula.
- *Source worksheet*: A worksheet that furnishes data to another (dependent) worksheet, the name of which is included in the external reference formula.
- *External reference formula*: A linking formula contained in at least one cell in a dependent worksheet that refers to a source worksheet. The formula is comprised of these parts:

  =Drive_name:Excel:Worksheet_name!:$Cell_address

In the formula, `Drive_name` is the name of the disk, `Excel` is the name of the Excel folder, `Worksheet_name` is the name of the worksheet, and `$Cell_address` is the absolute reference cell address or name. An exclamation point always follows the worksheet name.

If the source worksheet is open, you don't need to specify the name of the drive or folder name (Excel) — only the worksheet name (with an exclamation point) and the cell address or name. But if the worksheet is closed, on another disk, and part of a workbook, the external reference formula format becomes the following:

=Drive_name:Folder_name:[Book_name]:Worksheet_name!:$Cell_address

The point to remember is to provide Excel with all the information necessary to help it locate the worksheet and cell you want to link to, including any subfolder names.

There are three ways to create links:

- ✦ Choosing Copy and Paste Link from the Edit menu
- ✦ Pointing from the dependent worksheet to the source worksheet
- ✦ Typing the external reference formula

The following section discusses how you create links using these methods.

Linking with Copy and Paste Link

Creating a link using Copy and Paste Link is the linking version of copying and pasting. It's the same idea only you're using Paste Link instead of Paste (or Paste Special), and working with two worksheets. It's best to use the Edit commands to create a link when you need to reference a single cell from another worksheet, as discussed earlier in the income statement example.

To create a link using Copy and Paste Link, do the following:

1. Make the *source* worksheet the active worksheet.
2. Select the cell you want to link to the dependent worksheet.
3. Choose Copy from the Edit menu or shortcut menu.
4. Make the *dependent* worksheet the active worksheet.
5. Select the cell to hold the link — the external reference formula.
6. Choose Paste Link from the Edit menu.
7. Save each worksheet before quitting Excel to preserve the link.

In Figure 11-3, cell B3 in the worksheet named `Dependent` shows you the link to cell C2 in its source worksheet, below.

To link to more than one cell, select a multiple cell range. Keep in mind that any existing data in the dependent worksheet beginning with the cell holding the link is overwritten by incoming source data.

DEPENDENT

	A	B	C	D	E
1			Formulas in Column B		
2					
3	Date	7/4/92	=SOURCE!$C$2		
4	Total	139	=SUM(SOURCE!$A$7:$E$7)		
5	Highest	42	=MAX(SOURCE!$A$7:$E$7)		
6	Lowest	15	=MIN(SOURCE!$A$7:$E$7)		
7					

SOURCE

	A	B	C	D	E	F
1	Weekly Sales Report					
2	For the week ending:		7/4/92			
3						
4	Monday	Tuesday	Wednesday	Thursday	Friday	
5	6/29	6/30	7/1	7/2	7/3	
6						
7	22	25	42	35	15	

Figure 11-3: Linking cells in two different worksheets using the Paste Link command.

Linking by pointing

Creating a link by pointing is similar to referencing one cell to another in the same worksheet. For example, to create a single-cell link in Figure 11-3 by pointing, do the following steps:

1. Make the *dependent* worksheet the active worksheet.
2. Select the cell you want to link to the source worksheet.
3. Type an equal sign (=).
4. Make the *source* worksheet the active worksheet.
5. Select the cell that contains the data you want to link to.
6. Click Enter or press Return.
7. Save each worksheet before quitting Excel to preserve the link.

Notice that with pointing you begin with the dependent worksheet instead of the source worksheet, as you would with Copy and Paste Link. And you create links without the use of commands. More importantly, however, pointing enables you to use functions in your external reference formulas. In Figure 11-3, the formulas in range B4:B6 in the worksheet named `Dependent` reference range A7:E7 in the source worksheet below.

Creating links manually

If you have to, you can create linking formulas by typing. This technique is vulnerable to typing errors, so be careful. You can create links to unopened worksheets in this manner, though it's easier to open a source worksheet to see what you're doing.

To create a link manually, select the cell that will hold the formula in the dependent worksheet. Type an equal sign (=), and then the formula, following the same format as shown in the external reference formula definition discussed earlier.

The only procedure you need to do differently when typing is to enclose the path in single quotation marks, as shown in the following formula:

='MacintoshHD:Excel:Worksheets:SALES_92'!A20

Clicking Enter or pressing Return creates the link. Remember to furnish Excel with the exact location of the cell you want to link to, including disk drives, folders, and subfolders. The cell address can be a range or name that is absolute, mixed, or relative.

If typing the external reference formula becomes too tedious, you can change your mind and select the cell or range by pointing — if the source worksheet is open.

Managing links

Once you have your worksheets set up and properly linked, your links provide you with many years of trouble-free service — if the location of source and dependent worksheets remains the same. If the worksheet system changes, or if you've become a linked worksheet convert, you'll want to read the next few sections — a type of linking owner's manual.

Updating linked worksheets

Updating dependent worksheets with current data is effortless if all source worksheets and the dependent worksheet are open — Excel automatically does this for you. And if you haven't made any changes to the source worksheets, you don't need to open or update the linked values.

However, if you open a dependent worksheet and the source worksheets aren't open but contain new data, you'll be greeted with the message box shown in Figure 11-4.

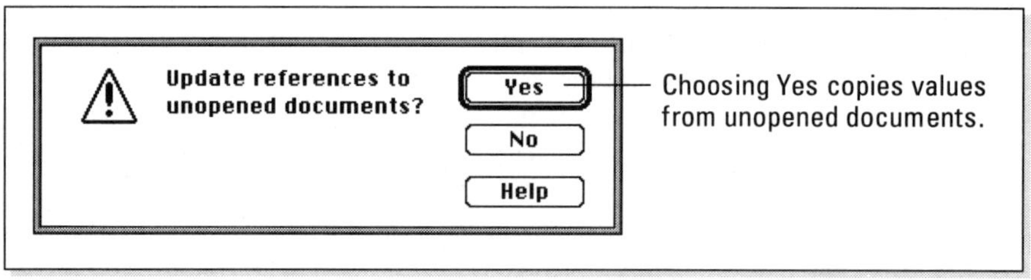

Figure 11-4: Opening a dependent worksheet without opening source worksheets that contain new data displays this message box.

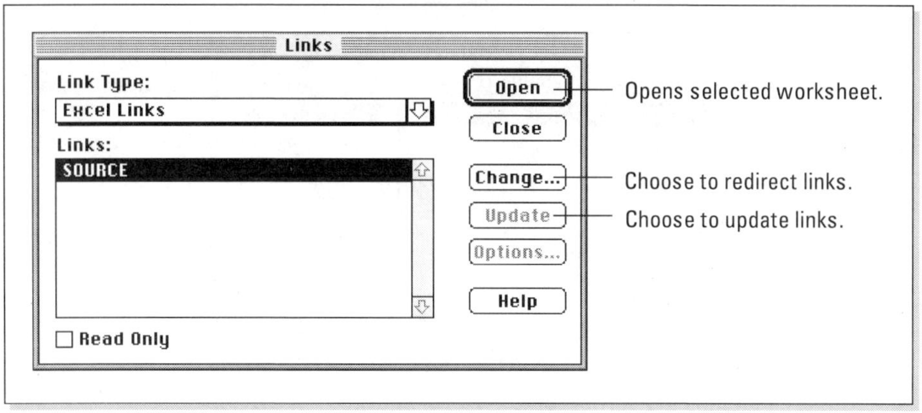

Figure 11-5: Choosing Links from the File menu displays the Links dialog box.

Choose Yes to have Excel update the dependent worksheet's linked values. You can also open the source worksheet, update links, or view a list of the dependent worksheet's source worksheets by doing the following steps:

1. Make the dependent worksheet the active worksheet.
2. Choose Links from the File menu.

   The Links dialog box shown in Figure 11-5 appears.
3. Select the source worksheet that contains the new data. Press Shift while dragging to select all worksheets; press Command and click on the worksheet name to select more than one worksheet.
4. Choose Open or Update.

Maintaining links

The key to successful linked worksheets is letting Excel know where to find a source worksheet, much like when you select a file by choosing Open from the File menu. As long as you don't change the drive, folder, worksheet name, or cell name in the external reference formula after you create the link, your linked worksheets will perform flawlessly.

If you or someone else, however, moves a source worksheet to another disk or folder, or renames a source worksheet name without reflecting the change in the dependent worksheet's external reference formula, Excel won't be able to find the source cell and update the linked value. If this happens, Excel displays the message box shown previously in Figure 11-4. Then, if you choose Yes, Excel displays the dialog box shown in Figure 11-6.

Select the source worksheet name from the dialog box options, and then choose Copy. Excel will update the dependent worksheet's linked cells. To make the dependent worksheet's external formulas reflect the change, you can use one of two methods available.

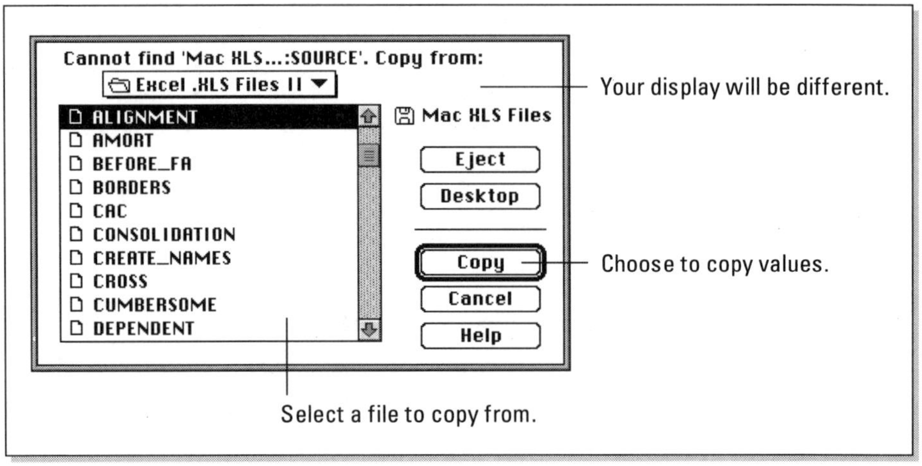

Figure 11-6: Choosing Yes from the message box shown in Figure 11-4 displays this dialog box, which allows you to select a file to copy data from.

The hard way is to edit the external formula in the formula bar. Make the dependent worksheet the active worksheet, select the cell containing the formula, and then activate the formula bar. Type the folder name or new name of the source worksheet, and click Enter or press Return. After you choose Save from the File menu (or click the Save tool), the link will be properly established for the current and future Excel sessions.

Avoiding the weak link

Creating a system of linked worksheets has many advantages over a single large worksheet that performs the same function. You should be careful, however, not to make a linked worksheet system overly complicated. For example, look at the linked worksheets in the following figure.

The worksheet named B is dependent on Worksheet C, and B is also a source worksheet to A. Thus, worksheet A is indirectly dependent on worksheet C, which means, unfortunately, that if you make a change to C and don't open or update B, A will not reflect the most current data. Worse, if B isn't open, you may not realize that A was not updated.

One way around this situation is to limit linked worksheets to two levels — a dependent worksheet that relies directly on worksheets that are source worksheets *only*. If you need or want to use source worksheets that also function as dependent worksheets, make sure you open all worksheets in the system to guarantee accurate results. Or use a separate worksheet as a log indicating which worksheets were updated if you're unable to open all worksheets in the linked system at the same time.

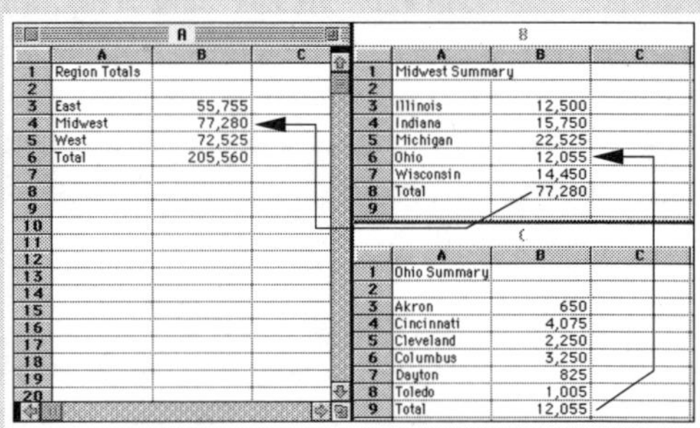

The easy way to make the dependent worksheet's external formulas reflect the changes is to choose Links from the File menu. Select the name of the link that needs redirecting from the Links box, and then click Update. The dialog box shown previously in Figure 11-5 appears so you can select the name of the worksheet and if necessary, the folder. Choosing Change redirects the link to the correct source worksheet. Be sure to save the dependent worksheet to disk before quitting Excel to preserve the updated link.

Ending a link

The day may arrive when you no longer want or need a source worksheet's data in the dependent worksheet. There are several ways to break the connection, depending on your data needs. To remove the link entirely, make the cell containing the link the active cell, and choose Clear from the Edit menu (or press Delete), and then choose OK when the dialog box appears. The external reference formula will be erased, leaving you with a blank cell.

A less severe option is to end the link but use the external formula's calculated result or value. In this case, select the cell, choose Copy from the Edit menu, and then choose Paste Special, also from the Edit menu. Finally, select the Values option button and choose OK. The link is broken, but you've entered the external reference formula's value into the cell.

If linking has whetted your appetite for multiple worksheets but doesn't quite fit the bill, consolidating data may be the tool you're looking for.

Consolidating data

Earlier in this Topic, I discussed the problem of adding similar worksheets together to arrive at a grand total. Excel's Data Consolidate command enables you to total up to 255 worksheets that are open (or closed) quickly and easily.

The first step is to open the worksheets you want to consolidate, and make the worksheet that will contain the totals (the summary) the active worksheet. Next, select the range where you want the totals to appear. Selecting a single cell is permissible as Excel enters values beginning with the selected cell as the upper-left cell of the consolidated data. Now, choose Consolidate from the Data menu. The Consolidate dialog box shown in Figure 11-7 appears.

Select the Reference box, and then select the first worksheet you want to consolidate. If your worksheets are structured identically to the summary worksheet, select only the range of values you want to consolidate, and then choose Add. Alternatively, you can type the name of the worksheet, an exclamation point, and the range address in the Reference box. Repeat this process for every open worksheet. When you're finished, each open worksheet and the range to include in the total will be listed in the All References box.

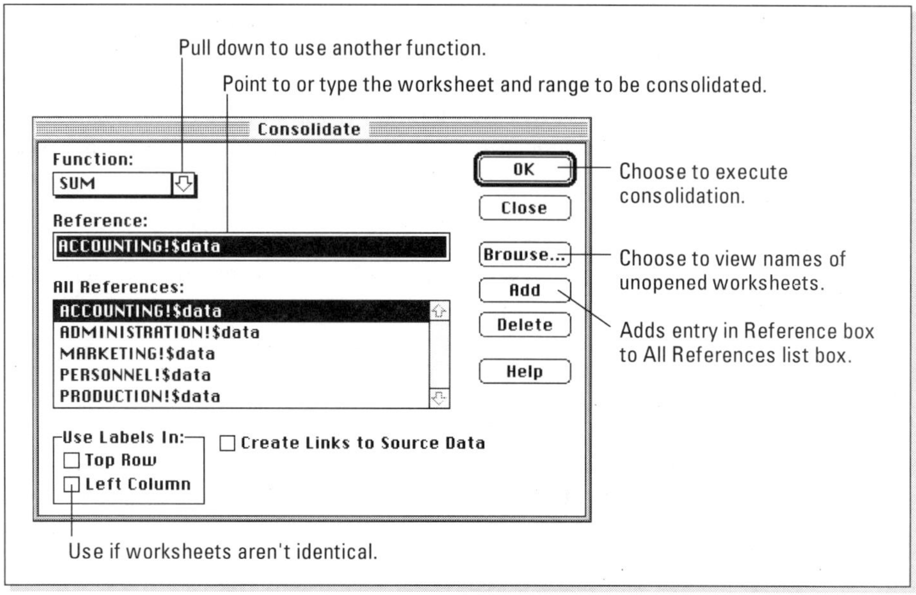

Figure 11-7: Choosing Consolidate from the Data menu displays the Consolidate dialog box.

When consolidating is better than linking

The most common uses of Excel are planning, budgeting, and forecasting. While there are several ways you can calculate grand totals from one or more worksheets, using Data Consolidate is the most elegant method. It *is* possible to perform a consolidation using worksheet linking (you can even have Excel create external reference formulas by selecting the Create Links to Source Data option from the Data Consolidate dialog box), but it's really not in your best interest to do so. For example, if you have 50 budget items in a 12-month budget worksheet template, your dependent (consolidation) worksheet will have 600 external reference formulas! Not to mention 13 SUM functions to total the months and the year, and 50 more SUM functions to total the individual budget items. A worksheet of this magnitude requires a lot of memory, time to open, and time to calculate.

Linked worksheets that are identical do provide you with the advantage of always having a current consolidation. But once you've set up reference areas for Data Consolidate and save the dependent worksheet to disk, updating the consolidation is a snap. Select Consolidate from the Data menu and choose OK. The dependent worksheet will reflect the most current data. Just remember to erase all cells containing data in the dependent worksheet first, or you'll have double expense amounts — something upper management won't appreciate. A macro that erases prior consolidated data and then executes Data Consolidate would be a good tool to add to your Excel toolbox.

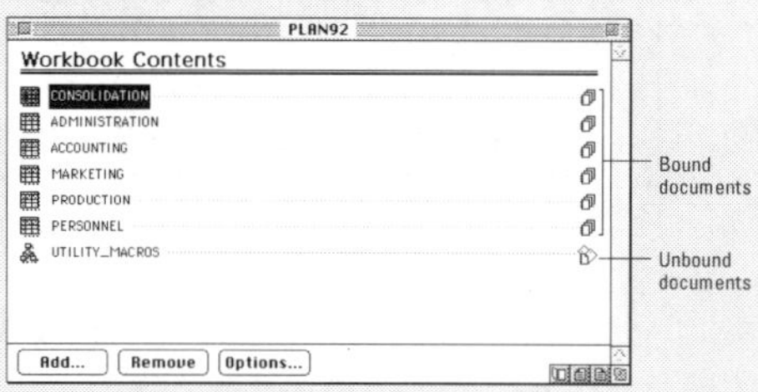

If your source worksheets are not structured identically to the dependent worksheet, you need to include the text in the left column and/or across the top row that encloses the data in the selected range. For example, your Sales department is the only department that will incur advertising expenses, so Sales is the only department with this item in its budget worksheet template (except for the consolidation worksheet). You need the amount in your consolidated total, but you don't give other departments the opportunity to budget for advertising in their respective worksheets. As a result, select either (or both, depending on the worksheets' structure) the Top Row or the Left Column option boxes so Excel can match the source worksheet labels with those in the dependent worksheet to consolidate correctly.

Choosing OK completes the consolidation process. The values in each worksheet's range are totaled and placed in the summary worksheet's destination range.

Managing multiple worksheets

OK, you've seen the light and want to plunge enthusiastically into the world of multiple worksheets, but the thought of managing more than one open worksheet at a time makes you cringe. No need to worry — Excel has several capabilities to help make your life with multiple worksheets easier.

Making changes simultaneously

You may find yourself in a situation where you're working with multiple worksheets that are identical and would like to make the same change to each worksheet at the same time. For example, you'd like all department budget totals to be formatted with a dollar sign with no decimal places. Excel's Group Edit mode enables you to do that easily, and much more.

To use Group Edit mode, open all the worksheets you want to edit at the same time. Then choose Group Edit from the Options menu. The Group Edit dialog box shown in Figure 11-8 appears.

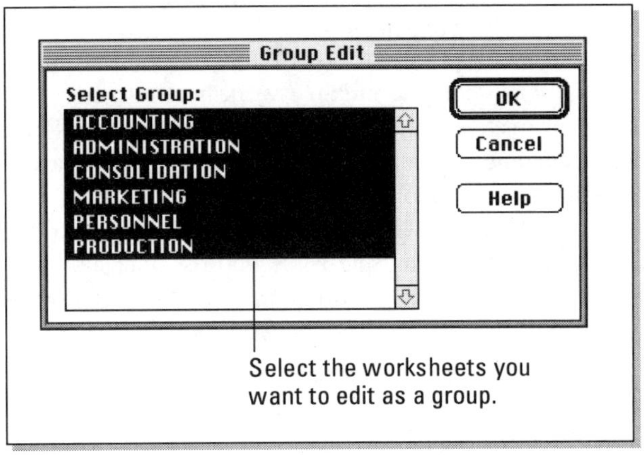

Figure 11-8: Choosing Group Edit from the Options menu displays the Group Edit dialog box.

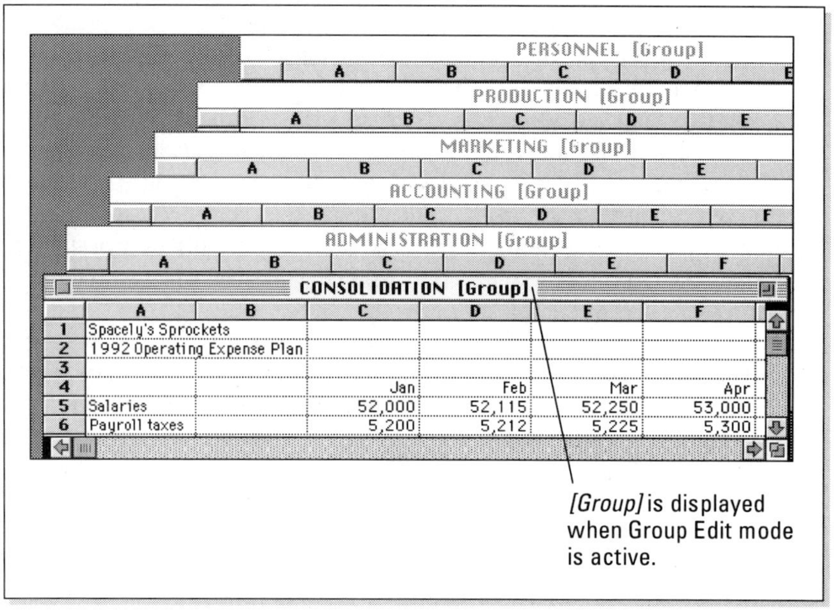

Figure 11-9: An example of a worksheet in Group Edit mode.

If this is your first group editing session, all the open worksheet names are selected. Press Command and click the worksheet name (if any) you don't want in Group Edit mode. Choosing OK activates Group Edit mode and the word *[Group]* is added to the worksheets' titles, as shown in Figure 11-9.

At this point, any changes to the active worksheet are reflected in all worksheets in Group Edit mode. If you enter or edit text, values, or formulas in the active worksheet, they are entered in all other group edit worksheets. For example, entering *January* in the active worksheet will also enter *January* in the other group edit worksheets. Changing row height or column widths, or formatting ranges in the active worksheet will affect all other group edit worksheets similarly.

Group edit mode has a corresponding multiple worksheet effect on Excel commands. Many Edit, File, Format, Macro, and some Data, Formula, and Window commands take on a multiple worksheet flavor. For instance, the Save command saves *all* worksheets that are in Group Edit mode — a great time saver. Of particular interest to multiple worksheeters is Fill Group from the Edit menu, which is available when Group Edit mode is active. Choosing Fill Group (or dragging on the cell's fill handle) copies the selected cell or range to the corresponding cell or range in each group edit worksheet, enabling you to get your work done a little faster.

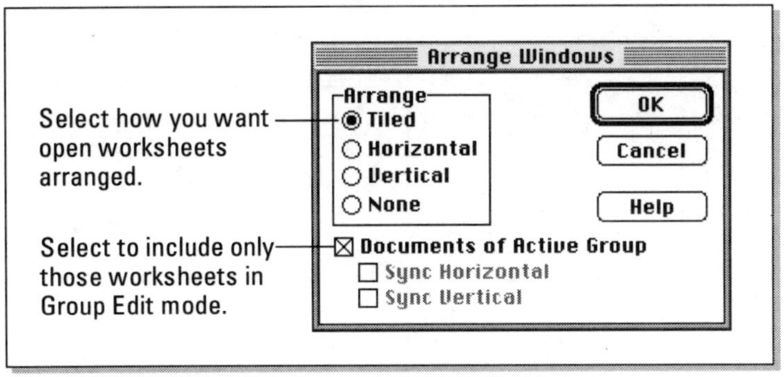

Figure 11-10: Choosing Arrange from the Window menu displays the Arrange Windows dialog box.

To exit from Group Edit mode, make another worksheet (even another group edit worksheet) the active worksheet. *Group* disappears from the worksheet titles and you can return to using worksheets as you would normally. Choosing Group Edit from the Options menu puts you back into Group Edit mode.

Seeing the big picture

Using multiple worksheets means having to open them all at one time or another (or at all times). Particularly if you're in Group Edit mode, you might like to see and feel more comfortable knowing what's going on — how changes in the active worksheet are affecting the other worksheets. Displaying open worksheets on screen simultaneously is as easy as choosing Arrange from the Window menu. When you choose Arrange, the Arrange Windows dialog box shown in Figure 11-10 appears.

You can display open worksheets in the following three ways :

Option	***Display***
Tiled	Horizontally and vertically (similar to ceramic tiles)
Horizontal	Stacked (landscape style)
Vertical	Side by side (portrait style)

Select one of these options and the Documents of Active Group check box in the Arrange dialog box. Choosing OK arranges the windows according to the options you selected. Figure 11-11 shows you tiled windows.

Filing worksheets in a workbook

You may feel having more than one worksheet open at a time is like having scattered paper all over your desk. It may be difficult to find the worksheet you need, or you may be worried you've lost it altogether.

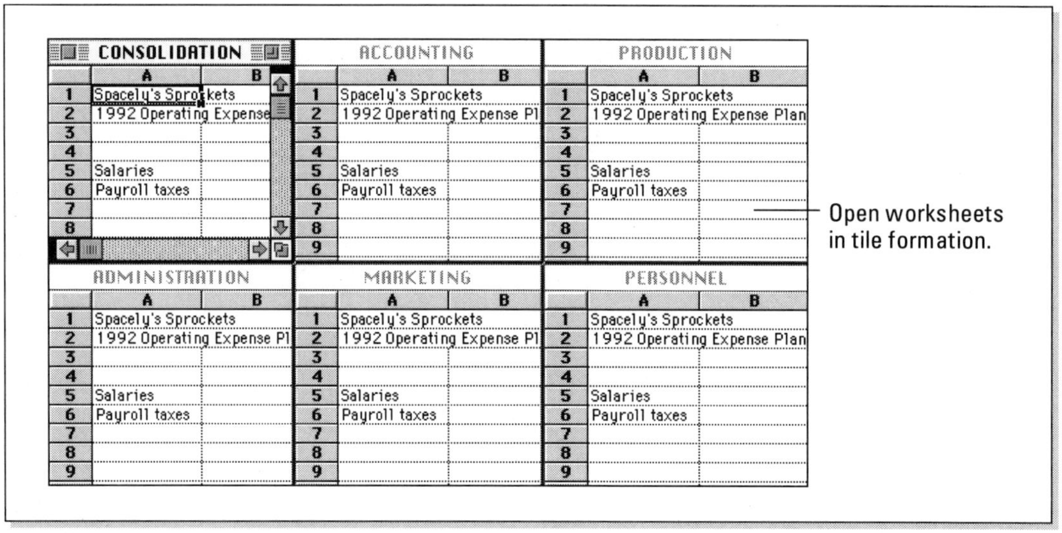

Figure 11-11: An example of worksheets arranged with the Tiled format.

You can allay those fears by keeping related worksheets together in a *workbook*. An Excel workbook is an electronic version of what you might distribute for a presentation to management — a booklet of reports and charts. Workbooks store individual documents in one file and can include worksheets, macro sheets, and charts. Some of the advantages of using workbooks include the following:

- ✦ Related documents are kept in one place (especially useful for linked worksheets), including macros and charts you want to use with the worksheets.
- ✦ It's easy to display a desired worksheet, and retain window display settings.
- ✦ File distribution is quicker and security is increased.

Creating a workbook is an easy process. Choose New from the File menu, select Workbook, and choose OK. Excel displays a new workbook contents window, as shown in Figure 11-12. The Window Contents window is the electronic version of a printed book's table of contents page.

Next, you add existing or new documents to the workbook. Click the Add button, and the Add To Workbook dialog box shown in Figure 11-13 appears.

You can add documents that are open to a worksheet by selecting from the "Select Documents to Add" box and then choosing OK. As when using the Links command from the File menu, pressing Shift and dragging through the filenames lets you select more than one worksheet at a time; pressing Command and clicking enables you to select more than one file when the names aren't in sequence. The New and Open buttons let you create a new document and display the Open dialog box, respectively, which then adds the document to the workbook.

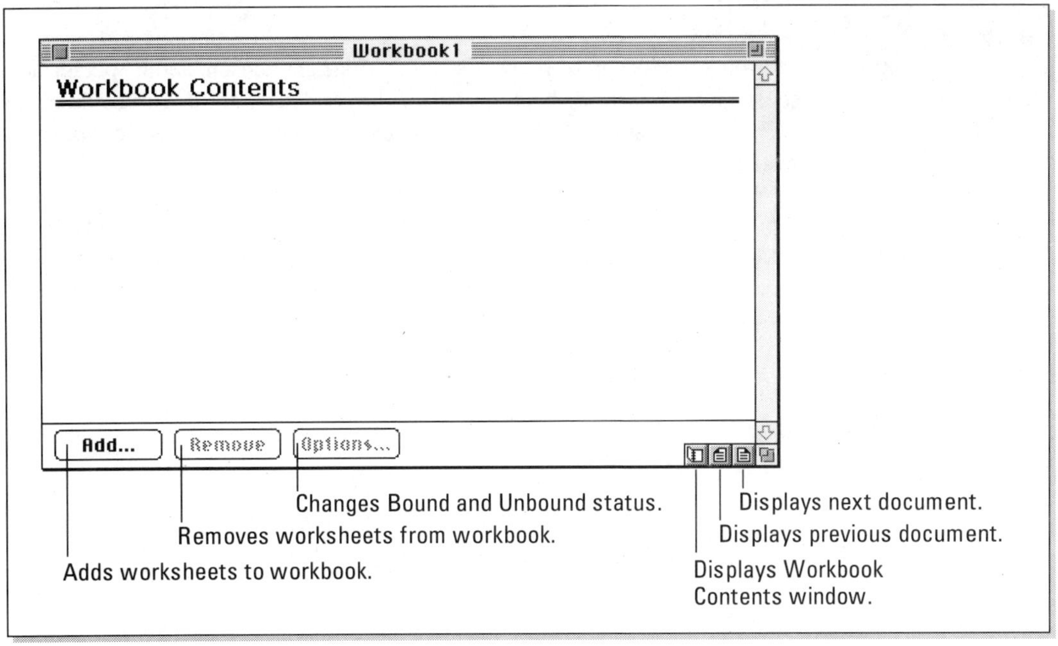

Figure 11-12: Choosing Workbook from the New dialog box displays the Workbook Contents window.

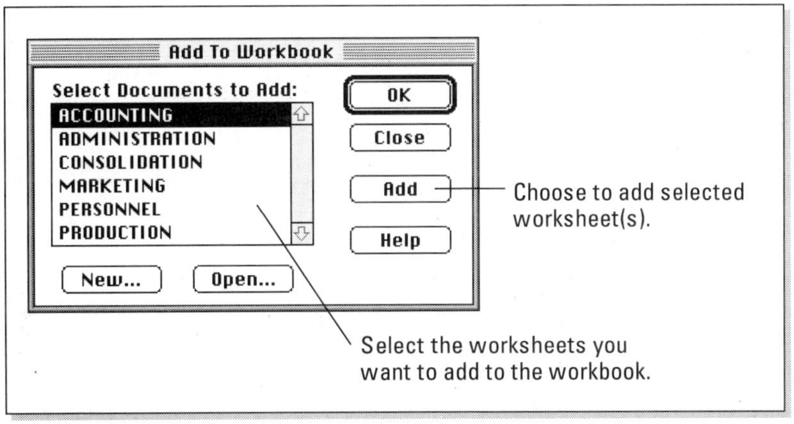

Figure 11-13: Clicking the Add button in the Workbook Contents window displays the Add To Workbook dialog box.

Left paging button

Right paging button

Contents button

Once you have your workbook up and running, displaying a document stored in the workbook is easy. Click the Right and Left Paging buttons to see the next and previous document, respectively. Or click the Contents button to display the Workbook Contents window. Double-clicking the document name displays that document. If you want to reorder the workbook's documents, drag the document's name in the Workbook Contents window to its new position.

Step-by-Step

In this section, you'll practice performing a simple worksheet consolidation. Specifically, you'll add the data from two worksheets and place the results in a third. You could easily do this using a single worksheet; the purpose, however, is to give you a taste of consolidating data from different worksheets.

You'll also experiment with Group Edit mode, and save your work in a workbook. This exercise will work best if you start (or restart) Excel to ensure that you have a single blank worksheet on screen. As always, if you make a mistake, choose Undo from the Edit menu or press F1.

To begin the exercise, do the following:

1. Start up or restart Excel.

   The Worksheet1 worksheet appears.

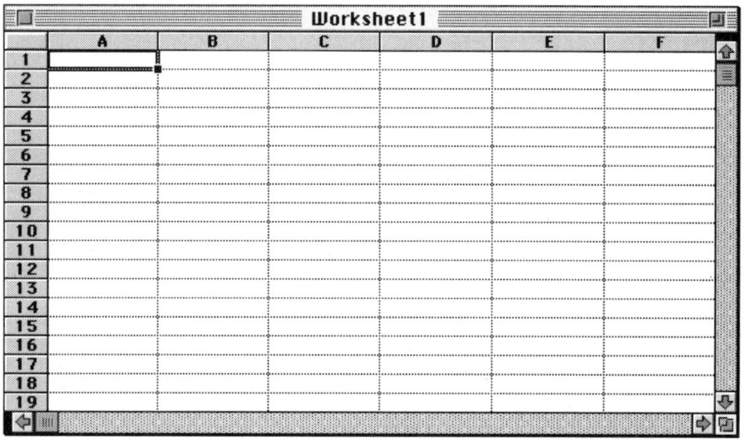

Figure 11-14: Starting up Excel displays the Worksheet1 worksheet.

Bound vs. unbound workbooks

You have a choice of having a workbook document being bound or unbound. Bound documents are stored in the workbook and can only be used with that particular workbook. Unbound documents are stored as separate files, though they're part of the workbook: a type of loose alliance. Unbound documents are utility players: They can be part of more than one workbook.

You can identify whether a document is bound or unbound by its icon in the Worksheet Contents window.

Changing from bound to unbound (or vice versa) is as easy as clicking on the document's icon (or clicking the Options button in the Worksheet Contents window).

Unless you need a document in another workbook, or need to use it with other single worksheets, you're better off binding the documents in the workbook. That way, you'll always know their location so they can be at your disposal in a moment's notice.

2. Click the File New tool two times.

   A total of three blank worksheets are displayed.

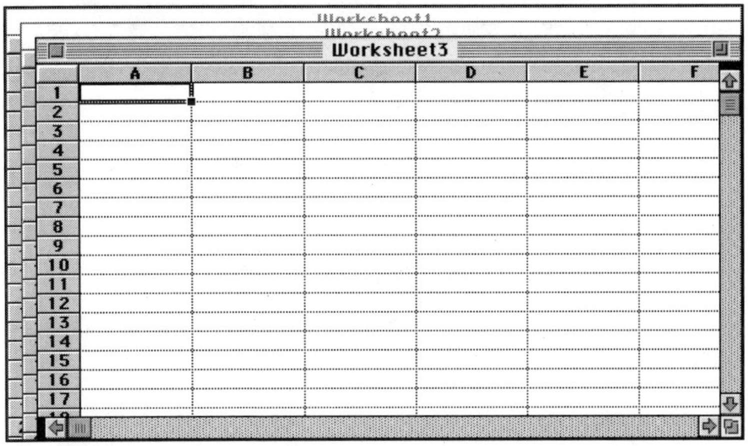

Figure 11-15: Clicking the File New tool two times displays a total of three worksheets.

Activating Group Edit mode:

Step 1. Choose Group Edit from the Options menu.

The Group Edit dialog box appears.

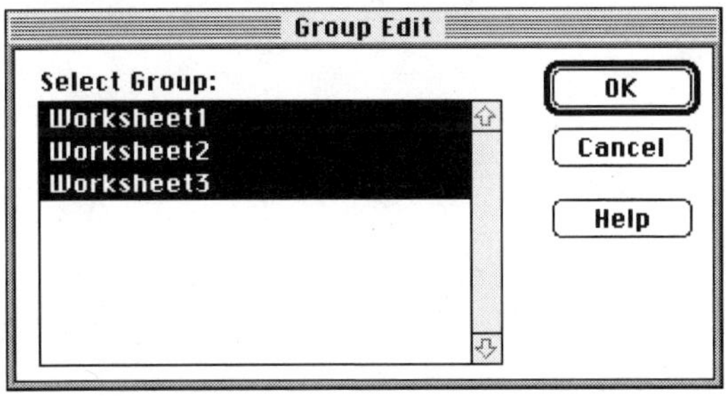

Figure 11-16: Choosing Group Edit from the Options menu displays the Group Edit dialog box.

Step 2. Choose OK.

[Group] appears in the worksheets' titles.

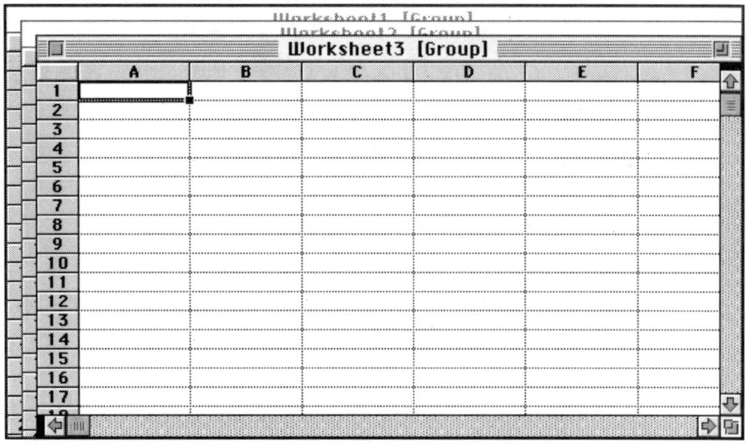

Figure 11-17: Choosing OK from the Group Edit box enters the selected worksheet into Group Edit mode and displays *[Group]* in the worksheets' title bar.

Step 3. Enter the labels exactly as shown in Figure 11-18. Next, select range B5:F5 and click the Right-align tool.

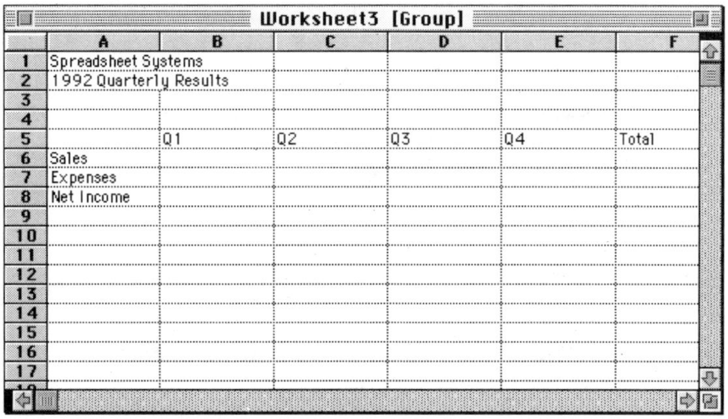

Figure 11-18: Sample text to be used for editing in Group Edit mode.

Step 4. Select Worksheet2, and enter the values and text as shown in Figure 11-19.

Group edit mode halts and Worksheet2 is displayed.

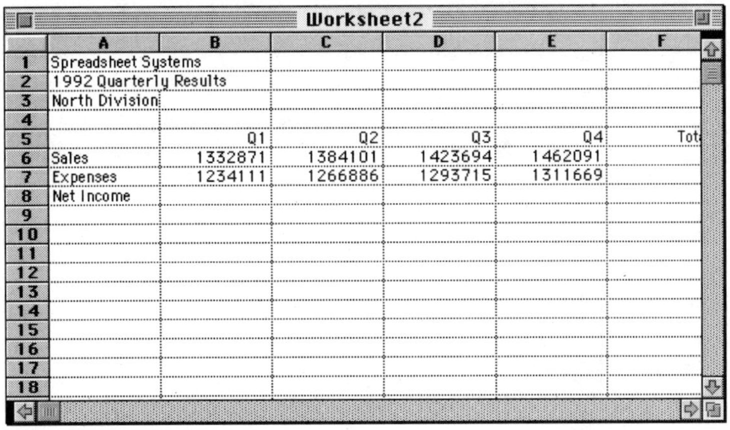

Figure 11-19: Selecting range B5:F5 and clicking the Right-align tool right aligns the selected text.

Step 5. Select Worksheet1, and enter the values and text as shown in Figure 11-20.

Worksheet1 with values is displayed.

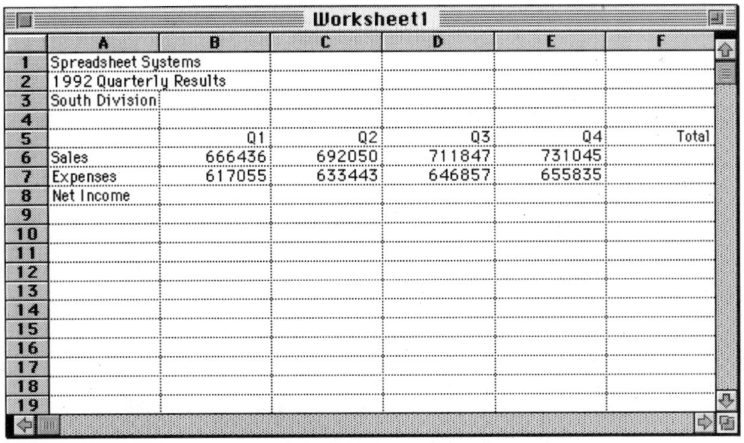

Figure 11-20: Sample text to be used for entering totals.

Entering totals:

Step 1. Choose Group Edit from the Options menu, and then make cell F6 the active cell.

Step 2. Click the Sum tool, and then click the Enter box.

Excel displays the total sales.

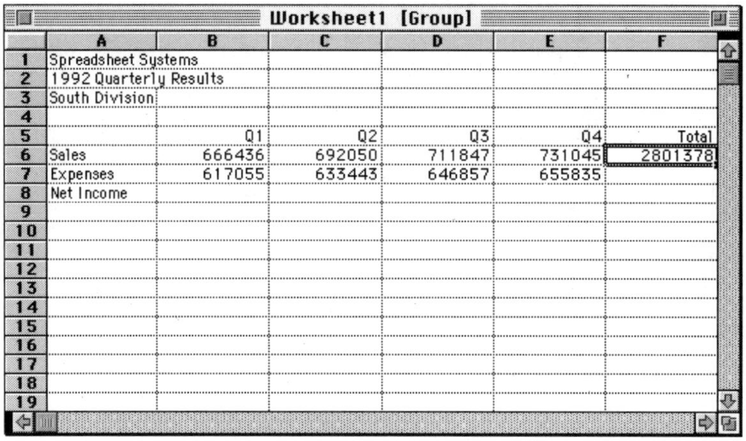

Figure 11-21: Entering a total using the Sum tool.

Step 3. Move the pointer to cell F6's fill handle. When the pointer appears as a cross, drag to F7:F8, and release the mouse button.

Excel displays the category totals.

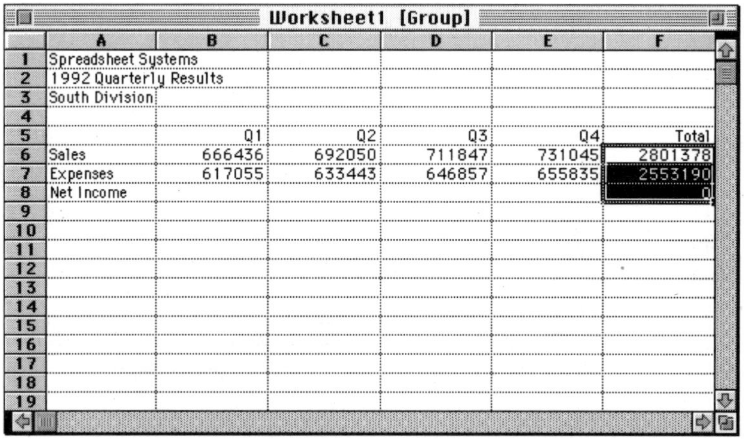

Figure 11-22: Entering totals by dragging the SUM function across a range.

Step 4. Make cell B8 the active cell, and enter the formula (by typing or pointing) `=B6-B7`, and click the Enter box.

Excel displays the first quarter net income.

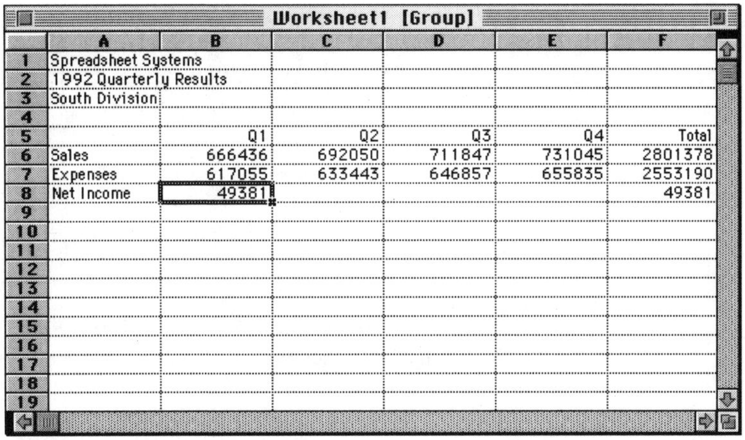

Figure 11-23: Entering the worksheet's first quarter net income by typing a formula into a cell.

Step 5. Move the pointer to cell B8's fill handle. When the pointer appears as a cross, drag to C8:E8, and release the mouse button.

Completed quarterly totals are displayed.

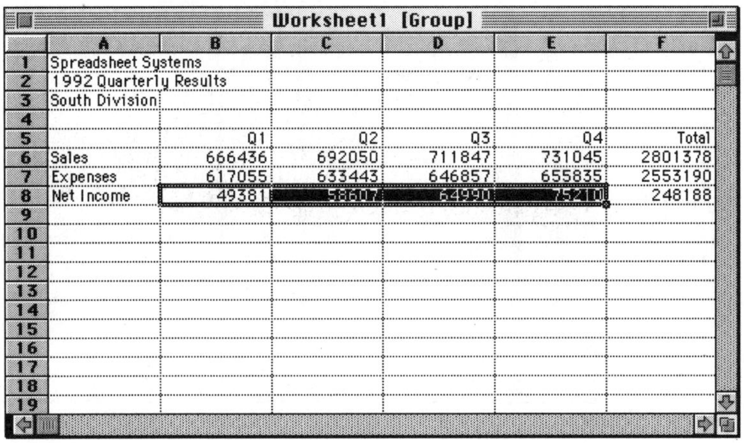

Figure 11-24: Entering all of the worksheet's quarterly totals by dragging a formula across a range.

Exiting from Group Edit mode:

Step 1. Select Worksheet2, and then select Worksheet1.

Naming ranges:

Step 1. Select range B6:E7 and choose Define Name from the Formula menu.

The Define Name dialog box appears.

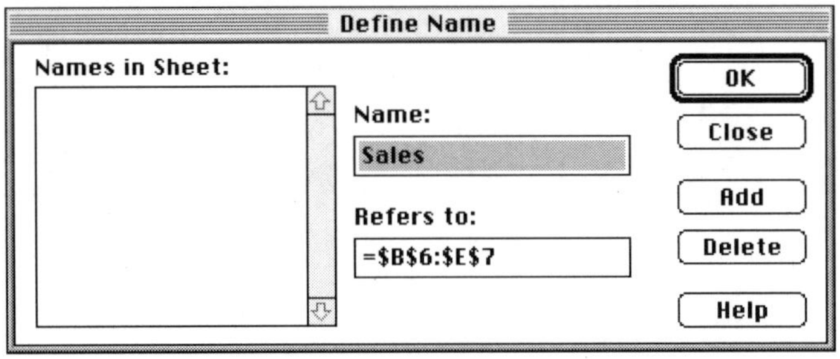

Figure 11-25: Choosing Define Name from the Formula menu displays the Define Name dialog box.

Step 2. Type data in the Name text box and choose OK.

Step 3. Select Worksheet2, and repeat steps 1 and 2.

Performing a consolidation:

Step 1. Select Worksheet3, and select cell B6.

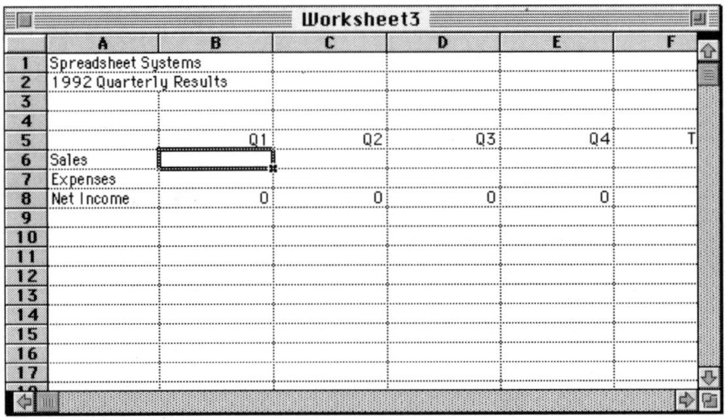

Figure 11-26: Preparing a worksheet for consolidation by selecting Worksheet3 and cell B6.

Step 2. Choose Consolidate from the Data menu.

The Consolidate dialog box appears.

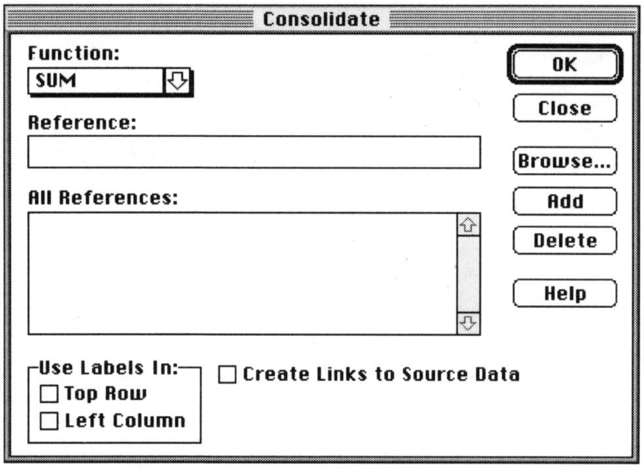

Figure 11-27: Choosing Consolidate from the Data menu displays the Consolidate dialog box.

Step 3. Type `worksheet1!data` in the Reference box, click the Add button, and then type `worksheet2!data`, also in the Reference box.

The Consolidate dialog box with reference areas is displayed.

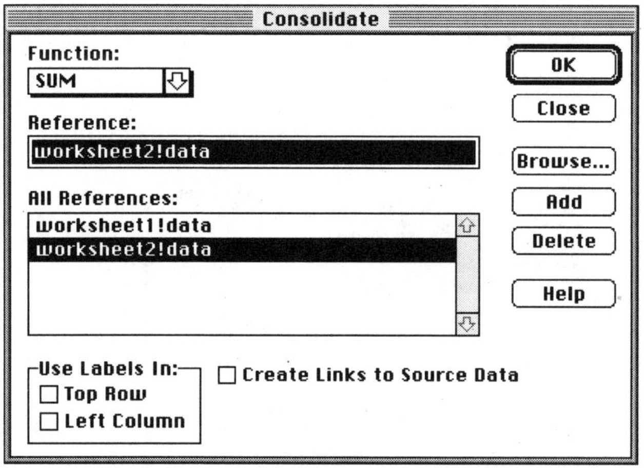

Figure 11-28: Adding reference areas to the Reference box and All References box in the Consolidate dialog box.

Step 4. Choose OK.

Excel totals the data from Worksheet1 and Worksheet2 to Worksheet3.

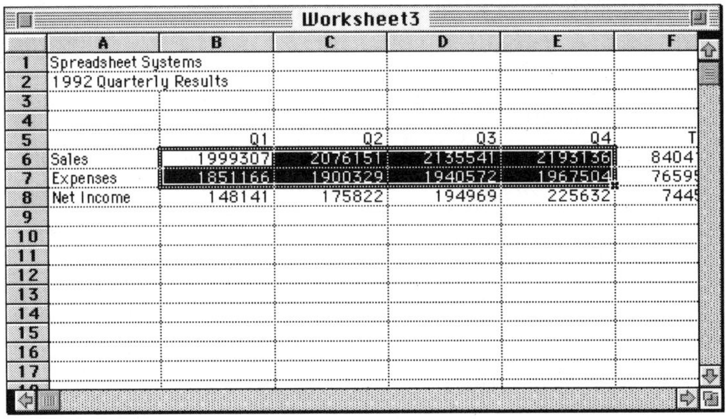

Figure 11-29: Totals from Worksheet1 and Worksheet2 consolidated into Worksheet3.

Saving worksheets in a workbook:

Step 1. Choose New from the File menu.

The New dialog box appears.

Step 2. Select Workbook and choose OK.

The Workbook Contents window appears.

Step 3. Choose the Add button.

The Add to Workbook dialog box appears.

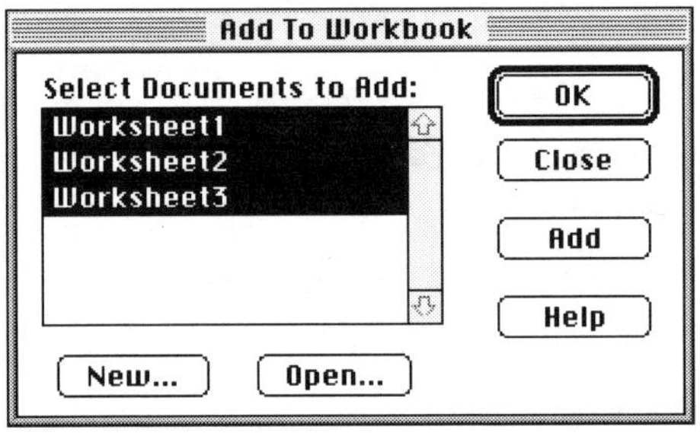

Figure 11-30: Choosing the Add button from the Workbook Contents window displays the Add To Workbook dialog box.

Step 4. Select Worksheet1 through Worksheet3 and choose OK.

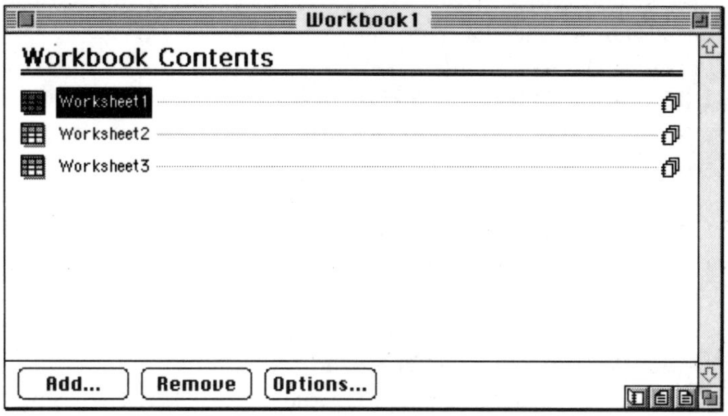

Figure 11-31: Adding worksheets to a workbook.

Step 5. Click the Save tool.

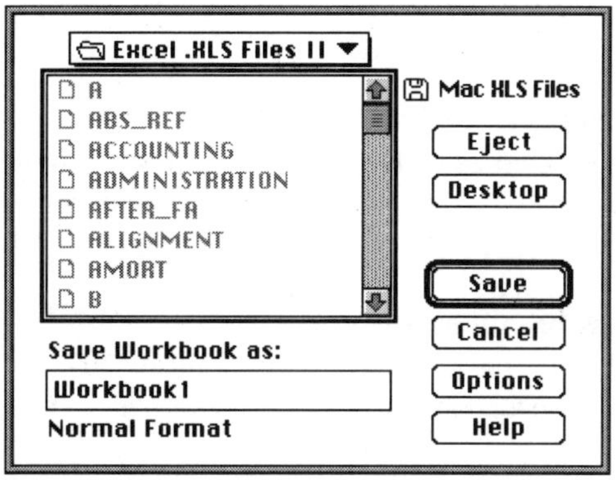

Figure 11-32: Clicking the Save tool displays the Save As dialog box.

Step 6. Type `TOPIC11` and choose OK.

Excel saves the workbook and worksheets to disk.

Quick Tips

This section provides you with tips on how to link and consolidate your worksheets in the most efficient way possible.

Opening worksheets as read-only

Opening worksheets as read-only allows you to open more worksheets than you would be able to open otherwise.

Changing cell addresses in external reference formulas

Changing the cell address from absolute to relative in an external reference formula enables you to copy the formula and create additional links to the source worksheet.

Consolidated worksheet subtotals

Worksheets that are consolidated usually contain subtotals. Only the subtotal's and other formula's values are consolidated in the summary worksheet. Text entries are not consolidated.

Consolidating other than totals

SUM is the worksheet function used by default to consolidate. The Function pull-down menu on the Consolidate dialog box contains other functions you can use for analysis purposes, such as AVERAGE, MAX, and MIN.

Formatting the first consolidated worksheet

Format the first worksheet to be consolidated as the way you want your summary worksheet to appear. Excel uses the formats from the first worksheet in the summary worksheet.

Ensuring an accurate consolidation

Creating and using names in external reference formulas and consolidation source areas ensures an accurate consolidation. Excel places the results of consolidated worksheets in the range named `Consolidate_Area` in the summary worksheet.

Summary

- Multiple worksheets that work interdependently have many advantages over using a single large worksheet, including less memory requirements, and faster opening, closing, calculating, and screen updating.
- Linking worksheets involves using a source worksheet to furnish data to a dependent worksheet.
- You can link worksheets through an external reference formula, a formula that contains the name of the source worksheet and a cell address or name.
- You can create external reference formulas by using Copy and Paste Link from the Edit menu, pointing, or typing the formula.
- You can create single-cell external reference formulas by using the Use Copy and Paste Link commands. Point to or type the formula when you want to link ranges or use functions and other formulas in the external reference formula.
- You can total data in worksheets, or consolidate data into another open worksheet.
- You total worksheets that do or do not have identical structures by using the Consolidate command from the Data menu.
- Consolidating dissimilar worksheets successfully requires that you include the text above rows or to the left of columns of values in ranges to be consolidated so Excel can match and total values correctly.
- Making a change in the active worksheet affects all open worksheets when Group Edit mode is active.
- The Arrange command from the Window menu enables you to display all open worksheets simultaneously.
- Worksheets that are used together repeatedly can be stored in a workbook.

Topic 12
Using Excel As a Database

Overview

Excel can do many things, and database tasks are no exception. If you need or always wanted a database, look no further. This Topic introduces you to databases, and how you might put Excel to work doing some database-like tasks.

What is a database?

A database is a collection of similar data stored in a structured manner. You already use databases, such as the white pages of a telephone book, a Rolodex, or your checkbook, for example. Database data is organized so you can easily analyze it, listing, sorting, or searching its contents for data meeting certain criteria.

Databases store their information as records. Each record contains separate items of information, or *fields*. In a telephone book, for example, each entry is a record, while each field contains similar information for every record (name, street address, and telephone number). Figure 12-1 shows you a spreadsheet that meets the requirements for a database.

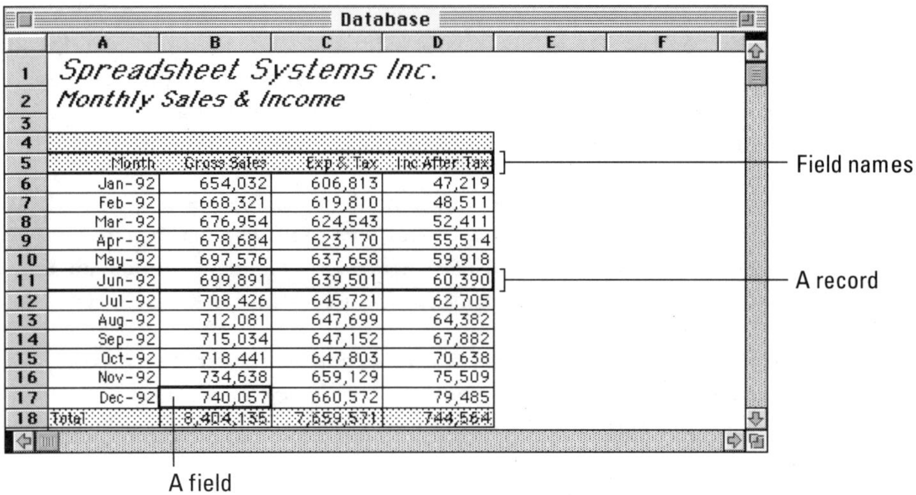

Month	Gross Sales	Exp & Tax	Inc After Tax
Jan-92	654,032	606,813	47,219
Feb-92	668,321	619,810	48,511
Mar-92	676,954	624,543	52,411
Apr-92	678,684	623,170	55,514
May-92	697,576	637,658	59,918
Jun-92	699,891	639,501	60,390
Jul-92	708,426	645,721	62,705
Aug-92	712,081	647,699	64,382
Sep-92	715,034	647,152	67,882
Oct-92	718,441	647,803	70,638
Nov-92	734,638	659,129	75,509
Dec-92	740,057	660,572	79,485
Total	8,404,135	7,659,571	744,564

Figure 12-1: An example of a spreadsheet that functions like a database.

There are plenty of uses for databases in your day-to-day work. For example, you can do the following:

- ✦ Calculate sales statistics
- ✦ Analyze stock market trends
- ✦ Monitor accounts receivable
- ✦ Target direct mail promotions

Database programs are available in a wide variety for all computer sizes and shapes. Some are dedicated to database management, such as Claris's Filemaker Pro and Acius's 4th Dimension. Excel can also be used for this purpose. Excel as a database manager? You must be joking. No, please read on.

Using a spreadsheet as a database

You *can* use Excel for database management operations, and what it does, it does well. But like anything else, there are pros and cons to doing so, as discussed in the follow section.

The good news

The good news of using Excel as a database is that you already have Excel and don't need to spend the time or money researching, comparing, shopping for, and buying another computer program. You can find out if you like or need database capability by trying it out with Excel first before you go out and plunk down your life savings.

Excel's row-and-column orientation make it a perfect candidate for database tasks, because each row in the database is a record of information, and each column in the record is a field.

If you've gotten this far in the book (this *is* Topic 12), you must have a fairly good comfort level with Excel by now. Since you're familiar with Excel's appearance and have a handle on how to use it, you don't need to learn another program to perform database operations.

And now that you're well on your way to becoming an Excel expert, you can take advantage of the Excel features you already know how to use and put them to work with your Excel database. These features include printing and charting, not to mention the database worksheet functions and commands that are specific to using Excel as a database.

Finally, Figure 12-1 shows you how you've already used Excel as a database. To perform calculations, you've entered data into your spreadsheet, and the data is in a structured arrangement in a range — a database! So there you have it. You've been using an Excel database all along.

The not so good news

As you may know, Excel loads a copy of your spreadsheet from disk when you choose Open from the File menu. Since your entire spreadsheet is in memory, your Macintosh's memory may limit the size of the database you can run. Most dedicated database management programs read and write records to and from the hard disk, and therefore don't face this limitation. But if your database needs are relatively simple, what you lose in capacity is more than made up in speed and flexibility. You won't have to wait around while your database is performing intensive disk operations. Because your database is in your Macintosh's memory, you'll enjoy very fast calculation and short task-completion times.

Now that you know the ground rules, you can tackle the first database step.

Designing a database

The first step in creating a database is to resist the urge to charge in and begin making entries in a blank Excel spreadsheet. Rather, as with any other spreadsheet application, you should invest some time in thinking about what you want your database to do and the best way to do it. Consider the type and quantity of data you're dealing with, the information you want to gain from your database, your ability to upgrade and enhance it, and so on. What you want to concentrate on are your fields: their selection, placement, and names in your database. After you determine that, you have the database bull by the horns.

Selecting fields

The fields you choose for your database are of paramount importance, as they determine the information in each database record, and ultimately, the database itself. You should decide what information you want in your database. For example, the accounts receivable database in Figure 12-2 should minimally include the name, amount, and date due.

You can, however, provide the database more firepower by breaking the fields down into more detail, or by adding additional fields. In Figure 12-3, for example, you could add invoice ID, days overdue, and so on. It all depends on what your current and future database uses are. In general, the more fields you have, the greater the flexibility of your database.

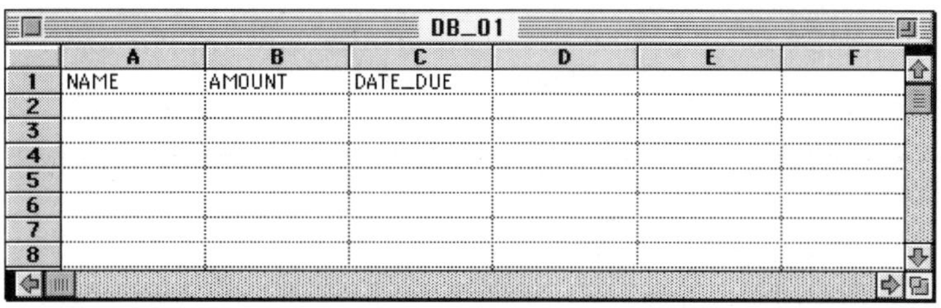

Figure 12-2: An example of an accounts receivable database with name, amount, and due date fields.

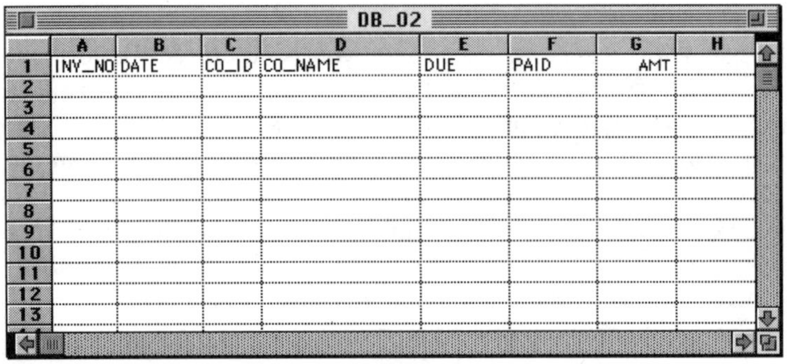

Figure 12-3: Adding additional fields to a database gives your database greater flexibility.

Placing fields

Field names comprise the top row of your database, so you need to place them across a contiguous row of cells. You should also place field names in logical order, grouping similar information together. For instance, descriptive information such as company ID and name should be adjacent to each other to make your database more understandable and useful.

Key fields

Each record in your database should be unique to ensure that your database is useful. A record is unique if one or more fields contains exclusive information, such as a date or amount. Such a field is called a key field, because the field identifies a unique feature of the record.

If you have records that aren't unique, you can create an extra field to make them unique. This field would include a serial number, a record number, or other entry that would make all the records unique. Many database programs, for example, automatically number a database's records beginning with the number 1.

Naming fields

Field names are a critical component of a database because Excel bases all its sort and search operations on field names. Thus, you should choose field names carefully.

Similar to range and filenames, database field names have their own set of rules, which include the following:

You must . . .	*You must not . . .*
Use text or text formulas (for example, ="100")	Use numbers, formulas, logical values, error values, or blanks
Use 1 to 255 characters per name	
Have names that are different from one another	

In general, shorter field names are easier to understand and permit you to display more fields on the screen at a time. You should also know that Excel is interested only in the row of field names directly above the first database record. You can have two or more rows of names to help you understand a field, but it's the single row above the database records that counts with Excel.

Creating your database

After you have a decided on a database design, you're ready to place the database in a spreadsheet. Begin by choosing a blank area of a spreadsheet with plenty of empty rows for database records. Better yet, use a new spreadsheet that will be dedicated to database duties. Then you're ready to enter data and specify the database.

Entering database data

Next, enter field names across a row in the spreadsheet. Make sure they're in the same row in adjacent cells and follow the rules described earlier. There are two ways to enter data: manually and with a form.

For now, I'll stick with the familiar and go with the first option. Later you'll learn how to have Excel create a fill-in-the-blanks form that you can use for data entry and other database tasks.

To enter the first database record, make the cell directly under the field names the active cell, specifically, in the cell that is the first field of the first record. Type the data for the field, and then press the right-arrow key. If you don't have data to enter into a cell, press the right-arrow key to continue. Database data can be text, values, or formulas, as with any other worksheet cell entry.

Repeat this process for each field in the record. For the last field, press the down-arrow key, and then press the left-arrow key repeatedly (or use the mouse) to make the first field of the second record the active cell. Continue this process for each record you want in the database. If you prefer, you can enter the same field for each record first (entering data by column) rather than by rows by pressing the Enter key, but it's a little easier to lose your place if you're entering data from a piece of paper. Figure 12-4 shows you some sample data in the database.

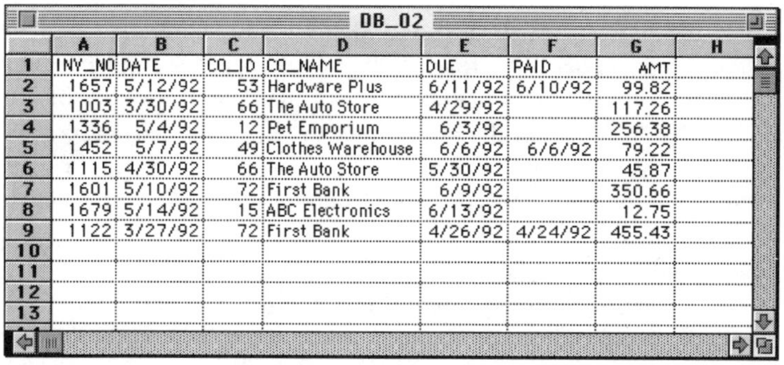
DB_02

	A	B	C	D	E	F	G	H
1	INV_NO	DATE	CO_ID	CO_NAME	DUE	PAID	AMT	
2	1657	5/12/92	53	Hardware Plus	6/11/92	6/10/92	99.82	
3	1003	3/30/92	66	The Auto Store	4/29/92		117.26	
4	1336	5/4/92	12	Pet Emporium	6/3/92		256.38	
5	1452	5/7/92	49	Clothes Warehouse	6/6/92	6/6/92	79.22	
6	1115	4/30/92	66	The Auto Store	5/30/92		45.87	
7	1601	5/10/92	72	First Bank	6/9/92		350.66	
8	1679	5/14/92	15	ABC Electronics	6/13/92		12.75	
9	1122	3/27/92	72	First Bank	4/26/92	4/24/92	455.43	
10								
11								
12								
13								

Figure 12-4: Sample data entered into a database.

Specifying the database

After you've finished entering data, you're ready to tell Excel that the spreadsheet contains a database. Select the database field names (exclude any cell entries above the field names) and all the records in the database. Then choose Set Database from the Data menu. When you do, Excel creates the range name Database and recognizes the range as such.

Be sure to save your spreadsheet to disk. Before putting the database to work, however, you may want to make a few changes to the database, so I'll cover that next.

Modifying a database

Someone may run up to you with another printout of database records you need to add to a database. Or you decide it would be helpful if your direct mailing list database included area code and telephone number data. As with any other spreadsheet application, from time to time you need to make changes to it, and databases are no exception. And because a database is stored on a worksheet, you use worksheet-type operations to modify it.

Changing fields

You may find as you work with your database that you need another field (to accommodate that telephone number) or can do without a field whose data all of a sudden becomes extraneous. Making a change to database fields isn't a difficult process, although, depending on the operation, you may change your database's fundamental structure.

If you want to change the name of a field, all you need to do is move the cell pointer to the cell containing the field name, click the formula bar or press Command-U, edit the name, and click Enter or press Return. Or you can type a completely new name. Either way, you have a new field name, and you can go on using the database as before.

Adding or deleting fields is a bit trickier, depending on the location of the field. Adding or deleting a field is as simple as adding a new column or removing an existing column from the database. To do so, choose Insert and Delete from the Edit menu, respectively. In both cases, choose the Entire Column option to ensure that the complete column (field) is inserted or deleted from the database.

Now comes the interesting part. If you're adding a field within the far left and far right columns, or deleting a field, you're home free — Excel adjusts the cell address of Database for you. But if you add a field adjacent to the database's extreme left or right columns, you'll need to select the entire range of your database and redefine it by choosing Set Database from the Data menu again. If you don't, Excel won't realize you've enlarged the database, and later you may be in for a surprise.

Changing records

Making a change to records is the converse of making a change to fields. Changing records has its own set of avoidable pitfalls, however. As with changing the name of a field, you change a record by making the field in the record you want to change the active cell; click the formula bar or press Command-U; and then edit the cell contents. You can also enter a completely different label, value, or formula.

VERSION 4 Microsoft

To add or delete a record, choose Insert and Delete from the Edit menu, respectively, and select the Entire Row option. As when adding or deleting fields, you'll want to ensure that you add or remove an entire row (record) from the database. You can also select the record (make sure you select every field) and choose Clear from the Edit menu, or drag on the selected range's fill handle to the upper-left corner of the first field, and release the mouse button.

Adding or deleting records has a similar pitfall to adding or deleting fields. If you add or delete a row (record) between your field names and the last record, Excel automatically makes the appropriate adjustment to the range name Database. If you add a record immediately following the last record at the bottom of your database, however, you won't need to insert a row to do so, but you'll need to select the entire range of the expanded database and choose the Set Database command from the Data menu again.

So far, you've seen how to create and fine-tune a database. Now you're ready to add some muscle to your Excel database.

Sorting your database

If you enter new records in the middle of a database, you'll realize that your records are out of order. Or perhaps you'd like to perform an analysis of an accounts receivable database that shows largest to smallest amounts owed, or longest to shortest in age.

Welcome to sorting, your first stop on the database productivity road. Sorting a database simply rearranges the order of the records. You can sort the rows of the database (the most common sort) or the columns (used less frequently, but still useful). The way a sort is performed is based on the sort keys you specify. If you want to sort the rows of a database, you select a cell in a column to specify the column to sort. If you want to sort the columns of a database, you select a cell in a row to specify the row to sort. You can specify up to three sort keys. You can also specify whether you want your records sorted in ascending order, where records are sorted from the lowest value to the highest value (for example, 1,2,3), or in descending order, where records are sorted from the highest value to the lowest value (for example, 3,2,1).

Many times you'll need more than one sort key to break "ties." A tie occurs when records with duplicate key fields remain unsorted. For example, suppose you have a wedding invitation list that includes names, addresses, and telephone numbers, and you'd like to have it in alphabetical order for easy envelope addressing. Before you enter into marital bliss, however, you'll need to specify the last name as the first sort key and the first name as the second sort key, for the list to be sorted in ascending order. That way, the Jones's (Irene, John, Paul, and Tom) are all in alphabetical order.

Excel sorts your records based on the following entries in your key field(s):

Ascending order	***Descending order***
Numbers (. . . –1, 0, 1 . . .)	Error values
Text (a, b, c . . .)	Logical values
Logical values	Text (z, y, x . . .)
Error values	Numbers (. . . 1, 0, –1 . . .)
Blanks	Blanks

Sorting a database, as with most operations in Excel, is an easy process once you know which button to push. And you don't need to specify a database in the worksheet to sort — any selected range will do. Sorting, however, is your biggest opportunity to make the greatest number of changes to a spreadsheet in one step, so be sure to save the spreadsheet to disk before beginning any sort operation.

After you've saved the spreadsheet, begin sorting by selecting the records of the database. Make sure you select every field of every record you want sorted, except field names. Next, choose Sort from the Data menu, and when the Sort dialog box appears, as shown in Figure 12-5, select Rows if you want to sort the order of the rows, or Columns if you want to sort the order of the columns.

Next, enter a cell reference in the 1st Key text box. You can enter the cell reference by clicking a cell or by typing its address. The cell reference can be any cell in the column or row to sort rows and columns, respectively. Now, select Ascending or Descending depending on the direction of the sort. Repeat this process if you plan on using 2nd and 3rd sort keys. When you're finished specifying sort key information, choose OK, and Excel sorts the selected records, as shown in Figure 12-6 (compare with Figure 12-4).

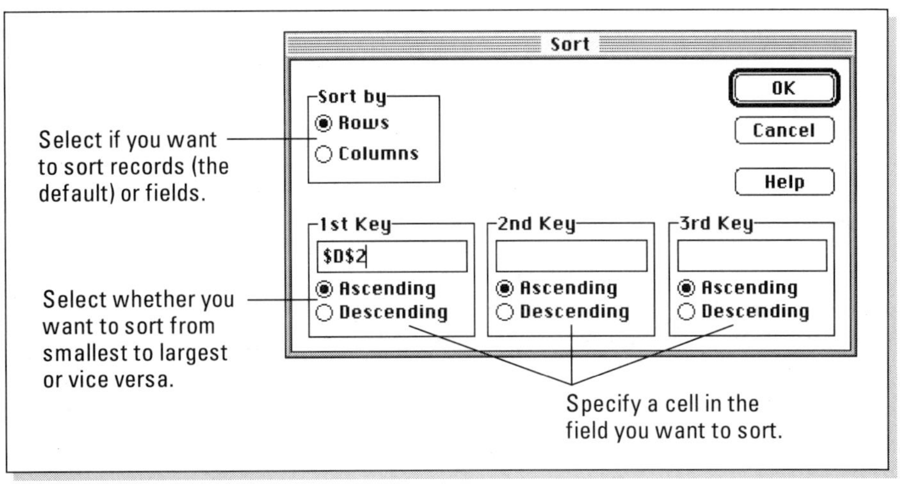

Figure 12-5: Choosing Sort from the Data menu displays the Sort dialog box.

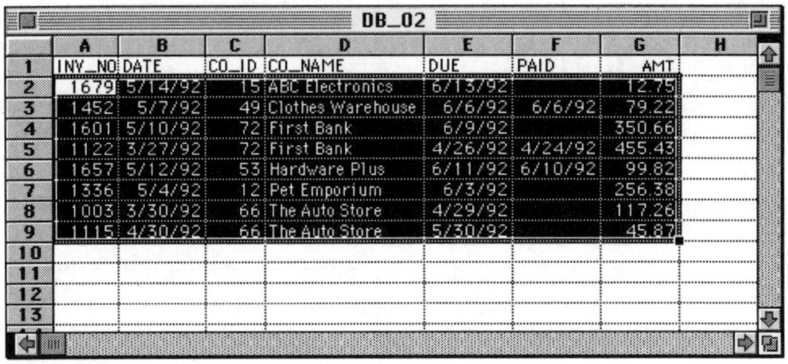

DB_02

	A	B	C	D	E	F	G	H
1	INV_NO	DATE	CO_ID	CO_NAME	DUE	PAID	AMT	
2	1679	5/14/92	15	ABC Electronics	6/13/92		12.75	
3	1452	5/7/92	49	Clothes Warehouse	6/6/92	6/6/92	79.22	
4	1601	5/10/92	72	First Bank	6/9/92		350.66	
5	1122	3/27/92	72	First Bank	4/26/92	4/24/92	455.43	
6	1657	5/12/92	53	Hardware Plus	6/11/92	6/10/92	99.82	
7	1336	5/4/92	12	Pet Emporium	6/3/92		256.38	
8	1003	3/30/92	66	The Auto Store	4/29/92		117.26	
9	1115	4/30/92	66	The Auto Store	5/30/92		45.87	
10								
11								
12								
13								

Figure 12-6: Sorting records in a database using the Sort dialog box.

Sorting on more than three keys

You may be delighted to know that you can sort on three keys with Excel. But what do you do if you need more than three keys? For example, recall your wedding invitation list. You have relatives, friends, and business associates who live in close proximity. You've sorted the list by last name, first name, and city, but it still isn't enough to sort all your records in ascending order. Now what?

You can sort on more than three keys with Excel by performing multiple sort operations. You start by sorting the *least* important key fields *first*, because the final sort takes precedence over all other sorts. In our example, then, you can choose to sort on the telephone number as your first sort. In effect, this is your "fourth key." Then do a second sort with 1st, 2nd, and 3rd sort keys as before. This multiple sort ensures that everyone in your close-knit group is alphabetized and gets their invitations on time.

If you don't like the results of a sort operation, or if you've inadvertently selected the database's field names with the range to be sorted, choose Undo from the Edit menu or press F1 immediately after the sort.

Asking your database to find data

In addition to sorting the records of the database, you can ask the database questions about its records. My example database contains only a few records, but what if the database you use (or will be using) has several hundred rows of information in it? It'll probably be a little more difficult finding records that need updating (editing), deleting, or that match a certain set of conditions. But you can have Excel find these records for you quickly and easily. You'll just need to give Excel a little head start first.

That head start is known as a criteria range. The criteria range contains conditions you specify that can be found in some or all of the database records. You can place the criteria range on the same spreadsheet as the database or on another open spreadsheet. Specifically, a criteria range is a multiple row range, with the first row containing a copy

Restoring order sequentially

All dedicated database programs number their records sequentially. You can do the same if, for example, a sort operation doesn't go as well as planned. You can sort the records on the field that contains the numbers, in ascending order, restoring the database records to their original order.

To number the records in the database in the following figure, insert a column in Column A, and then move the cell pointer to cell A2, type the number 1, press Enter, type the number 2, and press Enter again. Place the mouse pointer over the selected range's fill handle, and when it appears as a black cross, drag to cell A9, and then release the mouse button. Excel enters the numbers 3 through 8.

To return the database records to numerical order, select the database records (including the new field) and choose Sort from the Data menu. Specify any cell in Column A as the 1st Key, choose Ascending, and then choose OK. Excel returns the database back to its original state.

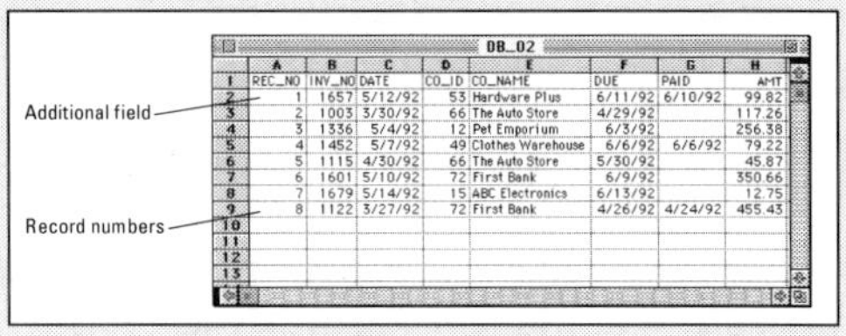

	A	B	C	D	E	F	G	H
1	REC_NO	INV_NO	DATE	CO_ID	CO_NAME	DUE	PAID	AMT
2	1	1657	5/12/92	53	Hardware Plus	6/11/92	6/10/92	99.82
3	2	1003	3/30/92	66	The Auto Store	4/29/92		117.26
4	3	1336	5/4/92	12	Pet Emporium	6/3/92		256.38
5	4	1452	5/7/92	49	Clothes Warehouse	6/6/92	6/6/92	79.22
6	5	1115	4/30/92	66	The Auto Store	5/30/92		45.87
7	6	1601	5/10/92	72	First Bank	6/9/92		350.66
8	7	1679	5/14/92	15	ABC Electronics	6/13/92		12.75
9	8	1122	3/27/92	72	First Bank	4/26/92	4/24/92	455.43
10								
11								
12								
13								

of the database's field names. The following rows (at least one) contain criteria characters or formulas. Figure 12-7 shows the example database with a criteria range ready to receive your criteria (with formatting so you can view the ranges easily).

The two types of criteria ranges, comparison and computed, are discussed in the following section.

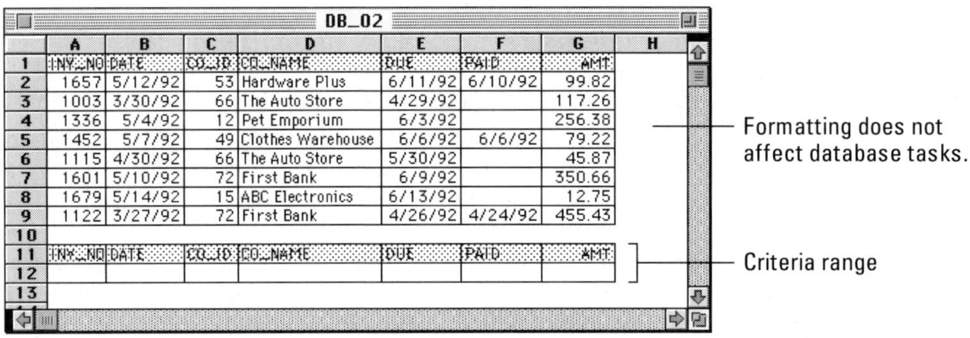

	A	B	C	D	E	F	G	H
1	INV_NO	DATE	CO_ID	CO_NAME	DUE	PAID	AMT	
2	1657	5/12/92	53	Hardware Plus	6/11/92	6/10/92	99.82	
3	1003	3/30/92	66	The Auto Store	4/29/92		117.26	
4	1336	5/4/92	12	Pet Emporium	6/3/92		256.38	
5	1452	5/7/92	49	Clothes Warehouse	6/6/92	6/6/92	79.22	
6	1115	4/30/92	66	The Auto Store	5/30/92		45.87	
7	1601	5/10/92	72	First Bank	6/9/92		350.66	
8	1679	5/14/92	15	ABC Electronics	6/13/92		12.75	
9	1122	3/27/92	72	First Bank	4/26/92	4/24/92	455.43	
10								
11	INV_NO	DATE	CO_ID	CO_NAME	DUE	PAID	AMT	
12								
13								

Figure 12-7: An example of a criteria range in a database.

Comparison criteria

You use comparison criteria when you want to find records that exactly match your criteria, or fall within a specified range. Comparison criteria consists of text, a value, or a date you want to search for, preceded by one of the following comparison operators shown in Table 12-1.

Table 12-1: Comparison criteria options

Operator	*Definition*	*Example criteria*	*Result*
=	Equal to	=500	Records with a field value equal to 500
>	Greater than	>500	Records with a field value greater than 500
<	Less than	<500	Records with a field value less than 500
>=	Greater than or equal to	>=500	Records with a field value value greater than or equal to equal to 500
<=	Less than or equal to	<=500	Records with a field value less than or equal to 500
<>	Not equal to	<>500	Records with a field value not equal to 500
?	Matches single character	="j?nes"	Records with a field with text and any single character at that position
*	Matches multiple characters	="j*nes"	Records with a field with text and any multiple characters at that position

If you want to use these criteria comparison operators with text, enclose the text in double quotation marks. For example, `="jones"` finds all records with a field containing the text jones. Dates operate similarly to values because Excel considers them as serial numbers. For example, `=10/31/92` finds records with a field that contains the date October 31, 1992. You can use dates in any date format you use to enter them into the spreadsheet.

When you enter your criteria in a single cell in the row below the criteria fields, it is known as *single* comparison criteria. In some instances, however, you'll need to use *multiple* comparison criteria — criterion that meets two or more sets of conditions. You can have multiple criteria that meets two or more conditions, or multiple criteria that meets one or another criteria.

In the first case, entering criteria in more than one field in the *same* row instructs Excel to search for records that meet *both* conditions. For example, entering `>500` under Amt (G12) and `>5/30/92` under Due (E12) in the second row of the criteria range tells Excel to search for records that are over $500 *and* due after May 30, 1992.

In the second case, entering criteria in *more* than one row instructs Excel to search for records that meet *either* condition. For example, entering `>500` under Amt (G12) in the second row and `>5/30/92` under Due in the third row (E13) of the criteria range tells Excel to search for records that are over $500 *or* over 60 days.

Computed criterion

Computed criterion is similar to comparison criteria, except in two ways: The computed criteria is a formula, and you need to use a name for the criterion that doesn't exist as a database field name. The formula should be the relative reference of the first database record (so all records are searched) and evaluate to TRUE or FALSE. Figure 12-8 shows the result of the criteria formula `=C3>B3*0.15`, which has Excel search the database for the poor souls paying greater than 15 percent of their income in taxes.

After you've set up the criteria range, you select it, and then choose Set Criteria from the Data menu. As with the Set Database command, this tells Excel where the criteria range is. Now you can search the database records and extract and delete records.

Finding records

Records in large databases can be found quickly using criteria you specify and by choosing Find from the Data menu. Excel selects the first record that meets the criteria (if no records meet the criteria, you'll be greeted by an alert box), and displays the message, *Use arrow keys to view records,* in the status bar at the bottom of the worksheet, as shown in Figure 12-9.

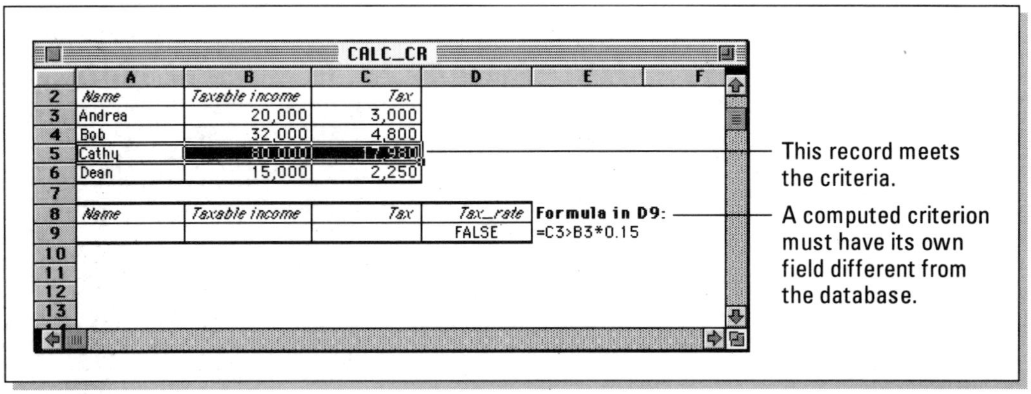

Figure 12-8: An example of a record that is found based on a criteria formula.

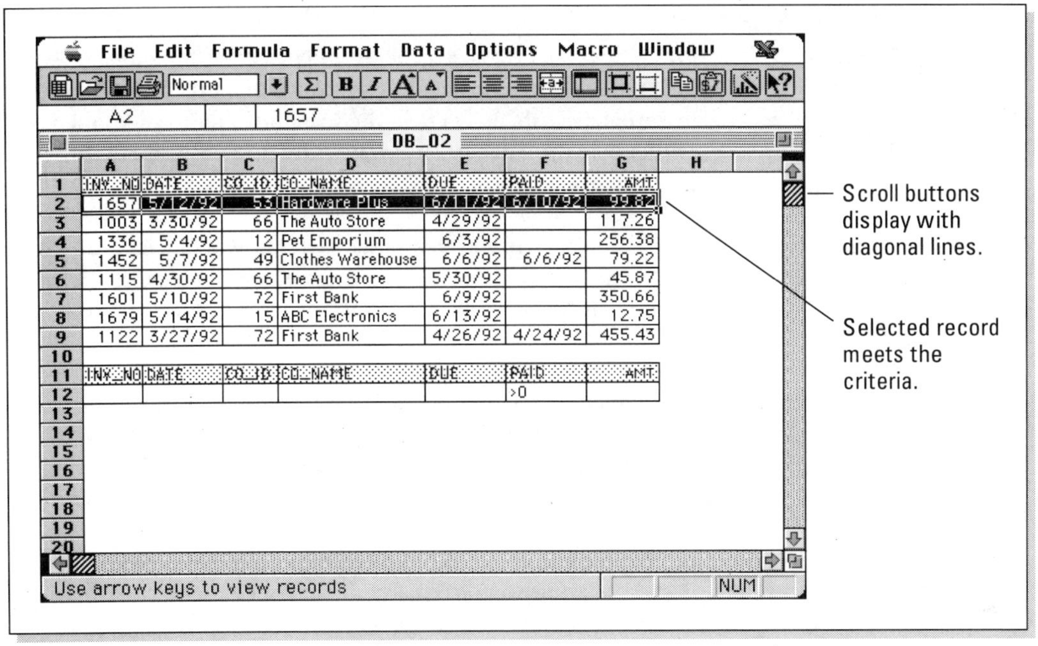

Figure 12-9: Finding records in a database using the Find command from the Data menu.

Table 12-2 lists the various ways to move to the next record that meets the criteria you have specified.

Table 12-2: Moving between records with matching criteria

To . . .	***Using mouse . . .***	***Using keyboard . . .***
Move to next/previous matching record	Click down/up scroll arrow	Press down/up arrow
Move to next/previous record one screen away	Click in vertical scroll bar	Press PgDn/PgUp
Scroll right/left	Click in horizontal scroll bar	Press right/left arrow

While a record is selected, you can edit it by selecting the cell, and then activating the formula bar, or by pressing Command-U. After you make changes, click Enter or press Return. Choose Find from the Data menu to restart finding records.

To exit from Find mode, choose Exit Find from the Data menu, press Esc, or select a cell outside the database range.

Extracting records

You can extract a copy of the records from a database and place the copied records in the same worksheet or another open worksheet. When you extract records, you create a copy of the records in the database that meet the criteria in the criteria range and place them in another area other than the database. In a way, extracting records is a database version of copying and pasting.

Before you extract records, you need to add another range to the worksheet — an extract range. The extract range must include at least one field name from the database field names, and should include all field names if you want to extract exact copies of the records.

After you've entered (or copied) the field names to be extracted, select the names and the rows beneath the names to hold the copied records. If you select only the field names, the extract range includes the names and all rows beneath the names to the bottom of the worksheet.

If you know how many records will be extracted, you can specify that number of rows in the extract range. If there are more records than rows in your extract range, however, Excel displays the alert box shown in Figure 12-10. Choose OK, select a larger extract range, and choose Extract from the Data menu to try again.

After you've created the extract range, choose Set Extract from the Data menu to let Excel know the whereabouts of the extract range. When you choose Extract from the Data menu, and then choose OK or press Return, Excel copies the records from the database that meet the criteria of the extract range, as shown in Figure 12-11.

Deleting records

If you work with databases frequently, especially accounts receivable databases, you know that every database requires maintenance to stay current. In the example in Figure 12-2, you need to remove a record when a company pays its bill in full. Earlier you learned how to delete records by choosing Delete from the Edit menu. You can also use the Delete command from the Data menu to remove records that are no longer needed. One advantage of using Delete from the Data menu instead of Delete Entire Row from the Edit menu is that Excel closes up any space in the database as a result of removing records.

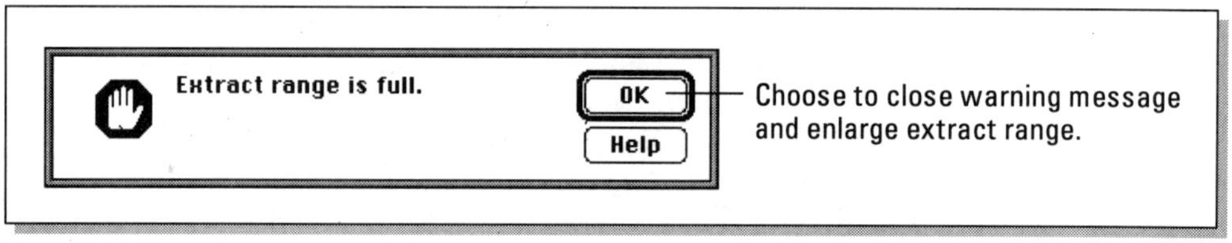

Figure 12-10: Extracting more records than rows to an extract range displays this alert box.

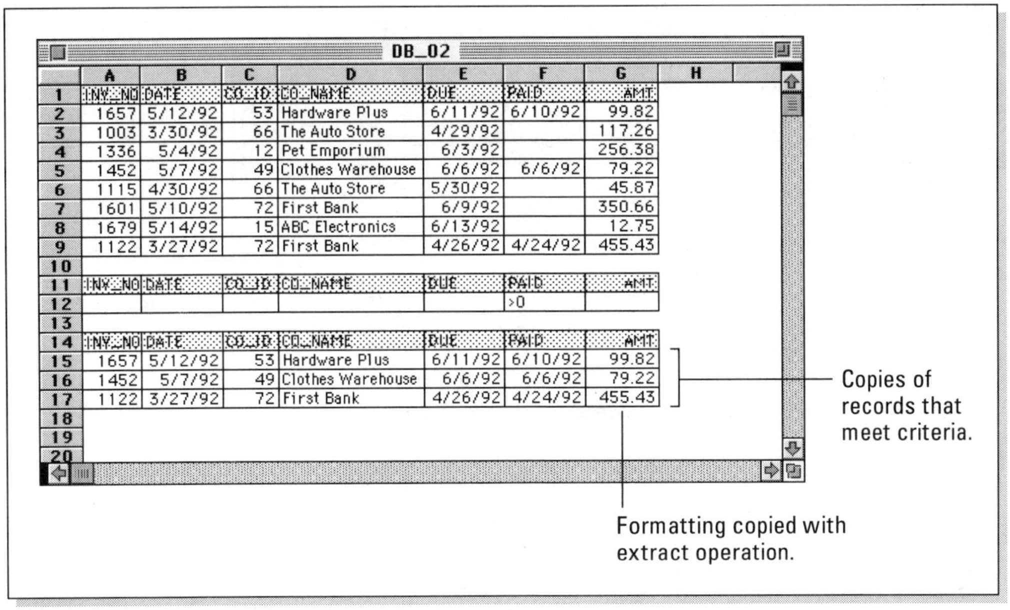

	A	B	C	D	E	F	G	H
1	INV_NO	DATE	CO_ID	CO_NAME	DUE	PAID	AMT	
2	1657	5/12/92	53	Hardware Plus	6/11/92	6/10/92	99.82	
3	1003	3/30/92	66	The Auto Store	4/29/92		117.26	
4	1336	5/4/92	12	Pet Emporium	6/3/92		256.38	
5	1452	5/7/92	49	Clothes Warehouse	6/6/92	6/6/92	79.22	
6	1115	4/30/92	66	The Auto Store	5/30/92		45.87	
7	1601	5/10/92	72	First Bank	6/9/92		350.66	
8	1679	5/14/92	15	ABC Electronics	6/13/92		12.75	
9	1122	3/27/92	72	First Bank	4/26/92	4/24/92	455.43	
10								
11	INV_NO	DATE	CO_ID	CO_NAME	DUE	PAID	AMT	
12						>0		
13								
14	INV_NO	DATE	CO_ID	CO_NAME	DUE	PAID	AMT	
15	1657	5/12/92	53	Hardware Plus	6/11/92	6/10/92	99.82	
16	1452	5/7/92	49	Clothes Warehouse	6/6/92	6/6/92	79.22	
17	1122	3/27/92	72	First Bank	4/26/92	4/24/92	455.43	
18								
19								
20								

Figure 12-11: Extracting records using the Set Extract command from the Data menu.

CAUTION!

Use Delete from the Data menu with caution, however, as it's a potentially destructive command. If you delete records inadvertently, you cannot use Undo to reclaim them. Instead, use Save or Save As from the File menu before you delete records regardless of which method you use. That way, you have a backup copy of the database on disk if the Delete operation goes awry.

To delete records from a database, you need only use the named database and a criteria range. Enter a criteria that represents an attribute about the records you want deleted. For example, if you want to delete the paid records, you'd enter >0 in the cell under the paid field of the criteria range (F12). After you've entered the criteria, choose Delete from the Data menu, and the alert box shown in Figure 12-12 appears.

Choose OK to proceed, and the records are removed, as shown in Figure 12-13.

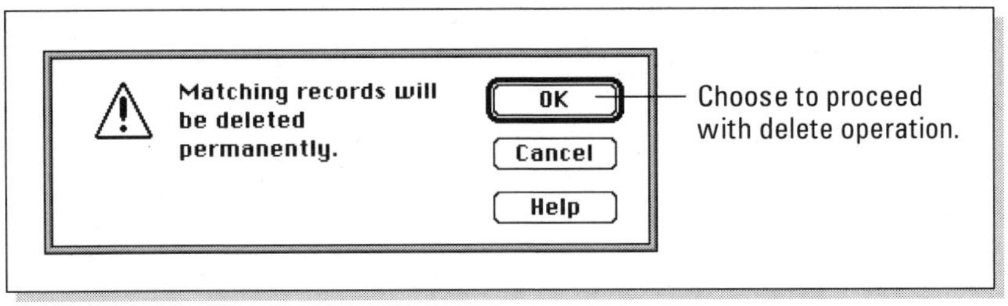

Figure 12-12: Excel displays this alert box when deleting records in a database.

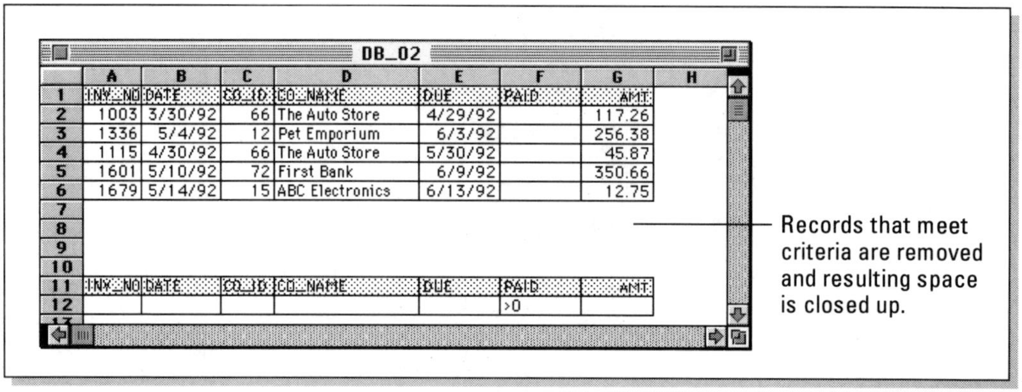

Figure 12-13: Deleting records in a database using a criteria range.

(In Figure 12-11, the criteria >0 was used in the cell beneath paid in the criteria range as a way for Excel to distinguish between a blank and nonblank cell, because a date is a serial number, and blank cells are evaluated as zero.)

Database forms

Excel, as with most database programs, has a feature that enables you to view, edit, add, or delete records one at a time using a fill-in-the-blanks form. Excel's data form is a dialog box (the title of the dialog box is the same as the worksheet title) and is created by Excel using the database field names. After you define the database by choosing Set Database from the Data menu, you can use the Form command from the Data menu at any time to create the form. The form for the example database is shown in Figure 12-14.

Here's how you can maintain a database with a form.

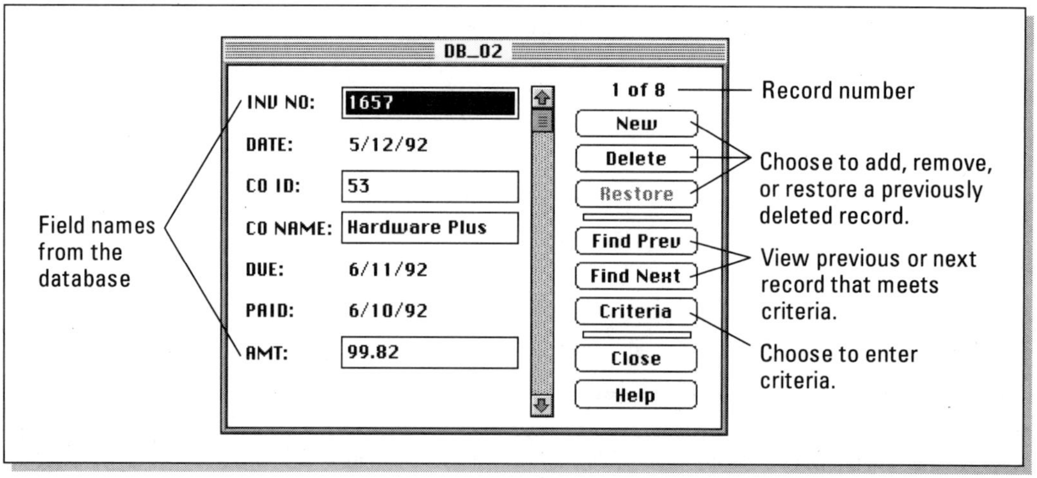

Figure 12-14: An example of a form for a database created by choosing Form from the Data menu.

Finding database records in a form

To search database records, click the Criteria button in the form, and then use criteria (as explained earlier in this Topic) appropriate for the search in the corresponding text box. (The record number indicator in the upper-right corner of the form changes to Criteria). To remove criteria from previous searches, click the Clear button, and to bail out of searching altogether, click the Form button.

Choose the Find Prev or Find Next button to move to the previous or next records, respectively, that meet the criteria. Excel displays the matching record's fields in the form's text boxes. When the last record is found, Excel beeps. Click the Close button to exit from the data form.

Because the data form is in its own window, you can move and close it like any other window. Table 12-3 lists the various ways to view other records in the data form.

Table 12-3: Viewing records in a data form

To . . .	*Do this . . .*
Move to next/previous matching record	Click down/up scroll arrow
Move to next/previous matching record 10 records away	Click below/above scroll box in vertical scroll bar
Move to last/first matching record	Drag scroll box to bottom/top of vertical scroll bar

Editing records

After you've found the record you're searching for, you can make changes to it. Move to the text box by clicking it or by pressing Tab. Edit the contents of the record in the form with the mouse and keyboard as you would any worksheet cell entry. If you change your mind about the edits you've made, make sure you click the Restore button before pushing on to the next record, although you can always recover by editing the record by clicking the Find Prev button to locate and display the record in the form.

Adding records

Adding new records to a database with a form helps you enter data properly — you don't need to worry about data going into the wrong field (cell). Forms are especially useful for data entry users who may not be well-versed in spreadsheets.

To add a record to a database, click the New button. The record number indicator displays New Record. Type the data for the first field, and then press Tab or click the next field. Repeat this for every field and press Return when you're through. Another blank record appears for you to fill out. If you're finished with data entry, choose the Close button. Excel extends the range name DATABASE to include the new records, and redisplays the database form.

Deleting records

Deleting records from a database with a form is similar to deleting them using Delete from the Data menu. In both cases, you should be very careful, because a backup copy of the spreadsheet on disk is the only way to recover from unwanted deletions.

To delete a single record using a form, find the record using the form, and then click the Delete button. After Excel displays an alert box, choose OK; the record is removed, and the resulting space in the database is closed up.

To delete multiple records in one step, enter appropriate criteria in the corresponding field's text box, and then proceed with the delete operation as before.

Are data forms for you?

Database data forms are great if your database needs are relatively simple, and are especially helpful if your database is used by another user primarily for data entry. If you need to extract records or use calculated criteria, however, you'll need to go the nonform route, unless you create a macro-driven custom application. You may also find searching for more than one record easier with the Data Find command.

Analyzing a database

Excel has several worksheet functions you can use with databases. These functions enable you to quickly calculate results that are otherwise tedious to perform. Table 12-4 lists the functions available to you.

Table 12-4: Database worksheet functions

Function	*Result*
DAVERAGE	Averages values
DCOUNT	Counts values
DCOUNTA	Counts nonblank cells
DGET	Extracts a single value
DMAX	Finds a maximum value
DMIN	Finds a minimum value
DPRODUCT	Multiplies numbers
DSTDEV	Calculates standard deviation of a population based on a sample
DSTDDEVP	Calculates standard deviation of a population based on the entire population
DSUM	Totals values
DVAR	Calculates variance of a population based on a sample
DVARP	Calculates variance of a population based on the entire population

All the database functions have the following format:

```
=Dfunction(Database,field,criteria)
```

In this function, *Database* is a range of cells, and *field* and *criteria* are as their name implies (you can use the range name *Database* and the name *criteria* if you've used Set Database and Set Criteria on the respective range).

As an example of the utility of database functions, it'd be a fairly easy process to determine the amount of money owed by *The Auto Store* in the example database. You could visually scan all the instances of amount owed and use (gasp!) your calculator, or enter the values in another area of the spreadsheet, and total the numbers. A faster and less error-prone solution is to use DSUM (especially if you're dealing with a database containing hundreds of records).

Figure 12-15 shows the result of using DSUM to quickly find the total. (Note that the extract range isn't a requirement to use with database worksheet functions). The DSUM function uses the name *Database* for the range database, *Amt* for the field, and the range D11:D12 as the criteria.

Note that you can specify a field name (as long as it's enclosed in quotation marks) from the database in database functions. You can also use the column number of the database as the field argument in a database function (database column numbers begin with 1). In the example database, INV_NO would be column number 1, so the function would then be =DSUM(DATABASE,7,D11:D12).

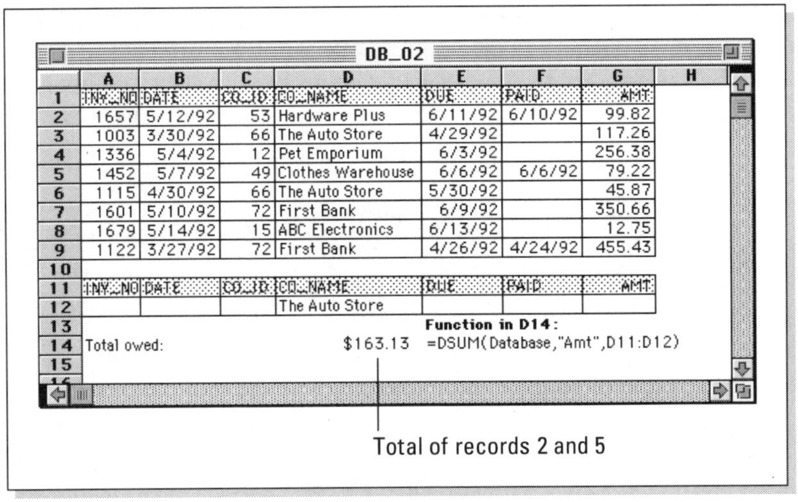
DB_02

	A	B	C	D	E	F	G	H
1	INV_NO	DATE	CO_ID	CO_NAME	DUE	PAID	AMT	
2	1657	5/12/92	53	Hardware Plus	6/11/92	6/10/92	99.82	
3	1003	3/30/92	66	The Auto Store	4/29/92		117.26	
4	1336	5/4/92	12	Pet Emporium	6/3/92		256.38	
5	1452	5/7/92	49	Clothes Warehouse	6/6/92	6/6/92	79.22	
6	1115	4/30/92	66	The Auto Store	5/30/92		45.87	
7	1601	5/10/92	72	First Bank	6/9/92		350.66	
8	1679	5/14/92	15	ABC Electronics	6/13/92		12.75	
9	1122	3/27/92	72	First Bank	4/26/92	4/24/92	455.43	
10								
11	INV_NO	DATE	CO_ID	CO_NAME	DUE	PAID	AMT	
12				The Auto Store				
13					Function in D14:			
14	Total owed:			$163.13	=DSUM(Database,"Amt",D11:D12)			
15								

Figure 12-15: Finding a total quickly using the DSUM function.

Step-by-Step

In this section, you'll practice creating, sorting, and querying a database. If you make a mistake, don't get flustered, just choose Undo from the Edit menu or press F1, or start over with a new worksheet.

To begin this exercise, do the following:

1. Start Excel if you haven't already.

   The Worksheet1 worksheet appears.

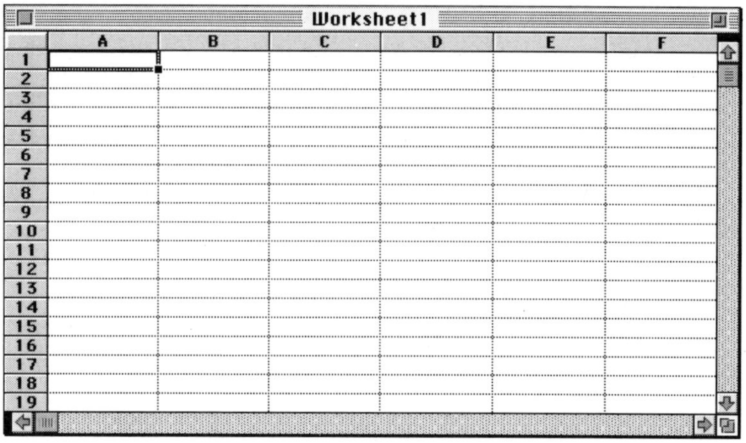

Figure 12-16: Starting up Excel displays the Worksheet1 worksheet.

2. Create a database by entering the text and values shown in Figure 12-17. Enter dates as displayed (for example, 5/12/92 in cell B2). To narrow the column widths, select all the columns and then double-click any line that separates the selected columns' letters. You can also format the database, as shown in Figure 12-11.

   You now have the completed database with criteria and extract ranges.

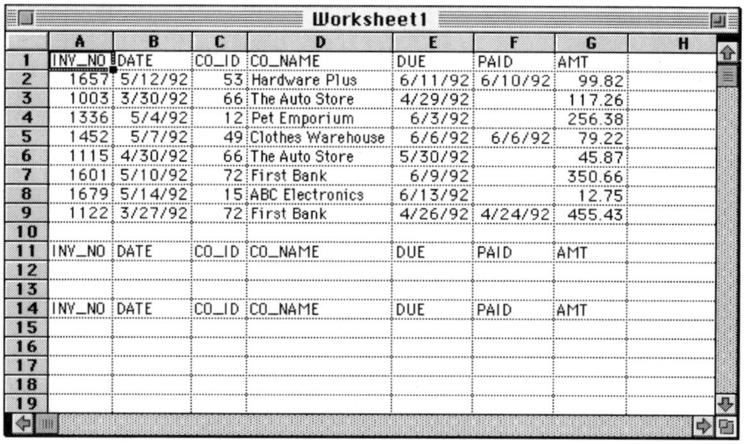

Worksheet1

	A	B	C	D	E	F	G	H
1	INV_NO	DATE	CO_ID	CO_NAME	DUE	PAID	AMT	
2	1657	5/12/92	53	Hardware Plus	6/11/92	6/10/92	99.82	
3	1003	3/30/92	66	The Auto Store	4/29/92		117.26	
4	1336	5/4/92	12	Pet Emporium	6/3/92		256.38	
5	1452	5/7/92	49	Clothes Warehouse	6/6/92	6/6/92	79.22	
6	1115	4/30/92	66	The Auto Store	5/30/92		45.87	
7	1601	5/10/92	72	First Bank	6/9/92		350.66	
8	1679	5/14/92	15	ABC Electronics	6/13/92		12.75	
9	1122	3/27/92	72	First Bank	4/26/92	4/24/92	455.43	
10								
11	INV_NO	DATE	CO_ID	CO_NAME	DUE	PAID	AMT	
12								
13								
14	INV_NO	DATE	CO_ID	CO_NAME	DUE	PAID	AMT	
15								
16								
17								
18								
19								

Figure 12-17: An example of a completed database with criteria ranges and extract ranges.

Specifying database ranges:

Step 1. Select the range A1:G9 and choose Set Database from the Data menu.

Step 2. Select the range A11:G11 and choose Set Criteria from the Data menu.

Step 3. Select the range A14:G14 and choose Set Extract from the Data menu.

Sorting a database from highest to lowest amount (AMT):

Step 1. Select the range A2:G9.

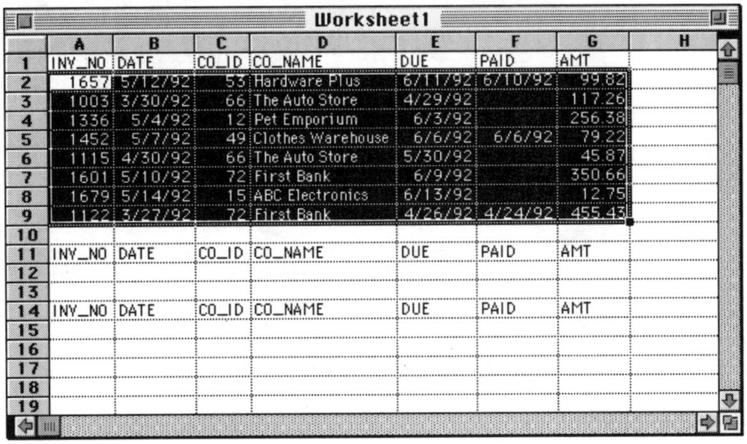

Figure 12-18: Selecting a database range to sort.

Step 2. Choose Sort from the Data menu.

The Sort dialog box appears.

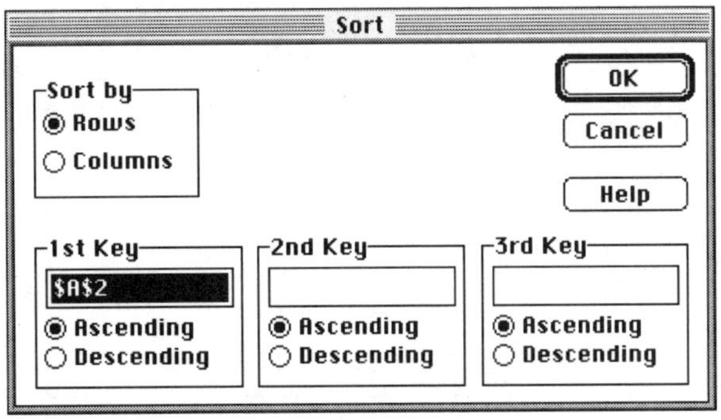

Figure 12-19: Choosing Sort from the data menu displays the Sort dialog box.

Step 3. Select cell G2, or type `G2` in the 1st Key text box; click the Descending button; and choose OK.

Excel sorts the database from largest to smallest amount owed.

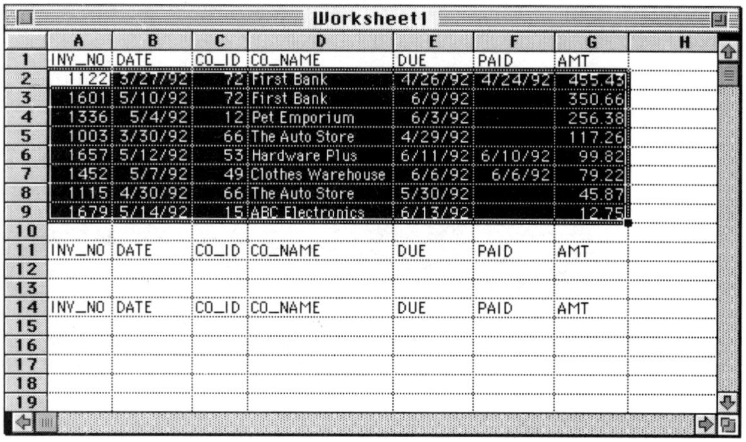

Worksheet1

	A	B	C	D	E	F	G	H
1	INV_NO	DATE	CO_ID	CO_NAME	DUE	PAID	AMT	
2	1122	3/27/92	72	First Bank	4/26/92	4/24/92	455.43	
3	1601	5/10/92	72	First Bank	6/9/92		350.66	
4	1336	5/4/92	12	Pet Emporium	6/3/92		256.38	
5	1003	3/30/92	66	The Auto Store	4/29/92		117.26	
6	1657	5/12/92	53	Hardware Plus	6/11/92	6/10/92	99.82	
7	1452	5/7/92	49	Clothes Warehouse	6/6/92	6/6/92	79.22	
8	1115	4/30/92	66	The Auto Store	5/30/92		45.87	
9	1679	5/14/92	15	ABC Electronics	6/13/92		12.75	
10								
11	INV_NO	DATE	CO_ID	CO_NAME	DUE	PAID	AMT	
12								
13								
14	INV_NO	DATE	CO_ID	CO_NAME	DUE	PAID	AMT	
15								
16								
17								
18								
19								

Figure 12-20: An example of a descending database sort.

Returning records to their previous order:

Step 1. Choose Undo Sort or press F1.

Excel returns the records to their original order.

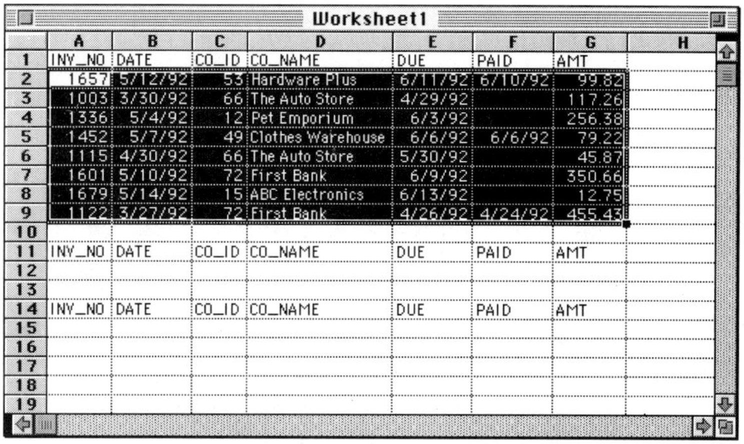

Worksheet1

	A	B	C	D	E	F	G	H
1	INV_NO	DATE	CO_ID	CO_NAME	DUE	PAID	AMT	
2	1657	5/12/92	53	Hardware Plus	6/11/92	6/10/92	99.82	
3	1003	3/30/92	66	The Auto Store	4/29/92		117.26	
4	1336	5/4/92	12	Pet Emporium	6/3/92		256.38	
5	1452	5/7/92	49	Clothes Warehouse	6/6/92	6/6/92	79.22	
6	1115	4/30/92	66	The Auto Store	5/30/92		45.87	
7	1601	5/10/92	72	First Bank	6/9/92		350.66	
8	1679	5/14/92	15	ABC Electronics	6/13/92		12.75	
9	1122	3/27/92	72	First Bank	4/26/92	4/24/92	455.43	
10								
11	INV_NO	DATE	CO_ID	CO_NAME	DUE	PAID	AMT	
12								
13								
14	INV_NO	DATE	CO_ID	CO_NAME	DUE	PAID	AMT	
15								
16								
17								
18								
19								

Figure 12-21: Returning records to their previous order using the Undo Sort command.

Searching records by criteria:

Step 1. Enter `>200` in cell G12.

The criteria over $200 is entered in cell G12.

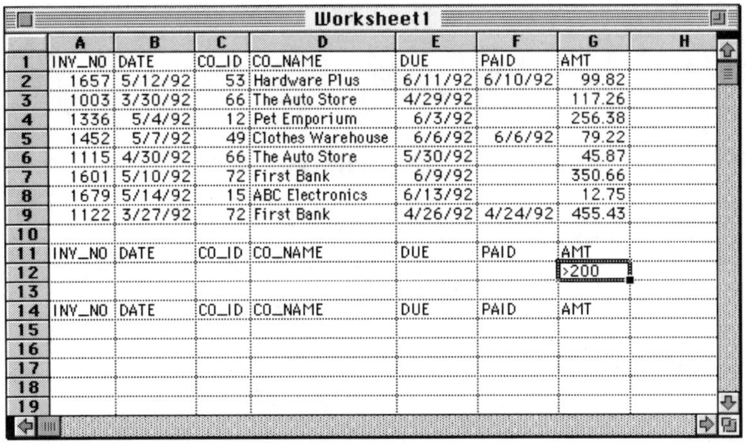

Worksheet1

	A	B	C	D	E	F	G	H
1	INV_NO	DATE	CO_ID	CO_NAME	DUE	PAID	AMT	
2	1657	5/12/92	53	Hardware Plus	6/11/92	6/10/92	99.82	
3	1003	3/30/92	66	The Auto Store	4/29/92		117.26	
4	1336	5/4/92	12	Pet Emporium	6/3/92		256.38	
5	1452	5/7/92	49	Clothes Warehouse	6/6/92	6/6/92	79.22	
6	1115	4/30/92	66	The Auto Store	5/30/92		45.87	
7	1601	5/10/92	72	First Bank	6/9/92		350.66	
8	1679	5/14/92	15	ABC Electronics	6/13/92		12.75	
9	1122	3/27/92	72	First Bank	4/26/92	4/24/92	455.43	
10								
11	INV_NO	DATE	CO_ID	CO_NAME	DUE	PAID	AMT	
12							>200	
13								
14	INV_NO	DATE	CO_ID	CO_NAME	DUE	PAID	AMT	
15								
16								
17								
18								
19								

Figure 12-22: Entering a criterion for a search operation.

Step 2. Choose Extract from the Data menu, and then choose OK.

Excel copies the records from the database to the extract range that are $200 or more.

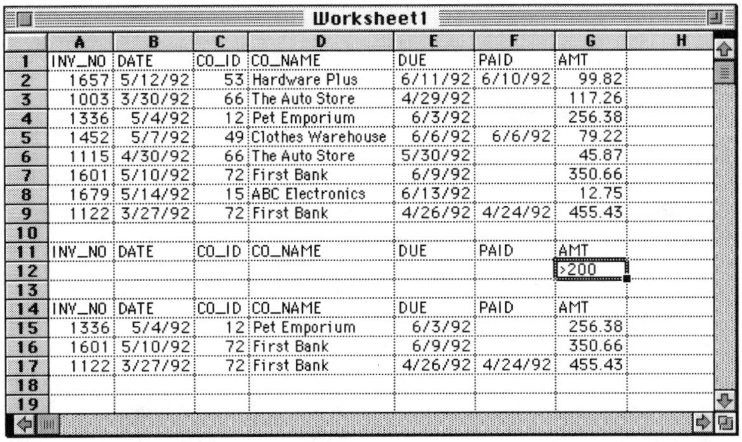

Worksheet1

	A	B	C	D	E	F	G	H
1	INV_NO	DATE	CO_ID	CO_NAME	DUE	PAID	AMT	
2	1657	5/12/92	53	Hardware Plus	6/11/92	6/10/92	99.82	
3	1003	3/30/92	66	The Auto Store	4/29/92		117.26	
4	1336	5/4/92	12	Pet Emporium	6/3/92		256.38	
5	1452	5/7/92	49	Clothes Warehouse	6/6/92	6/6/92	79.22	
6	1115	4/30/92	66	The Auto Store	5/30/92		45.87	
7	1601	5/10/92	72	First Bank	6/9/92		350.66	
8	1679	5/14/92	15	ABC Electronics	6/13/92		12.75	
9	1122	3/27/92	72	First Bank	4/26/92	4/24/92	455.43	
10								
11	INV_NO	DATE	CO_ID	CO_NAME	DUE	PAID	AMT	
12							>200	
13								
14	INV_NO	DATE	CO_ID	CO_NAME	DUE	PAID	AMT	
15	1336	5/4/92	12	Pet Emporium	6/3/92		256.38	
16	1601	5/10/92	72	First Bank	6/9/92		350.66	
17	1122	3/27/92	72	First Bank	4/26/92	4/24/92	455.43	
18								
19								

Figure 12-23: Searching records by criteria by choosing Extract from the Data menu.

Step 3. Click the Save tool or choose Save As from the File menu.

Step 4. Type `TOPIC12` in the Save Worksheet As box and choose OK.

Quick Tips

This section provides you with tips on how to organize your worksheet data into a database using Excel.

Anticipating your database design

Before creating database fields, examine the data you'll be working with. Create the fields for your database based on the type of data that appears most often, and consider whether you need to separate these fields into smaller units, or add additional fields for calculations or other database operations.

Using correct field names

Steer clear of field names that resemble cell addresses, such as ab1, as Excel and your macros may become confused and calculate database results improperly.

Moving the cell pointer automatically

Select the row (or column) that you want to enter data into your database. Type the data for the first cell and press Return. Excel moves the cell pointer to the next cell for you.

Creating a template file

If you deal with similarly structured data on a periodic basis, you can create a template file with the database field names and then add data from another file using Copy from the Edit menu and Paste or Data Consolidate.

Using multiple databases on a spreadsheet

You can have more than one database on a spreadsheet at a time, but only one can be defined as a database. To specify another range as the database, select the range, and choose the Set Database command from the Data menu. Excel then recognizes the new range as the database. You may be better off, however, placing multiple databases on separate spreadsheets and creating a workbook file of the databases.

Avoid losing data integrity

If you use Insert or Delete from the Edit menu with a Shift Cells option, and you haven't selected all the records in the database, adjacent fields in the database records do not line up properly, which ruins the integrity of the data.

Avoid having to redefine a database

You can dodge the redefining-the-database bullet every time you add a new record to the bottom of a database if you: 1) Define your database with an extra blank row at the bottom of the database; 2) Insert a new row at the location of the blank row; and 3) Enter the new record where you've inserted the new row. Excel automatically expands the range name for you when you insert the new row.

Ensuring the success of your query operations

Your database and criteria field names must match exactly for any query operation to work properly. To ensure that they do, copy and paste the database field names to the criteria and extract ranges.

Searching a database in reverse

To search a database in reverse, press Shift, and then choose Find from the Data menu.

Extracting records deletes cell entries

Any existing cell entries below an unlimited extract range (an extract range that includes only field text) are overrun by extracted records without warning from Excel.

Copying nonduplicate records to an extract range

Select Choose Unique Records Only from the Data Extract dialog box to copy non-duplicate records to an extract range.

Determining what is removed from a database

You can determine which records are removed from a database using Find from the Data menu. The Find command selects all records that qualify for removal based on the criteria if you choose Delete from the Data menu.

Understanding criteria in a data form

Criteria you set in the data form work independently of any criteria defined with Set Criteria from the Data menu on your spreadsheet.

Summary

- A database is a collection of similar data organized in a structured manner.
- Database data consists of *records*, which is a row of data. Each cell in the record, or *field*, contains a unique data item.
- You can use Excel for database management, thereby taking advantage of Excel's analytical, charting, and printing capability, a familiar environment, and avoiding the expense and learning time of using a dedicated database program.
- Database design is the first and crucial step toward creating a useful database.
- You can enter database records using the normal data-entry manner, a form, or by creating a macro-driven dialog box (see Topic 15).
- You can modify the structure of a database by adding, deleting, or moving fields (columns).
- You can modify the contents of a database by editing, adding, or deleting records.
- You can rearrange the order of database records by sorting them.
- You can find, extract, and delete database records that match specified criteria.
- You can use a fill-in-the-blanks form in a database to perform simple find, add, and delete operations.
- You can analyze information from a database using Excel's worksheet functions.

Part V: Customizing Excel

Topic 13
Managing Excel's Display

Overview

Your company no doubt has a few resident Excel gurus. If you've peeked over their cubicle walls, you've probably been dazzled by their Excel displays — rainbows of colors, windows, and more than one toolbar! If you yearn for such special but useful effects, this is the Topic for you. This Topic shows you how to select colors for various Excel screen regions, how to use windows to help you get your work done with less effort, and how to get the most out of the toolbars.

Choosing colors

You have wide latitude on the regions and colors you can display in Excel. You can change the color of the following:

- ✦ Cell contents
- ✦ Ranges
- ✦ Borders
- ✦ Patterns of shades
- ✦ Gridlines
- ✦ Row numbers and column letters

The following section discusses how to select the color of each of these items.

Choosing colors for cells

You can add color to the contents of cells in two ways: by a predefined or custom numeric format, or by changing the color of the font.

Setting colors by numeric format

Creating a custom numeric format can display a particular color based on a condition, such as when results are above or below expectations. You can use a numeric format that includes color for date formats as well as values.

For example, if you have a range of values that are positive and negative, and you want to display negative values in red (and both positive and negative values with a dollar sign and two decimal places), you'd use the following Excel format:

```
$#,##0.00_);[Red]($#,##0.00)
```

You can change the color red to something else by selecting from one of the following sixteen available colors:

Color name	***Color number***
Black	1
White	2
Red	3
Green	4
Blue	5
Yellow	6
Magenta	7
Cyan	8
Dark Red	9
Dark Green	10
Dark Blue	11
Light Brown	12
Purple	13
Dark Cyan	14
Light Gray	15
Gray	16

The pound sign (*#*) is the color number, numbered from 1 through 16, beginning with black as color 1 and dark gray as color 16 as displayed on the Color Palette dialog box.

You can also change the format by adding a color symbol at the point in the format that represents what you want to color. In the above example, suppose you have a holiday version of your worksheet, and you want to display positive values as green. The new format would be the following:

```
[Green]$#,##0.00_);[Red]($#,##0.00)
```

If you prefer another color set to work with, you can customize one or more of the colors on the color palette. This process is explained later in this Topic.

Changing the color of a font

Changing the color of fonts is done through the Font dialog box, as shown in Figure 13-1.

You may recall that the Font command lets you change many aspects of the fonts in your worksheet. To select another color, you simply select a range, and then choose Font from the Format menu. The Color pull-down list is your ticket to changing colors.

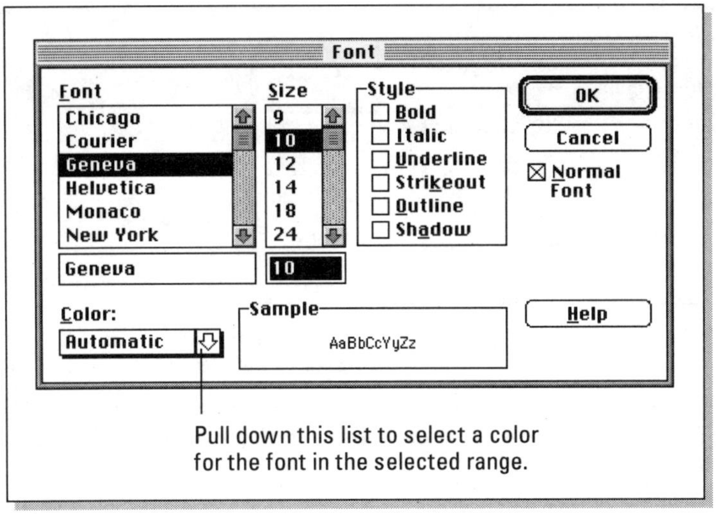

Figure 13-1: Choosing Font from the Format menu displays the Font dialog box.

Select a color from the list, and notice how the color looks with the font type and size shown in the Sample box. If you're satisfied with your choice, choose OK or press Return, and the data in the range you've selected now sports the new color.

Choosing colors for borders

Choosing a color for borders is similar to choosing a color for fonts. The Border dialog box shown in Figure 13-2 also has a Color pull-down list from which you can select a color. You can add a color to borders as you're applying them to spreadsheet cells or

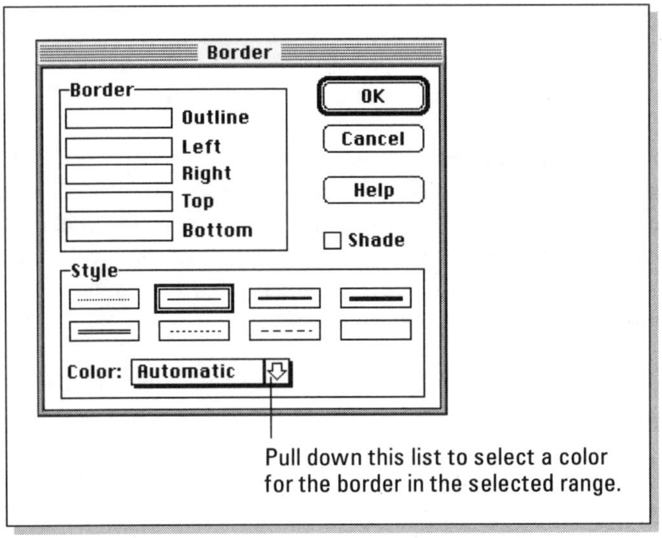

Figure 13-2: Adding color to borders using the Border dialog box.

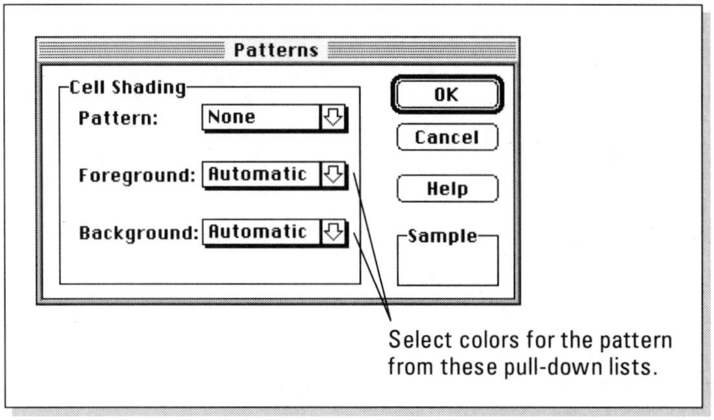

Figure 13-3: Choosing Patterns from the Format menu displays the Patterns dialog box.

after you have the lines the way you want them. In either case, select the range of cells that contains borders, choose Border from the Format menu, choose Color, and select the color for the lines. When you choose OK or press Return, Excel displays the borders around the selected cells with the color you selected.

Choosing colors for ranges

Topic 7 acquainted you with selecting a color for the shade pattern applied to ranges. First, after you select a range, choose Patterns from the Format menu or shortcut menu, and the Patterns dialog box shown in Figure 13-3 appears. Pull down the Pattern drop-down list to select the type of pattern (horizontal, vertical, diagonal lines, and so on). Second, select Foreground and Background colors from the corresponding drop-down color list. Make sure you select colors that won't cause the data to become illegible. Watch the Sample box to see beforehand how the colors look before you choose OK or press Return. If you pull down the Patterns list a second time you can see how the various patterns appear with the color combination you've chosen.

Choosing the gridline and headings color

The final two areas of the worksheet that you can control the color of are the gridlines and the headings. Headings are the row numbers and column letters along the left side and on top of the worksheet, respectively. To change a heading's color, choose Display from the Options menu, and then pull down the Gridline & Heading Color list from the Display Options dialog box shown in Figure 13-4.

Select the color you want, and then choose OK or press Return. That's all there is to it. Excel displays the worksheet's gridlines and headings with the selected color.

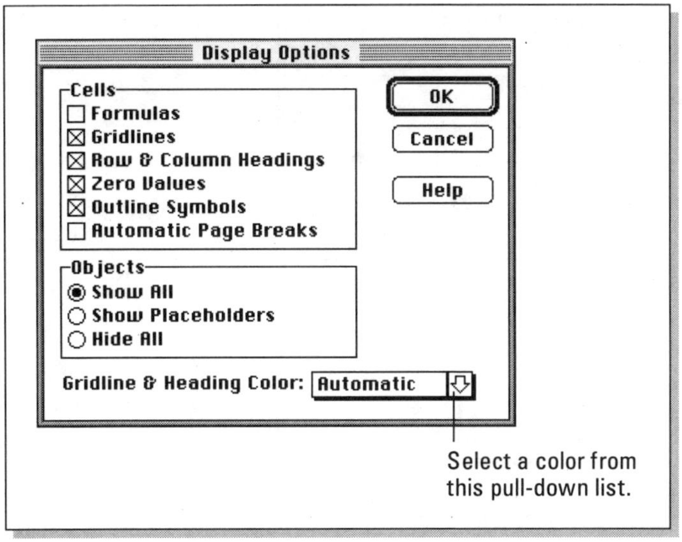

Figure 13-4: Changing the color of a heading using the Display Options dialog box.

What is an automatic color?

The Automatic color found on all Color pull-down lists is based on the color selected from Control Panels. You can easily select another Automatic color by selecting Control Panels from the Apple menu. When you do, the Control Panels window shown in the following figure appears.

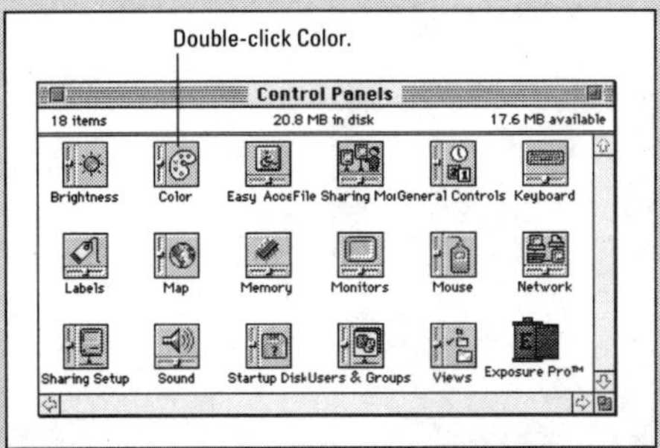

Double-clicking the Color icon displays the window shown in the following figure.

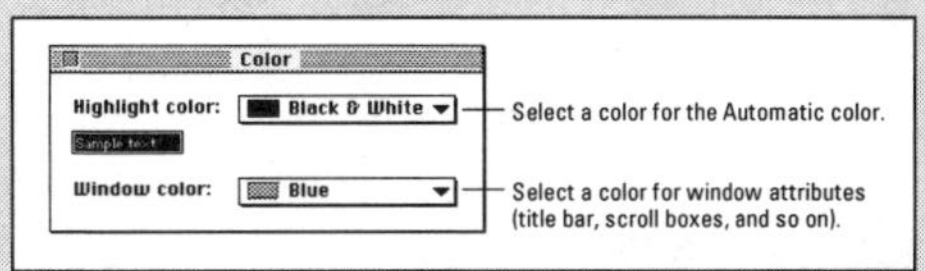

Select another color by pulling down the Highlight color list. Watch how the color appears in the Sample text box. In addition, you can customize the color by selecting Other from the pull-down list. You can also select a color for windows from the Window color pull-down list.

When you're finished changing or customizing colors, choose OK or press Return. You'll be returned to the Control Panels window. Close the window, and Excel displays the color you selected.

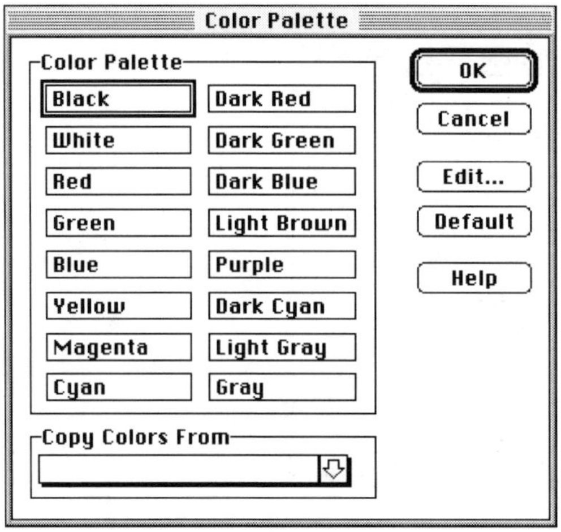

Figure 13-5: Choosing Color Palette from the Options menu displays the Color Palette dialog box.

Modifying colors

Excel comes with 16 standard colors that you can customize or use out-of-the-box. If you use a different set of 16 colors, you can keep this modified set in a template worksheet for use in other Excel models. Creating your own custom set of colors is a relatively painless process, as you'll see. First, activate the worksheet that contains the color palette you want to modify. Next, choose Color Palette from the Options menu and the Color Palette dialog box shown in Figure 13-5 appears.

Now, choose the color you want to change by clicking on it or by using the arrow keys. When you've selected the one you want, choose Edit. The dialog box in Figure 13-6 appears.

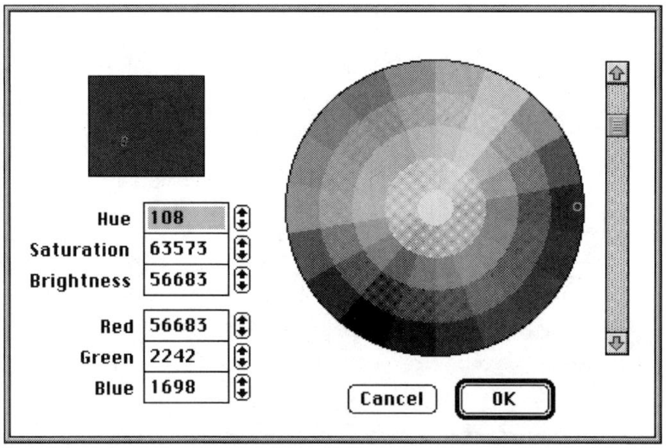

Figure 13-6: Modifying Excel's standard colors.

Circular pointer

Move the mouse pointer over the small circle contained in the color wheel. When the pointer resembles a circle, click and drag the mouse around the color wheel while watching the square in the upper-left corner of the dialog box. As you drag the mouse, the upper half of the square changes color according to the location of the mouse pointer on the wheel (the lower half of the square remains the same for purposes of comparison). When the color appears the way you want, choose OK; you return to the Color Palette dialog box where you can choose OK to implement the color or edit another color.

You can also copy color palettes from one worksheet or chart to another, so only once will you need to modify a palette that contains colors you like. Copying color palettes from one worksheet to another is similar to copying named styles among worksheets.

To copy color palettes between worksheets, do the following:

1. Open the source and target worksheets (or charts).
2. Make the target worksheet the active worksheet.
3. Choose Color Palette from the Options menu (from the Chart menu for charts).
4. Select the name of the source worksheet from the Copy Colors From pull-down list.
5. Choose OK.

When you choose OK or press Return, the target (active) worksheet (or chart) receives the source worksheet's color palette. Fonts, borders, ranges, gridlines and headings, and objects in the target worksheet display colors based on the new palette.

Choosing the elements to display

You have many choices for which areas of the worksheet, and even Excel itself, to display on screen. If you've completed setting up a large worksheet, for example, you might want to hide the Standard toolbar or status bar to display more rows on screen. The next two sections show you how you can select what you want displayed on screen.

Displaying parts of Excel

When you change how Excel appears on screen, you make changes to the window Excel resides in. In general, this is the area that surrounds your open worksheets, and includes the following screen regions:

- Standard toolbar
- Formula bar
- Vertical and horizontal scroll bars
- Status bar

The Toolbar command from the Options menu lets you control the display of the Standard toolbar, discussed later in this Topic. The display of the other three areas are controlled by choosing Workspace from the Options menu, which is discussed in the next section. Note that by default, Excel displays all these screen areas.

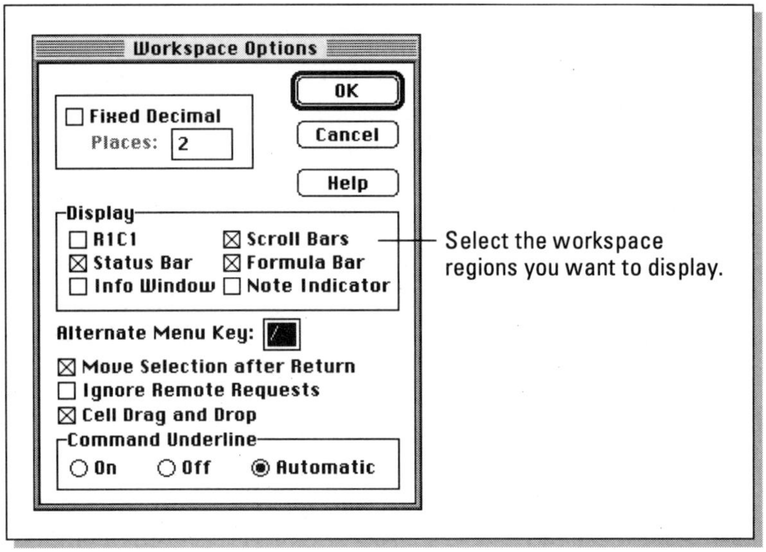

Figure 13-7: Hiding bars in a worksheet using the Workspace Options dialog box.

Hiding the formula, scroll, and status bars

Choosing Workspace from the Options menu displays the dialog box shown in Figure 13-7.

Simply unselect the corresponding box of the element you don't want displayed. When you choose OK or press Return, Excel removes that element from the display. Although you can see more of a worksheet by hiding these bars, in general, however, hiding the formula bar isn't a good idea. Hiding the formula bar forces you to edit cell contents directly in the cell, which can be tedious, because you can't see a formula in its entirety.

Displaying parts of a worksheet

When you choose what you want a worksheet to display, you're changing those elements of the worksheet's window — the area where you enter data and perform calculations. These elements include the following:

- ✦ The display of a formula's results, or the formula itself
- ✦ Worksheet gridlines
- ✦ Row numbers and column letters
- ✦ Zeros
- ✦ Outline symbols
- ✦ Page break symbols

By default, Excel displays each of these elements, except formula results.

Changing any of these options is much like using the Options Workspace command. When you choose Display from the Options menu, the Display Options dialog box shown in Figure 13-8 appears, and you need only select or unselect the option of the corresponding element you want displayed or hidden.

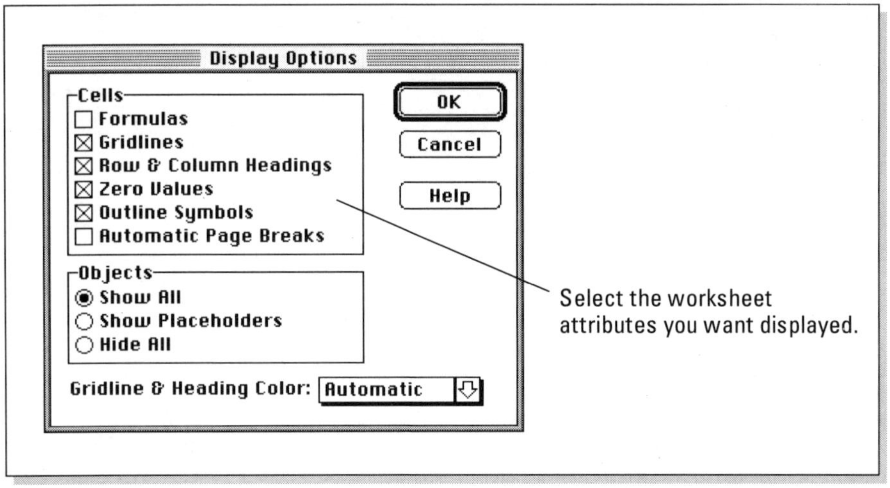

Figure 13-8: Choosing Display from the Options menu displays the Display Options dialog box.

Choosing OK or pressing Return completes the operation and Excel makes the changes you want.

Taking advantage of multiple views

Thus far you've displayed a worksheet in a single window. In the sections that follow, you'll learn how you can benefit from looking at different areas of the worksheet simultaneously. You can do this by creating panes of the worksheet, creating additional windows of the single worksheet window, or by using a combination of both.

Creating window panes

You may have a large Excel application that doesn't lend itself well to multiple worksheets. If this is the case, you can view different areas of the worksheet window at the same time. For example, in Figure 13-9, you can see range A1:H7 and A18:H27 at the same time. Creating different views of a worksheet is known as creating panes, because you're separating the worksheet's window into sections, much like the windows in a house.

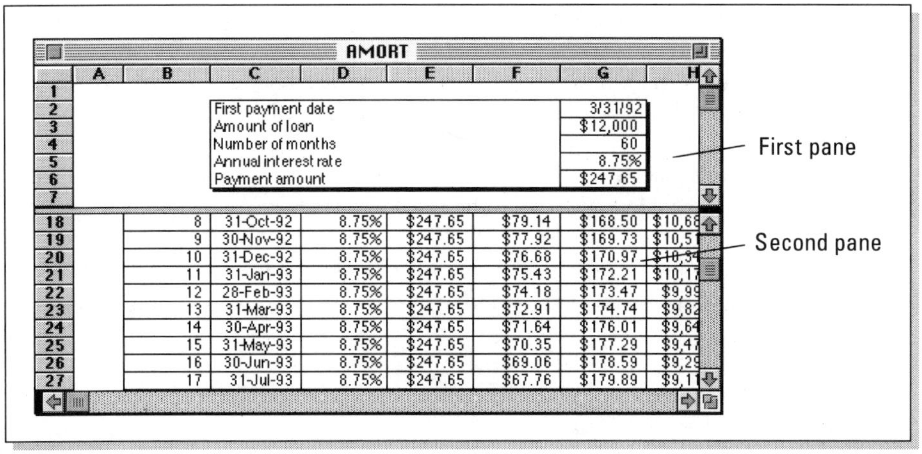

Figure 13-9: Viewing different areas of a worksheet using panes.

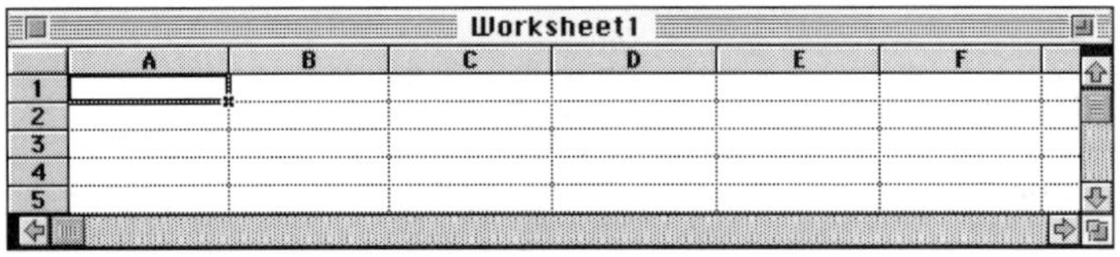

Figure 13-10: An example of the horizontal and vertical split bars.

Two-headed arrow

Creating window panes is no sweat. Unlike many Excel commands, you don't have to select a range before completing this procedure. It's helpful, however, to have the portion of the worksheet that you want to view most of the time through one of the panes on screen before creating panes. You also want to decide ahead of time if you want two vertical panes, two horizontal panes (such as in Figure 13-9), or four panes. In any event, notice the small black rectangle at the top of the vertical (right) scroll bar, and the far left of the horizontal (bottom) scroll bar, as shown in Figure 13-10. If you move the mouse pointer to one of these areas, the pointer changes to a black two-headed arrow.

To create two horizontal panes, move the mouse pointer to the rectangle above the vertical scroll bar — the horizontal split box — and then click and drag. As you drag, a gray horizontal line appears on the worksheet and follows the direction (up and down) of the mouse movements. Stop and release the mouse button when the gray line is at the point in the worksheet where you'd like the two panes to appear. You now have two horizontal panes on the worksheet window.

To create two vertical panes, you use the same procedure to create horizontal panes, only you click and drag on the rectangle to the far left on the horizontal scroll bar — the vertical split box.

If you already have two panes on the window, you can quickly add two panes of the opposite orientation by pressing and dragging on the appropriate split box. For example, if you decide you need four panes on a worksheet, and you already have two horizontal panes, click and drag on the vertical split box (on the far left on the horizontal scroll bar) to add two vertical panes.

Moving between panes

Moving the cell pointer between window panes is easy. If you use a mouse, just click any cell in the pane you want to move to. To use the keyboard, press F6. Each press of F6 moves the cell pointer to the next pane in clockwise order.

Removing panes

Removing window panes is the reverse of creating them. Simply click the vertical split box and drag all the way to the left, to the row numbers, and then release the mouse button to remove vertical panes. Click the horizontal split box and drag all the way to the top, to the column letters, and then release the mouse button to remove horizontal panes.

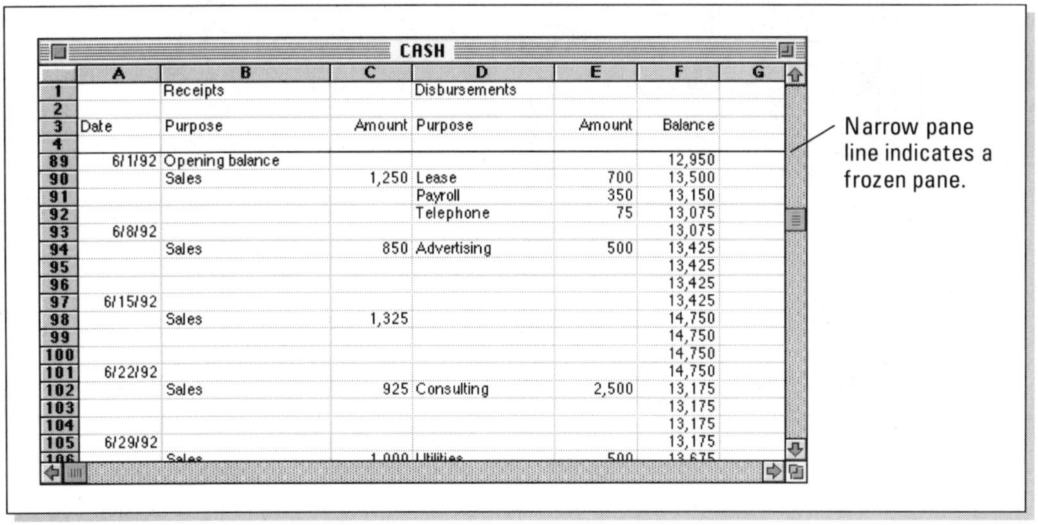

Figure 13-11: A example of how you can lose your place in a worksheet when scrolling in two separate panes.

Holding a pane in place

When you display window panes and scroll a worksheet, both panes scroll in the same direction together. For example, if you display two vertical panes on a worksheet and click the vertical scroll bar or press PgDn, both window panes scroll down. At times, however, you may want to hold one pane in place while the other scrolls. For example, you may have a worksheet with many line items. As you move down the worksheet, it's easy to lose your place, as shown in Figure 13-11.

You can create a horizontal pane that displays the text (more often than not, the months of the year) over values in columns, and freeze the upper pane in place, so it doesn't scroll with the lower pane. This is also known as freezing titles, because you're freezing them in place so you can view them at all times. Table 13-1 lists how to freeze text over columns of data, freeze text to the left of data, or both.

Table 13-1: Freeze text options

To freeze . . .	*Create . . .*	*And choose . . .*
Text in rows	A vertical pane that encloses text down a column (usually Column A)	Freeze Panes from the Options menu
Text in columns	A horizontal pane that encloses text across a row	Freeze Panes from the Options menu
Both	A vertical pane that encloses row labels, and a horizontal pane that encloses your column labels	Freeze Panes from the Options menu

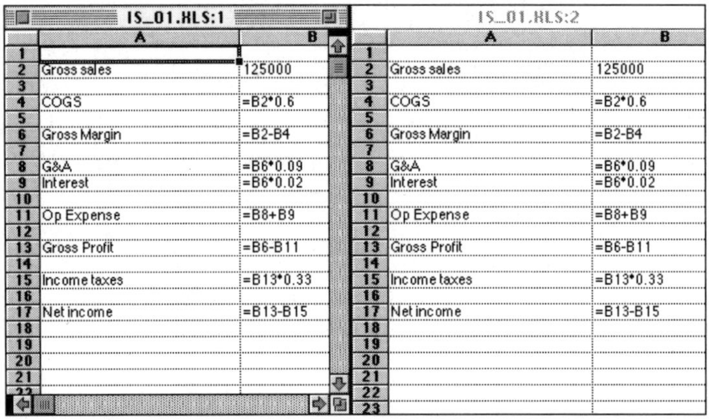

IS_01.XLS:1

	A	B
1		
2	Gross sales	125000
3		
4	COGS	=B2*0.6
5		
6	Gross Margin	=B2-B4
7		
8	G&A	=B6*0.09
9	Interest	=B6*0.02
10		
11	Op Expense	=B8+B9
12		
13	Gross Profit	=B6-B11
14		
15	Income taxes	=B13*0.33
16		
17	Net income	=B13-B15
18		
19		
20		
21		

IS_01.XLS:2

	A	B
1		
2	Gross sales	125000
3		
4	COGS	=B2*0.6
5		
6	Gross Margin	=B2-B4
7		
8	G&A	=B6*0.09
9	Interest	=B6*0.02
10		
11	Op Expense	=B8+B9
12		
13	Gross Profit	=B6-B11
14		
15	Income taxes	=B13*0.33
16		
17	Net income	=B13-B15
18		
19		
20		
21		
22		
23		

Figure 13-12: An example of a display option that enables you to see the results of formulas and the formulas themselves.

Creating windows

A tool you can use to view other distant portions of a worksheet is, appropriately enough, a window. Though a new worksheet comes in one window, you can create multiple windows to display other areas of a worksheet. The number of windows you can create is limited only by the computer's memory and your imagination. And because your new windows are bona fide windows, you can move and size them like any other window.

Keep in mind when you create new windows that you're not creating new worksheets (as you do with the New command). Rather, you're looking at different parts of the same worksheet, and changes to a cell are reflected in every window, if that cell is displayed. You can, however, change the display options of the window. For example, you can see the results of formulas, and the formulas themselves, in Figure 13-12. Notice that each window is numbered: The original window is 1, the new window is 2, and so on.

Creating another window of your worksheet is easy. Just choose New Window from the Window menu, and Excel does the rest, creating and numbering the new window for you.

Arranging windows

You can move and size worksheet windows by clicking and dragging the window's resize box with the mouse. If you need to display all windows simultaneously on screen in a hurry, choosing Arrange from the Window menu (as shown in Figure 13-13) is your ticket (you may remember the Arrange command from Topic 11). The Arrange command options include the following:

Option	***Window display***
Tiled	Small rectangles or squares
Horizontal	Windows are stacked evenly from top to bottom as wide rectangles
Vertical	Windows are placed from left to right as tall rectangles

Using panes vs. windows

Using window panes or additional windows to view different areas of a worksheet boils down to, once again, personal preference, and what you need to do. Remember, panes let you view rows and columns you've labeled continuously, and additional windows may make it a little easier to see disparate areas of the worksheet, especially if they're diagonal to each other. Your best bet may be to experiment and see which method works best for you.

You shouldn't look at window panes and multiple windows as an either-or proposition, however. You can team them up so you can gain the benefits of both. For example, if you have a large budget worksheet, you may want to create horizontal and vertical frozen panes to view row and column labels, a second window to view row totals, and even a third window to view column totals.

Specifying window scroll synchronization

Unlike window panes, windows of the same worksheet do not scroll together by default. If you select the Windows of Active Document box from the Arrange Windows dialog box, the Sync Horizontal and Sync Vertical options become available. Check the appropriate box for the direction you want your windows to scroll — horizontal for left and right scrolling, vertical for up and down scrolling.

Hiding and unhiding windows

You may have one or more windows you want to hide from casual or deliberate snooping, such as a salary planning worksheet. You can keep confidential windows from being displayed, whether those windows are from the same or other open worksheets.

To hide a window, first make the window you want to hide the active window. Next, choose Hide from the Window menu, and the window and its contents disappear from view. If you want to redisplay a hidden window, choose Unhide from the Window menu and select the name of the window you want to display from the list box, as shown in Figure 13-14. When you choose OK or press Return, Excel displays the hidden window you selected.

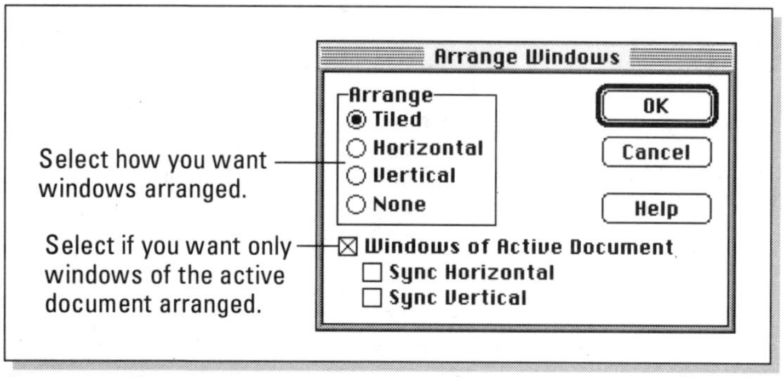

Figure 13-13: Choosing Arrange from the Window menu displays the Arrange Windows dialog box.

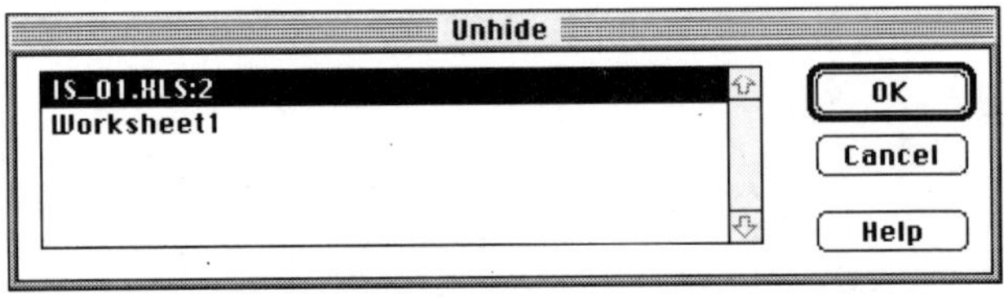

Figure 13-14: Unhiding windows in Excel using the Unhide dialog box.

Saving windows

Saving the number, size, and position of open windows is done for you automatically when you save a worksheet to disk. Nothing more is required other than choosing Save or Save As from the File menu. The next time you open the worksheet, the windows will be displayed just as you left them — like any other modification (such as data, formulas, and range names) to the worksheet.

Closing windows

If you no longer need a window, you can remove it from the worksheet. First, make the window you want to remove the active window (by clicking it or selecting it from the Window menu). Then, click the window's close box; the window is permanently removed from the worksheet.

Sizing a worksheet by a percentage

You can expand or contract the display of a worksheet by a percentage by choosing Zoom from the Window menu. Zooming a worksheet is helpful when you want to position a chart or object precisely, or want to see it in its entirety to determine what you're dealing with if you inherit a worksheet the size of an aircraft carrier. When you choose Zoom from the Window menu, the Zoom dialog box shown in Figure 13-15 appears.

Select one of the factors from the dialog box, or enter a percentage from 10 to 400 percent in the Custom text box. When you choose OK or press Return, Excel expands or contracts the worksheet's display size by the percentage you specified. Figure 13-16 shows a condensed view (75 percent) of Figure 13-9.

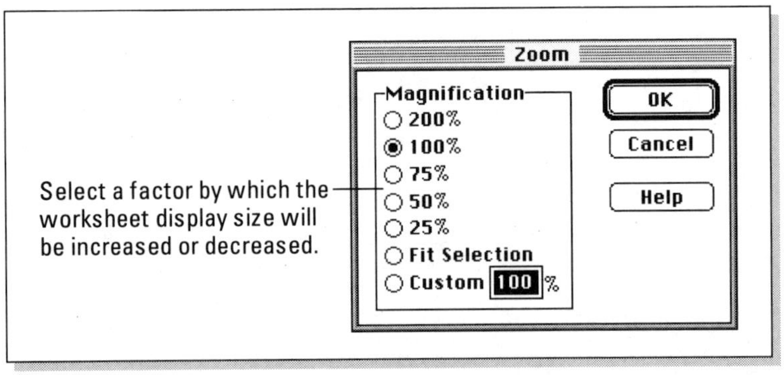

Figure 13-15: Choosing Zoom from the Window menu displays the Zoom dialog box.

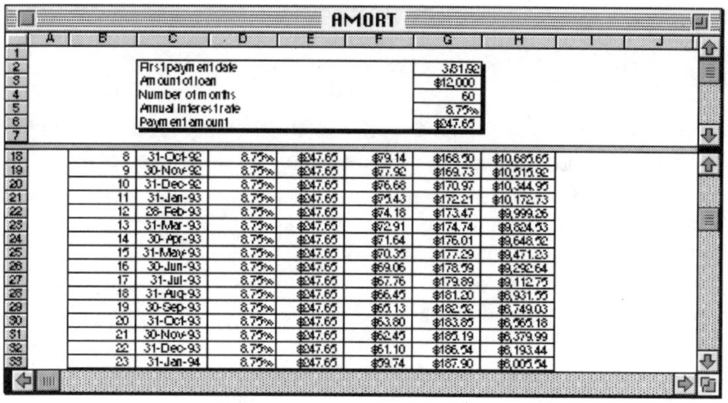

Figure 13-16: An example of a worksheet condensed to 75 percent of its original size.

To redisplay the worksheet at normal size, choose the Zoom command again, choose 100% from the Zoom dialog box, and then choose OK or press Return. The worksheet appears as it did prior to zooming.

Displaying and hiding toolbars

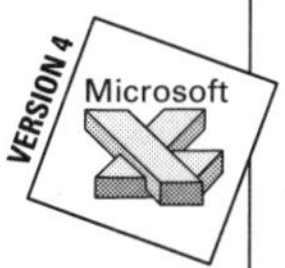

By default, Excel displays the Standard toolbar between the command menu bar and the formula bar. You can, however, hide or display as many toolbars as you want, choose where you want the toolbars displayed, and select the tools you want on an existing or new toolbar you create.

In several earlier Topics you learned how to display toolbars to accomplish a task, such as adding objects to a worksheet with the Drawing toolbar. Choosing Toolbar from the Options menu displays the Toolbars dialog box shown in Figure 13-17. Select the toolbar you want to display or hide from the Toolbars dialog box. Depending on the display status of the toolbar you select, the Show and Hide button toggles to the appropriate option. Selecting Show or Hide displays or hides the toolbar you selected, closes the dialog box, and gets you back to work.

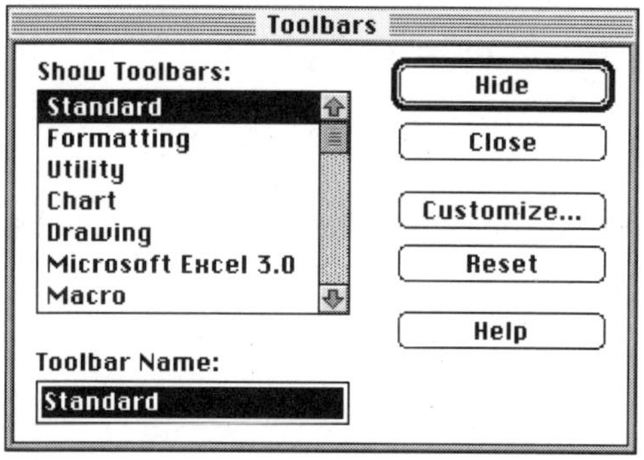

Figure 13-17: Choosing Toolbar from the Options menu displays the Toolbars dialog box.

A toolbar shortcut

If you position the mouse pointer in a toolbar displayed horizontally and press Command-Option and click the mouse, you'll display the toolbar shortcut menu, which is similar to other Excel shortcut menus. The toolbar shortcut menu displays the names of the first six toolbars, as shown in the following figure, and the commands that lead to the Toolbars and Toolbars Customize dialog boxes.

Notice that the upper portion of the menu is similar to the bottom portion of Excel's Window menu — a check mark appears to the left of the name of the toolbar that is displayed. To display or hide a toolbar, simply select its name.

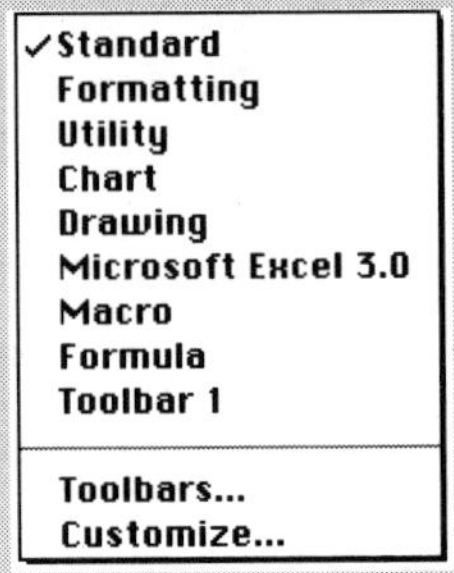

Moving and sizing toolbars

Toolbars are displayed in a window, thus you can move and size them like any other Excel window. Consequently, to move a toolbar, position the mouse pointer in a blank area in the toolbar, and then click and drag. As you drag, a gray outline of the toolbar appears. What happens next depends on where you're moving the toolbar from and to. Some terminology is now in order.

Docking toolbars

You can move toolbars anywhere in the Excel application window or worksheet window. If you place a toolbar above the formula bar, or along an edge of the Excel application window, Excel displays the toolbar in a toolbar dock. The four toolbar docks are the following:

- To the left of the worksheet row numbers
- To the right of the vertical scroll bar
- Below the horizontal scroll bar
- Between the Command menu and formula bars

Figure 13-18 displays an assortment of toolbars.

After you've displayed a toolbar, you can move it into a toolbar dock or float it over your worksheet. The placement of toolbars has a direct bearing on their size.

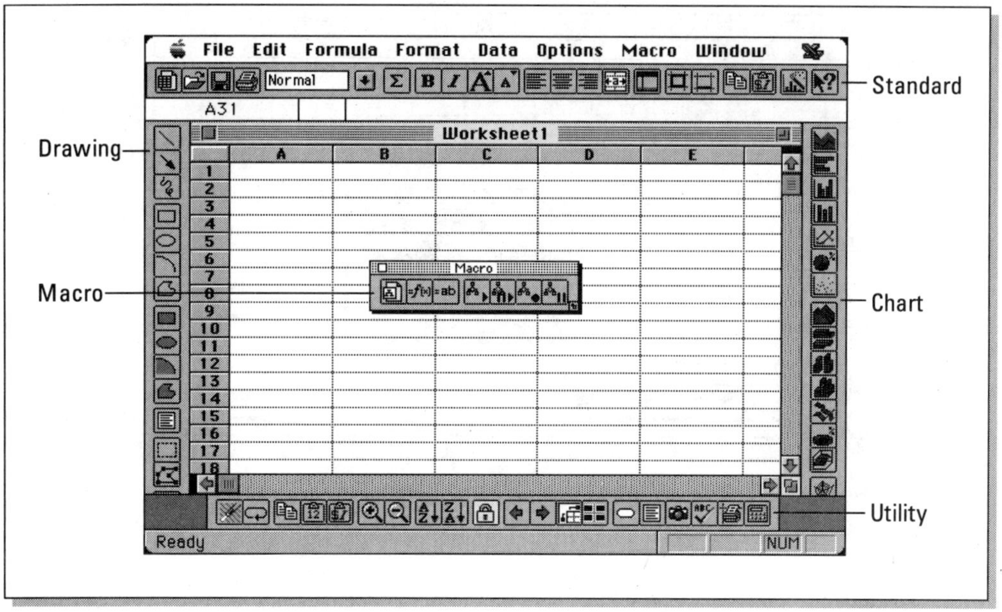

Figure 13-18: An example of Excel's various toolbars.

Toolbar dock	*Drag to . . .*
Top	Above the formula bar
Left	Left edge of the worksheet, below the bottom line of the formula bar
Right	Right edge of the worksheet, below the bottom line of the formula bar
Bottom	Above the status bar

To move a toolbar to a toolbar dock, drag the toolbar to the following screen regions:

If the toolbar dock is occupied, the next toolbar is positioned relative to the first toolbar depending on the location of the second toolbar's outline when you released the mouse button.

Floating toolbars

Figure 13-18 also displays a *floating toolbar*. Floating toolbars have a title bar and close box over the worksheet. You can display floating toolbars across columns or down rows.

Moving a toolbar float is easy. If a toolbar is in a dock, point to a blank area of the toolbar, and then click and drag it to the location over the worksheet. When you release the mouse button, the gray outline disappears and the toolbar reappears with a title bar and close and resize boxes.

You can also resize floating toolbars by clicking and then dragging the toolbar's resize box. Dragging to the right changes the window's length, and dragging down changes its

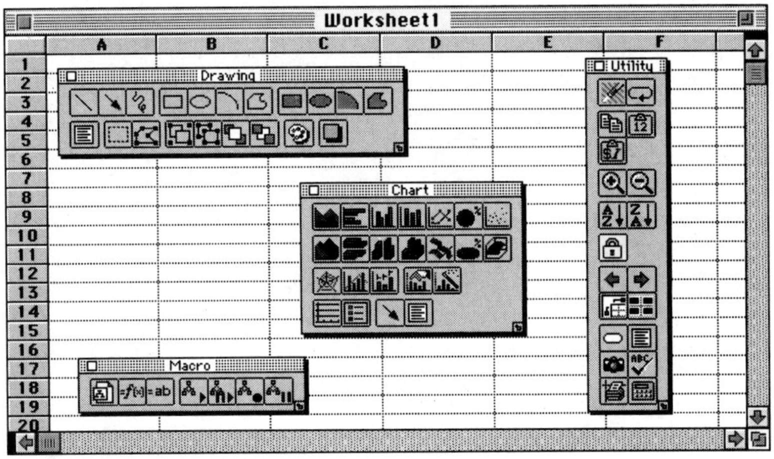

Figure 13-19: An example of the many shapes a floating toolbar can take on.

height. A toolbar window can appear as a wide rectangle, a square, or a long rectangle. Figure 13-19 shows some of the various shapes your floating toolbars can have.

Customizing toolbars

Excel provides a great deal of flexibility with toolbars. You can create new toolbars or change the composition of toolbars that ship with Excel so that they better fit the way you use Excel. You do this by adding, deleting, and changing the order in which the tools appear on one or more of the toolbars. Table 13-2 lists the various ways you can customize toolbars.

Table 13-2: Toolbar customization options

To . . .	*Do this . . .*	*Excel does this . . .*
Add a tool	Select a tool category, and then drag a tool from the Tools box to the location on the toolbar.	Adds the tool and resizes the toolbar
Delete a tool	Drag the tool off the toolbar to anywhere other than a toolbar or the dialog box.	Deletes the tool and resizes the toolbar
Move a tool	Drag the tool to its new location on the existing toolbar or another displayed toolbar.	Changes the order the tools are displayed on the toolbar and closes up any extra space
Copy a tool	Press Control and drag the tool to its new location on the existing toolbar or another displayed toolbar.	Inserts a copy of the tool and resizes the toolbar to accommodate the duplicate

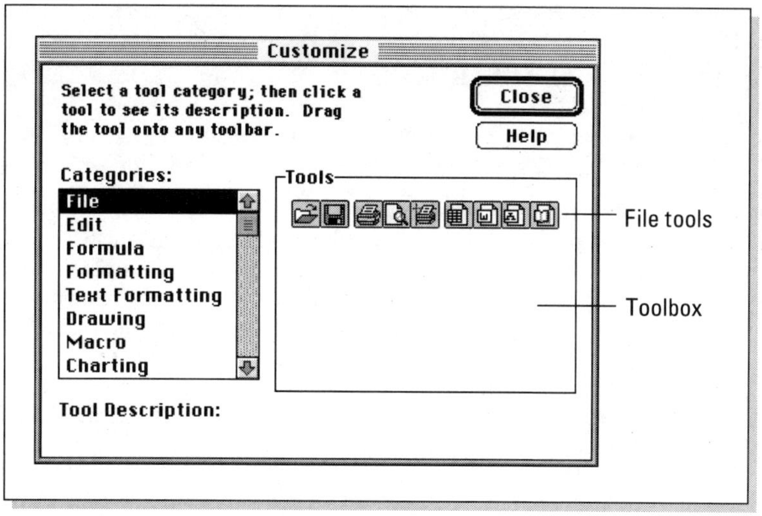

Figure 13-20: Choosing Customize from the Options toolbar or from the toolbar shortcut menu displays the Customize dialog box.

To customize an existing toolbar, do the following:

1. Display the toolbar by selecting the name of the toolbar after choosing the Toolbar command from the Options menu or the toolbar shortcut menu.
2. Select Customize from the Options toolbar or toolbar shortcut menu. The Customize dialog box in Figure 13-20 appears.
3. Do one of the operations listed in Table 13-2.
4. Choose Close.

To create a new toolbar, do the following:

1. Choose Toolbars from the Options menu or shortcut menu.
2. Type a name for the toolbar in the Toolbar name box.
3. Select Add or Customize. A blank toolbar appears, as well as the Customize dialog box, as shown in Figure 13-20.
4. Follow the directions in step 3 for customizing existing toolbars (given above).
5. Choose Close.

Creating toolbars on the run

You can create new toolbars in rapid-fire fashion, using either of the following methods:

- ✦ Drag a tool from the Tools box and place it anywhere over the worksheet (as long as it isn't on another toolbar).
- ✦ Press Control and drag a tool from a displayed toolbar anywhere over the worksheet.

In either case, Excel creates a toolbar for the tool, with its own title bar and close and resize boxes, and names it Toolbar1, Toolbar2, and so on. You can continue to add tools from the Tools box or another toolbar, or forge ahead and put the toolbar to work (remember, however, you'll need to assign a macro to a custom tool for it to operate).

To rename a new toolbar with a more descriptive name, choose Toolbars from the Options menu and select the name of the toolbar in the Show Toolbars list box. Type a new name in the Toolbar Name text box and choose Add. Repeat the process again but select the original toolbar name and Delete from the Toolbars dialog box to remove the original name.

Step-by-Step

In this section, you'll create window panes. You'll also create a toolbar that helps you create formulas quickly. If you make a mistake, remember that the worksheet is saved to disk, so close it without saving it and open it again when you feel like trying again, or use Undo.

To begin the exercise, do the following:

1. Start Excel.

   The Worksheet1 worksheet appears.

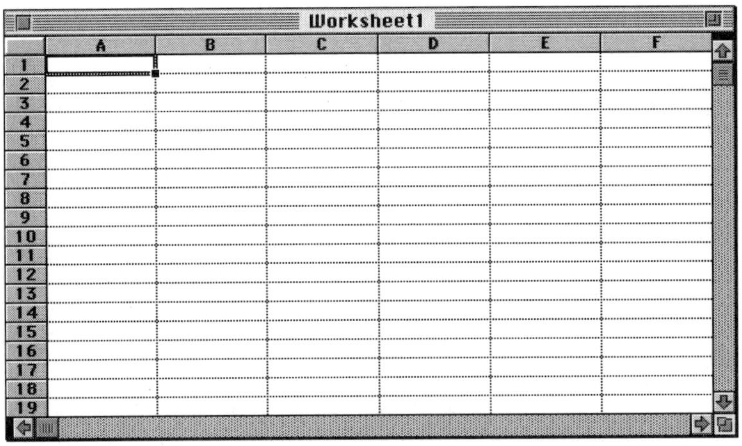

Figure 13-21: Starting up Excel displays the Worksheet1 worksheet.

2. Choose Open from the File menu, or click the File Open tool.

   The Open dialog box appears.

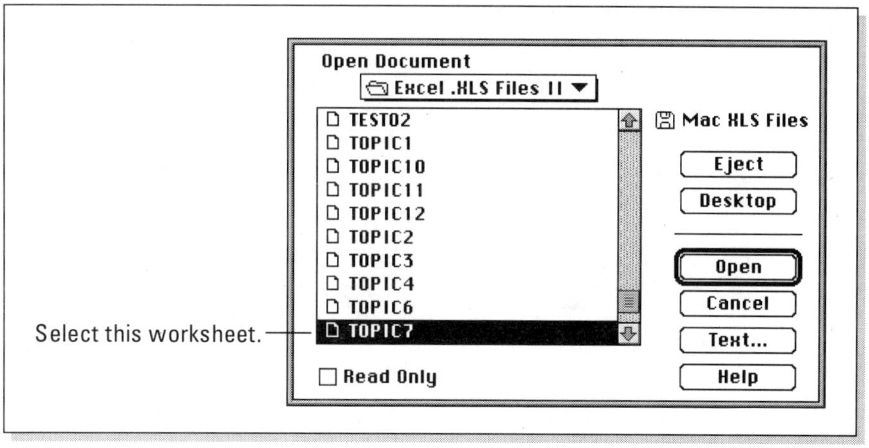

Figure 13-22: Choosing Open from the File menu, or clicking the File Open tool displays the Open dialog box.

3. Select TOPIC7, and choose OK.

   The TOPIC7 worksheet appears.

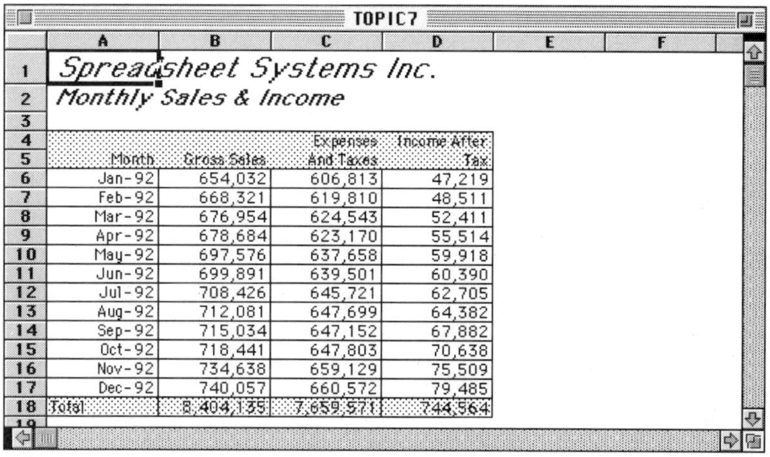

Figure 13-23: Selecting TOPIC7 from the Open dialog box displays the TOPIC7 worksheet.

Creating a vertical pane:

Step 1. Move the mouse pointer to the vertical split box. When the pointer resembles a black two-headed arrow, drag the mouse to the right so the split bar is on the far side of the line separating column letters A and B, and then release the mouse button.

Excel displays two vertical window panes.

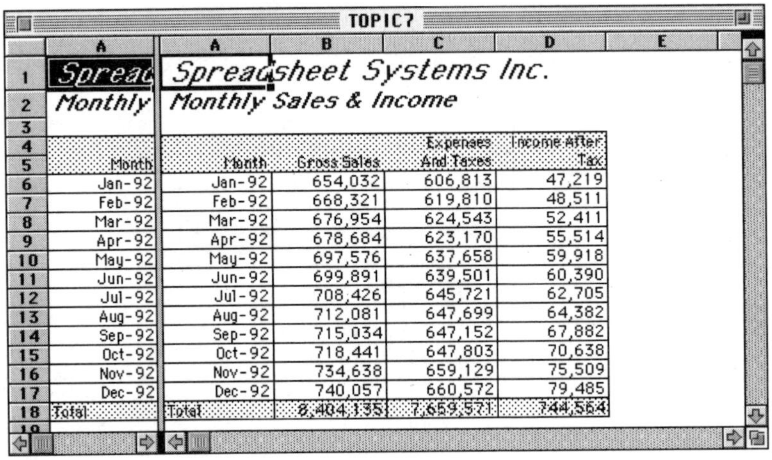

Figure 13-24: Creating vertical panes in a worksheet.

Step 2. Click on the right pane's horizontal scroll bar.

Excel displays the left pane while scrolling the second.

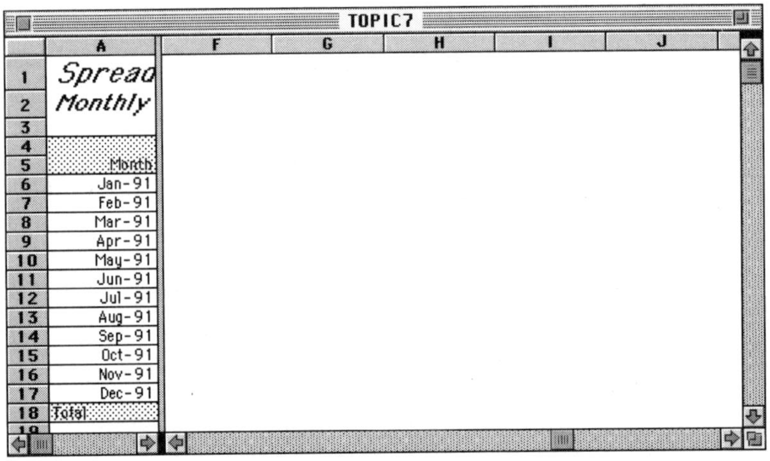

Figure 13-25: Scrolling in one vertical pane while viewing data in another vertical pane.

Removing vertical panes:

Step 1. Move the mouse pointer to the vertical split box. When the mouse pointer resembles a black two-headed arrow, drag the mouse to the left until it touches the row numbers, and then release the mouse button.

Excel removes the panes.

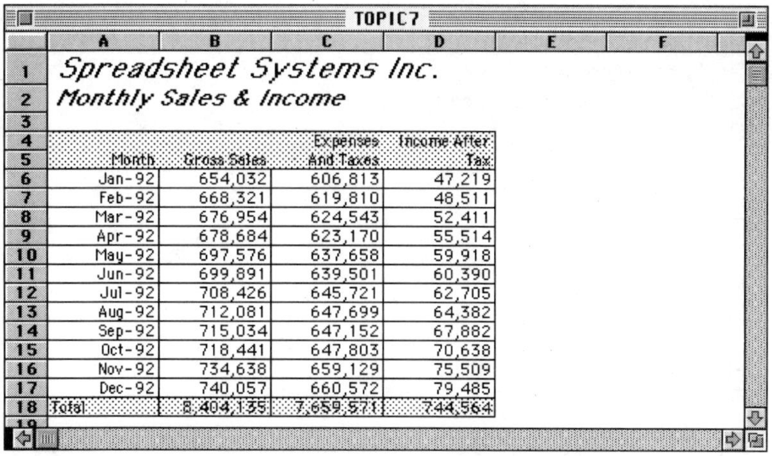

Month	Gross Sales	Expenses And Taxes	Income After Tax
Jan-92	654,032	606,813	47,219
Feb-92	668,321	619,810	48,511
Mar-92	676,954	624,543	52,411
Apr-92	678,684	623,170	55,514
May-92	697,576	637,658	59,918
Jun-92	699,891	639,501	60,390
Jul-92	708,426	645,721	62,705
Aug-92	712,081	647,699	64,382
Sep-92	715,034	647,152	67,882
Oct-92	718,441	647,803	70,638
Nov-92	734,638	659,129	75,509
Dec-92	740,057	660,572	79,485
Total	8,404,135	7,659,571	744,564

Figure 13-26: A worksheet after the vertical panes have been removed.

Creating a horizontal pane:

Step 1. Move the mouse pointer to the horizontal split box. When the pointer resembles a black two-headed arrow, drag the mouse down until the split bar is on the line separating row numbers 5 and 6, and then release the mouse button.

Excel displays two horizontal panes.

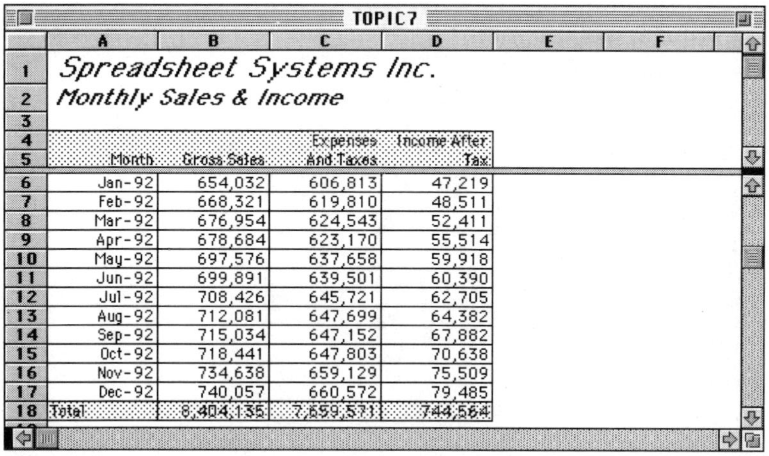

Month	Gross Sales	Expenses And Taxes	Income After Tax
Jan-92	654,032	606,813	47,219
Feb-92	668,321	619,810	48,511
Mar-92	676,954	624,543	52,411
Apr-92	678,684	623,170	55,514
May-92	697,576	637,658	59,918
Jun-92	699,891	639,501	60,390
Jul-92	708,426	645,721	62,705
Aug-92	712,081	647,699	64,382
Sep-92	715,034	647,152	67,882
Oct-92	718,441	647,803	70,638
Nov-92	734,638	659,129	75,509
Dec-92	740,057	660,572	79,485
Total	8,404,135	7,659,571	744,564

Figure 13-27: Creating horizontal panes in a worksheet.

Step 2. Click on the lower pane's vertical scroll bar.

Excel displays the top pane while scrolling the lower.

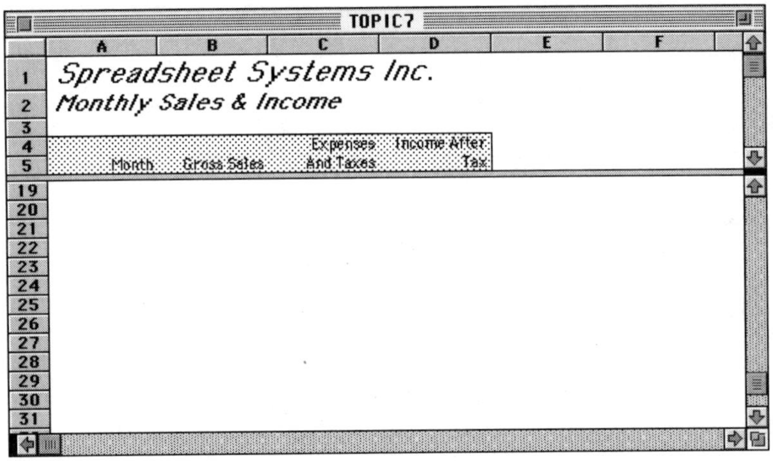

Figure 13-28: Scrolling in one horizontal pane while viewing data in another horizontal pane.

Removing horizontal panes:

Step 1. Move the mouse pointer to the horizontal split box. When the pointer resembles a black two-headed arrow, drag the mouse to the top until it touches the column letters, and then release the mouse button.

Excel displays the worksheet window without panes.

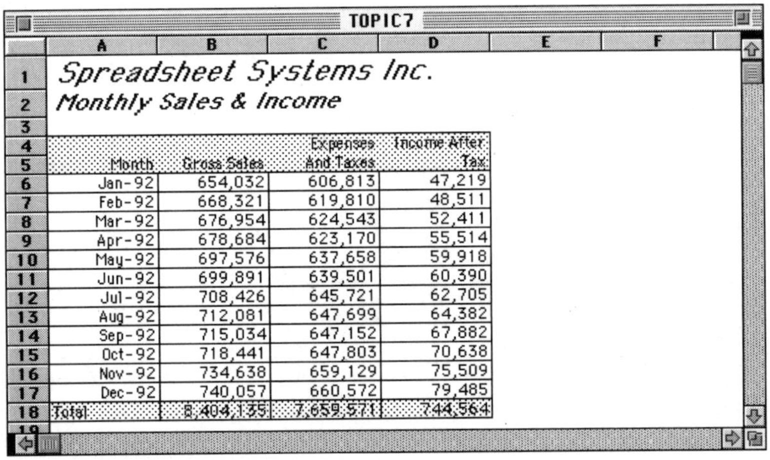

TOPIC7

Spreadsheet Systems Inc.

Monthly Sales & Income

Month	Gross Sales	Expenses And Taxes	Income After Tax
Jan-92	654,032	606,813	47,219
Feb-92	668,321	619,810	48,511
Mar-92	676,954	624,543	52,411
Apr-92	678,684	623,170	55,514
May-92	697,576	637,658	59,918
Jun-92	699,891	639,501	60,390
Jul-92	708,426	645,721	62,705
Aug-92	712,081	647,699	64,382
Sep-92	715,034	647,152	67,882
Oct-92	718,441	647,803	70,638
Nov-92	734,638	659,129	75,509
Dec-92	740,057	660,572	79,485
Total	8,404,135	7,659,571	744,564

Figure 13-29: A worksheet after the horizontal panes have been removed.

Creating a toolbar:

Step 1. Choose Toolbars from the Options menu or shortcut menu.

Excel displays the Toolbars dialog box.

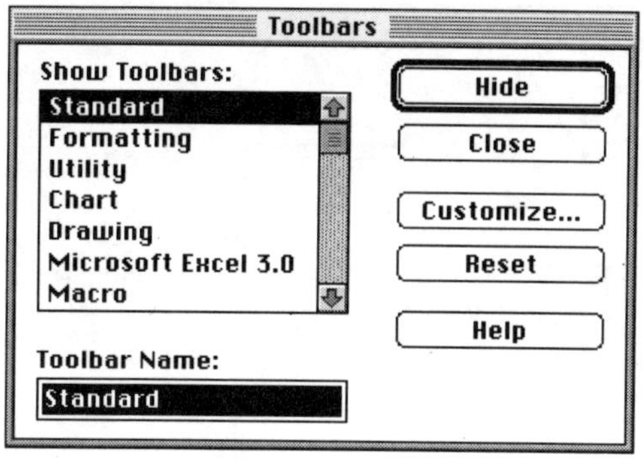

Figure 13-30: Choosing Toolbars from the Options menu displays the Toolbars dialog box.

Step 2. Type `Formula` in the Toolbar Name text box, and then choose Customize.

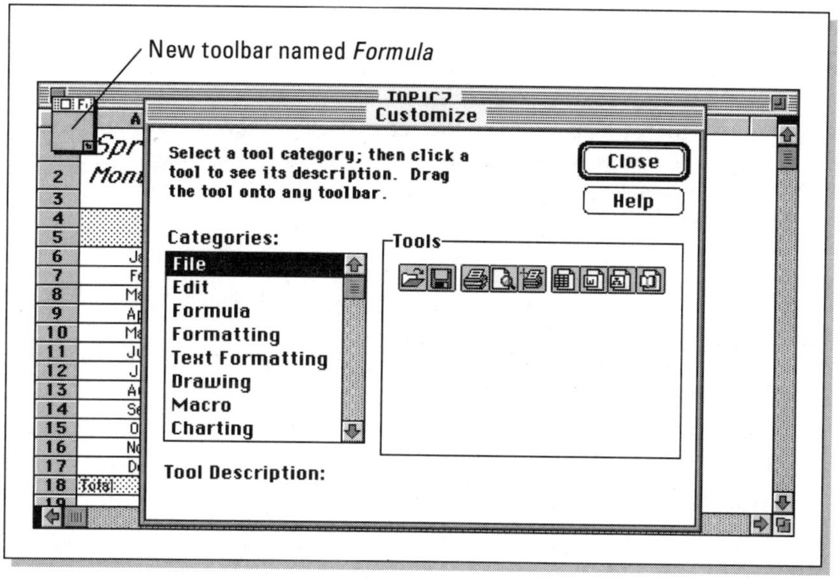

Figure 13-31: Typing Formula into the Toolbar Name text box and choosing Customize displays a new, blank toolbar and the Customize dialog box.

Step 3. Select Formula from the Categories list box.

Excel displays the Formula toolbar tools.

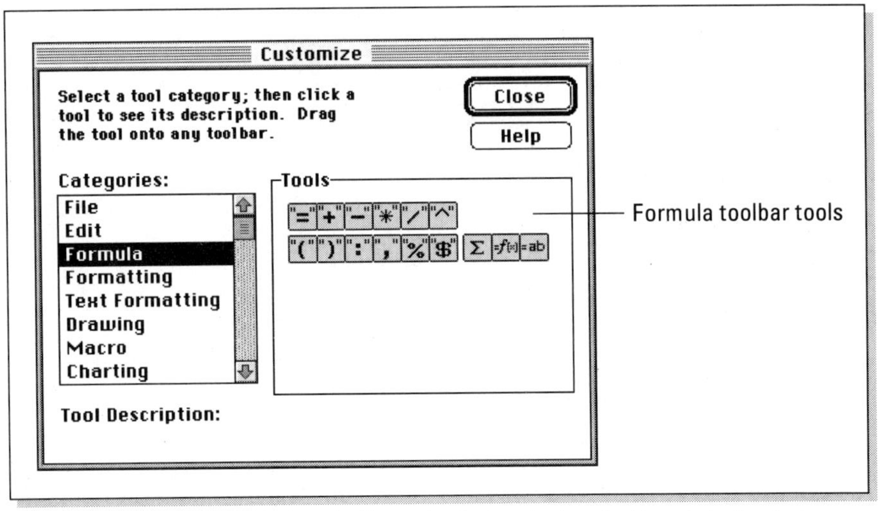

Figure 13-32: Selecting Formula from the Categories list box displays the Formula toolbar tools.

Step 4. Click and drag a tool from the Formula toolbox to the Formula toolbar. Select the tools which represent the arithmetic operators and symbols you use most often to create formulas. Group tools together by dragging a tool halfway over a tool already on the toolbar, and then release the mouse button.

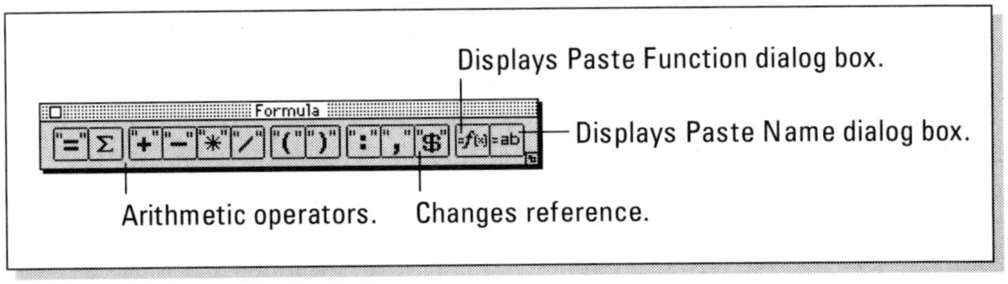

Figure 13-33: An example of a Formula toolbar.

Step 5. Choose Close from the Customize dialog box.

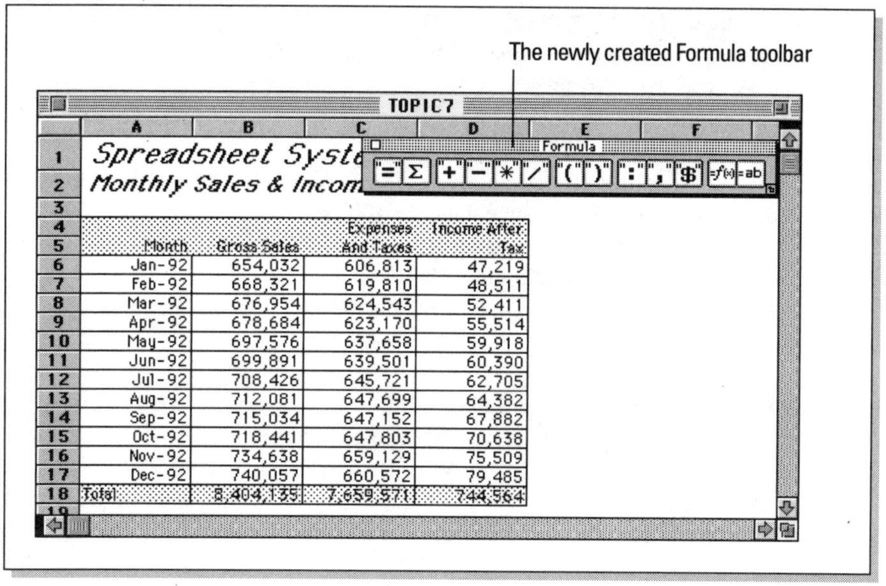

Figure 13-34: Choosing Close from the Customize dialog box displays the worksheet and the Formula toolbar.

Quick Tips

This section provides you with tips on how to effectively manage Excel's display.

Selecting a color for your borders

Select a color for your borders that won't be obscured if you've shaded the range that contains the borders.

Selecting foreground and background colors

Select pattern background and foreground colors that are different from the color of the fonts so your data doesn't fade out.

Zapping zeroes from a worksheet

If you have a worksheet with many formulas that calculate to zero, the worksheet may be more attractive and understandable if you suppress their display by choosing Display from the Options menu.

Using color with a black-and-white printer

A black-and-white printer may not be able to accurately reproduce a display with an assortment of colors. If this is the case, select Black and White Cells from the Page Setup dialog box.

Unfreezing and removing panes

Choose Unfreeze and Unsplit from the Window menu to unfreeze and remove panes from worksheets, respectively.

Arranging your windows

Choose None from the Arrange box if you only want your windows to scroll together and do not want Excel to arrange them for you.

The effects of the Zoom command

The Zoom command affects only the display of the worksheet on screen, and not how it appears on paper.

Using the More Toolbars command

If you've caught toolbar mania and have created more toolbar names than the toolbar shortcut menu can display, the More Toolbars command appears on the shortcut menu. Choosing More Toolbars displays the Toolbar dialog box so you can select the name of the toolbar from the Show Toolbars list box, and display or hide the toolbar as needed.

Moving toolbars carefully

CAUTION!

Make sure you position the mouse pointer carefully when moving a toolbar. If you don't, and you click an icon, you may experience unplanned results. If this occurs, choose Undo immediately.

Undockable toolbars

You cannot place the standard, formatting, and Microsoft Excel 3.0 toolbars in the left or right toolbar docks because of their pull-down list boxes.

Replacing deleted tools

You can replace tools deleted from a toolbar by selecting them again from the appropriate toolbox in the Customize dialog box.

Returning a toolbar to its former location

Double-clicking the background of a previously moved toolbar returns it to its former location.

Summary

- You can change the color of values you've entered into a worksheet through predefined or custom formats.
- You can change the color of your data by changing the color of a font in a worksheet.
- You can change the color of borders using the Border Color command from the Format menu.
- You can apply color to ranges by shading them, and selecting the color from the Foreground and Background commands available from the Pattern menu.
- You can select the color for your gridlines and worksheet headings from the Options menu's Display Gridline & Heading Color pull-down list.
- You can customize the 16 colors available to worksheets using Color Palette from the Options menu.
- You can choose whether you want to display Excel's toolbar, formula bar, the scroll bars, or the status bar. You can also specify which toolbars, if any, you want to display.
- You can choose to display worksheet attributes, such as formulas or the results of formulas, worksheet gridlines, and worksheet headings.
- You can view a worksheet through two or four window panes, which also can be frozen to prevent scrolling.
- You can view worksheets through more than the one default window. You can move, size, close, and save multiple worksheet windows with a worksheet.
- You can increase or decrease the display size of a worksheet with the Zoom command from the Window menu.
- Toolbars hold the tools and you can locate them in four toolbar docks located along the edges of the Excel workspace. You can also have floating toolbars that hover over the worksheet.
- Floating toolbars can be moved or sized just like any other window, and have close and resize boxes, plus a title bar.
- The Standard toolbar appears in the top toolbar dock, between the menu and formula bars.
- You can hide or show toolbars using Toolbars Hide and Show from the Options menu, respectively.
- You can access the toolbar shortcut menu by pointing to a blank area of a toolbar and pressing Command-Option and while clicking the mouse.
- You can customize existing toolbars or create new ones by adding and/or deleting tools that come with Excel.

Topic 14
Creating Macros

Overview

Well, here it is, the Topic you've been waiting for — macros. If you've been using a computer for any length of time, you've probably heard of macros, and how they can speed up tasks and generally make your life easier. This Topic introduces you to the world of Excel macros. Whatever your spreadsheet experience, you won't be disappointed with Excel's rich macro capability.

Introducing the macro

In Excel, macros come in two flavors: *command* and *function*. Command macros, which you're more likely to be familiar with, speed up or automate repetitive spreadsheet tasks by executing a series of Excel menu commands. Command macros can be of the simple keystroke variety (such as entering or selecting data), or can be advanced macros that use subroutines or custom dialog boxes.

Function macros calculate results from values, much like a worksheet function. Since Excel has over 100 functions (over 350 if you open the Analysis Toolpak add-in [see Topic 15]), it's likely Excel already provides you with the worksheet function you're looking for, so this Topic concentrates on creating, executing, and correcting command macros.

Macros in Excel

Excel macros are stored in their own document, just like worksheets and charts. Macro documents are very similar to worksheet documents, as you can see from Figure 14-1.

The major differences between a worksheet document and a macro document are the following:

- ✦ The standard column width is larger.
- ✦ Formulas, rather than results, are displayed.
- ✦ The Paste Function dialog box contains command-equivalent macro functions.

You can store macros on a macro sheet you name (like you name a worksheet document) or on Excel's global macro sheet. Macros stored on the global macro sheet are always available during an Excel session, making it a good place to store macros you use frequently.

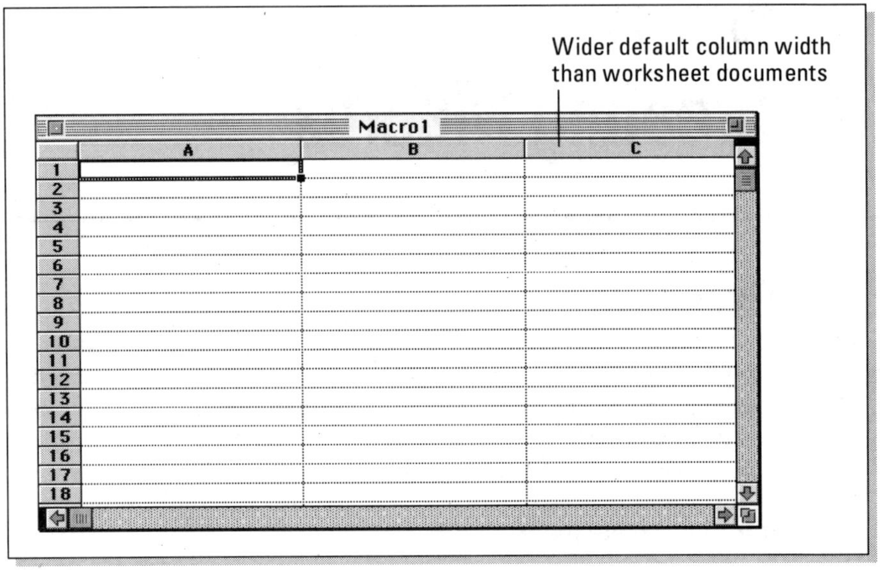

Figure 14-1: Macro documents are similar to worksheet documents.

Creating macros

You have two choices available for creating macros. You can perform a sequence of menu commands while Excel records them, thus creating the macro automatically, or you can type the macro commands manually. The following discussion describes how you do each.

Recording macros

Letting Excel create a macro for you is the easier of the two methods. The Record command on the Macro menu lets you record keystrokes and mouse selections, and stores them as macro command equivalents on a macro sheet. For example, suppose you want to enter the date and time on your worksheets (not a bad idea during budget time or other multiple-iteration activity) rather than have this information in a header or footer.

To create a macro that does this for you automatically, do the following:

1. Choose Record from the Macro menu.

   The Record Macro dialog box shown in Figure 14-2 appears.

2. Type `Info` (or some other descriptive name) in the Name text box.
3. Type `d` (or another letter) in the shortcut key box.
4. Select Global Macro Sheet from the Record Macro dialog box.
5. Choose OK.

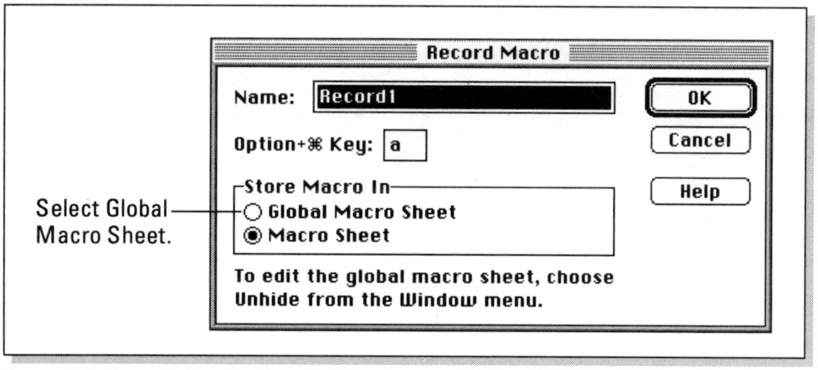

Figure 14-2: Choosing Record from the Macro menu displays the Record Macro dialog box.

6. Choose Paste Function from the Formula menu; select Date & Time from the Function Category list box; select Now from the Paste Function list box and choose OK; and then click Enter.
7. Choose Number from the Format menu or shortcut menu, select Date from the Value type list, select *m/dd/yy* from the Format Codes list box, and then choose OK.
8. Select the next cell immediately below the current cell.
9. Repeat steps 6 and 7, except in step 6, select Time from the Value type list box and h:mm AM/PM from the Format Codes list box, and then choose OK.
10. Choose Stop recorder from the Macro menu.

Excel records all your keystrokes. If you choose Unhide from the Window menu, the Unhide dialog box shown in Figure 14-3 appears. Select Global Macros, and then choose OK. The macro equivalent of your recorded keystrokes should resemble those shown in Figure 14-4.

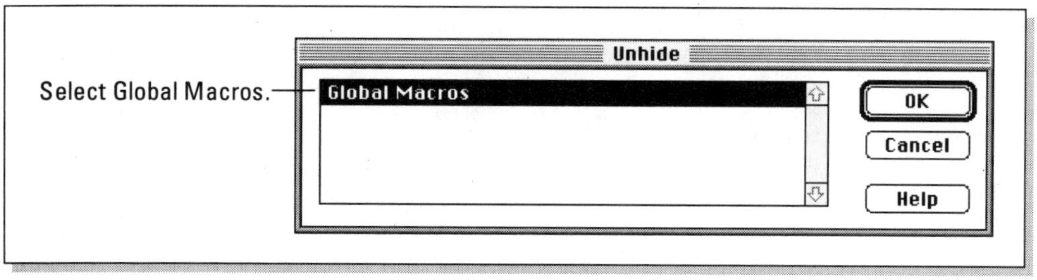

Figure 14-3: Choosing Unhide from the Window menu displays the Unhide dialog box.

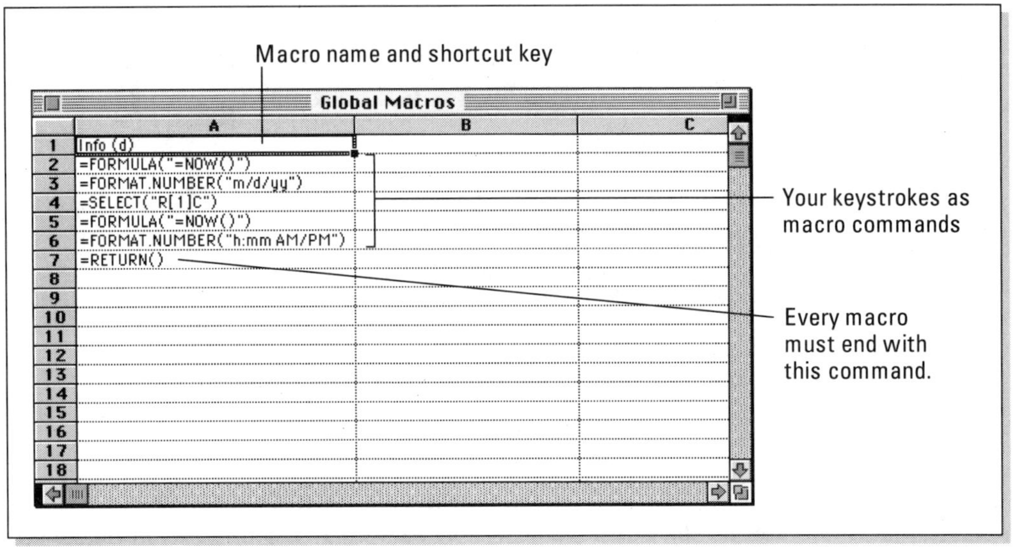

Figure 14-4: Selecting the Global Macros option in the Unhide dialog box displays the macro equivalents of your keystrokes.

Typing macros manually

Just as you would when entering worksheet functions manually, you can forego the macro recording route and type the macro functions yourself. In some cases, you need to do this anyway, if the macro function is of the more advanced type, such as if you need to create a subroutine to perform a certain task.

RC: Cola, or spreadsheet jargon?

In Figure 14-1 you may have noticed some different-looking notation in the select macro command. Actually, this is the way Excel refers to the location of the cell pointer, based on the cell that was selected when you started the macro, or the next time the macro moves the cell pointer.

The following list should help you crack RC (row-column) notation:

Symbol	***Meaning***
R	Row
C	Column
-	Row *above* or Column to the *left*
No brackets	Same row or column

For example, if C10 is the selected cell, and the macro sends the cell pointer off around the worksheet, here are some row-column equivalents:

RC notation	***Cell address***
RC[-2]	A10
RC[3]	F10
R[-9]C	C1
R[-9]C[-2]	A1
R[2]C	C12

Other spreadsheet programs handle row-column notation differently. For instance, if you want to move the cell pointer from C10 to F10 in some other spreadsheet's macro language, you use a {LEFT 3} or {L 3} statement.

Row-column notation takes some getting used to, but it won't take long before you have it under your belt.

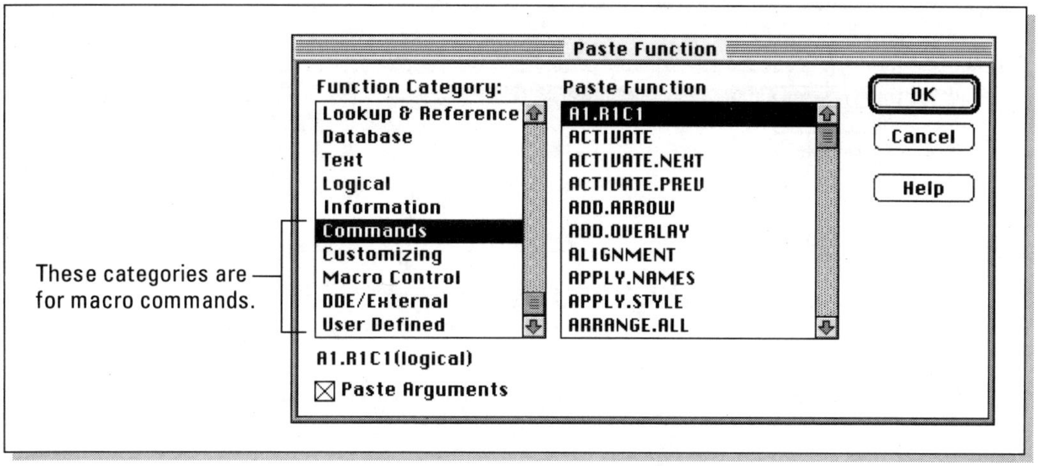

Figure 14-5: An example of the macro functions available in the Paste Function dialog box.

If the thought of creating an automatic process manually is unpalatable to you, choosing Paste Function from the Formula menu makes the task easier to swallow (and perform). When a macro sheet is active, choosing the Paste Function command displays the macro functions shown in Figure 14-5.

Selecting a function and choosing OK enters the function in the selected cell. You can also use both methods together to create a macro if necessary: Record the parts that are recordable, and then manually enter the rest. Just make sure you begin a command with an equal sign and end the macro with the last statement as =RETURN().

When you finish creating a macro, be sure you save it to disk by choosing Save from the File menu or by clicking the File Save tool.

Executing a macro

Executing a macro is an easy process. Open the macro sheet containing the macro by choosing Open from the File menu or by clicking the File Open tool. If the macro you want to run is stored on the global macros sheet, however, all you need to do is make the worksheet you want the macro to operate on the active worksheet, and select the worksheet cell where the macro should begin performing. Then choose Run from the Macro menu. The Run Macro dialog box shown in Figure 14-6 appears.

Select the name of the macro you want to use from the list in the Run Macro dialog box and choose OK. Excel runs the macro as recorded. Alternatively, you can press Option-Command and the shortcut key assigned to the macro to run the macro.

Recording subsequent macros

You can place more than one macro on a macro sheet to keep your macros in one convenient location and minimize the number of macro sheets you need. Storing a second, third, or more macros on the same macro sheet is similar to creating the first macro, with a few exceptions.

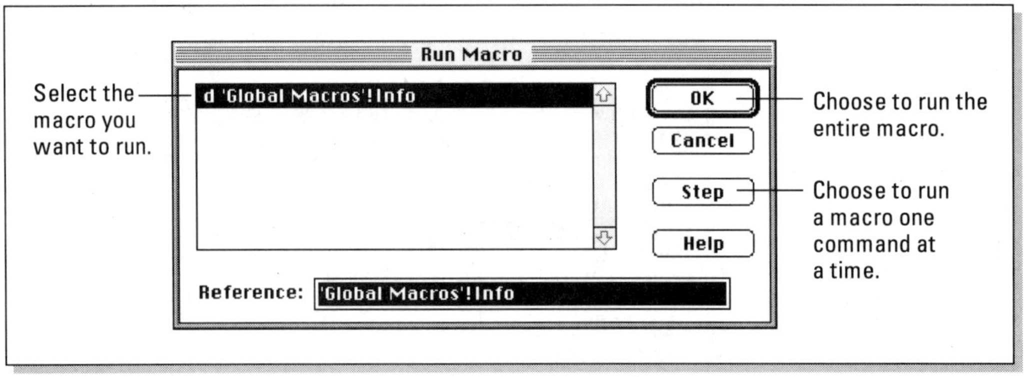

Figure 14-6: Choosing Run from the Macro menu displays the Run Macro dialog box.

Start by opening the worksheet you want to use the macro with, and the macro sheet that will store the macro. Make the macro sheet the active document, and select the first cell that will store the macro, preferably two cells below the previous macro. Type a name for the macro and click Enter or press Return. Choose Set Recorder from the Macro menu, and then make the worksheet the active document.

Next, choose Start Recorder from the Macro menu, and perform the worksheet operation the way you want Excel to record it. Choose Stop Recorder from the Macro menu when you're finished.

Now, make the macro sheet the active document, and select the first cell of the new macro. Choose Define Name from the Formula menu, and when the Define Name dialog box appears (as shown in Figure 14-7), type a name in the Name text box, select Command, and enter a shortcut key for the macro. When you choose OK, you're ready to put the macro to work or continue creating other macros.

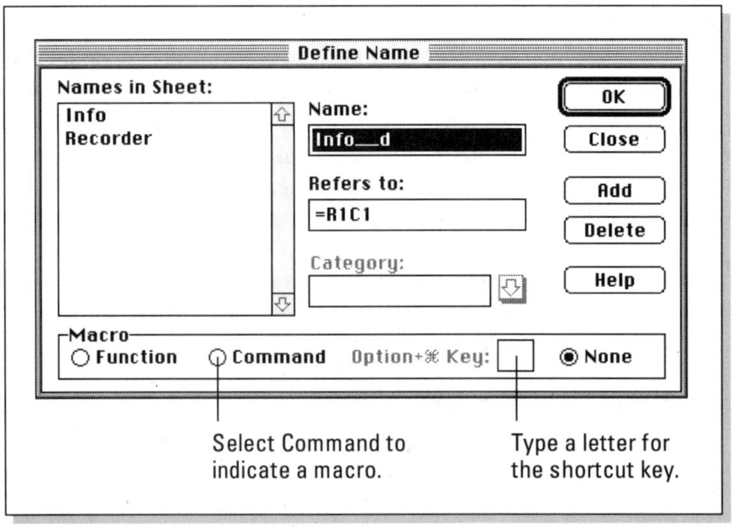

Figure 14-7: Choosing Define Name from the Formula menu displays the Define Name dialog box.

Relative vs. absolute revisited

You may recall from Topic 6 that absolute or relative cell references can have a huge impact on the accuracy of copied formulas. So too is it the case with macros.

By default, Excel records and plays back macros in an absolute mode. For example, suppose your company's financial statements have worksheet titles formatted in a certain way, and to save time, you've created a macro that enters the titles into a worksheet and then formats them in company style. If you record the macro with the titles in cells A1 through A3, the titles will always be in this range when you run the macro.

To enter the titles in a range of your choosing, you need to create the macro in *relative* mode. After you choose Record from the Macro menu and complete the Record Macro dialog box, choose Relative Record from the Macro menu. The macro will be recorded on a relative basis and will run with more flexibility, if that's what the macro needs to execute properly.

Correcting macros

Once in a blue moon you create a macro that won't run properly the first time, an experience we've all shared at one time or another. Some of the common macro problems are listed in Table 14-1.

Table 14-1: Common macro miscues

Problem	***Possible cause***
The macro won't run	No shortcut key assigned to macro Macro assigned to another shortcut key Macro is not named Macro sheet is not open
The macro isn't listed in the Macro Name dialog box	Macro not named Macro sheet not open
The macro is performing tasks on the wrong cells	Didn't select Relative Record after selecting Start Recorder
The wrong macro runs	Two macros share the same shortcut key Macro was previously assigned the shortcut key combination
Macro stops running in midstream	Misspelled macro command
Macro runs OK occasionally	All possible worksheet conditions haven't been taken into account
Macro no longer runs	Macro relies on cell contents whose addresses have changed

There are two categories of errors that can cause a macro to fail: syntax and logical. Syntax errors are the easier of the two to repair and occur when a macro function is misspelled, arguments are missing or inappropriate, parentheses are omitted, or cell contents are referenced that are no longer there because they've been moved (use names instead of addresses).

Logical errors are a little harder to track down and require you to put on your thinking cap. Logical errors develop when the macro does something you didn't expect; you then need to take into account all possible conditions.

To correct macro errors, switch to the open macro sheet. Scan the wayward macro statement for syntax errors, and if one exists, activate the formula bar and edit it like any other cell entry. Click Enter or press Return, and then run the macro. If the macro fails again, you may have another syntax error in another macro statement, or you may have a logical error. To correct a logical error, you may need other macro commands, subroutines, or you may need to start over from scratch, depending on the macro's purpose.

If you still have trouble finding the problem, you can step through the macro one line at a time, as discussed in the next section.

Single-stepping through macros

Macros normally run from start to finish without pausing, and at high speed. You can, however, run a macro one macro command at a time to help you identify a problem command. To do so, open the worksheet and macro documents you want to work with. Make the worksheet the active document, and then choose Run from the Macro menu. Select a macro to run, and then instead of choosing OK, choose Step. When you do, the Single Step dialog box appears, as shown in Figure 14-8.

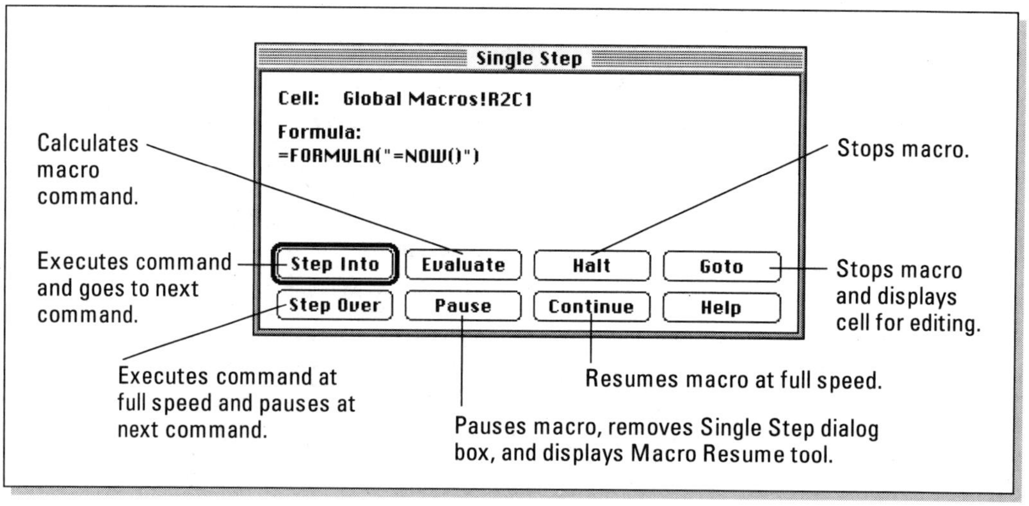

Figure 14-8: Choosing the Step option in the Run Macro dialog box displays the Single Step dialog box.

The Single Step dialog box displays the contents of the cell that's next in line to be executed and its address or name. Click the button that represents what you want to do next.

Usually single-step mode is enough to help you locate the error and get the macro up and running. On the other hand, if the macro still refuses to cooperate, consider using the Debug add-in, discussed in the next Topic.

Assigning macros

You can assign a macro to an object on the worksheet or to a tool. This gives you two more ways you can execute a macro.

Assigning macros to an object

Assigning a macro to an existing object is easy. Select the object, and then choose Assign To Object from the Macro menu. The Assign To Object dialog box shown in Figure 14-9 appears.

The Assign Macro list box displays all macros on the open macro sheet. Select the macro you want to attach to the object and choose OK. Whenever you click the object, the macro runs (if the macro sheet is open).

If you don't currently have any objects on a worksheet, display the drawing toolbar to add the object of your choice to the worksheet: a square, circle, rectangle, and so on — any of these objects can have a macro assigned to them. In addition, the Utility toolbar shown in Figure 14-10 has a Button tool with which you can add a button object. Clicking the Button tool displays the mouse pointer as cross-hairs, which allows you to draw the button on the worksheet. Releasing the mouse completes the button and displays the Assign Object dialog box, so you can assign a macro to it.

Assigning macros to a tool

When you assign a macro to a tool, you're really reassigning it, because it already has a macro attached to it. You begin by displaying the toolbar that contains the tool, and then choosing Customize from the Toolbar menu or toolbar shortcut menu.

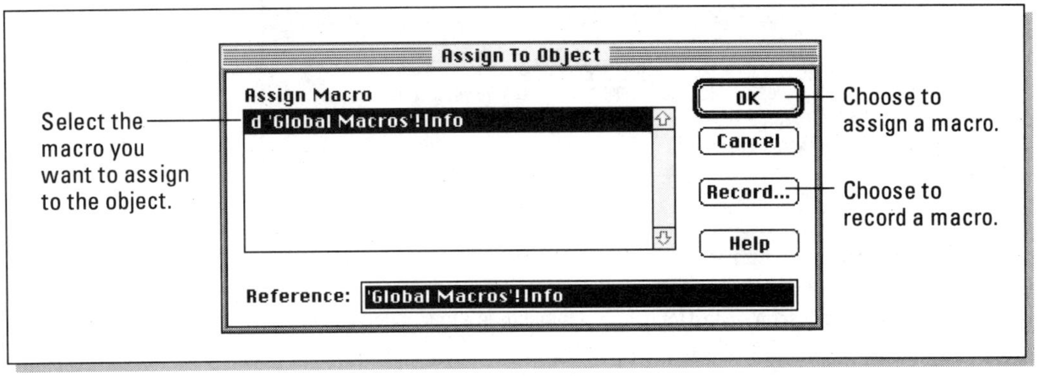

Figure 14-9: Choosing Assign To Object from the Macro menu displays the Assign To Object dialog box.

Figure 14-10: The Button tool on the Utility toolbar enables you to add a button object to a worksheet.

When the Customize dialog box appears, click the tool you want to assign the macro to, and then choose Assign to Tool from the Macro menu. A dialog box similar to the one shown in Figure 14-9 appears so you can select the macro you want to assign to the tool.

Documenting macros

It goes without saying that macros can be very powerful and useful, as well as complicated. It's always a good idea to not only document your worksheets, but your macros also. You can never be sure who'll eventually end up using your worksheets and macros, and documentation does reduce those untimely telephone calls (or visits) for help.

You can document a macro in two ways, but in either case, make the macro sheet containing the macro the active document. First, you can use Formula Note to attach a note to each cell containing a macro command. To view the documentation, choose Note from the Formula menu or double-click the cell that contains the note.

Second, you can enter descriptive text for each macro command in the corresponding cell in Column B (or C), as shown in Figure 14-11.

Select the method that appeals to you most, keeping in mind that worksheets and macros can never have enough explanation or instructions.

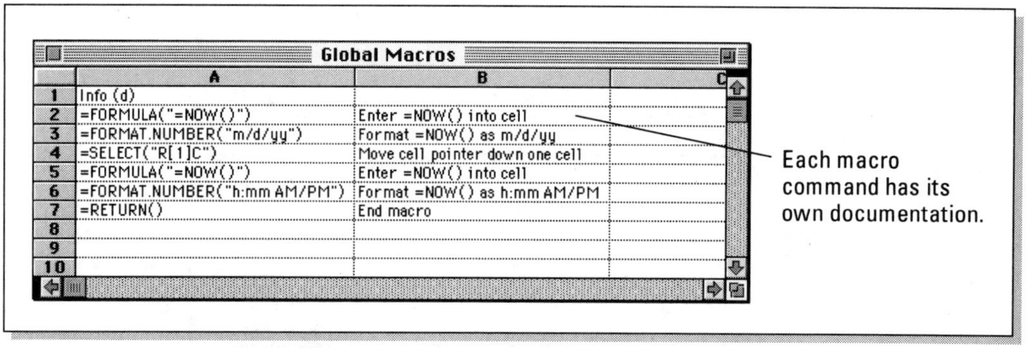

Figure 14-11: Entering descriptive text for macro commands in a macro document.

Step-by-Step

In this section, you'll practice creating macros. You'll use the macro recorder to create a pair of macros that quickly hide and redisplay worksheet gridlines.

As always, if you make a mistake, remember the first rule of thumb: Don't panic. But because you'll be recording macros, if you make a mistake, you'll need to start over without saving the macro sheet. Or you can try your hand at debugging the macro. Either way, don't get flustered. Hang in there and you should have two simple but useful macros when you're finished.

To begin the exercise, do the following:

1. Start Excel.

The Worksheet1 window appears.

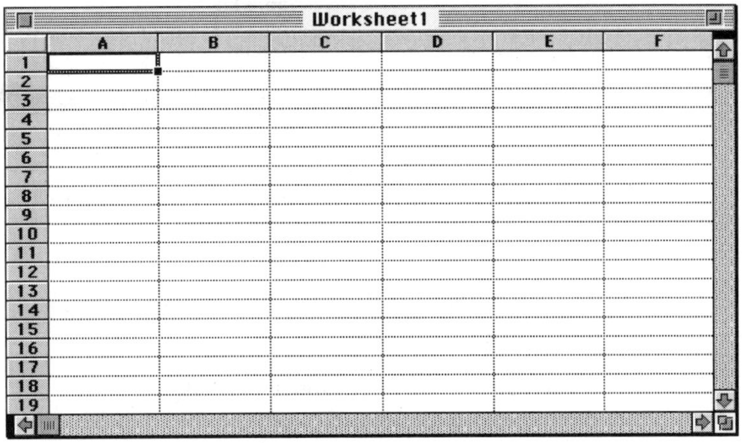

Figure 14-12: Starting up Excel displays the Worksheet1 worksheet.

Creating a macro by recording:

Step 1. Choose Record from the Macro menu.

The Record Macro dialog box appears.

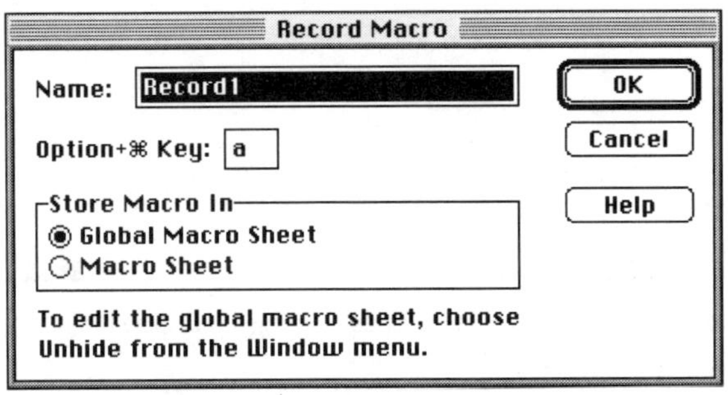

Figure 14-13: Choosing Record from the Macro menu displays the Record Macro dialog box.

Step 2. Enter Gridoff in the Name text box, type g in the shortcut key text box, select Global Macro Sheet, and then choose OK.

Step 3. Choose Display from the Options menu.

The Display Options dialog box appears.

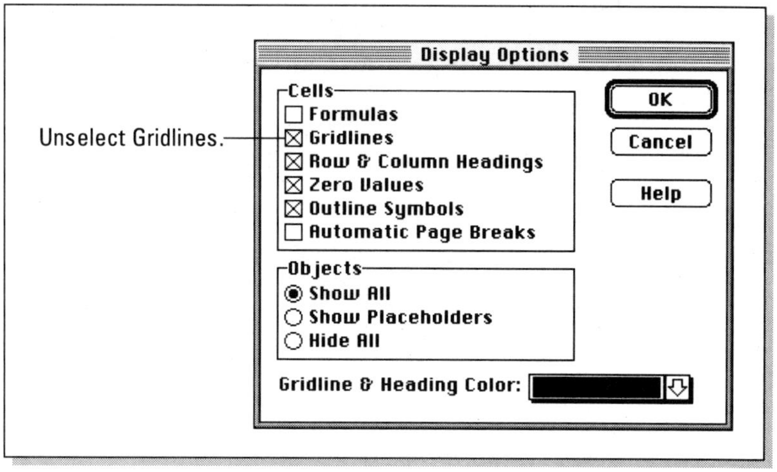

Figure 14-14: Choosing Display from the Options menu displays the Display Options dialog box.

Step 4. Unselect Gridlines and choose OK, and then choose Stop Recorder from the Macro menu.

The worksheet appears without gridlines.

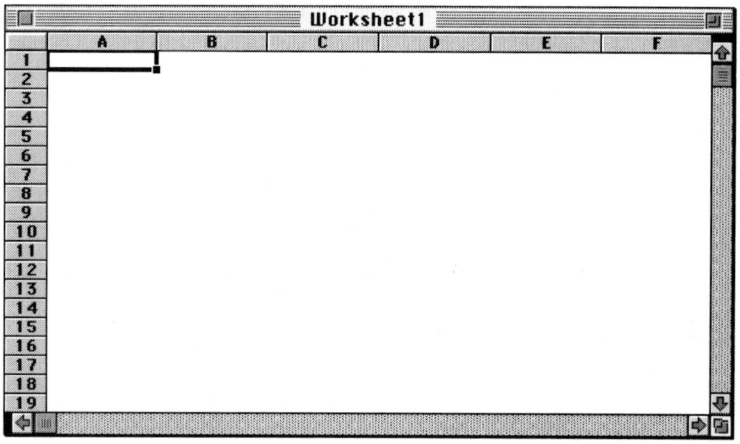

Figure 14-15: Unselecting the Gridlines option in the Display Options dialog box displays the worksheet without gridlines.

Displaying the Global Macros sheet:

Step 1. Choose Unhide from the Window menu.

The Unhide dialog box appears.

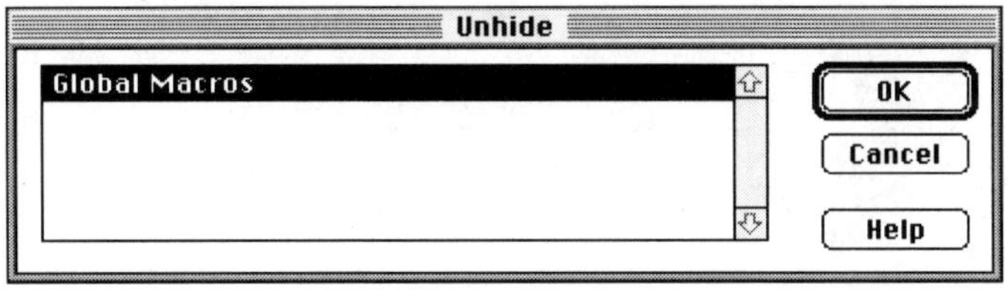

Figure 14-16: Choosing Unhide from the Window menu displays the Unhide dialog box.

Step 2. Select Global Macros and choose OK.

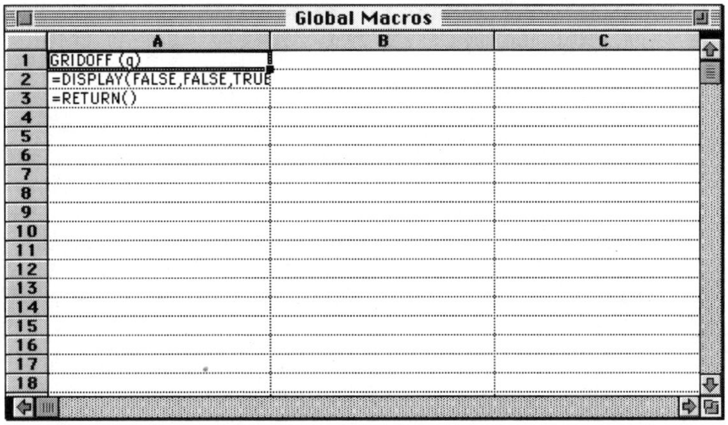

Figure 14-17: Selecting the Global Macros option in the Unhide dialog box displays the Global Macros macro sheet.

Recording a subsequent macro:

Step 1. Double-click the line separating Columns A and B, move the cell pointer to cell A5, type `GRIDON`, press Return, and then choose Set Recorder from the Macro menu.

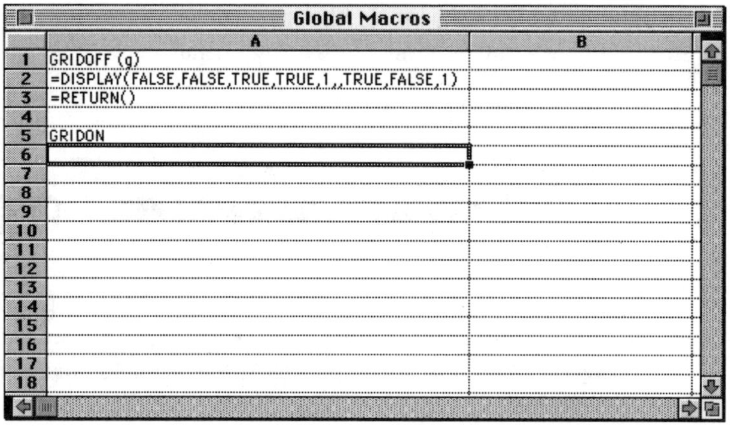

Figure 14-18: Preparing a macro sheet for recording of subsequent macros.

Step 2. Make the worksheet the active window and choose Start Recorder from the Macro menu.

Step 3. Choose Display from the Options menu.

The Display Options dialog box appears.

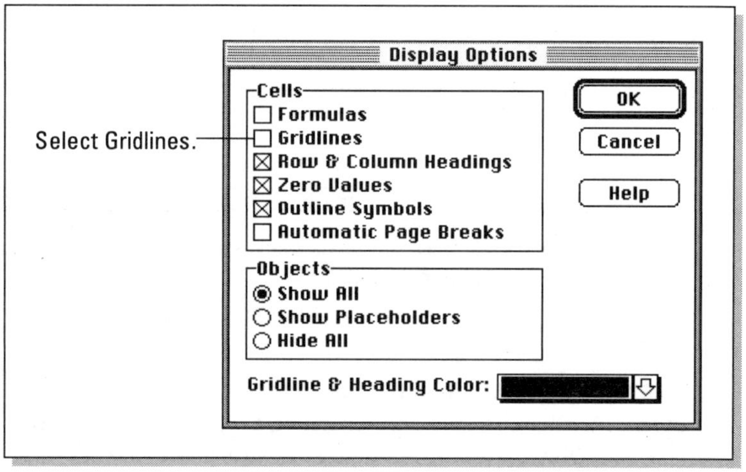

Figure 14-19: Choosing Display from the Options menu displays the Display Options dialog box.

Step 4. Select Gridlines from the Display Options dialog box and choose OK, and then choose Stop Recorder from the Macro menu.

The worksheet appears with gridlines.

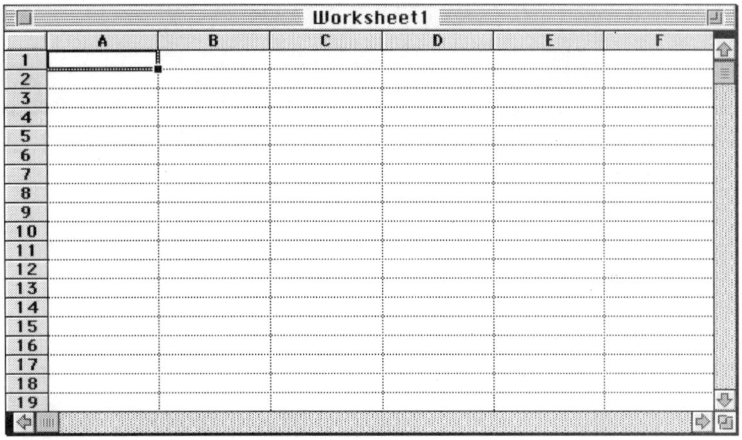

Figure 14-20: Selecting the Gridlines option from the Display Options dialog box displays the worksheet with gridlines.

Step 5. Make Global Macros the active document.

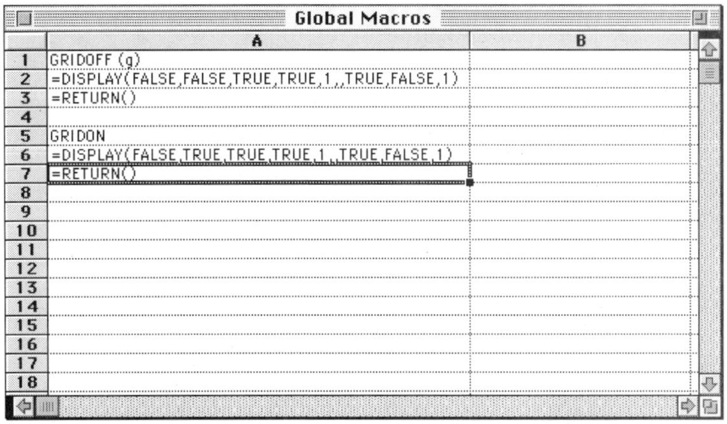

Figure 14-21: Clicking on the Global Macros document makes it the active document.

Step 6. Select cell A5, and then choose Define Name from the Formula menu.

The Define Name dialog box appears.

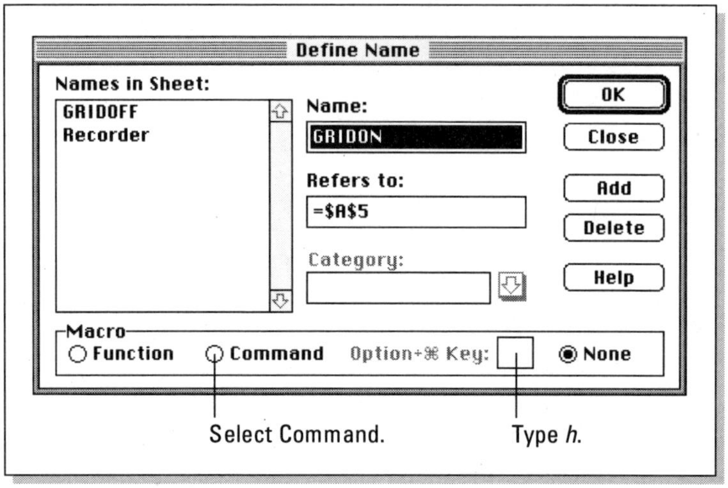

Figure 14-22: Choosing Define Name from the Formula menu displays the Define Name dialog box.

Step 7. Select Command, type h in the shortcut key box, and then choose OK.

Your macros appear, ready to go.

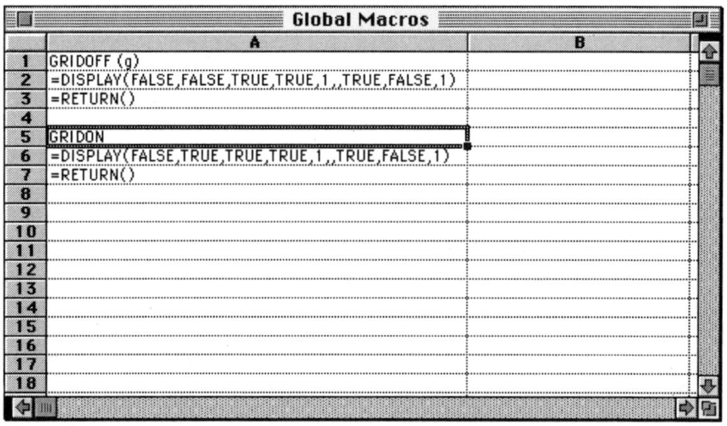

Figure 14-23: An example of subsequent recorded macros that are ready for operation.

Saving macros:

Step 1. Choose Save from the File menu or click the File Save tool.

The Save dialog box appears.

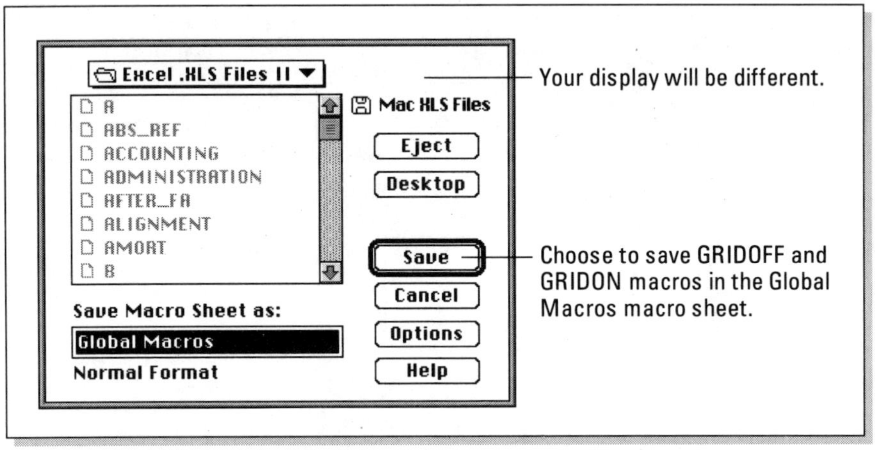

Figure 14-24: Choosing Save from the File menu displays the Save dialog box.

Step 2. Choose OK.

Excel saves the Global Macros macro sheet to disk.

Quick Tips

This section provides you with tips on how to effectively use macros to automate tasks that you routinely perform in your Excel sessions.

Assigning letters to shortcut keys

When assigning letters to macro shortcut keys, make sure you specify either an uppercase or lowercase letter as Excel considers a and A different keys.

Interrupting a macro recording

If you need to take a break and stop recording a macro, choose Stop Recorder from the Macro menu. When you're ready to get rolling again, choose Start Recorder from the Macro menu.

Learning about macros

You can gain a better understanding of macros by choosing Arrange from the Window menu. This technique enables you to view the worksheet and macro sheets simultaneously, and see how Excel translates your worksheet operations into macro commands as you do them, as shown in Figure 14-25.

Using the Macro toolbar

Excel's Macro toolbar, shown in Figure 14-26, enables you to quickly access many of the common macro commands found on the Macro menu.

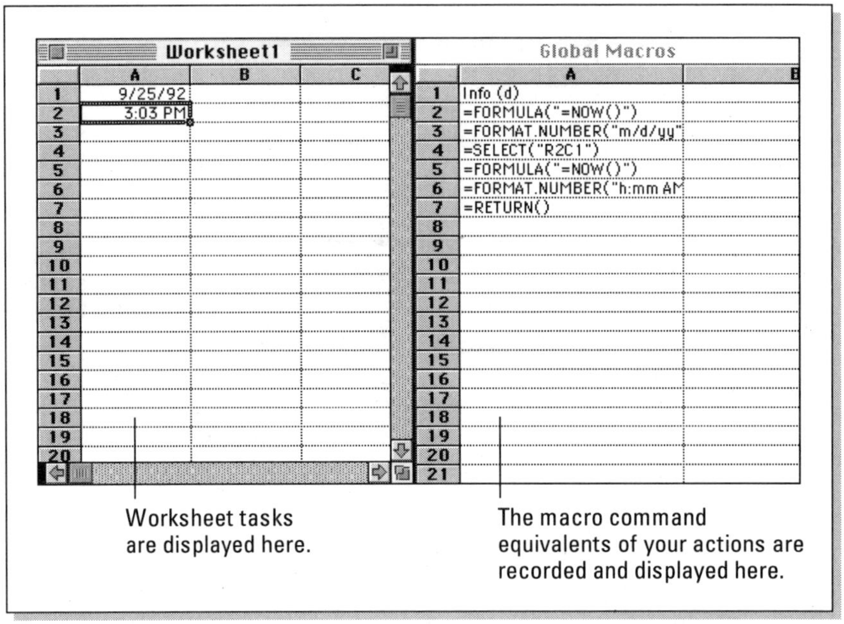

Figure 14-25: Viewing worksheets and macro sheets simultaneously enables you to see how macros relate to worksheet operations.

Suppressing a macro

If a worksheet contains the name Auto_Open, the macro that Auto_Open refers to automatically executes each time you open the worksheet. Hold down Shift before you click OK in the Open dialog box to prevent the Auto_Open macro from running.

Displaying the Assign to Tool dialog box automatically

Dragging a tool from the Custom toolbox automatically displays the Assign to Tool dialog box, because the tool doesn't have a macro assigned to it.

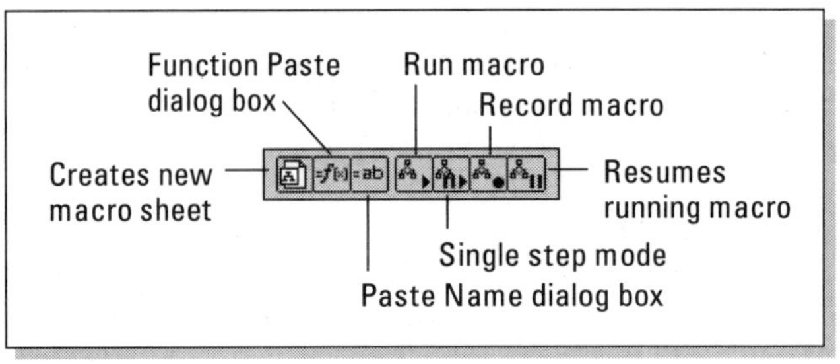

Figure 14-26: You can quickly access macro commands using the Macro toolbar.

Summary

- Macros enable you to automate repetitive worksheet tasks and create custom Excel applications.
- Macros reside in their own macro sheet.
- A macro sheet must be open to be able to use a macro.
- You can create a macro by having Excel record your worksheet operations, typing the macro commands, or using a combination of both.
- You can execute macros using a shortcut key combination or by selecting its name from the Macro Run dialog box.
- Macros, like other computer programs, need to be tested and corrected. Step mode helps you find errors in macros.
- Macros can be assigned to objects and tools.
- You and your users will thank you for liberally documenting your macros.

Topic 15
Excel Add-Ins

Overview

Just when you thought Excel could do anything, along come add-ins. Add-ins extend the functionality of Excel for specialized needs. This Topic catalogs the add-ins that come with Excel and describes each so you can determine which ones may be helpful in your spreadsheet sessions.

What is an add-in?

An Excel add-in is a separate program that "adds in" more functionality to Excel. Add-ins come in all stripes, ranging from general-purpose, such as Name Changer, to high-powered specialized uses, such as the Analysis ToolPak. Add-ins can include those provided by Microsoft and included with Excel, those from other software companies besides Microsoft (third-party vendors), and those you create yourself.

You use an add-in by loading it into memory, like a worksheet, chart, or macro sheet. Once an add-in is loaded, you won't know it's there until you use it. Most add-ins add another command to a menu, and the worksheet functions provided by the Add-in Functions and the Analysis ToolPak appear in the Paste Function dialog box.

Making add-ins part of your spreadsheet regimen is easy, as you'll find in the next section.

Putting add-ins to work

You need to take care of two things before you can use an add-in: Like Excel, you must install it on your Macintosh's hard disk, and you must place a copy of it in memory. The following describes how you do each.

Installing add-ins

If you chose the complete installation when you (or someone else) installed Excel, all the add-ins that come with Excel are automatically installed for you on your Macintosh's hard disk, in a Macro Library subfolder in the Excel folder. The custom installation, on the other hand, gives you the opportunity *not* to install the Analysis ToolPak, Solver, CrossTab ReportWizard, Data Access, or Macro Library (all other add-ins). If you find that you need one or more of these add-ins, place the Excel Setup disk in your Macintosh, double-click the Microsoft Excel Setup icon, and then select Custom. Select the add-in you need and the Microsoft Excel 4.0 folder. Choosing Setup displays a window with instructions about which disk to insert into your Macintosh next so the add-in files can be copied to disk. Appendix A has more information about installing Excel on your Macintosh.

Loading an add-in into memory

The following choices enable you to load an add-in to memory:

1. Choose Open from the File menu, click the File Open tool or press Command-O.
2. Through the Add-in Manager.
3. Moving the add-in from the Macro Library subfolder to the Startup folder.

If you only have occasional use for an add-in, you may want to open it only when needed. In this case, open the add-in using one of the options in the first choice above. Select the Macro Library folder, and then the name of the add-in from the Open dialog box shown in Figure 15-1.

Choosing OK loads a copy of the add-in into memory from disk.

You may prefer to have an add-in automatically load every time you start Excel, which is convenient if you depend on the functionality the add-in provides. You can have Excel do this for you through the Add-in Manager or by using the third choice above.

The Add-in Manager (which is also an add-in) helps you . . . well, manage your add-ins. The Add-in Manager maintains add-ins that open automatically with Excel, known as your *working set*. Figure 15-2 lists several add-ins that are part of the working set.

Several add-ins, although they may appear in the Add-in Manager dialog box and are part of the working set, won't open until you choose the command from the menu. These include the add-ins listed in the following table.

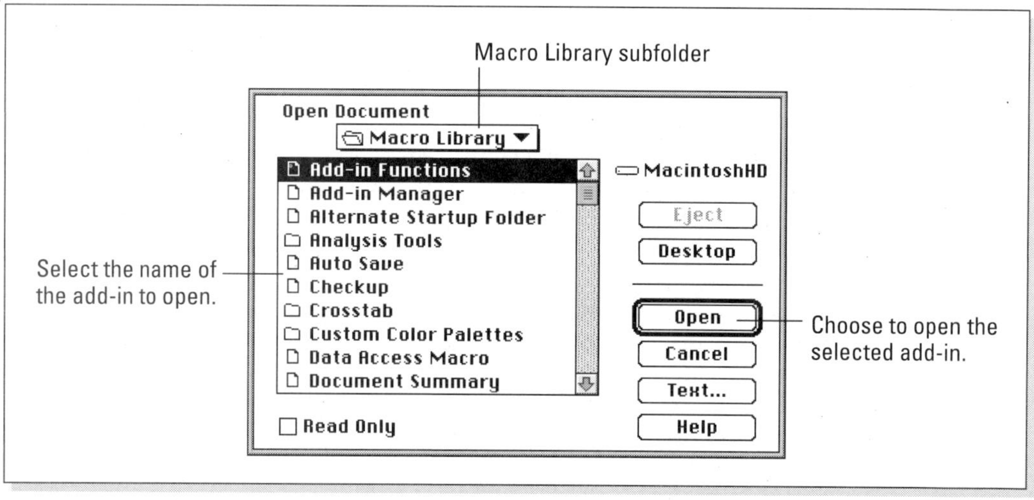

Figure 15-1: Loading an add-in into memory using the Open dialog box.

Where is the Startup folder?

You won't find the Startup folder in the Excel folder or in any Excel subfolders. Rather, you'll find it lurking in the Preferences subfolder (System 7.*x*) or in the Excel Startup folder (4) (System 6.0 and under) of the System Folder.

If you want an add-in (or other document) to load automatically immediately after Excel loads, drag the add-in's icon to the desktop. Then open the System Folder, and drag the add-in icon to the Startup folder appropriate for the System software you're using. The next time you start Excel, the add-in will be loaded and ready to go.

Add-in	***Menu***	***Command***
Add-in Manager	Options	Add-in
Analysis ToolPak	Options	Analysis Tools *
CrossTab	Data	CrossTab
Report Manager	File	Print Report
Solver	Formula	Solver
View Manager	Window	View

* Analysis ToolPak worksheet functions are available without selecting a command.

If you've installed one of the above add-ins (except for the Add-in Manager), selecting the name of the add-in from the Add-in Manager dialog box and choosing OK removes the add-in from your working set frees up memory for future sessions.

As an add-in is loaded into memroy, Add-In appears in the Reference area with the completion percentage, similar to opening other Excel documents. When the mouse

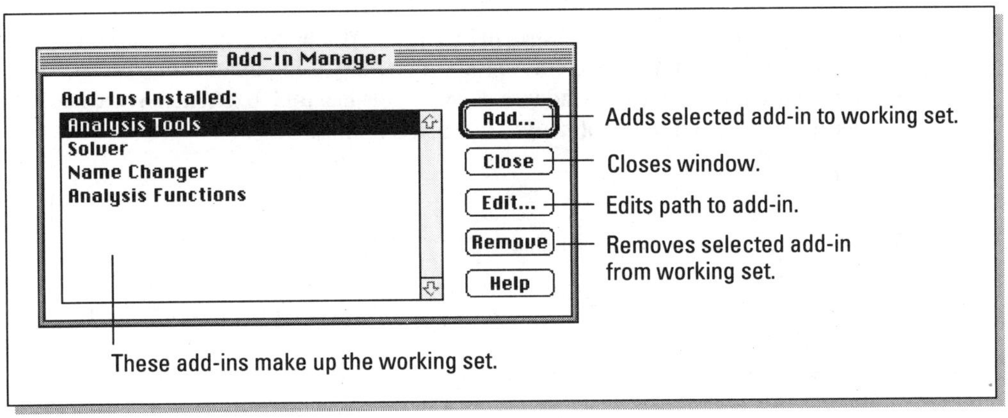

Figure 15-2: An example of a working set of add-ins.

pointer changes from the watch to the black arrow or white cross (depending on the location of the pointer), choose the command from the appropriate menu to use the add-in.

Removing an add-in from memory

You may find that you only need an add-in for a short time during an Excel session, and then you would like to put it away. Unfortunately, removing an add-in from memory requires some jumping through hoops (attention Microsoft). While not particularly elegant, the following add-in removal technique gets the job done. It also gives you an opportunity to see the macro commands that comprise an add-in.

First, choose Open from the File menu, or click the File Open tool. When the Open dialog box appears, select the name of the add-in you want to remove. Hold down Shift and choose Open. The alert message box shown in Figure 15-3 appears.

Choosing OK replaces the first copy of the add-in with a second copy, only this time it is in its own window (you may need to choose Unhide from the Window menu to see it). Make the window containing the add-in the active window and click the close box, choose Close from the File menu, or press Command-W. Be sure to choose No when the alert message box appears, as shown in Figure 15-4. If you make changes to the add-in and then save it to disk, it may not function properly the next time you use it, which requires you to copy it from the Excel disks to your Macintosh again. In any event, closing the add-in's window removes the add-in from memory, making more memory available for your Excel session.

Reducing the memory usage of add-ins

Like any other computer program, add-ins need some of your Macintosh's memory to operate, which may be a problem if your Macintosh has limited resources for the task at hand. Or maybe you prefer to have as much memory available as possible while you're spreadsheeting. Whatever the reason, you can make more memory available to Excel by not making the add-in part of the working set. That way, a copy of the add-in won't be loaded into memory when you start up Excel.

If a copy of the add-in *is* currently in memory, and you no longer have a need for it during an Excel session, you can remove it from memory using the technique described above. That way, you can use add-ins like the tools in a toolbox: Take out the add-in you need and use it, and then put it away when you're finished.

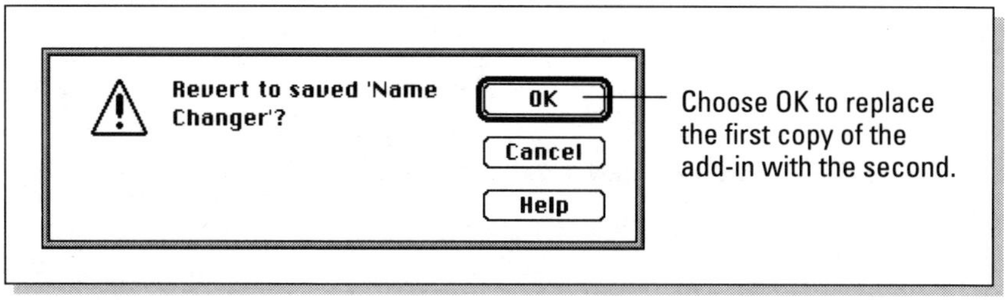

Figure 15-3: Removing an add-in from memory using the Open menu displays this alert message box.

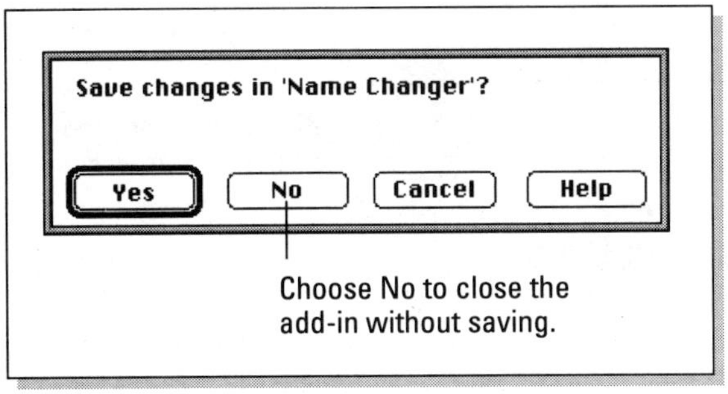

Figure 15-4: Closing out of a window containing an add-in displays this alert message box.

Introducing Excel's add-ins

The following section describes the add-ins that come with Excel in alphabetical order. Remember, to use any add-in it must be installed on your Macintosh's hard drive, with a copy loaded into memory, using one of the techniques described earlier.

Add-in Functions

Add-in Functions provides you with the five functions listed in Table 15-1.

Table 15-1: Add-in Functions

Function	*Action*
BASE	Converts a number from base 10 to another specified base
DEGREES	Converts radians to degrees
FASTMATCH	Returns the relative position of an element in an array of numbers that matches a specified number
RADIANS	Converts degrees into radians
RANDBETWEEN	Returns a random integer within a specified range of integers

Add-in Manager

The Add-in Manager enables you to add or delete add-ins from the working set of add-ins, as described above. Choose Add-ins from the Options menu.

Alternate Startup folder

VERSION 4 Microsoft

Documents and files that reside in the Excel Startup folder (4) (System 6.0 and under) and Preferences folder (System 7.*x*) are opened automatically each time you start Excel. Documents and files you can have Excel open for you include the following:

- Worksheets
- Workbooks
- Charts
- Add-ins
- Macro sheets

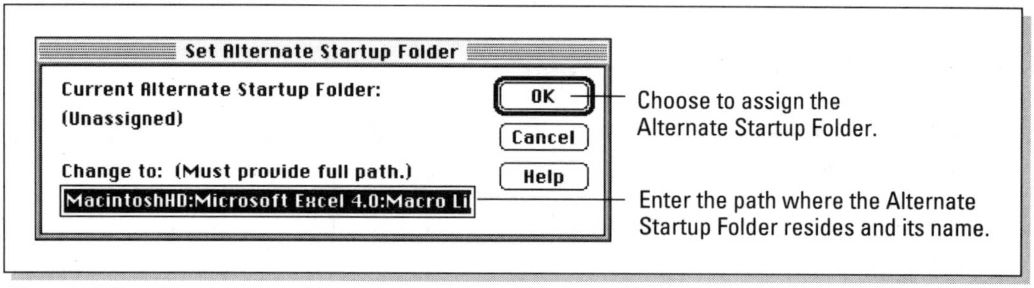

Figure 15-5: Specifying the disk and the name of the Alternate Startup Folder.

The Alternate Startup Folder add-in enables you to specify a second startup folder. Figure 15-5 displays the Set Alternate Startup Folder dialog box, in which you can specify the disk and the name of the folder that will be the alternate startup folder.

The startup folder is useful when you have worksheets, templates, or macros you use frequently. An alternate startup folder is especially valuable if you use Excel on a network and want to use a shared startup folder.

Analysis ToolPak

The Analysis ToolPak adds many advanced financial, statistical, and engineering worksheet functions in Excel. In addition, the Analysis ToolPak adds several statistical tests and procedures to Excel, several of which are listed in the Analysis Tools dialog box shown in Figure 15-6. Use this add-in if you need a sophisticated analysis of your data.

Select the worksheet function from the Paste Function dialog box as you would normally. Choose Analysis Tools from the Options menu to select a statistical test.

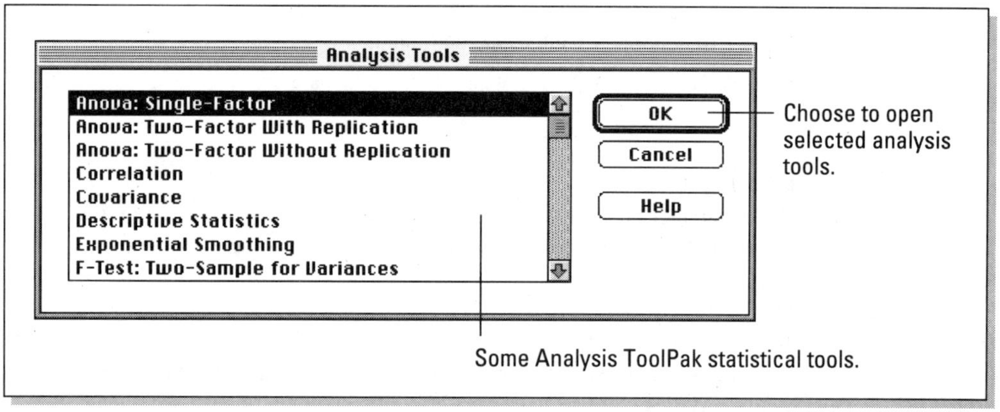

Figure 15-6: Using the Analysis Tools dialog box from the Analysis ToolPak add-in to add statistical tests and procedures to Excel.

AutoSave

The AutoSave add-in automatically saves all open documents to disk at an interval you specify. The following settings are available:

Interval	*Minutes*
High	3
Medium	9
Low	30

The AutoSave dialog box shown in Figure 15-7 enables you to select the interval as well as whether you want to save only the active document, or all open documents. Choose AutoSave from the Options menu.

Checkup

Checkup displays a window containing Excel, System software (System 6.*x* or 7.*x*), and Macintosh technical information, as shown in Figure 15-8.

Keep Checkup in mind before you call Microsoft Technical Support or if you just have a thirst for knowledge.

Crosstabs

Crosstabs starts CrossTab ReportWizard, a step-by-step program that totals and compares related data in an Excel database. For example, you can summarize a monthly sales report by product, region, and salesperson. CrossTab ReportWizard operates similarly to ChartWizard. Choose Crosstab from the Data menu.

Custom Color Palettes

Custom Color Palettes offers you a quick way to change the color palette that the active document uses. The dialog box shown in Figure 15-9 gives you several palette choices. Choose Custom Palettes from the Options menu or Chart menu.

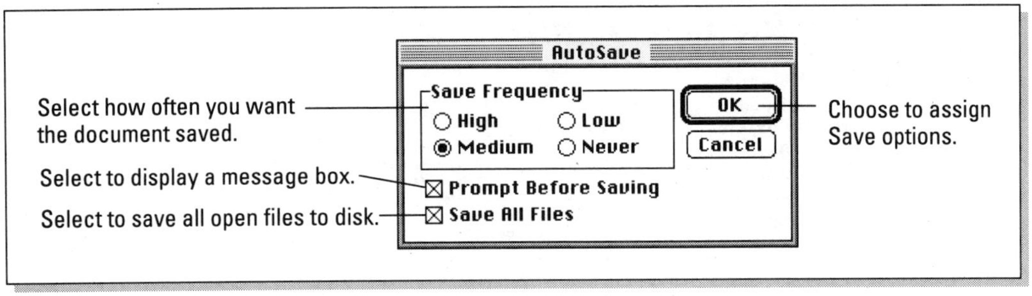

Figure 15-7: Setting save options using the AutoSave dialog box.

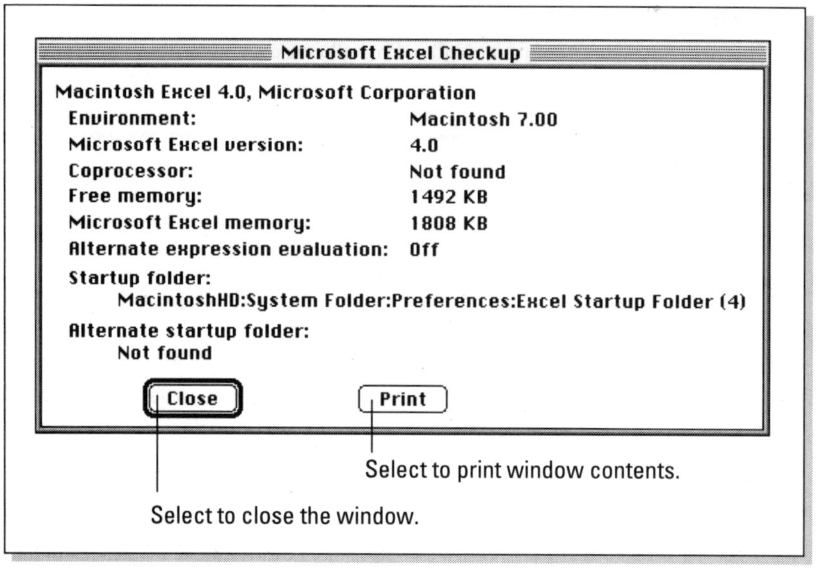

Figure 15-8: Accessing information about your Macintosh, system software, or Excel using the Microsoft Excel Checkup dialog box.

Data Access

Data Access enables you to access data from a non-Excel database. To use Data Access, the following requirements must be met:

- ✦ Your Macintosh must be part of a computer network.
- ✦ You must have an account and a password to access the network's host computer and database program.

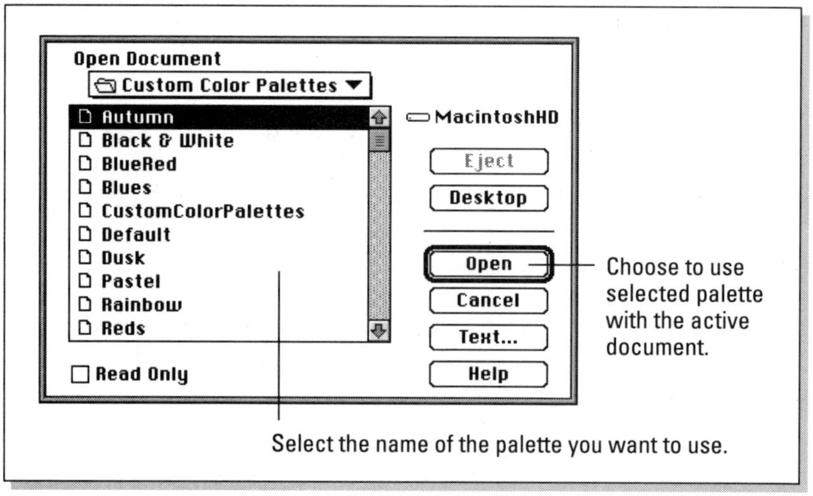

Figure 15-9: An example of the various palette choices available from the Custom Color Palettes add-in.

- ✦ The network's host computer must have Apple's Data Access Language (DAL) server program installed.
- ✦ Your Macintosh must use System 7.0 (or later), *or* have DAL installed.

Data Access provides you with the following additional commands so you can query the host computer's database and pass the query results to an Excel worksheet:

Menu	***Command***
Data	Paste Fieldnames
Data	SQL Query
Data	Close Connection
Data	Query Assistant
Options	Query Destination

Document Summary

Document Summary gives you a way to electronically jot down information about a worksheet. The Summary Info dialog box, shown in Figure 15-10, tells you what summary information can be stored.

Note that the worksheet's creation date cannot be changed (sorry). Choose Document Summary from the Edit menu.

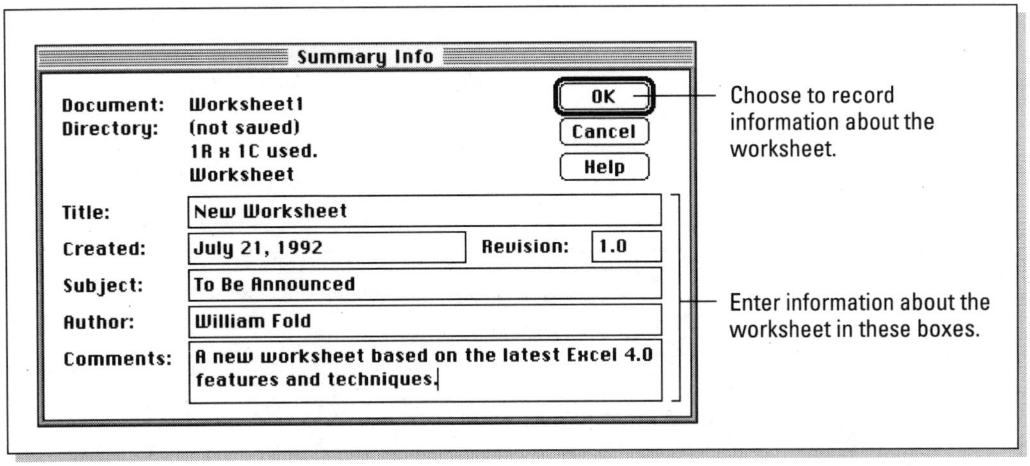

Figure 15-10: Storing electronic information about Excel worksheets using the Summary Info dialog box.

File Functions

File Functions provides you with six additional macro functions (see Table 15-2), relating to file operations.

Table 15-2: File Functions

Macro function	*Purpose*
CREATE.DIRECTORY	Creates a new folder
DELETE.DIRECTORY	Deletes an empty folder
DIRECTORIES	Places a list of folders in the current folder or specified path
FILE.EXISTS	Determines whether a file or folder exists
OPEN.DIALOG	Displays the Open dialog box
SAVE.DIALOG	Displays the Save dialog box

Use File Functions if you create macros that include file tasks as part of their operation.

Flat File

Flat File provides you with the capability to easily use the information contained in text files with Excel. Flat File furnishes you with two commands: the Export command, which transfers selected cells to a space-delimited (separated) text file, and the Smart Parse command, which separates data contained in each line of text and places it in its own cell in the row.

Figures 15-11 and 15-12 display the Export and Smart Parse dialog boxes, respectively.

Data Export is more flexible than choosing Save or Save As from the File menu and selecting the Text file format. This is because Data Export enables you to select whether you want the text file to retain text alignment and number formats of the selected Excel data.

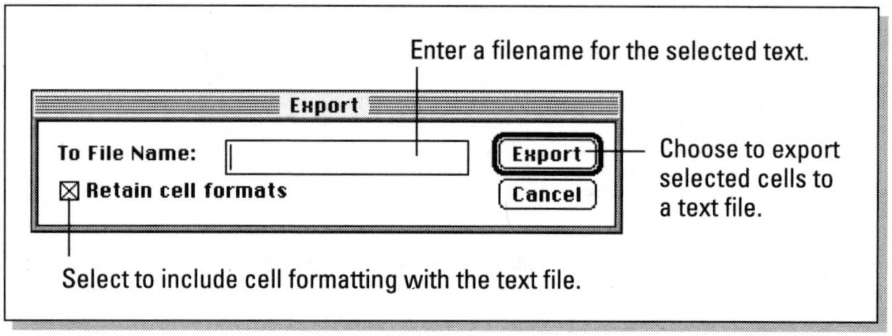

Figure 15-11: Transferring selected cells to a space-delimited text file using the Export dialog box.

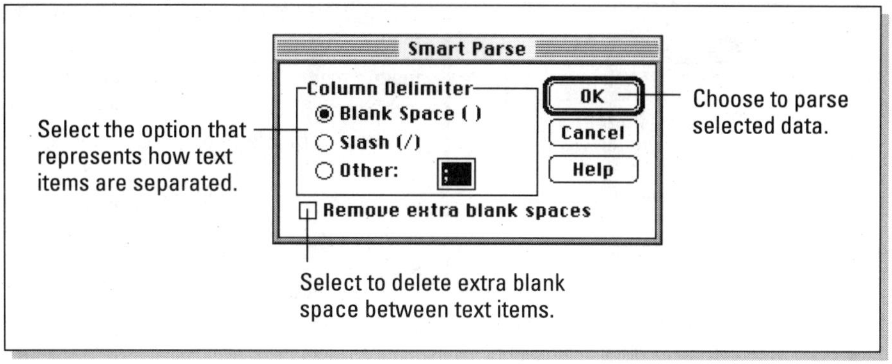

Figure 15-12: Separating lines of data and placing them in cells within rows using the Smart Parse dialog box.

Smart Parse enables you to import variable-length data, while Data Parse enables you to import fixed-length data. Choose Export and Smart Parse from the Data menu.

Glossary

Glossary enables you to quickly paste text, values, and formulas you use frequently in worksheets and macro sheets. You can use Glossary entries as many times as needed, which are stored until you delete them. Figure 15-13 displays the Glossary dialog box. Choose Glossary from the Edit menu.

Macro Debugger

Macro Debugger helps you find and correct errors in your macros. Macro Debugger places Excel in Debug mode, where the menu bar only displays Debug, Formula, and Display. Figure 15-14 displays the Debug menu.

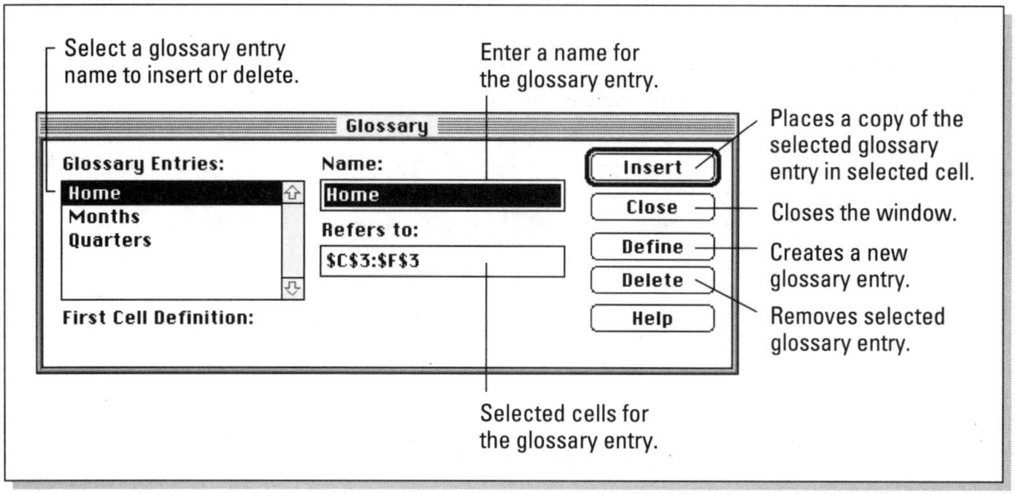

Figure 15-13: Pasting text, values, and formulas into worksheets and macro sheets using the Glossary dialog box.

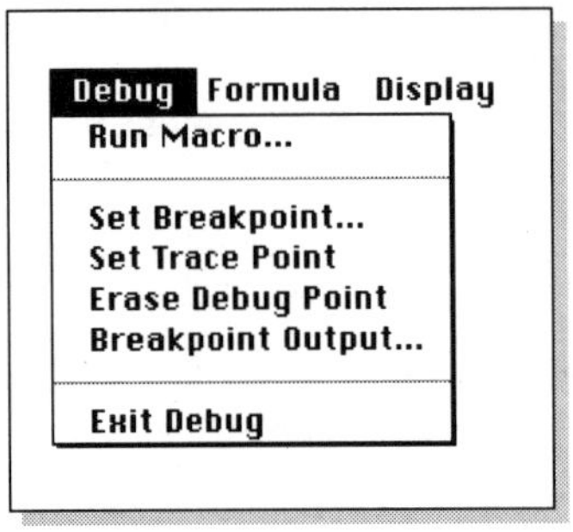

Figure 15-14: An example of the Debug menu when Excel is in Debug mode.

The two central capabilities of Macro Debugger are that it allows you to set *tracepoints* (one or more points in a macro where you want execution paused and entered into Single-Step mode) and *breakpoints* (one or more points in a macro where execution is paused and the current value of the cell(s) specified in advance are displayed). When Macro Debugger encounters a tracepoint, Excel pauses the macro and enters into Single-Step mode. At this time, you can interactively trace through the macro in Single-Step mode, continue running at full speed, or stop the macro.

When Macro Debugger encounters a breakpoint, on the other hand, Excel pauses the macro and displays the values of cells and the names specified before you ran the macro in Debug mode. At this time, you can run the macro at full speed, enter Single-Step mode, or stop the macro. Macro debugger operates only on command macros and not function macros.

Name Changer

Name Changer quickly deletes names from a worksheet or macro sheet. Name Changer also searches and replaces one name with another in a document. Figure 15-15 shows you the dialog box that appears when you choose Change Name from the Formula menu.

Name Changer is useful if you use names extensively in worksheets or macros (be sure to use names instead of cell addresses in macros). Choose Change Name from the Formula menu.

Movie Maker

Movie Maker enables you to animate Excel charts and requires the following additional software:

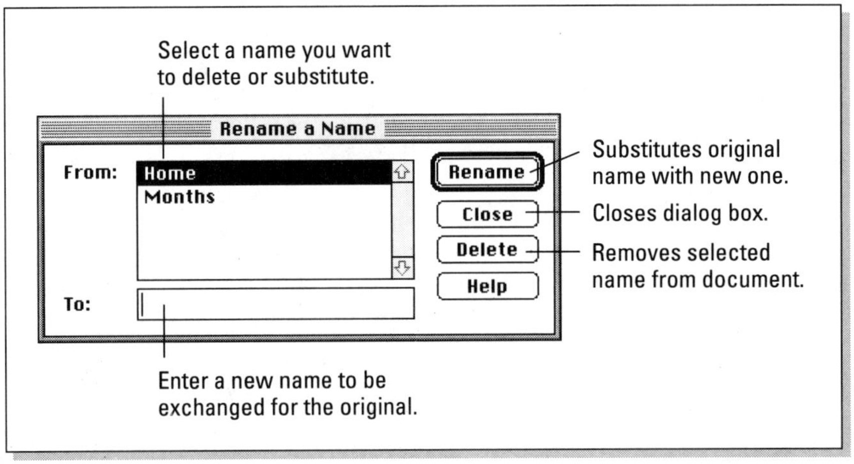

Figure 15-15: Choosing Change Name from the Formula menu displays the Rename a Name dialog box.

- ✦ Your Macintosh must use System 7.0 (or later).
- ✦ You must have Apple's QuickTime extension in the Extensions subfolder in your Macintosh's System Folder.
- ✦ You must have Apple's MoviePlayer or other similar playback software installed on your Macintosh.

Movie Maker adds animation to charts in the following ways:

- ✦ Rotates the chart 360 degrees
- ✦ Displays each data series of the chart separately
- ✦ Adds each data series in the chart in sequence
- ✦ Adds the data points in a series in sequence

Movie Maker can be particularly useful for creating presentations. Choose Movie Maker from the Edit menu.

Report Manager

Report Manager lets you print reports from analyses and views created by the Scenario Manager and the View Manager, respectively. Report Manager automatically loads the Scenario Manager and View Manager into memory if they haven't been already. Choose Print Report from the File Menu.

Scenario Manager

Scenario Manager lets you perform what-if analyses with multiple sets of variables. The scenarios can be viewed individually or in a separate summary. Use Report Manager to print scenarios as part of a report. Choose Scenario Manager from the Formula menu.

Slide Show

Slide Show uses a Slide Show template to create on-screen slide shows from worksheets and charts. Slide Show is particularly effective for presentations involving large-screen projection.

Solver

Solver enables you to find the best answer to a problem by specifying inputs that can be adjusted up or down within limits you set. Choose Solver from the Formula menu.

Switch

Switch enables you to quickly make another Microsoft program the active application. Figure 15-16 shows you three tools on a custom toolbar you can create to quickly switch to another application.

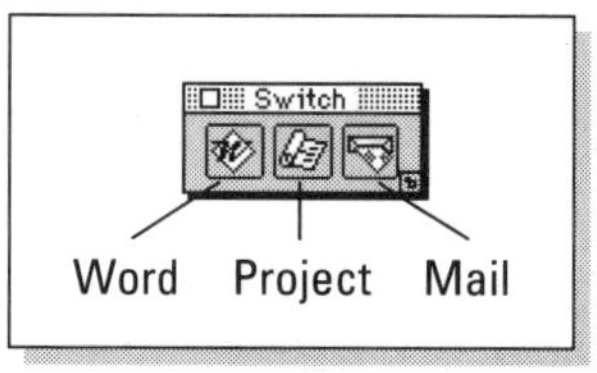

Figure 15-16: Switching between applications using a custom toolbar from the Switch add-in.

For the Switch add-in to work, it must be loaded in memory, the tool must be on a toolbar, a macro must be assigned to the tool, and a copy of the application you want to run must be installed on your Macintosh and open in memory.

View Manager

View Manager enables you to see a worksheet in various formats, without saving each format as a separate document. The following settings comprise a view, which you can name:

- Print settings
- Hidden rows and columns
- Display settings
- Selected ranges
- Window size and placement

The Views dialog box is shown in Figure 15-17.

Named views are saved along with the worksheet. Choose View from the Window menu.

What If

What If inputs a series of data into a worksheet creating up to 64 different scenarios. What If requires two open worksheets — one that contains the model, and another that contains the data. Choose What If from the Formula menu when the model worksheet is the active document.

Worksheet Auditor

Worksheet Auditor generates reports that identify errors and display information about a worksheet. In addition, Worksheet Auditor provides an interactive trace facility to help you understand how cells depend on each other in the worksheet. Figure 15-18 shows the Worksheet Auditor dialog box.

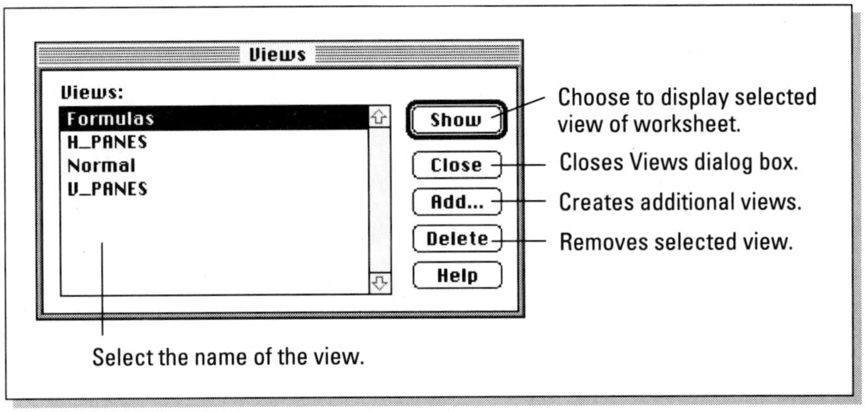

Figure 15-17: Setting a format to view a worksheet in using the Views dialog box.

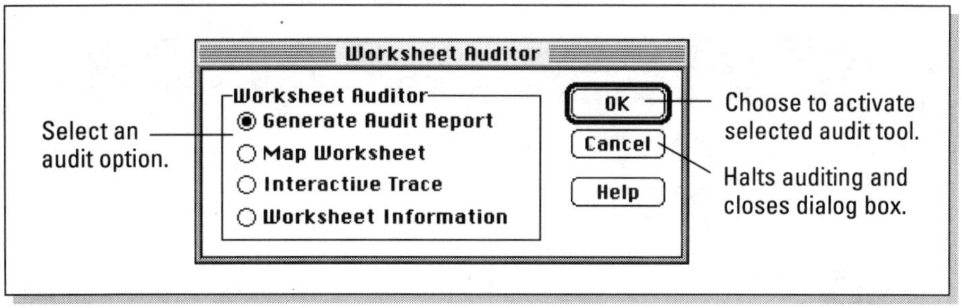

Figure 15-18: Identifying errors and displaying information about a worksheet using the Worksheet Auditor dialog box.

The Worksheet Auditor options provide the auditing tools listed in Table 15-3:

Table 15-3: Worksheet Auditor options and tools

Option	*Purpose*
Generate Audit Report	Creates several reports including cells containing error values, circular references, and names
Map Worksheet	Displays a condensed view of the worksheet using codes to identify cell contents
Interactive Trace	Enables you to trace through cells that depend on one another so you can understand the worksheet's logic
Worksheet Information	Displays details about the worksheet

Choose Worksheet Auditor from the Formula menu.

Worksheet Comparison

Worksheet Comparison enables you to determine the difference between two versions of the same worksheet. Both worksheets must be open to use Worksheet Comparison. Figure 15-19 displays the Worksheet Comparison report. Choose Compare from the Formula menu.

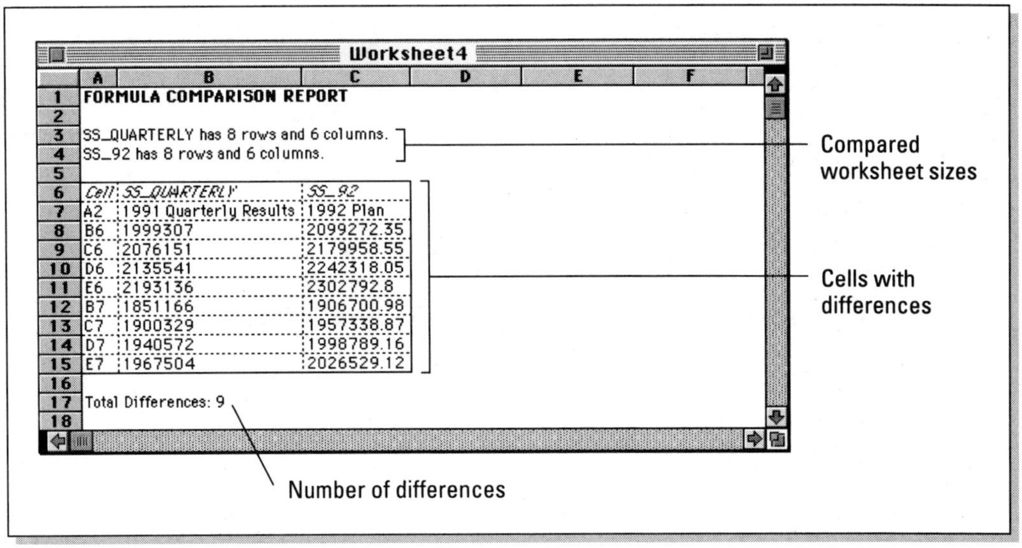

Figure 15-19: Comparing two versions of the same worksheet using the Worksheet Comparison add-in.

Step-by-Step

In this section you'll practice using the Views Manager add-in. The Views Manager is a particularly good add-in to become acquainted with because you can create multiple views of a worksheet, and quickly change to a view, bypassing the need to create multiple versions of the same worksheet to look at it from a different perspective.

As you learned earlier, the View command already appears on the Window menu, and the View Manager should load automatically after you choose the View command, unless another user has removed it from the working set (shame on them). If this is the case, load the View Manager by selecting Open from the File menu or by clicking the File Open tool, and then selecting View Manager from the Macro Library subfolder.

There's no way you can damage the worksheet as a result of this exercise, so if you make a mistake or lose track of where you were, simply close the file without saving and start over.

To begin this exercise, do the following:

1. Start Excel.

   The Worksheet 1 window appears.

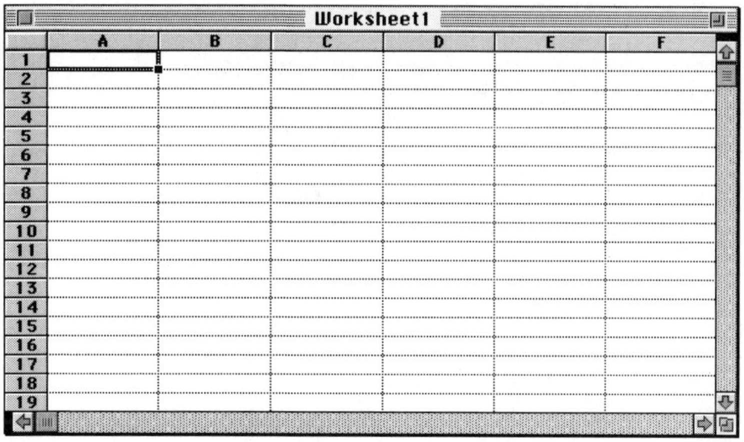

Figure 15-20: Starting up Excel displays the Worksheet1 worksheet.

2. Choose Open from the File menu or click the File Open tool.

   The Open dialog box appears.

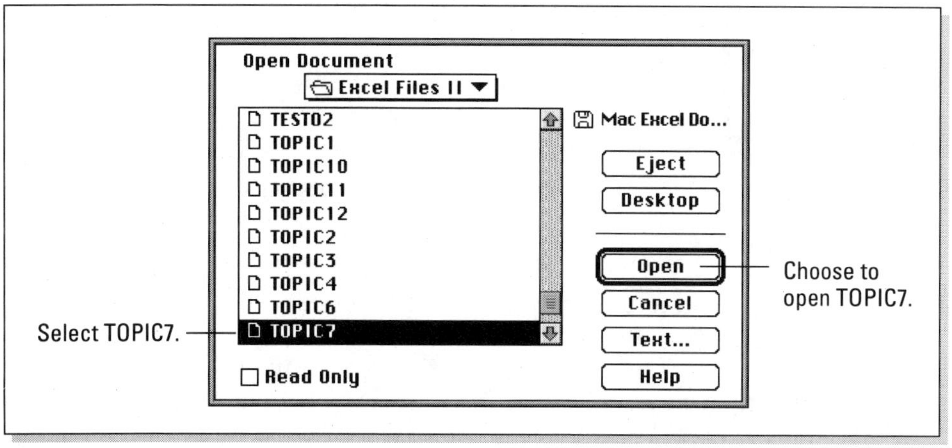

Figure 15-21: Choosing Open from the File menu, or clicking the File Open tool displays the Open dialog box.

3. Select TOPIC7 and choose OK.

   The TOPIC7 worksheet appears.

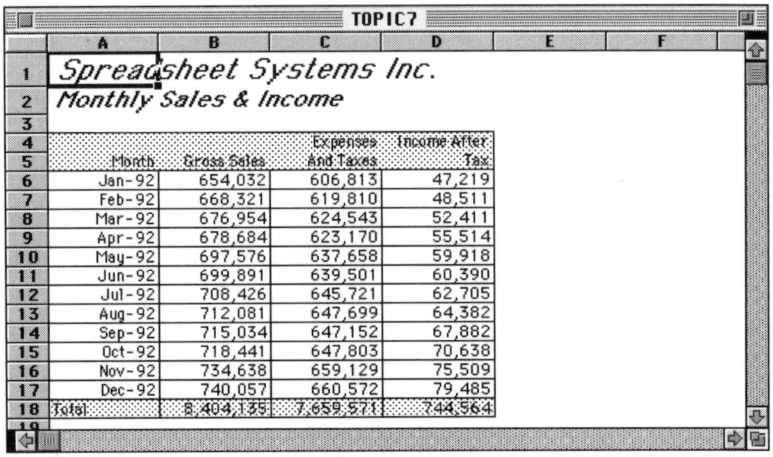

Figure 15-22: Selecting TOPIC7 from the Open dialog box displays the TOPIC7 worksheet.

Loading the View Manager into memory:

Step 1. Choose View from the Window menu.

The Views dialog box appears.

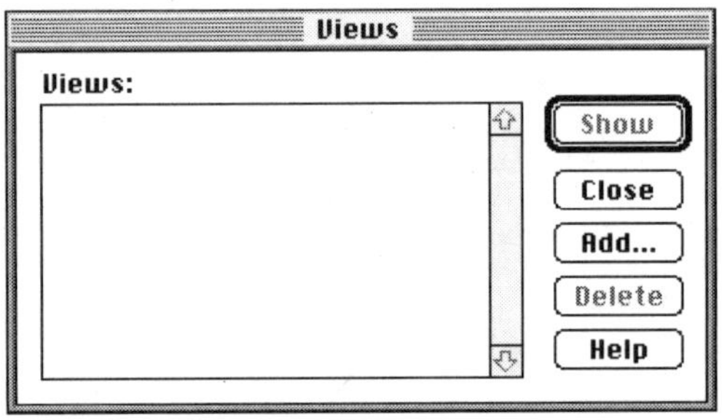

Figure 15-23: Choosing View from the Window menu displays the Views dialog box.

Adding a view:

Step 1. Click Add.

The Add View dialog box appears.

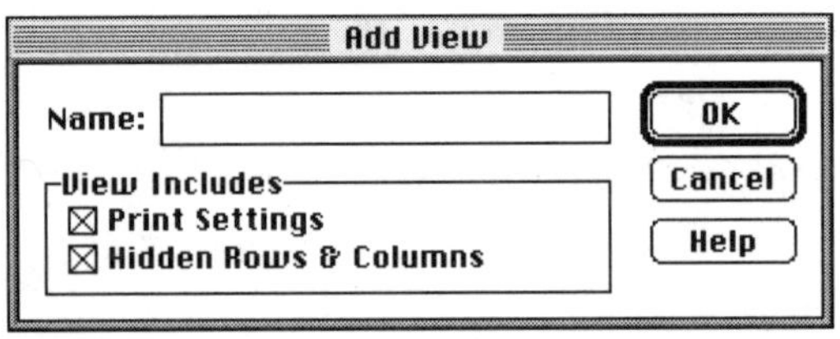

Figure 15-24: Clicking the Add option in the View dialog box displays the Add View dialog box.

Step 2. Type `Normal` in the Name box, and choose OK.

Step 3. Choose Display from the Options menu.

The Display Options dialog box appears.

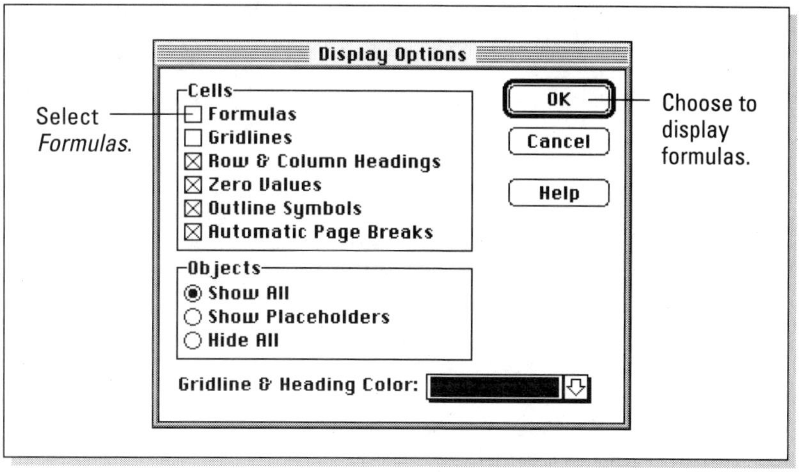

Figure 15-25: Choosing Display from the Options menu displays the Display Options dialog box.

Step 4. Select Formulas and choose OK.

TOPIC7 displays with formulas.

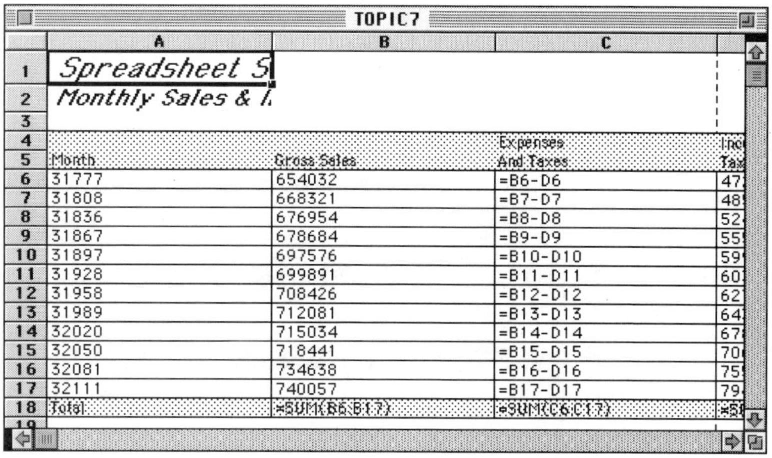

Figure 15-26: Selecting the Formulas option from the Display Options dialog box displays the TOPIC7 worksheet with formulas.

Adding another view:

Step 1. Choose View from the Window menu.

The Views dialog box appears.

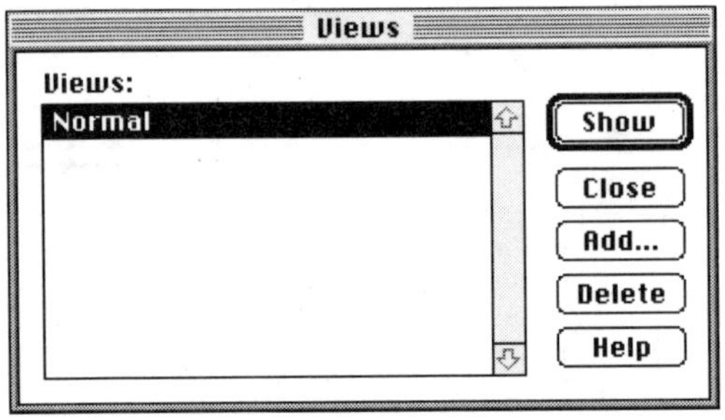

Figure 15-27: Choosing View from the Window menu displays the Views dialog box.

Step 2. Click Add.

The Add View dialog box appears.

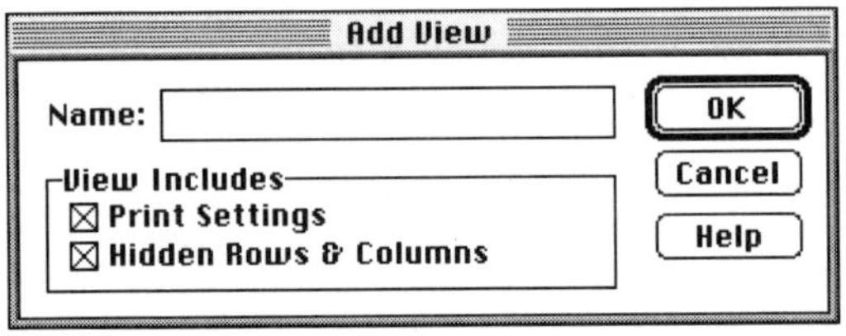

Figure 15-28: Clicking the Add option in the Views dialog box displays the Add View dialog box.

Step 3. Type `Formulas` in the Name box, and choose OK.

Displaying a view:

Step 1. Choose View from the Window menu.

The Views dialog box appears.

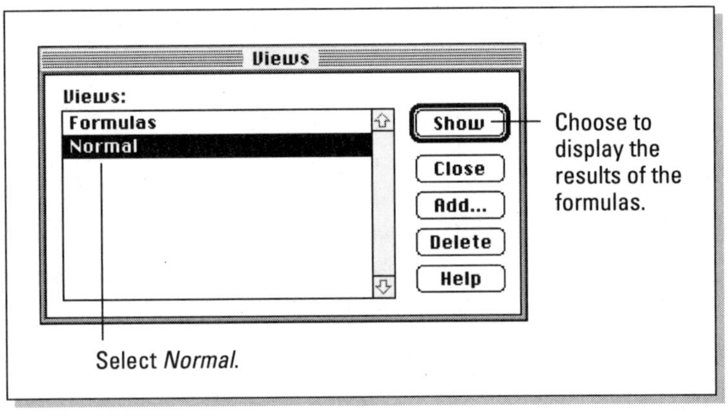

Figure 15-29: Choosing View from the Window menu displays the Views dialog box.

Step 2. Select Normal, and then choose Show.

TOPIC7 displays with the results of the formulas.

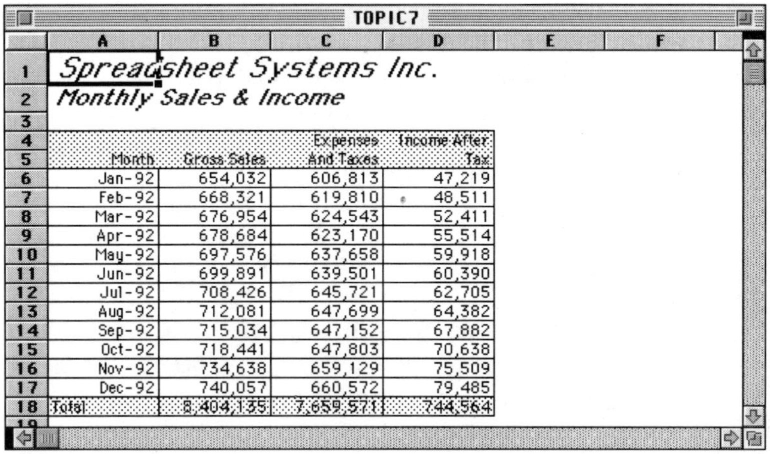

Figure 15-30: Selecting Normal from the Views dialog box displays the TOPIC7 worksheet with the results of formulas.

Saving views:

Step 1. Choose Save As from the File menu or press F12.

The Save As dialog box appears.

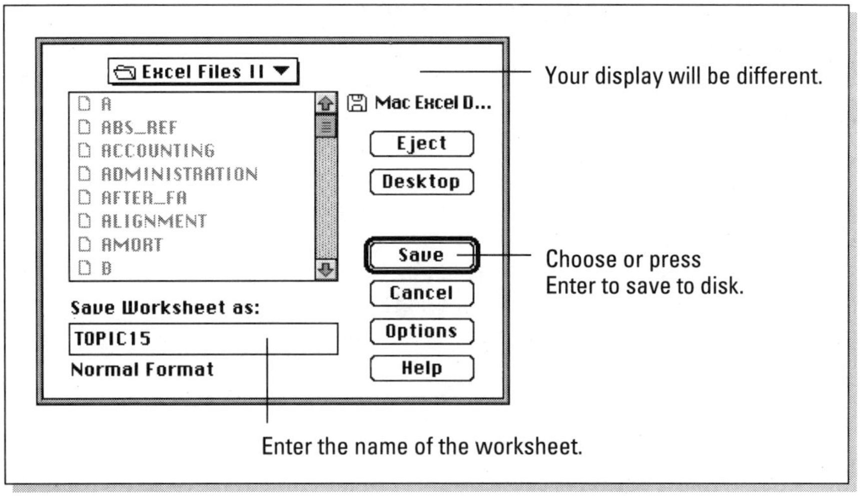

Figure 15-31: Choosing Save As from the File menu displays the Save As dialog box.

Step 2. Type `TOPIC15` and choose OK.

Excel saves the worksheet and views to disk.

Quick Tips

This section provides tips on how to use add-ins to add functionality to your Excel sessions.

Understanding the startup hierarchy

Excel opens documents and files in the startup directory first, and then opens the documents and files in the Alternate Startup Folder.

Using correct column widths

Make sure the width of columns is at least equal to the largest cell entry when you use Data Export (through the Flat File add-in). Data in cells less than the width of the column are truncated.

Using Macro Debugger with caution

CAUTION!

As a precaution, save your macro sheet to disk before using Macro Debugger. While in Debug mode, you can alter formulas, but the formulas are returned to their original state when you exit Debug mode.

Viewing slide shows

You can view slide shows with the Slide Show add-in on the screen only, not printed.

Adding add-ins to the working set

If you have the wherewithal to create your own add-ins, you can make them part of your working set through the Add-in Manager.

Opening add-ins automatically

Formulas that depend on functions provided by the Add-in Functions or Analysis ToolPak display #REF if the add-in is not open. Similarly, macros that depend on the macro commands in the Flat File add-in fail if the add-in is not open. If you create worksheets that depend on other add-ins, have Excel automatically open the add-ins for you through the Startup folder or the Add-in Manager.

Saving macros as an add-in

You can save macros as an add-in by making the macro sheet the macro resides on the active document, and then choosing Save As from the File menu. From the Save As dialog box, select Options, and then pull down the File Format list and select Add-in, and then choose OK.

Summary

- An add-in is a separate program that adds functionality to Excel.
- Add-ins perform a variety of functions, and are available with Excel, from other software firms, and from you (if you create them).
- You must install an add-in on the Macintosh's hard disk and load it into memory for the add-in to function.
- You can load add-ins automatically by placing them in the Startup folder, or by making them part of the working set through the Add-in Manager.
- The working set of add-ins are those add-ins that are automatically loaded when you start Excel.
- You add and delete add-ins from the working set using the Add-in Manager.
- For occasional use, you can load add-ins into memory by choosing Open from the File menu or by clicking the File Open tool, and then selecting the name of the add-in from the Macro Library subfolder.

Topic 16
Exchanging Data

Overview

Everyone wants to get a job done as quickly as possible, and exchanging data can help you accomplish that goal. Exchanging data with other programs enables you to use information directly with Excel, eliminating the need to perform one of the biggest money and time wasters in business today — taking data from one computer and manually entering it into another.

In some cases, exchanging data enables you to create Excel documents that ordinarily wouldn't be possible with Excel alone. For example, you can include a graphic object created with Aldus PageMaker, or a table of information created with Microsoft Word in an Excel worksheet.

If you work alone and only use Excel, you can skip this Topic. On the other hand, if you work in a corporate or other type of environment where you need, or could use, data from sources other than what you or someone else enters manually, it's well worth your while to window-shop this Topic. Exchanging data is one of the Macintosh's less-publicized strengths, but it is also a strength that you can easily tap into.

Sharing the wealth

You can access data from other sources in the following ways:

- ✦ Opening a file on disk
- ✦ Using the Clipboard

System 7 users can exchange data in the following ways:

- ✦ Using Publish and Subscribe
- ✦ Linking
- ✦ Embedding

Table 16-1 summarizes the Macintosh data exchange options and can help you decide which ones are right for you.

Table 16-1: Data exchange options

Option	Requirement						
	Additional hardware/ software	**System 7**	**Network**	**More than one program per disk**	**More than one program open**	**Automatic updating**	**Access by other users**
Disk files: IBM to Mac	No	No	No	No	No	No	No
Disk files: Mac to IBM	Yes	No	No	No	No	No	No
Clipboard	No	No	No	Yes	No	No	No
Publish & Subscribe	No	Yes	Yes	No	No	Yes	Yes
Linking	No	Yes	No	Yes	Yes	Yes	No
Embedding	No	Yes	No	Yes	No	Yes	No

Each of these options has its own set of pros and cons. Sometimes one method is better than another. These methods are explored in the next section.

Opening a file on disk

You can read a variety of file formats directly in Excel by selecting Open from the File menu or by clicking the File Open tool. Simply select the name of the file from the file's folder or subfolder from the File Open list box. Excel can read the following file formats:

Program	*File format*
Excel for Windows 4.0, 3.0, 2.2	xls
MultiPlan	sylk
Lotus 1-2-3 1A	WKS
Lotus 1-2-3 2.01, 2.2, 2.3, 2.4	WK1
Lotus 1-2-3 3.0, 3.1, 3.1+	WK3
Lotus 1-2-3 for Windows 1.0, 1.1	WK3
Lotus Symphony	WRK, WR1
VisiCalc	DIF
dBASE	DBF2, DBF3, DBF4

You can also open text files with no formatting and text files with comma separated values (CSV) created by a DOS, Windows, or OS/2 program.

In addition, if a format file accompanies a Lotus 1-2-3 worksheet file (.ALL files for 1-2-3 2.01 and 2.2, .FMT files for 1-2-3 3.0, 3.1, 3.1+, or .FM3 files for 1-2-3 for Windows), Excel applies the corresponding formatting to the worksheet's contents.

Timing is everything

Excel's ability to open a file in just about any format, especially worksheet files, is a terrific but under appreciated ease-of-use feature. If you've ever had to reenter volumes of data or formulas, you'll understand what a timesaver this overlooked capability is. But there's something you should keep in mind if you decide to forge ahead and let the computer do the work for you.

Excel uses a serial numbering system for calculating dates. In Excel for Macintosh, January 2, 1904 equals 1, January 3, 1904 equals 2, and so on. In Excel for Windows, the date system begins with January 1, 1900, so as to be compatible with Lotus 1-2-3. If you use worksheets with formulas that calculate dates, such as accounts receivable applications, Excel automatically changes to the date system used by that version. For example, if you open an Excel for Windows file with your Macintosh, Excel for Macintosh uses the 1904 date system, and vice versa. You should, however, use the 1900 date system if you develop worksheets for 1-2-3, and to be on the safe side, so should Excel for Windows users. To do so, choose Calculation from the Options menu. When the Options Calculation dialog box appears, as shown in the following figure, unselect 1904 Date System and click OK or press Return.

Dates entered after changing date systems aren't converted to the new system; the formulas that depend on the dates return different results. The moral of the story is you should choose a date system appropriate for your intended audience before entering dates and thereby ensuring accurate calculations.

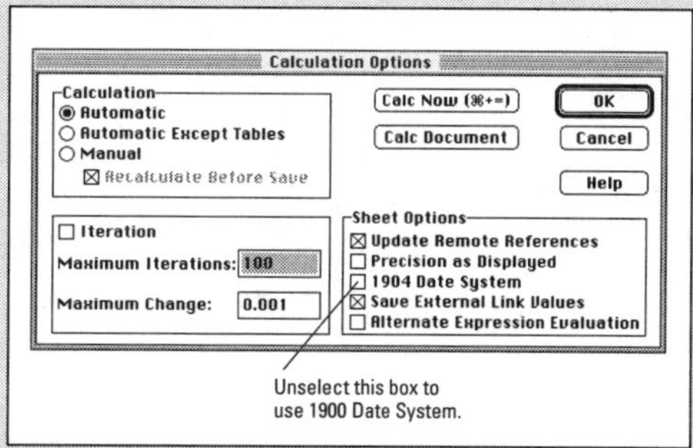

If the file format isn't recognized, Excel tries to open the file by displaying the warning message shown in Figure 16-1. Choosing OK reads the file into memory as a text file.

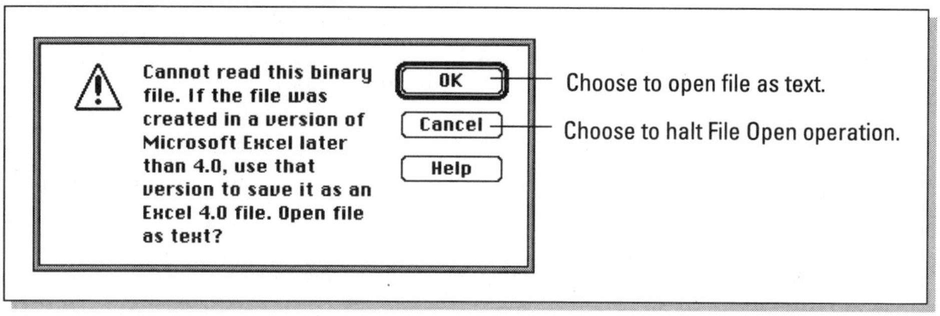

Figure 16-1: If a file is in a format that Excel doesn't recognize, Excel displays this warning message.

Opening a file created by another program is usually a quick and easy way to get data and applications into Excel, thereby eliminating tedious reentry of the data into Excel. The capability of computers to use the disk containing the file is another story, however, depending on whether you're transferring data from an IBM PC or compatible computer to the Macintosh, or vice versa.

Exchanging different file formats

If the file you want was saved to disk in your Macintosh or another Macintosh, you're home free. Any Macintosh can easily open the file you need. If you want to share data with friends who use an IBM PC (or compatible), you'll need to navigate heavier seas.

Actually, moving data from a PC to the Macintosh isn't too difficult if the PC has a 3½-inch disk drive. Fortunately, the floppy drive in all Macintoshes that came out in the late summer of 1990 read 3½-inch MS-DOS disks. Consequently, in Excel you can choose Save As from the File menu and save an Excel document to a 3½-inch disk on the PC.

The Apple File Exchange application (in the Apple File Exchange Folder, which is in your System Folder), enables you to use files contained on a 3½-inch disk from an IBM PC (normally, a dialog box appears asking you if you want to format the disk if you put it in the drive), and transfer the data to the folder of your choosing. Choosing Quit from Apple File Exchange's File menu, ejects the disk from the Macintosh. Figure 16-2 shows the Apple File Exchange dialog box.

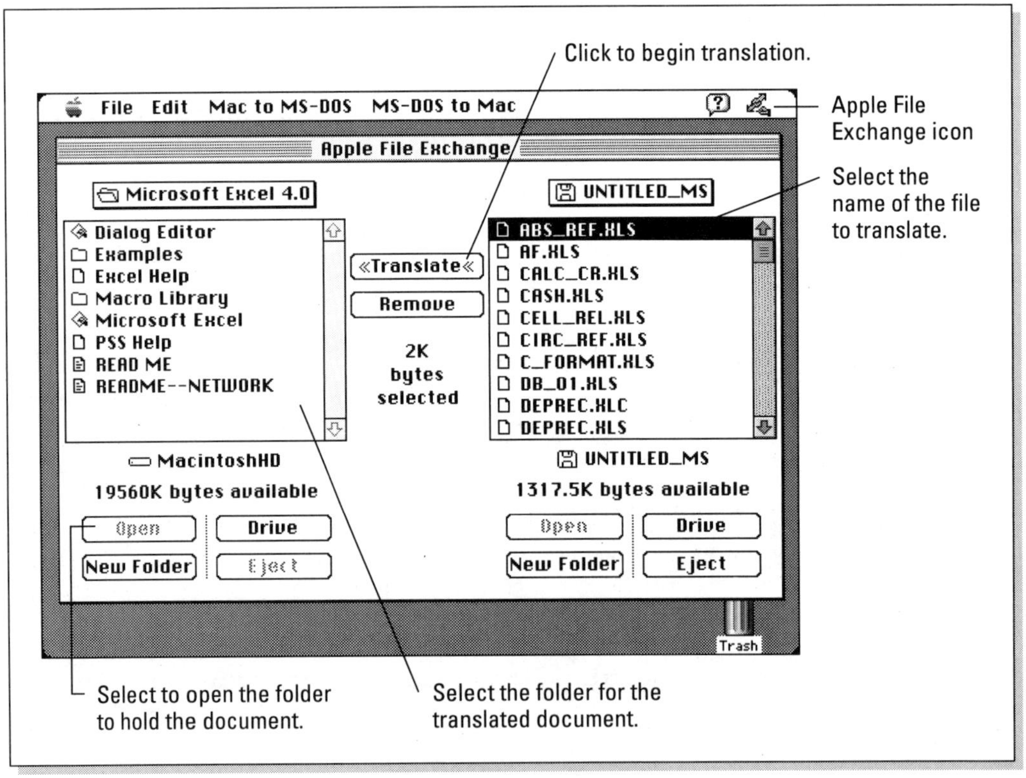

Figure 16-2: An example of the Apple File Exchange dialog box.

If you want to keep the disk in the Macintosh, or see the disk on the desktop, you'll need to use a third-party utility, such as Dayna Communications' DOS Mounter or Insignia Solutions' DOS Access.

If you exchange files frequently, you should consider transferring data by connecting two (or more) computers together. For Macintosh-to-PC data transfer, this is your only option because PC disk drives unfortunately don't recognize the Macintosh floppy disk format. Several companies have cabling and communication software that enable you to move data from the Macintosh to the PC (and vice versa) with or without the use of a modem. Dataviz's MacLink Plus/PC and Traveling Software's LapLink/Mac contain everything you need to transfer files back and forth between the Mac and PC.

Another option is to share files via a network. Adding a LocalTalk expansion board to the PC, and file-server software (Tops or AppleShare) to the Mac, enables both camps to talk to each other quickly and conveniently.

If you'd like to learn more about transferring files between the Macintosh and PC, read Jim Heid's *Macworld Complete Mac Handbook*, published by IDG Books, 1991.

Using the Clipboard to exchange data

Using the Clipboard is the simplest method of exchanging data between open Excel worksheets, or other open Macintosh applications, such as Microsoft Word. As you know from Topic 5, to use the Clipboard, you first select the data you want to transfer, and then choose Copy from the Edit menu to copy the data to the Clipboard. Now activate the application you want to receive the data. If the application is Excel, move the cell pointer to the cell that will be the upper-left corner of the data to be pasted in, preferably a blank area of the worksheet. For other applications, move the blinking cursor to the location where you want the data.

In either case, choose Paste from the Edit menu. The data is pasted from the Clipboard to the location in the active application's document. As long as you don't use the Copy and Cut commands a second time, you can paste the same data again as many times as you need.

Using System 7.*x* to exchange data

One of the many and more useful features of System 7 is its new data exchange capabilities. System 7 brings DDE/OLE (Dynamic Data Exchange and Object Linking and Embedding) capability to the Macintosh. DDE enables you to link data from one application to another so that when the linked data changes in the source document, it is instantly updated in the dependent document. OLE enables you to embed data from one application to another while enabling you to edit or format the data in the source document. You can link or embed information from one Excel worksheet to another, or between Excel and another Macintosh application — if that application supports DDE/OLE.

You can exchange data using System 7 by employing any one of the following techniques:

Publish and Subscribe You can make all or part of an Excel spreadsheet you're using available to others by *publishing* it. Conversely, when you *subscribe* to another user's Excel worksheet or other Macintosh document, you insert that information into your Excel worksheet.

Linking Similar to creating links between Excel worksheets, linking joins files created by dissimilar Macintosh programs to exchange data within a single computer.

Embedding Embedding is placing an object on a worksheet, such as an arrow or other drawing. In this case, an object contains information from another Macintosh application. If you double-click the object, the Macintosh opens a window and switches to or starts the application so you can edit the information. When you close the window, the object is updated with the new information.

The following section describes each of these System 7 data exchange features.

Publishing and subscribing

Publishing and subscribing enables you to automatically update information from other sources, avoiding the manual updating required if you use the Clipboard. With publish and subscribe, you can do the following:

- ✦ Use text from Word to explain a monthly financial statement on an Excel worksheet. Publish and subscribe allows you to update the explanation to reflect the current month's results.
- ✦ Link supporting worksheets to a summary Excel worksheet. You may need to do this if you want to put together quarterly summary reports from each of your company's departments, for example.

The key advantage to publish and subscribe is that you can access information from other Macintoshes on a network, making a collaborative effort possible and thereby eliminating duplicated work.

Not all Macintosh software supports publishing and subscribing, although you can easily identify those that do by pulling down the Edit menu. If the Create Publisher and Subscribe To commands appear, as they do in Excel and Word, you're set (in Excel they appear below Paste Link and above Delete, as shown in Figure 16-3).

Publishing and subscribing is a little more complex than using the Clipboard, but it isn't a difficult process. To publish information, which can be text, values, an object, or a chart, you select the data or item, and then choose Create Publisher from the Edit menu. By doing so, you create an edition, which is a file containing the selected data and

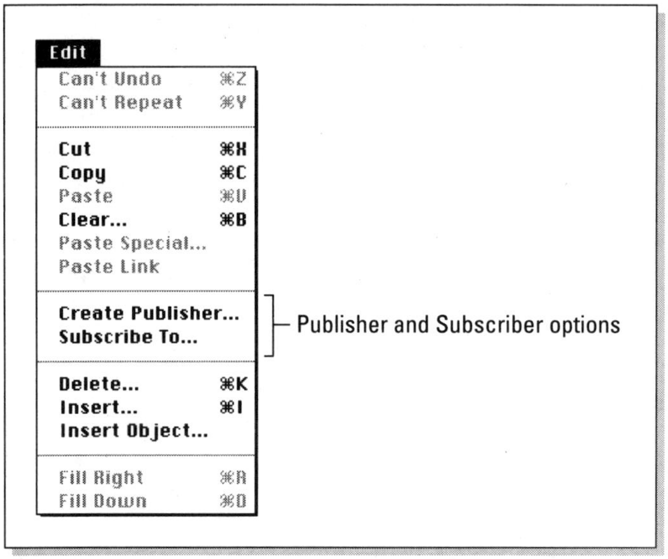

Figure 16-3: Macintosh software that supports publishing and subscribing displays the Create Publisher and Subscribe To commands in the Edit menu.

information about the file, such as where it originated. An edition file is the gateway between publishing and subscribing — the data you want to exchange travels through the edition. Choosing Save or Save As from the File menu also saves an edition, though the worksheet (and edition) doesn't have to be open for one or more users to subscribe to it.

To subscribe to data, you place an edition on the worksheet. Select the cell that you want to be the upper-left corner of the range that holds the data, and then choose Subscribe To from the Edit menu. After you select the name of the edition and choose OK, the data is placed beginning with the selected cell.

Double-clicking a range that is part of the subscribed information displays a dialog box that enables you to specify how often editions are updated. In some cases, you'll want the most current data immediately, such as when changes to department budgets are available, so you'd select Automatically. In other cases, you'll want the latest edition only when the information is final, such as when the accounting department closes for the month, so you'd select Manually. Manual updating enables you to control when you receive the changes of an edition. Choosing the Manually option requires that you click the Get Edition Now button to use the most recently created edition.

Linking

Linking is similar to publishing and subscribing, except for the following key differences:

- ✦ You can only link to information in your own computer.
- ✦ The programs that furnish and receive the data must be open to create a link.

Creating a link in System 7.*x* is similar to linking one worksheet to another worksheet in Excel. To link data from another program to Excel, make that program active, select the information, and choose Copy from the Edit menu. Then switch to Excel and select the cell that will be the upper-left corner of the data, preferably a blank area of the worksheet. Choose Paste Link from the Edit menu to establish the link. Any time you change data in the source document, the new data will automatically be reflected in the Excel worksheet.

You use the reverse procedure to send Excel data to another open application. First, select the Excel data you want to appear in the other program, choose Copy from the Edit menu, and then switch to that program. Move the blinking cursor to the point in the document where you want the Excel data, and then choose the appropriate link command from the program's Edit menu.

Managing links

After you've established a link, the link requires no further maintenance on your part. Unless, of course, you move the document to another folder or drive, or want to manually update links. Choosing Links from the File menu displays the Links dialog box shown in Figure 16-4. This is your link management tool.

To manage your links, pull down the Link Type menu and select the type of link you want to change or update. Select DDE/OLE to update or change information linked to Excel from another Macinstosh application. Click the Change button to redirect the link; click Update to use the most current data from an unopened application.

To remove a link, place the cell pointer on the cell containing the link, and choose Clear from the Edit menu or press Delete.

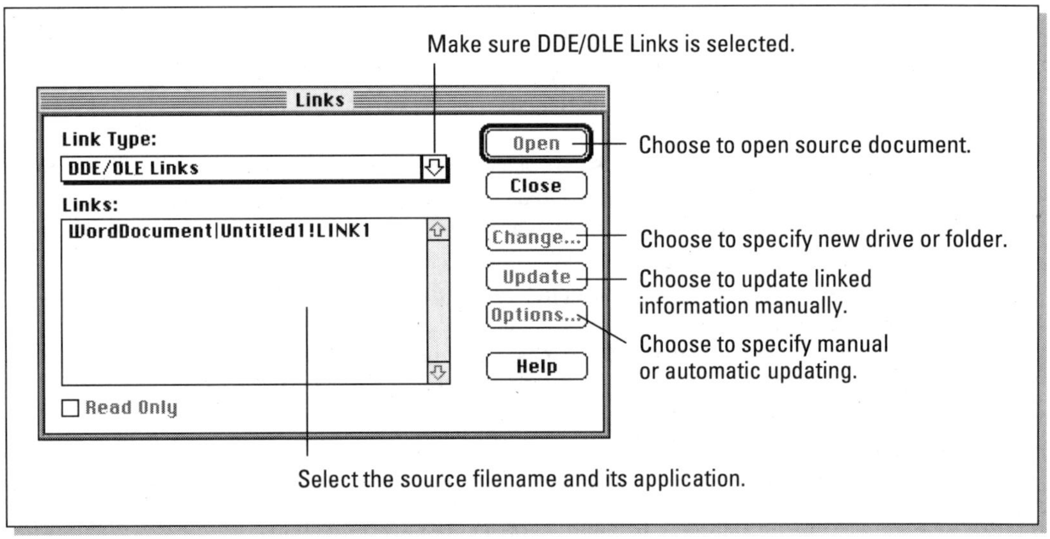

Figure 16-4: Choosing Links from the File menu displays the Links dialog box.

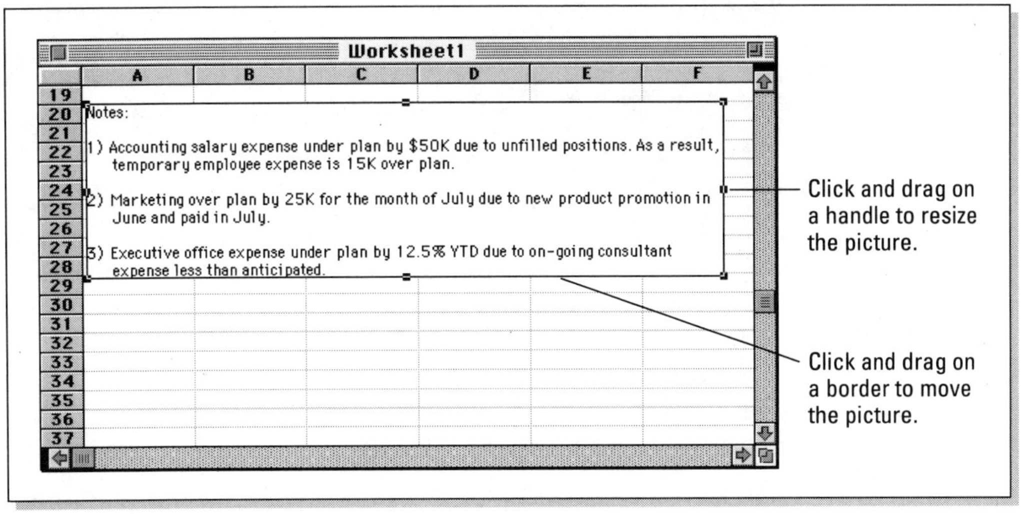

Figure 16-5: An example of data from another program embedded into an Excel worksheet.

Embedding objects

The Embedding feature in System 7.*x* takes selected data from another program (such as Word) and places a picture of it on an Excel worksheet, as shown in Figure 16-5.

Double-clicking the object that's embedded on the Excel worksheet starts the application and displays the object so you can edit it. After you finish editing the object and exit the application, the object on the Excel worksheet is updated. The object is saved with the worksheet when you choose Save or Save As from the File menu, or when you click the File Save tool.

To remove the object, select the object and then choose Clear from the Edit menu or shortcut menu and press Delete.

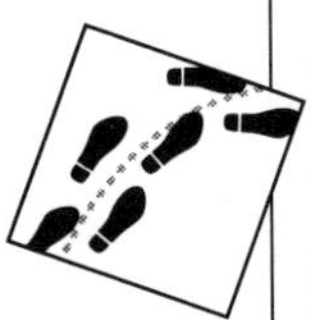

Step-by-Step

This section outlines how to save Excel documents in other file formats and open files created by other programs. In addition, this section contains instructions for publishing and subscribing, linking, and embedding.

Saving a document in a different file format:

Step 1. Choose Save As from the File menu.

The Save As dialog box appears.

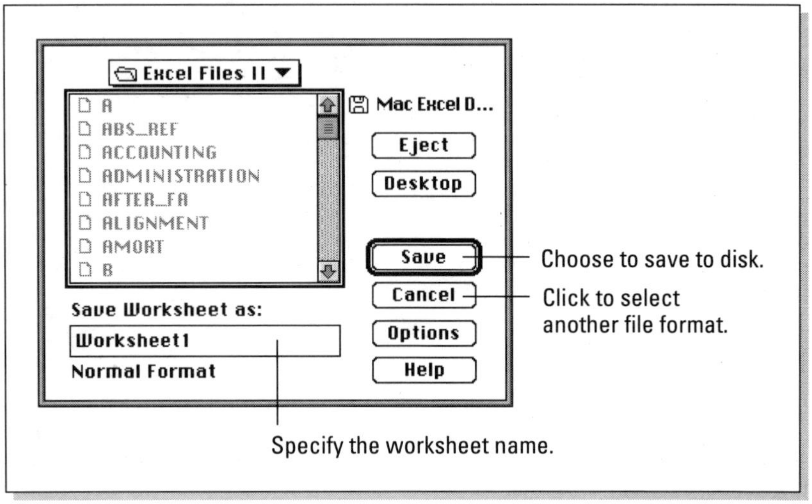

Figure 16-6: Choosing Save As from the File menu displays the Save As dialog box.

Step 2. Click the Options button.

The Save Options dialog box appears.

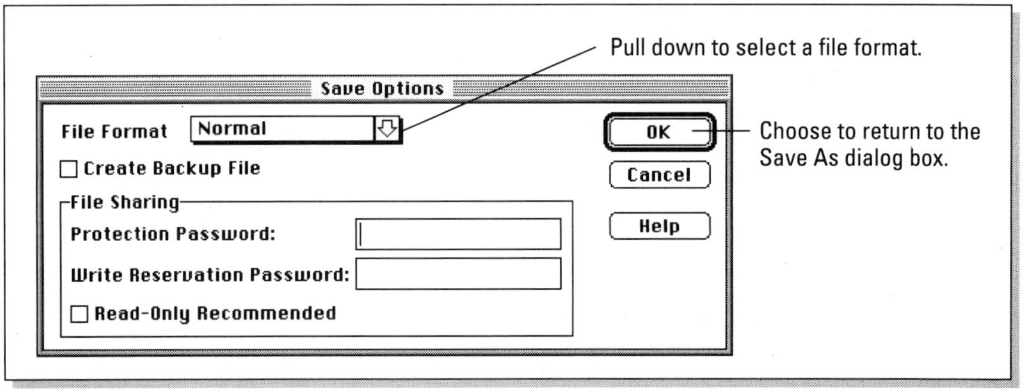

Figure 16-7: Clicking the Options button on the Save As dialog box displays the Save Options dialog box.

Step 3. Pull down the File Format list, select a format, and choose OK.

The Save Options dialog box closes and the Save As dialog box reappears. Make sure you enter a new name for the file, otherwise Excel will overwrite the old file with the new one.

Step 4. Choose Save.

Excel saves the document in the file format you selected.

Opening a document in a nonExcel format:

Step 1. Choose Open from the File menu, or click the File Open tool.

The Open dialog box appears.

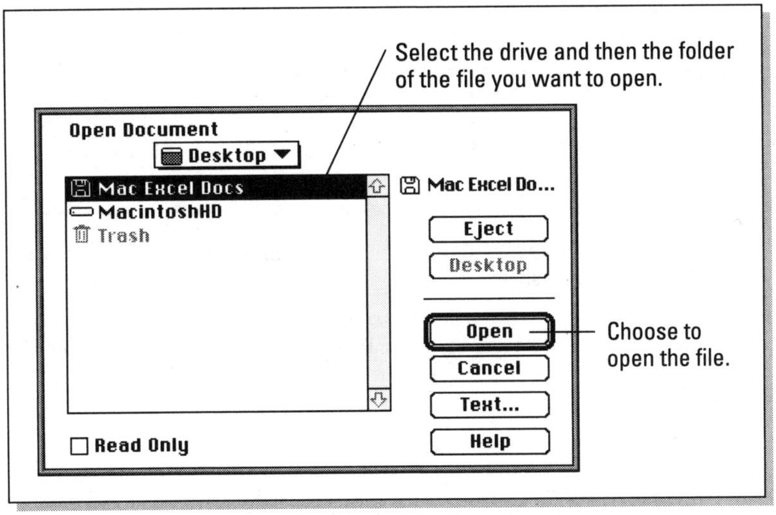

Figure 16-8: Choosing Open from the File menu or clicking the File Open tool displays the Open dialog box.

Step 2. Select the folder where the file resides and choose Open, and then select the name of the file and choose Open, or double-click the filename.

Excel opens the file.

Publishing data:

Step 1. Select the cell or range you want to publish.

Step 2. Choose Create Publisher from the Edit menu.

The Create Publisher dialog box appears.

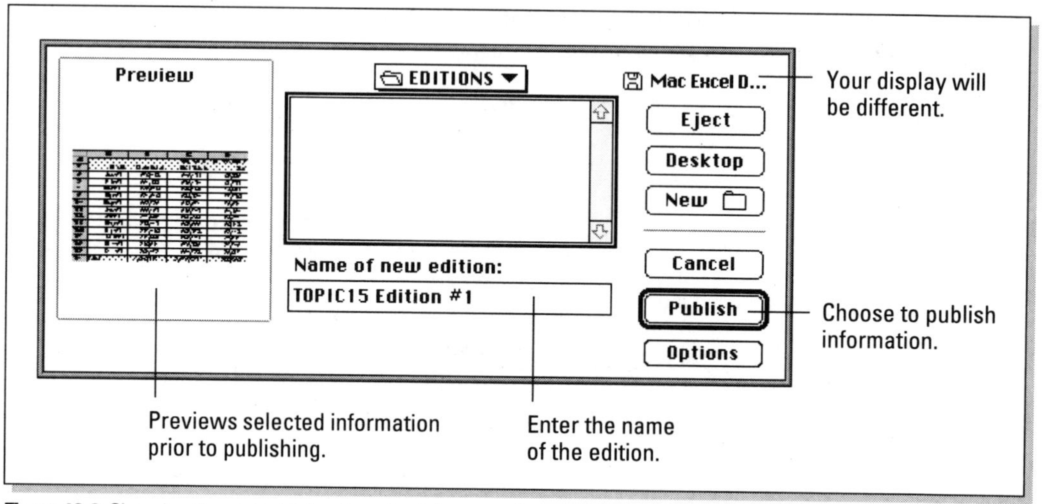

Figure 16-9: Choosing Create Publisher from the Edit menu displays the Create Publisher dialog box.

Step 3. Type a name for the edition file in the "Name of new edition" box.

Step 4. Choose Publish or press Return.

Excel creates the publisher.

Specifying publisher options:

Step 1. Position the cell pointer within the published information and double-click.

The following dialog box appears:

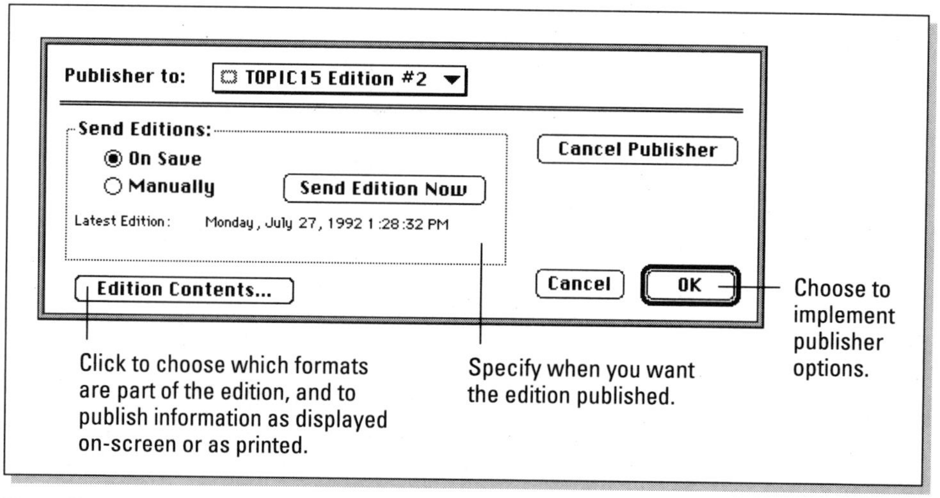

Figure 16-10: Double-clicking within the published information displays this dialog box.

Step 2. Select the options you need and click OK or press Return.

Excel makes the changes you requested.

Subscribing to data:

Step 1. Move the cell pointer to the cell where you want the upper-left corner of the published information to appear.

Step 2. Choose Subscribe To from the Edit menu.

The following dialog box appears:

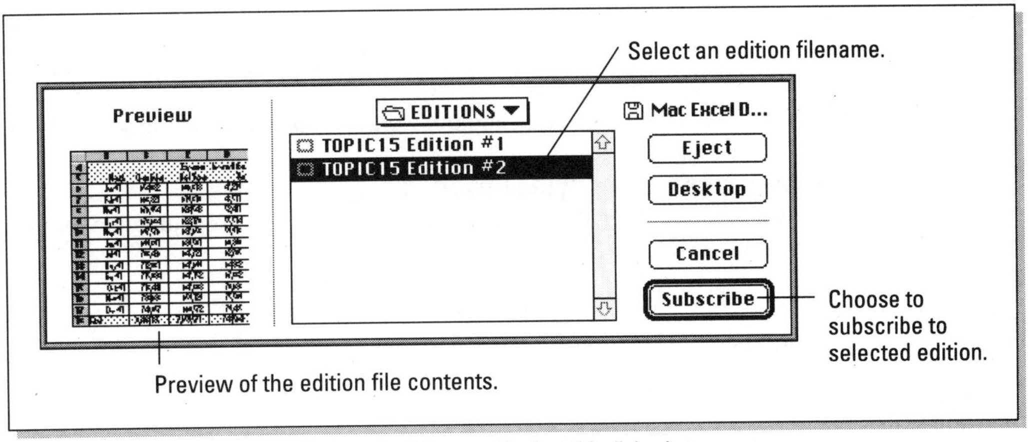

Figure 16-11: Choosing Subscribe To from the Edit menu displays this dialog box.

Step 3. Select the name of the edition, and then choose Subscribe or press Return, or simply double-click its name.

Excel subscribes to the edition by inserting its contents beginning at the location of the active cell.

Specifying subscriber options:

Step 1. Position the cell pointer within the subscribed information and double-click.

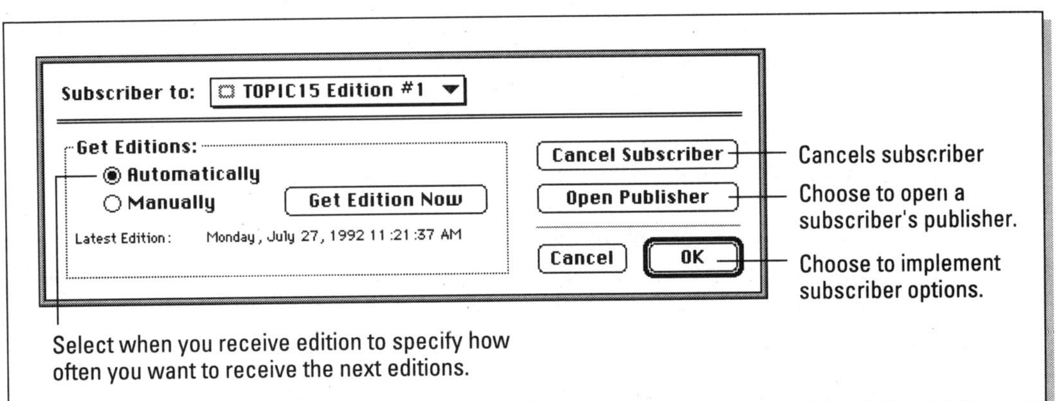

Figure 16-12: Double-clicking within the subscribed information displays this dialog box.

Step 2. Select the options you need and click OK or press Return.

Excel makes the changes you requested.

Creating a link to another application:

Step 1. From the source program (the program that furnishes the information), select the information you want in your Excel worksheet, and then choose Copy from the Edit menu.

Step 2. Switch to Excel and make the worksheet you want to link active.

Step 3. Move the cell pointer to the cell where you want the upper-left corner of the linked information to appear.

Step 4. Choose Paste Link from the Edit menu.

Excel inserts the information into the worksheet beginning at the selected cell.

Redirecting links or specifying updating:

Step 1. Make the Excel worksheet containing the link to the other application the active document.

Step 2. Choose Links from the File menu.

The Links dialog box appears.

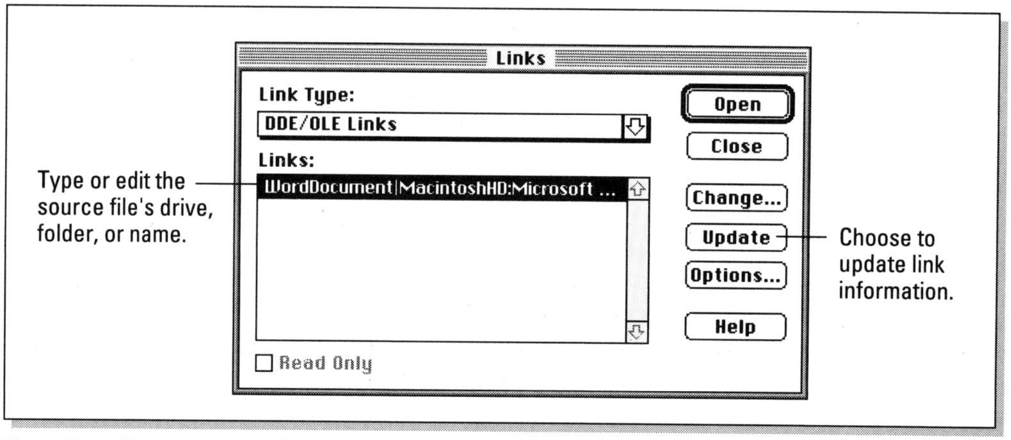

Figure 16-13: Choosing Links from the File menu displays the Links dialog box.

Step 3. Specify the options you need, and then choose OK or press Return.

Embedding an object in an Excel worksheet:

Step 1. In the other application that you are embedding from, select the information you want to embed and choose Copy from the Edit menu.

Step 2. Switch to Excel.

Step 3. Click in the upper-left cell of the range that you want to hold the data.

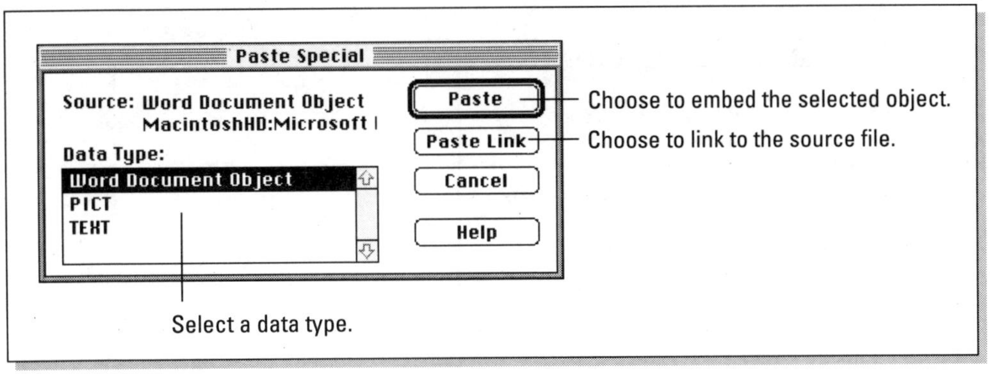

Figure 16-14: Choosing Paste Special from the Edit menu displays the Paste Special dialog box.

Step 4. Choose Paste Special from the Edit menu.

The Paste Special dialog box appears.

Step 5. Select the data type, including the name of the program you used to create the object, such as Word Document.

Step 6. Choose Paste.

The information appears on the Excel worksheet.

Editing an embedded object:

Step 1. Double-click the object.

Step 2. Edit the object as needed.

Step 3. Click the close box, choose Close from the File menu, or press Command-W.

Excel is the active application and the object is updated.

Quick Tips

This section provides you with tips on how to quickly and easily exchange data between application programs and between computer platforms.

Making imported text usable

When importing a text file, you need to use Data Parse or the Flat File add-in's Smart Parse to make the data usable. These parse options separate a line of text and place each item into its own cell in the same row so you can manipulate the data.

Memory requirements for exchanging data

To run System 7.*x*, Excel, and one other application, your Macintosh needs a minimum of 4MB of memory. Even then, your data exchange capabilities are probably limited. To help you get the job done until you can run out to your nearest Apple Macintosh supplier for additional memory, you can specify the amount of memory available to Excel.

Open the Excel folder and select the Excel icon. Next, choose Get Info from the Apple File menu. The Microsoft Excel Info dialog box shown in Figure 16-15 appears.

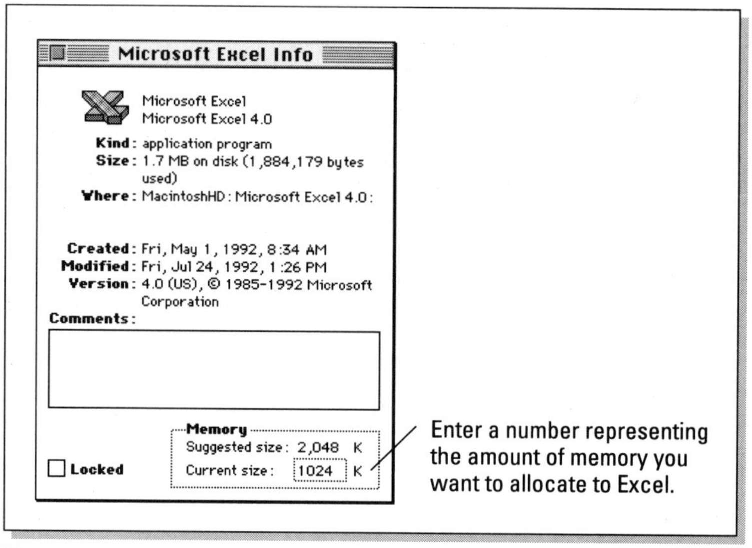

Figure 16-15: Specifying the amount of memory available to Excel by choosing Get Info from the Apple menu.

Specify the amount of memory you want available for Excel in the Memory box. This limits the amount of memory for your worksheet, but may get you over the hump until you can add additional memory to your computer. If you plan on doing extensive linking or embedding, consider a minimum of 6MB and preferably 8MB of RAM.

You may, however, be able to increase the amount of memory available to you through the use of virtual memory. Virtual memory uses a portion of your hard disk as memory, and is available to System 7.*x* users with Macintoshes that have a paged memory management unit (PMMU). Most Macintoshes, except for the Mac Plus, SE, Classic, and Portable, either come equipped with a PMMU or can be upgraded with an accelerator card that includes one. Readers interested in learning the ins and outs of virtual memory should read Lon Poole's *Macworld Guide To System 7.1, 2nd Edition*, 1993, IDG Books.

Text linked and embedded from Word

Linked or embedded text from Word appears without formatting in Excel — sorry.

Summary

- Exchanging data saves you time and keeps you from having to manually reenter text, values, and formulas.
- Excel can open and save files in most popular Macintosh, Windows, and DOS file formats.
- You can directly read Excel (and other file formats) from an IBM PC or compatible computer if your Macintosh contains a SuperDrive floppy disk drive.
- You need additional hardware and software to use Excel files from the Macintosh with IBM PCs or compatibles.
- Apple System 7.*x* users can exchange data through publishing and subscribing, linking, and embedding.
- Publishing and subscribing enables others on a network to exchange information through edition files.
- Linking data is similar to linking worksheets. Excel and one other application that supports linking need to be open simultaneously to exchange linked data.
- Embedding places an object created from data in another application on an Excel worksheet (and vice versa).

Part VI:

Appendixes

Appendix A
Installing Excel

Excel's installer program makes installing the program a no-brainer. The Installer, however, does give you a few choices about what you'd like to install and where. So it's worth your while to review this appendix if you (or another user) haven't installed Excel, or want to install a missing Excel capability.

Getting started

Before you begin installation, you should make sure your Macintosh has adequate disk space and memory to install and use Excel. At a minimum, you'll need at least 2MB of hard disk space to install Excel, and roughly another 2MB to install the Excel Help system. System 7 and MultiFinder users need a minimum of 2MB of RAM; System 6.0.2 (and up) users need 1MB. You can determine the amount of memory your Macintosh is using by pulling down the Apple menu and choosing About this Macintosh. Available hard disk space information is shown in the window that appears when you double-click the hard disk icon, choose Open from the Desktop's File menu, or press Command-O.

Keep in mind that these RAM figures are the bare minimum. To get adequate performance, especially if you plan to use Excel for some heavy-duty applications, you should probably double the above memory numbers, or have at least 4MB of memory, though you'll be happier with 6 or 8MB. Fortunately, the price of memory is pretty reasonable; MacConnection (800-800-2222) and MacZone (800-248-0800), for example, carry easy-to-install SIMMS (single in-line memory modules) that'll give you a fairly decent bang for your buck.

If your Macintosh meets these system requirements, you're ready for action.

Installing the software

You begin installation by placing the Disk-1 Setup disk in the Macintosh's disk drive. After a few seconds, the contents of the disk appear in a window (just as if you'd chosen Open from the File menu). Double-click the Microsoft Excel Setup icon, and the window shown in the figure on the following page appears.

Type your name and the name of your organization in the Name and Organization boxes. Click the OK button or press Return, and a confirmation message appears. At this point, you have the opportunity to correct spelling errors or change your mind about what you've entered. Click Change to correct errors or click Proceed to continue installing, keeping in mind that this is your only chance to make some of the information that appears in the Excel startup screen the way you want. When you choose Proceed, the window shown in the second figure on the following page appears.

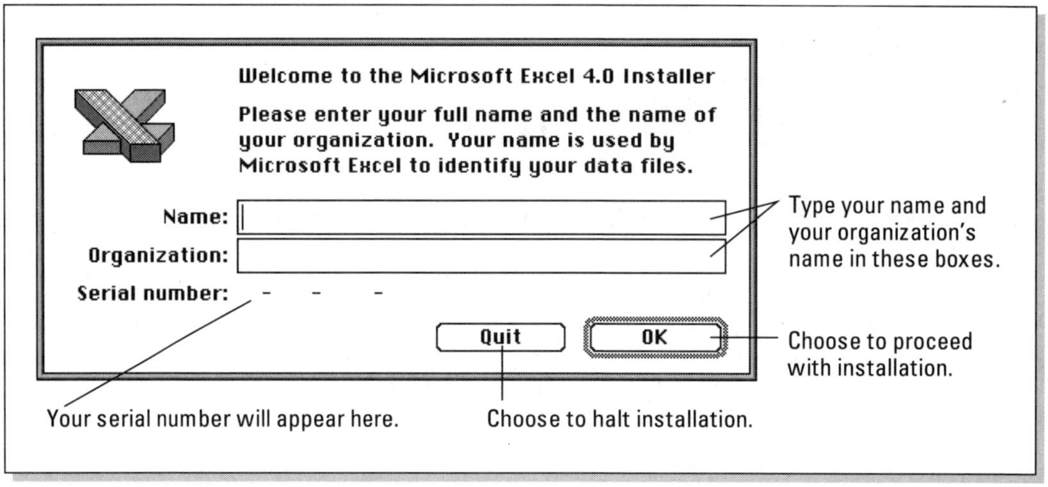

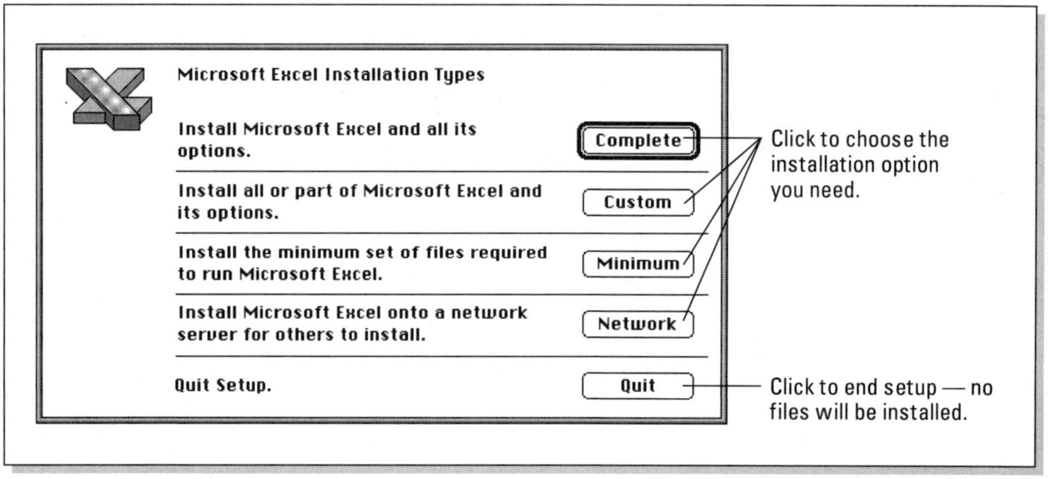

This window enables you to choose the type of Excel installation that's right for you. Choose Complete if you want all Excel program files and example files copied to your hard disk; choose Custom if you'd like to pick and choose what gets installed; choose Minimum if you want only the essential Excel files installed; or choose Network if you are installing Excel in a multiuser computer environment.

If you choose Custom or Minimum, don't worry that you might miss out on some of the capabilities the installation leaves out — you can go back and install the additional Excel capabilities you need later. Just run through the installation procedure again, but choose Custom. If you do choose Custom (during an initial or subsequent install session), the dialog box shown in the following figure appears.

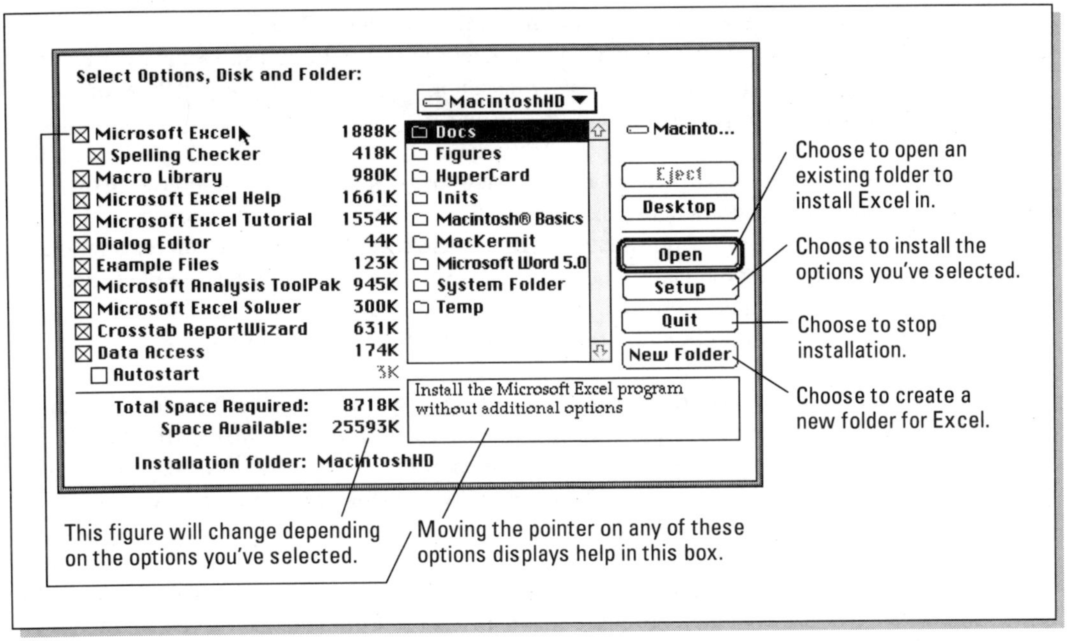

The Complete and Minimum options install the files listed in Table A-1.

Table A-1: Complete and Minimum installation options

Install option	*Files*	*Disk space (K)*
Complete	All	8,718
Minimum	Excel	1,888
	Spelling Checker	418
	Macro Library	980
	Help	1,661
	Example	123
	Solver	300
	Other (Readme, TeachText)	84
	Total	5,454

The disk space required by a Custom installation depends on the options you select. And remember that by installing some of the options (such as the Analysis ToolPak or Solver), they automatically become part of your working set, which requires more memory than if you hadn't installed the option. (You can always choose Add-in from the Options menu and remove the add-in from your working set later if you find you don't use the add-in as often as you thought you would.)

If you need to save disk space, use the Minimum option. To save even more disk space, you can install just Excel, which needs only 1.8MB of disk space, by using the Custom option. In addition, consider installing Help, for a total of 3.2MB. A spreadsheet without Help is only half a spreadsheet.

When you choose an install option, the Macintosh displays a window indicating the installation progress, and prompts you to change disks as necessary. The top portion of the screen displays a window encouraging you to complete and mail your registration card (which you've already done, right?), and shows you some of the ease-of-use and analytical capabilities new with Excel 4.0. A window appears when installation is complete, and choosing OK closes the window and returns you to the desktop.

You should not, of course, choose Network unless you are the network administrator or supervisor of your company. If you are the network boss, be sure to read the Network Readme file on Setup Disk 1. And to get the most from Excel on a network, you should consider installing the System 7 Tune-Up utility, available from your Apple dealer or local Macintosh user group.

After you've successfully installed Excel, make sure you store the installation disks in a secure, easy-to-remember place that is dry, away from magnetic fields, and has a moderate temperature.

Appendix B
Keyboard Shortcuts

Command	*Key sequence*	*Menu*
Activate formula bar	Command-U	
AutoSum	Command-Shift-T	
Border (remove)	Command-Option- - (hyphen)	Format
Border-Bottom (Toggle)	Command-Option-down arrow	Format
Border-Left (Toggle)	Command-Option-left arrow	Format
Border-Outline (Toggle)	Command-Option-0 (zero)	Format
Border-Right (Toggle)	Command-Option-right arrow	Format
Border-Top (Toggle)	Command-Option-up arrow	Format
Calc Document Calc Document	Command-Shift-= Shift-F9 (Extended keyboard)	Options Options
Calc Now Calc Now	Command-= F9 (Extended keyboard)	Options Options
Cancel action Cancel action	Command-. (period) Esc (Extended keyboard)	
Clear	Command-B	Edit
Clear-Selection (selected cell or range)	Delete	Edit
Close	Command-W	File
Column width-hide (Toggle)	Command-0	Format
Column width-unhide (Toggle)	Control-Shift-)	Format
Copy Copy	Command-C F3 (Extended keyboard)	Edit Edit
Copy Picture	Command-Shift-C	Edit
Create Names	Command-Shift-F3 (Extended keyboard)	Formula
Cut Cut	Command-X F2 (Extended keyboard)	Edit Edit
Define Name Define Name	Command-L Command-F3 (Extended keyboard)	Formula Formula
Delete	Command-K	Edit

(continued)

(continued)

Command	Key sequence	Menu
Demote	Command-Shift-K	
Display-Form/values	Command-' (apostrophe)	Options
Display-Objects	Command-6	Options
Display-Outline symbols	Command-8	Options
Extract	Command-E	Data
Fill Down	Command-D	Edit
Fill Right	Command-R	Edit
Find	Command-J	Formula
Find (data)	Command-F	Data
Find	Shift-F5 (Extended keyboard)	Formula
Find (Next)	F7 (Extended keyboard)	Formula
Find (Prev)	Shift-F7 (Extended keyboard)	Formula
Find Next (data)	Command-F	Data
Font-Bold	Command-Shift-B	Format
Font-Italic	Command-Shift-I	Format
Font-Outline	Command-Shift-D	Format
Font-Plain text	Command-Shift-P	Format
Font-Shadow	Command-Shift-W	Format
Font-Strikeout	Command-Shift-_ (underline)	Format
Font-Underline	Command-Shift-U	Format
Goto Goto	Command-G F5 (Extended keyboard)	Formula Formula
Help-Context sensitive Help-Context sensitive	Command-Shift-? Shift-Help (Extended keyboard)	
Help-Open window Help-Open window	Help (Extended keyboard) Command-/	Window Window
Insert	Command-I	Edit
Move to cell A1	Command-Home	
Move to cell in Column A	Home	
Move to last cell with an entry	End-Return	
Move to last cell with an entry	Command-End	
Move to next pane	F6 (Extended keyboard)	
Move to previous pane	Shift-F6 (Extended keyboard)	
New	Command-N	File
New-Chart	F11 (Extended keyboard)	File

(continued)

(continued)

Command	Key sequence	Menu
New-Macro sheet	Command-F11 (Extended keyboard)	File
New-Worksheet	Shift-F11 (Extended keyboard)	File
Note	Shift-F2 (Extended keyboard)	Formula
Number-#,##0.00	Control-Shift-!	Format
Number-$#,##0.00_); ($#,##0.00)	Control-Shift-$	Format
Number-0%	Control-Shift-%	Format
Number-0.00E-00	Control-Shift-^	Format
Number-d-mmm-yy	Control-Shift-#	Format
Number-General	Control-Shift-~	Format
Number-h:mm AM/PM	Control-Shift-@	Format
Open Open	Command-O Command-F12 (Extended keyboard)	File File
Paste Paste	Command-V F4 (Extended keyboard)	Edit Edit
Paste Function	Shift-F3 (Extended keyboard)	Formula
Paste Special	Command-Shift-V	Edit
Print Print	Command-P Command-Shift-F12 (Extended keyboard)	File File
Promote	Command-Shift-J	
Quit	Command-Q	File
Reference	F4 (Extended keyboard)	Formula
Repeat	Command-Y	Edit
Row height-hide	Control-9	Format
Row height-unhide	Control-Shift-(	Format
Save Save	Command-S Shift-F12 (Extended keyboard)	File File
Save As Save As	Command-Shift-F5 (Extended keyboard F12 (Extended keyboard)	File
Scroll left one window	Command-Page Up (Extended keyboard)	
Scroll one column left	Left arrow key	
Scroll one column right	Right arrow key	
Scroll one row down	Down arrow key	
Scroll one row up	Up arrow key	
Scroll one window down	Page Down (Extended keyboard)	
Scroll one window up	Page Up (Extended keyboard)	

(continued)

(continued)

Command	Key sequence	Menu
Scroll right one window	Command-Page Down (Extended keyboard)	
Select chart	Command-A	Chart
Select Special Notes	Command-Shift-O	Formula
Select Special Current Region	Control-Shift-*	
Select Special Current Region	Command-* (Numeric keypad)	Formula
Select Special Current Array	Control-/	Formula
Select Special Column Differences	Command-Shift-I	Formula
Select Special Row Differences	Command-\	Formula
Select Special Prec: Dir Only	Command-[	Formula
Select Special Prec: All Levels	Command-Shift-{	Formula
Select Special Dep: Direct Only	Command-]	Formula
Select Special Dep: All levels	Command-Shift-}	Formula
Select Special Vis: Cells Only	Command-Shift-Z	Formula
Select Special Last Cell	Command-End	Formula
Show/hide Standard toolbar	Command-7	Options
Show Info Window	Command-F2 (Extended keyboard)	Options
Style box	Command-Shift-L	
Undo	Command-Z	Edit
Undo	F1 (Extended keyboard)	Edit

Appendix C
Glossary

This glossary contains definitions of words associated with spreadsheets and terms related to Excel. The glossary also includes definitions of italicized words throughout the sixteen Topics of this book. The index at the back of the book shows you where you can learn more about each term.

absolute address A cell address that has a dollar sign preceding both the column letter and the row number of the address. The address is not changed when copied.

active cell The cell that is selected; it is surrounded by a border. The active cell's address is displayed in the Excel reference area.

add-in A macro or custom program that enhances or extends Excel's functionality. Add-ins that come with Excel are located in the Macro Library folder. Macros you create can be saved as an add-in by choosing Options from the Save As dialog box, and then selecting Add-in from the File Format pull-down list.

application A software program, such as Excel, or a file created by a software program, such as an Excel worksheet application.

argument A unit of information a worksheet function needs to calculate a result. An argument can be a value or calculated value, referenced by a name or cell address. Some arguments are optional but most are required to calculate properly.

attached text Chart text that is attached to a chart item, such as a data marker (*see* data marker). Attached text is limited in movement (if it can move at all).

border A line around at least one side of a cell or range.

breakpoint Available through the Macro Debugger add-in, breakpoints let you stop a macro from running when the macro encounters previously specified values or names, displays the current value(s), and switches to Single-step mode. You can continue in Single-step mode, run the macro at full speed, or stop the macro altogether.

CSV An acronym for Comma Separated Value. A text file that contains only values, where each value is separated by a comma.

cell The intersection of a row and column of the worksheet. A cell can hold a value, text, a worksheet function, or a formula.

cell address The location of a cell on a worksheet, as a result of the intersection of a column and row. The cell's address is comprised of the column's letter and row number.

cell format The attributes you apply to the contents of a cell or range. Formatting can be as simple as aligning the cell entry, or as thorough as coloring, shading, bordering, and bolding. Formats affect what appears on screen as well as on paper.

cell pointer The rectangular border that highlights the active cell.

chart Worksheet data displayed in a picture format. Excel can display data in eight two-dimensional, six three-dimensional, or several combination chart types, also known as graphs.

choose The process of picking a command from a pull-down menu or closing a dialog box. Commands can be chosen with the mouse or a keyboard shortcut. See *close* for dialog box options.

clicking Pressing the mouse button.

Clipboard An area of the Macintosh's memory that is set aside to hold information you've cut or copied.

close To remove a window or dialog box from display. Close windows by clicking the close box or by pressing Command-W. Close dialog boxes by clicking Open or Cancel, or by pressing Return or Esc.

column A vertical range of cells beginning in Row 1 and extending to Row 16,384. Columns are normally identified by a letter, ranging from A to IV.

command An instruction you issue from an Excel pull-down menu, shortcut menu, or tool. The task is normally carried out on the selected cell or range.

criteria Formulas in the criteria range that act as filters so you can find, extract, or delete records that meet the criteria conditions.

criteria range The range in the worksheet you've specified by choosing Set Criteria from the Data menu. The criteria range contains formulas that represent conditions you want met during a database find, extract, or delete operation.

data Text and/or values that have meaning to you. Excel uses data to compute other values (results). Data can be entered manually from the keyboard, by opening a file stored on disk, or by transferring files from another computer.

data marker A symbol that represents a value on the worksheet, such as a bar, dot, or pie wedge.

data series The symbols that represent the values of a row or column of data in the worksheet.

database A range of continuous cells on an Excel worksheet. Each record (row) of the database is made up of fields (cells) that contain unique information. Each field (column) of the database contains the same type of information in each record. Databases can be sorted, printed, queried, and charted.

default An action or setting automatically performed unless changed by the user.

delimiter A separator character between items of data in a row of text in text files. The character can be a tab, comma, space, semicolon, or other character.

dependent worksheet A worksheet that depends on another (source) worksheet for data.

document An Excel worksheet, macro sheet, or chart you create.

drag Slide the mouse while the mouse button is depressed.

edition A file created by publishing and used by subscribing. An edition file contains data and information about the file.

embed An object that is placed on a worksheet. Embedding an object enables you to receive information from another open program.

export Saving a document in another format other than an Excel format for use with another program.

external reference formula A linking formula that resides in a cell of a dependent worksheet that refers to a source worksheet. *See* dependent worksheet *and* source worksheet.

extract range The range in the worksheet you've specified by choosing Set Extract from the Data menu. Database records that meet the criteria specified in the criteria range are copied to the extract range. *See* criteria range.

field A vertical range of information in an Excel database. The same field in each record contains the same type of data.

file Information stored as separate units on disk. You create a file when you choose Save or Save As from the File menu, which copies the information in memory as displayed on screen in a worksheet, macro sheet, or chart file.

file format The way a program arranges data as a unit on disk. Excel can read file formats from most popular software programs.

floating toolbar A toolbar that is positioned over the worksheet, and contains a title bar and close box.

font A complete collection of characters (letters, numbers, punctuation marks) in a specific design or typeface.

font family A group of fonts that are of the same type but have different sizes and other attributes.

footer Information, such as date, time, or page number, that appears at the bottom of each printed page. Choose Page Setup from the File menu to specify footer information.

formula A mathematical expression you create with arithmetic operators, worksheet functions, values, text, cell or range references, or names. Each formula must begin with an equal sign, one formula per cell.

formula bar The rectangular area between the menu bar and the worksheet's title bar. The formula bar enables you to enter new or edit existing cell contents.

function A built-in formula provided by Excel. Functions need arguments to calculate, but calculate faster and more accurately than a formula counterpart. Excel has over 130 worksheet functions and over 350 if you install the Analysis ToolPak add-in.

freezing panes The process of holding a pane in place on screen. Freezing a pane is helpful when you need to see row text or column text displayed continuously while another pane scrolls.

handles Small squares that surround objects or chart items when selected. Objects with black handles can be moved or sized, but objects with white handles cannot.

header Information, such as date, time, or page number, that appears at the top of each printed page. Choose Page Setup from the File menu to specify header information.

import Opening a file created by a program other than Excel. Importing text files requires that you parse the data to make it usable in Excel. *See* parse.

linking The process where one worksheet depends on another for information, or where an Excel worksheet is linked to another Macintosh application program or vice versa.

macro A list of commands in a continuous range down a column of a macro sheet. Macros can be created by Excel's macro recorder or entered manually. A macro sheet must be open to use the macros with a worksheet. Macros can be as simple as keystroke reducers or as complex as custom dialog boxes.

marquee The counter-clockwise moving dashed line that surrounds selected cells when they are cut or copied.

menu bar The narrow rectangle at the top of the Macintosh display that contains Excel's pull-down command menus, as well as the Apple and Finder menus.

mixed address A cell address that has a dollar sign preceding the column letter or the row number of the address, but not both. Only the portion of the address that does not have a dollar sign (the relative portion) changes when copied.

object A graphical item placed on a worksheet or chart. You can create an object by using the Drawing toolbar, or embed an object from another open program. You can add arrows and lines to charts, as well as move and size objects.

open To retrieve a copy of a worksheet, macro sheet, or chart saved on disk to memory and display it on screen.

page break The dashed lines displayed on the worksheet indicating where printing of the next page begins. Page breaks do not print and can be set automatically by Excel, or manually.

palette The group of sixteen colors available in Excel documents. The palette can be customized, copied among documents, or substituted with a palette from the Custom Color Palette add-in.

pane A worksheet window segment. A worksheet window can have two horizontal, two vertical, or four window panes.

parse The process of taking a text file and making it usable by Excel. Text files normally contain many rows of information, one row per cell in Column A. Parsing separates each data item in the row into its own cell in the same row. Choose Parse from the Data menu or use the Flat File add-in (Smart Parse) to parse text files.

pointer The symbol displayed on screen that moves as the mouse is moved. The pointer changes shape as you move it to different areas of the Excel display. The pointer can resemble, among other things, a black pointer, white cross, and black cross hairs. The pointer enables you to select commands, ranges, and objects, and to move and resize windows.

print titles Text in rows and/or columns that are printed along the left side and top of the paper, respectively.

publish To create an edition file from a selected range of the worksheet for use by others on a network.

RAM An acronym for random-access memory. The Macintosh's main memory that interacts with its central processing unit. Information stored in memory is lost when power is turned off, so save to disk frequently.

range A group of cells on a worksheet. A range can be as small as a single cell or as large as an entire worksheet. A selected range can be comprised of contiguous or noncontiguous cells. You must select a cell or range before carrying out most Excel operations.

record A horizontal range of information in an Excel database. Each field in the record contains a different type of information.

reference area The small rectangle to the left of the formula bar. The reference area displays information about a task in progress, such as the size of a selected range, percent of add-in loaded, and so on.

relative address The address of a cell that changes when copied.

row A horizontal range of cells from Column A to Column IV in the worksheet. Rows are numbered from 1 to 16,384.

sans serif A font without the short line at the ends of the strokes of each character.

scroll bars The narrow bar on the right side and along the bottom of a worksheet window. The vertical scroll bar enables you to move the screen display up or down, and the horizontal scroll bar enables you to move the screen display left or right.

select To use the mouse (or Shift and arrow keys) to mark a cell, range, object, chart item, or other Excel item for editing, formatting, or other action.

serif A font with a short line at the ends of the strokes of each character.

Single-step mode A macro running one command at a time, rather than at full speed. Single-step mode helps you spot and correct errors in macros by seeing problems you wouldn't ordinarily see because the macro is running at full speed.

source worksheet A worksheet furnishing data to another (dependent) worksheet.

split bar The black box at the top and to the left of the vertical and horizontal scroll bars, respectively. Dragging from the split bar creates two worksheet window panes.

status bar The rectangle along the bottom of the Excel display, directly below the worksheet window. The status bar displays Excel's current mode (Ready, Edit, Help), and whether SCROLL, CAPS, or NUM is on.

style A combination of fonts, borders, shading, and other format attributes. Styles can be created and named for repeated use in any worksheet.

subscribe To include information contained in an edition file in a worksheet.

syntax Rules a worksheet or macro function contains to calculate properly.

text Characters entered into a cell using the keyboard primarily to describe values and results of functions and formulas.

text file A file that contains only text characters and no formatting. When opened in Excel, each line of text is an entry in Column A. A text file must be parsed to be of any use in Excel. *See* parse.

toolbar An on-screen rectangle that holds tools. Toolbars can be displayed, hidden, and customized. The Standard toolbar appears by default between the Command menu and the formula bars.

toolbar dock One of the four areas of the Excel display where you can position a toolbar. Toolbars can be docked between the Command menu and formula bars, above the status bar, and along the left and right sides of the screen.

tracepoint Available through the Macro Debugger add-in, tracepoints let you stop a running macro at logical points and switch to Single-step mode. You can continue in Single-step mode, run the macro at full speed, or stop the macro altogether.

unattached text Chart text that you've added and can move.

value A number entered into a cell in a worksheet from the keyboard, or as a result of a worksheet function or formula calculation.

virtual memory The capability of using a portion of a computer's hard disk as an extension of random access memory.

workbook A file that can contains worksheets, charts, and macro sheets.

working set The add-ins that automatically load into the computer's memory when you start Excel.

Appendix D
Task Index

Index

— B —

— C —

Index

— D —

Index

—F—

—H—

—I—

—J—

—K—

—L—

—M—

— N —

— O —

— P —

—Q—

—R—

— S —

— T —

— U —

—V—

—W—

—X—

—Z—

Notes

Notes

Notes

Notes

Notes

Notes

Notes

Notes

Notes

Notes

Notes

Notes

Notes

Notes

Notes

International Data Group (IDG), and IDG Books Worldwide, Inc., an affiliate of IDG based in San Mateo, CA, are committed to directing the power of business and industry toward improving the environment.

▲▼▲

This book was printed on recycled paper, and can be recycled.

Macworld Guide To Microsoft Works 3

by Barrie Sosinsky

Macworld Guide To Microsoft Works 3 is your definitive guide to mastering Works' individual modules and integrating them effectively to produce powerful documents. A step-by-step approach, expert tips, and task-oriented examples teach you to use Works in the context of your own particular needs. You'll master word processing, database, spreadsheet, draw, charting, and communications modules. Then find out how to use the macro recorder and to share data between programs.

Learn how to use Works for business publishing, with templates, or running on a network. A special section even shows you how to use Works on the road with your PowerBook. And you'll also receive special instructions for using the program with System 7. 434 pages.

Book **ISBN: 1-878058-42-8** **$22.95 US/$29.95 Canada**

Macworld Guide to Microsoft Word 5/5.1

by Jim Heid

Just like a travel guide, *Macworld Guide To Microsoft Word 5* is well-illustrated, organized for quick reference, and packed with tips from a knowledgeable insider. You can start your excursion through Word 5.1 with basic editing and formatting techniques, or jump directly to more advanced formatting with frames and sections.

Want to improve your accuracy through Word's built-in spelling, style, and grammar checkers? Create footnotes, tables of contents, and indexes? Save keystrokes with Word's glossary features? Just turn right to the appropriate chapter for complete, easy-to-follow instructions. You'll even learn to exchange information with other programs and to customize Word to design your own stationery, menu commands, and keyboard shortcuts. 408 pages.

Book **ISBN: 1-878058-39-8** **$22.95 US/$29.95 Canada**

For more information or to order by mail, call 1-800-762-2974. Call for a free catalog!
For volume discounts and special orders, please call Tony Real, Special Sales at 415-312-0644.

IDG Books — *Macworld* Authorized Editions

Macworld Networking Handbook

by David Kosiur, Ph.D. and Nancy E.H. Jones

Whether you've got a couple of Macs hooked up to a printer, or a sophisticated network linking Macs, DOS and Windows PCs, DECs, even IBM mainframes — you'll benefit from this authoritative hands-on reference.

You'll find expert tips on networking printers, working with networked databases, sharing modems and files, and using electronic mail and groupware. You'll also be able to diagnose and correct common network problems, optimize your network's performance, secure your data, and manage resources. The added benefit of an extensive glossary ensures that this comprehensive handbook is your first and only networking reference. 176 illustrations, 584 pages.

Book **ISBN: 1-878058-31-2** **$29.95 US/$39.95 Canada**

Mac For Dummies®

Bestseller

by David Pogue

David Pogue, *Macworld* magazine columnist and personal trainer of hundreds of former Mac Dummies, blasts through the techno-jumbo — and helps you build your Mac IQ without trying to turn you into a power user. You'll learn do it-it-yourself Mac maintenance: what to do when bad things happen to good computers; how to fake your way through the top ten programs; how to buy or upgrade a Mac; and David Pogue's Top Ten List of Tips on printers, word processing, fonts major software programs, and more! 100 illustrations, 336 pages.

"Enjoyed the humor. Loved the format. Absolutely well written. David Pogue is a marvel." — *Virginia Kochanek, Plant City, Florida*

"Great — I'm off to buy a new Mac!!" — *Paul Barry, Toronto, Ontario, Canada*

"The writer is excellent! He can make dull material lively." — *Christina Markuras, New York, New York*

Book **ISBN: 1-878058-31-2** **$29.95 US/$39.95 Canada**

For more information or to order by mail, call 1-800-762-2974. Call for a free catalog!
For volume discounts and special orders, please call Tony Real, Special Sales at 415-312-0644.

Order Form

Order Center: (800) 762-2974 (8 a.m.-5 p.m., PST, weekdays) or (415) 312-0650

For Fastest Service: Photocopy This Order Form and FAX it to : (415) 358-1260

Quantity	ISBN	Title	Price	Total

Shipping & Handling Charges

Subtotal	U.S.	Canada & International	International Air Mail
Up to $20.00	Add $3.00	Add $4.00	Add $10.00
$20.01-40.00	$4.00	$5.00	$20.00
$40.01-60.00	$5.00	$6.00	$25.00
$60.01-80.00	$6.00	$8.00	$35.00
Over $80.00	$7.00	$10.00	$50.00

In U.S. and Canada, shipping is UPS ground or equivalent.
For Rush shipping call (800) 762-2974.

Subtotal ________

CA residents add applicable sales tax ________

IN residents add 5% sales tax ________

Canadian residents add 7% GST tax ________

Shipping ________

TOTAL ________

Ship to:

Name ________________________________

Company ________________________________

Address ________________________________

City/State/Zip ________________________________

Daytime Phone ________________________________

Payment: ❑ Check to IDG Books (US Funds Only) ❑ Visa ❑ MasterCard ❑ American Express

Card # ________________ Exp. ________ Signature ________________

Please send this order form to: IDG Books, 155 Bovet Road, Suite 310, San Mateo, CA 94402.
Allow up to 3 weeks for delivery. Thank you!

BOBMW

IDG BOOKS WORLDWIDE REGISTRATION CARD

RETURN THIS REGISTRATION CARD FOR FREE CATALOG

Title of this book: MW Guide To Microsoft Excel 4

My overall rating of this book: ❑ Very good [1] ❑ Good [2] ❑ Satisfactory [3] ❑ Fair [4] ❑ Poor [5]

How I first heard about this book:

❑ Found in bookstore; name: [6] ❑ Book review: [7]

❑ Advertisement: [8] ❑ Catalog: [9]

❑ Word of mouth; heard about book from friend, co-worker, etc.: [10] ❑ Other: [11]

What I liked most about this book:

What I would change, add, delete, etc., in future editions of this book:

Other comments:

Number of computer books I purchase in a year: ❑ 1 [12] ❑ 2-5 [13] ❑ 6-10 [14] ❑ More than 10 [15]

I would characterize my computer skills as: ❑ Beginner [16] ❑ Intermediate [17] ❑ Advanced [18] ❑ Professional [19]

I use ❑ DOS [20] ❑ Windows [21] ❑ OS/2 [22] ❑ Unix [23] ❑ Macintosh [24] ❑ Other: [25] ______ (please specify)

I would be interested in new books on the following subjects:
(please check all that apply, and use the spaces provided to identify specific software)

❑ Word processing: [26] ❑ Spreadsheets: [27]

❑ Data bases: [28] ❑ Desktop publishing: [29]

❑ File Utilities: [30] ❑ Money management: [31]

❑ Networking: [32] ❑ Programming languages: [33]

❑ Other: [34]

I use a PC at (please check all that apply): ❑ home [35] ❑ work [36] ❑ school [37] ❑ other: [38] ______

The disks I prefer to use are ❑ 5.25 [39] ❑ 3.5 [40] ❑ other: [41] ______

I have a CD ROM: ❑ yes [42] ❑ no [43]

I plan to buy or upgrade computer hardware this year: ❑ yes [44] ❑ no [45]

I plan to buy or upgrade computer software this year: ❑ yes [46] ❑ no [47]

Name: Business title: [48] Type of Business: [49]

Address (❑ home [50] ❑ work [51]/Company name:)

Street/Suite#

City [52]/State [53]/Zipcode [54]: Country [55]

❑ **I liked this book!** You may quote me by name in future IDG Books Worldwide promotional materials.

My daytime phone number is ______

IDG BOOKS
THE WORLD OF COMPUTER KNOWLEDGE

❑ **YES!**

Please keep me informed about IDG's World of Computer Knowledge. Send me the latest IDG Books catalog.

SECRETS™

...FOR DUMMIES™ COMPUTER BOOK SERIES FROM IDG

MACWORLD MW AUTHORIZED EDITION

AUTHORIZED PC WORLD EDITION

NO POSTAGE NECESSARY IF MAILED IN THE UNITED STATES

BUSINESS REPLY MAIL
FIRST CLASS MAIL PERMIT NO. 2605 SAN MATEO, CALIFORNIA

IDG Books Worldwide
155 Bovet Road Suite 310
San Mateo CA 94402-9833